Urban Transport and Planning

A bibliography with abstracts

David Banister and Laurie Pickup

An Alexandrine Press Book

MANSELL PUBLISHING LIMITED
London and New York

First published 1989 by
Mansell Publishing Limited, *A Cassell Imprint*
Artillery House, Artillery Row, London SW1P 1RT, England
125 East 23rd Street, Suite 300, New York 10010, U.S.A.

© David Banister and Laurie Pickup, 1989

This book was commissioned, edited and designed by
Alexandrine Press, Oxford

All rights reserved. No part of this publication may be reproduced or transmitted in any form or by any means, electronic or mechanical, including photocopy, recording or any information storage or retrieval system, without permission in writing from the publishers or their appointed agents.

British Library Cataloguing in Publication Data
Banister, David, *1950-*
   Urban transport and planning: a bibliography
with abstracts.——(An Alexandrine Press book).
   1. Urban regions. Transport. Planning——
bibliographies
   I. Title   II. Pickup, Laurie
016.711'7'091732
   ISBN 0-7201-1627-9

Library of Congress Cataloging-in-Publication Data
Banister, David.
   Urban transport and planning : a bibliography with abstracts / David Banister and Laurie Pickup.
     p. cm.
   "An Alexandrine Press book."
   Includes indexes.
   ISBN 0-7201-1627-9 : $72.00 (U.S. : est.)
   1. Urban transportation——Bibliography. 2. Urban transportation——Planning——Bibliography. I. Pickup, Laurie. II. Title
Z7164.U72B36   1989
[HE305]
016.3884——dc19   88-30454
                                                                  CIP

This book has been printed and bound in Great Britain: typeset in 10/12 pt Compugraphic Baskerville by Colset Private Limited, Singapore
and printed and bound by Biddles Ltd., Guildford, on Onslow Book Wove paper.

Contents

Acknowledgements	vii
Introduction	1
1. The context	**5**
1A The urban context	10
1B The transport context	19
2. Policy and planning in transport	**41**
2A Great Britain	45
2B The United States of America	55
2C Europe	66
2D Organizational and institutional issues	71
2E Management and labour practices	75
3. Social issues	**81**
3A Land-use patterns	87
3B Technological change	93
3C Social groups	97
3D Impact of transport on lifestyle, commuting and shopping	113
3E Health effects, stress and crime	127

4. Travel modes 130

4A Bus services 140
4B Urban rail 163
4C Unconventional public transport and taxis 171
4D Cars 178
4E Freight transport 190
4F Walking and cycling 192

5. Methods and evaluation 198

5A Theoretical frameworks 204
5B Analysis methods 217
5C Investment appraisal and evaluation 250
5D Energy 260
5E Environment and safety 269
5F Engineering 283

6. Area studies 288

7. Bibliographies and research registers 298

7A In English 298
    In German 302
    In French 304
7B Database search system 304
    Selected periodicals 306

8. Additional entries 312

Subject index 327

Author index 343

Acknowledgements

When putting together a volume such as this the authors always depend to a great extent on the numerous researchers in transport to supply much of the information. Surveys were carried out in Britain, Europe and further afield to gather the base information from which the representative material presented here was selected. Our thanks go to all those who made time to respond to our investigation –

Steve Atkins, Chris Banister, George Banjo, Alain Bieber, B Boi, Tunji Bolade, Tilman Bracher, John Brotchie, Peter Chapman, Martyn Cordey-Hayes, Marie-Antoinette Dekkers, Donald Fillinger, J R Fradin, Keith Gardner, David Gillingwater, Phil Goodwin, Shalom Hakkert, Dilip Halder, Peter Hall, Wolfgang Heinze, Vincent Hilderbrandt, Mayer Hillman, Peter Hills, Jean Hopkin, B Horn, H Jenkinson, Russ Kilvington, Pierre Laconte, Peter Matthews, Birgit Maxe-Ericson, Jurgen von Muralt, Stephen Nutley, Kate Oliver, Paul Ove Pedersen, Tom Rallis, Karl Ribbeck, Birgitta Sandstedt, Bernard Schaeffer, Brian Turton, Peter White, John Whitelegg.

In addition to our respondents there are other individuals who have made the book a reality. Ann Rudkin has provided the stimulus to start, continue and finish. Tris Freeman has typed the manuscript and Ann Heath compiled the author and subject indexes. Our respective wives, Lizzie and Chris, have not escaped as they have been involved in typing our handwriting and proof reading our mistakes.

David Banister and Laurie Pickup
September 1988

Introduction

When Henry Ford was giving evidence in the witness box in a libel case in July 1919, he stated that 'history is bunk'. However, even he did not realize the impact that his mass-production techniques at the Highland Park plant would have on the twentieth century. Lifestyles and social patterns have been revolutionized with the advent of the car; it has proved to be a powerful facilitator of change with the spread of urban areas; and it has provided major employment opportunities in both the manufacturing and service sectors. An environment devoid of the car is hard to imagine. Commensurate with the growth in the numbers of cars has been the growth of the numbers of publications on urban transport.

This annotated bibliography attempts to cover the enormous range of recent literature on urban transport and planning. It is a companion volume to *Rural Transport and Planning: A Bibliography with Abstracts* produced by David Banister in 1985. However, the task in the urban sector is vast and it has proved more problematical than the rural bibliography. Coverage here has necessitated reviewing over 10,000 references, even after a series of constraints upon the search have been imposed. So only about one in twenty of the references has been included. Consequently, the selection criteria have been severe. The intention is to give a flavour of the range of material and sources available. Where one author has written a series of papers on the same topic, then only one or two have been included in full, with the others being cross referenced. Throughout the compilation of this bibliography we have been in what chess grandmasters would call a 'Zugswang'. We are only in a good position if it is not our turn to move. There is a need for such a bibliography, and we have taken the initiative to make our move!

The search has focused on published literature since 1980 in the English language. Much useful material is presented as conference papers, or produced by consultants, governments, pressure and interest groups, and academics as working papers or discussion documents. We have resisted the temptation to include this material. Similarly, our contacts overseas have provided a tremendous amount of fascinating source information, much of it in their own language. Reluctantly, this material has also been omitted as space is limited. Hence, the coverage from countries which do not publish most of their research in the English language has been less comprehensive.

The same structure has been used in this volume as in *Rural Transport and Planning*, there being six major sections. Each section has a short introduction that attempts to describe and highlight the main themes together with the principal publications. The abstracts are mainly descriptive, with comments and recommendations being restricted to the introductory text. The first section is the shortest, and outlines the urban context with some seminal texts that cover the main changes which have taken place in urban society as a whole over the past twenty years. This section is complemented by a similar review of the major transport texts in urban areas.

The second section covers the policy-making framework as it relates to urban transport in Great Britain, the United States of America and, briefly, Europe. Other topics covered in this section include organizational and institutional issues, management and labour practices, and the process of participation and consultation. Certain policy themes such as finance, liberalization and privatization are given prominence. This emphasis reflects the radical changes in transport policy which have been implemented in many countries in the last eight years. In the third section the social issues are highlighted. This essentially is a complement to the section in *Rural Transport and Planning* on access and mobility. Within the heading of social issues are land-use patterns and technological change, as well as social groups (e.g. the elderly, women, the disabled) and the impacts of transport on lifestyles, commuting and

INTRODUCTION

shopping. References are also included on health effects, stress and crime as they relate to transport.

The fourth section covers modes (including bus, rail, metro, unconventional public transport, the private car, car sharing, the company car, bicycles, pedestrians, and, briefly, freight). With the flexibility brought about by recent policy changes there now exists the potential for a much wider range of modes to be used within urban areas. Also included in this section are a wide range of economic considerations such as pricing, fares, subsidy, elasticities, ticketing and taxation. Analysis methods and evaluation have really formed the central part of the contribution of urban transport planning research, and the fifth section selectively covers the principal publications. In addition to references on analytical frameworks, models, investment appraisal, impact analysis and evaluation, there are short subsections on energy, environment and safety, and engineering aspects including traffic management and restraint. The final section has grouped together those studies that have an explicit area-based focus.

Selection and allocation have been difficult as particular publications could have been put into more than one section. Cross referencing and comprehensive indexing attempt to get round this problem. Section seven covers bibliographies and computer retrieval information systems together with a list of the principal periodicals abstracted.

The system of numbering is consecutive and continuous, and is identical to that used in the *Rural Transport and Planning*. Each major section has a number which is followed by a letter to indicate the subsection. Similarly each reference in the bibliography is uniquely defined by one or more digits and the section and subsection identifiers. Hence 3B always comes before 4B and 3C28 before 3C38. The similarities between the two bibliographies should allow the reader to switch from one to the other as the numbering system is parallel; for example, section 4D in the Rural bibliography is on private transport whilst section 4D in the Urban bibliography is entitled cars, car sharing and company cars. Some of the key references are in both volumes, but in most cases there is very little overlap. As a reference work this arrangement will help readers to find their way round both volumes quickly and efficiently and avoid duplication between the two.

1 The context

1A The urban context

Many of the cities in the Western World are facing similar problems, namely the flight of capital and population, the decline in employment in traditional industries, the need to renew the urban fabric and infrastructure, and a dramatic increase in social and cultural questions caused by the concentrations of disadvantaged people within particular locations in the city. Some authors would say that this decline is inevitable (Hall [1A16], Ewers *et al.* [1A9]) with the switch from an industrial society to a technologically based one. The driving force in this process is technical and can be linked with long-term economic cycles of activity. Others suggest that the process is socio-economic as developing countries have undermined the profitability of industrial countries which in turn have had to lose labour (Massey and Meegan [1A21]). Coupled with these factors is a physical dimension as cities have an ageing capital stock with respect to housing, factories and infrastructure. Again, much renewal of the urban fabric has taken place in the last thirty years with massive construction programmes, but this has not kept pace with the ageing process. Recently there has been a switch back to rehabilitation and the notion of the community as local resistance has built up against large-scale redevelopment.

The functions of the city have been radically changed. Gone are the days of the industrial base with employment centrally located and short journeys to work and other facilities. Cities are taking on much more complex and diversified functions. They are still the centres for transactions which require face to face contact, and provide much of the essential back-up to technological developments such as software production, research, consultancy and advertising. Availability of information and skills will be the key ingredients for success. Cities will maintain the functions of being the centres for the arts, culture and education, as well as shopping and the staging of international events. Capital cities may have additional roles as centres of government with their massive support structures, a financial role both national and international, and a role as the hub of the communications network.

Superimposed on these structural changes is the social imperative which is a crucial part of urban regeneration. The affluent and mobile middle classes are the catalysts for change with respect to housing and environmental conditions, and they have also been influential in maintaining local services such as education and health care. However, there has also been an increase in the inequalities in wealth as the population has become polarized into the mobile rich and the constrained poor. This social inequality also has a spatial dimension. Similarly, the family structure has become much more loosely defined and there has been a tremendous growth in female and part-time participation in the labour force (Meltzer [1A22]).

In developing countries the picture is also one of rapid change, but with a lag of a few years. Cities are still expanding at a phenomenal rate with large peripheral squatter settlements. Unskilled rural immigrants are looking for city-based employment. These people are prepared to accept low wage levels, poor working conditions and long journeys to work. Planning has a different set of problems to tackle, but even here the familiar questions of priorities in education, health, housing, employment and transport are dominant (Taylor and Williams [1A29], Linn [1A20], Thomson [1B49]).

The response of governments to the urban revolution have been varied. The traditional methods of stimulating urban regeneration through subsidizing capital investment has been questioned, and there has been a switch to governments playing more of a facilitating role which in turn has been seen as an attack on local government and the planning system. Governments have encouraged local authorities to sell land for development, and in some cases favourable tax exemptions have been given to firms locating in inner-city areas. The powers of local authorities have been further weakened by the Urban Development Corporations and the involvement of large multinational companies in the financing and development of office, industrial, commercial and residential sites (Barrett and Fudge [1A1], Goldsmith [1A12], Self [1A27]).

Planning has also come full circle with the recent moves away from strategic long-term planning to shorter-term incremental planning (Friend [1A11]). Plans to control and guide the spread of cities have been produced for many of the world's great cities – the Abercrombie Plan for London in 1944, the New York Regional Plan of 1928–31, and the Schema Directeur for the Paris Region in 1965. Now the emphasis is on redirecting growth back into the inner cities, but it is unclear whether this redirection does in practice result in a net benefit to the urban economy as a whole, or whether it is only a matter of relocating a given amount of development with an urban area; a distribution question. Government policy has become the major agent in urban development with financial incentives, the setting up of development corporations and through the placing of research contracts. Planning seems to have become less important. This has happened in Silicon Valley (Hall and Markusen [1A17]) and similar direct intervention may occur elsewhere in the economy. Technological changes may have as fundamental an effect on the structure of cities as did the industrial revolution (Brotchie *et al.* [1A5]), and these changes are apparent in most Western economies with the shortening of the working week, the increase in leisure time and travel distances, and the consequent changes in lifestyle (Meltzer [1A22], Williams [1A32]).

The urban context presented here is a vast canvas of change and the intention is to give the reader a feel for what is happening. The references in the text are selective, but they represent some of the principal contributions to the debate.

1B The transport context

Within the urban context transport has been a facilitator of change. The railways facilitated the industrial revolution with the switch from primary agricultural-based employment to a manufacturing-based economy. The car has enabled the switch from manufacturing to a service-based economy. Technology now permits a movement to quaternary (knowledge-based industry) and quinary activities (home services). Each of these transitions has involved an infrastructure and the development of a network. The principal difference between the technological revolution and all previous revolutions is that it is aspatial and not distance related, even though it will have spatial impacts (Altshuler *et al.* [1B2], Dickey [1B20]).

The car has altered the way in which we live and think, and will continue to do so as car ownership levels increase. To the user the car offers real advantages which alternative forms of transport can never match except in congested urban areas. The car has a unique flexibility in that it is always available, it offers door to door transport, it has a high level of privacy and comfort, and it really forms an extension to the home. It is in effect a part of the home that can be detached and reattached at will (Altshuler *et al.* [1B3], Flink [1B26], Meyer and Gomez-Ibanez [1B32]).

These private benefits conceal considerable costs that car ownership and high levels of mobility have brought. As a result of the increase in car ownership, the demand for public transport has fallen. This decline reflects both the direct transfer of passengers from bus and rail to the car, and the secondary effects such as increased fares and declines in service levels on public transport to compensate for the loss of patronage – the so-called downward vicious spiral (Webster *et al.*[1B56]). The car has also brought considerable social and environmental costs to society as a whole. The environmental problems of pollution, noise and vibration from transport are very apparent as are the personal and social costs caused by road accidents (Sections 5D and 5E).

The car is also a significant user of resources. Consumption of finite energy resources has continued to increase with many motorists either being insensitive to increases in petrol prices or being shielded from the direct costs through subsidies from employers for petrol and company cars (Button and Gillingwater [1B16], Studnicki-Gizbert [1B48]).

Superimposed on these issues is the basic inequality of the car. Not everyone has equal access to it and this will always be the case. Some will be too old or too young to drive, whilst others will have some physical disability and others will not be able to afford to buy and run the car. There is a polarization between those with unrestricted access to the car and those who are in some way disadvantaged (Barker [1B7]). Public transport, taxis, the bicycle and unconventional transport, mainly in voluntary sector, offer some compensation, but none provides the unique advantages of the car (Section 4).

Similar arguments can be made with respect to freight transport and the switch from rail to road and from public operators to private ones (Button and Pearman [1B17]). The advantages to the individual firm of having its own fleet are again the flexibility and the control which can be exerted. Often, as with the car user, only marginal costs are considered as fixed costs have already been paid. As with the dispersal of population, the dispersal of industry to peripheral and road accessible sites has made rail less appropriate. However, the public costs imposed by road-based freight industry are also considerable. Their impact individually, particularly for the largest vehicles, is greater than that for cars in environmental, social and energy terms.

Analysis has mainly focused on the land use and transport interrelations and on the journey to work. However, other issues are becoming more important as the structure of cities changes. Decentralization and deindustrialization has led to increased journey to work distances and times in all large cities. Workplaces are no longer concentrated in the city centres but have also become dispersed so that more travel is now orbital, not radial. Public transport provision becomes problematical under these demand conditions. Conversely, there has been a counter trend towards concentration and specialization in other facilities such as shops, schools and health facilities. These activities, together with leisure related activities, have become more important and may form the principle source of patronage for public transport, and analysis methods have been adapted to take account of them (Banister and Hall [1B5], Blunden and Black [1B11], Meyer and Miller [1B34]). Increasing interest is being placed not in the traditional relationships between transport and land use, but in the impact that transport investments will have on local economies, employment and development measures in inner-city areas. In a very different context the same relationships are seen as important in developing countries, namely the role of transport in development (Owen [1B40]).

Reactions to the car-based city have been strong (Adams [1B1], Bendixson [1B9], Plowden [1B42]). Many governments and planners have invested heavily in maintaining compact and accessible cities (Starkie [1B46], Thomson [1B49]). The choice seems clear, either to move inexorably towards the car-dominated city as in the United States (St Clair [1B47]), or to maintain urban structure and restrict the car through physical and economic policy measures. European cities have tended to follow the second alternative and have chosen to subsidize public transport and to invest in rail-based systems (Dunn [1B20]). However, good public transport has to be coupled with restraint on the use of the car. Some cities have gone further and implemented extensive pedestrian schemes in city centres or have introduced management systems that favour local, non-motorized traffic – the *Woonerfs* (Hass-Klau [1B28]).

A The urban context

1A1 BARRETT, S. and FUDGE, C. (eds.) (1981) *Policy and Action*. London: Methuen.

This book is about the relationship between public policy and action, the processes at work within and between agencies involved in making and implementing public policy and the factors affecting those processes. It consists of a collection of case studies and essays which have been grouped into three sections linked with text from the editors. The first part is an introductory review which examines the policy-action relationship, and this is followed by ten case studies. The final section explores policy and action together with analysis methods.

1A2 BOURNE, L.S., SINCLAIR, R. and DZIEWONSKI, K. (eds.) (1984) *Urbanisation and Settlement Systems: International Perspectives*. Oxford: Oxford University Press.

Urbanization is a global phenomenon involving not only the creation of distinct settlement patterns, but the transformation of society. In this volume, a panel of international experts demonstrates the immense diversity of that phenomenon as represented by cities in their own countries. The unifying theme of the volume is the concept of settlement systems, which emphasizes the inter-relationship of urban settlements of varying size and function.

1A3 BRACKEN, I. (1981) *Urban Planning Methods: Research and Policy Analysis*. London: Macmillan.

This book explains a range of concepts so that methods can be applied to urban planning problems. The first part outlines the emergence of the strategic urban plan and policy-making over the past fifteen years and reminds the reader of the broader context – political and administrative – within which planning is placed. Different approaches to plan-making are covered, and this forms the basis for the other two substantive sections, which focus on urban research and policy studies. There is also an extensive set of appendices with practical methodological examples.

1A4 BREHENY, M.J. (1983) A practical view of planning theory. *Environment and Planning B*, **10** (1), pp. 101–115.

In this paper the author identifies a widening gulf between theory and practice in planning during the last decade, in Britain at least. The reasons for, and implications of, this gulf are discussed. He begins by attempting to 'identify' planning and to clarify the meanings of 'theory' and 'prescription'. He argues that both theory and practice are undermined by their separation and that it is essential for the development of planning that the two come back together. The theory-practice link needs to become a major focus of attention both for academics and for practitioners.

1A5 BROTCHIE, J., NEWTON, P., HALL, P. and NIJKAMP, P. (1985) *The Future of Urban Form: the Impact of New Technology*. London: Croom Helm.

The indications seem to be that the information revolution will cause fundamental changes in patterns of work and living. This book presents a range of views on the impact of new technology on urban form. The technological changes covered include automation in the secondary sector, the combination of microprocessors and telecommunications, the impact of energy shortfall, and a range of socio-economic factors. In particular the concern is with the means by which socio-technical changes can alter the direction of urban development through space and location requirements of industry and transport as well as individuals and families.

1A6 CULLINGWORTH, J.B. (1988) *Town and Country Planning in Britain*, 10th ed. London: Unwin Hyman.

This standard review of the British planning system is now in its tenth edition. The chapters cover every aspect of planning and take the reader through the evolution of town and country planning, central and local government, the legislative framework and development control. This broad introduction is followed by more specific issues such as planning and the environment, planning for traffic, planning and land values, recreation and the countryside and new towns. There are also chapters on urban renewal, regional planning and planning and the public. The latest edition updates the significant changes which have taken place in British planning over the last eight years, and new material is included on environmental concerns and conservation in the countryside.

1A7 ELLIOTT, T.B. and MCCRONE, D. (1982) *The City: Patterns of Domination and Conflict*. London: Macmillan.

This book takes a Weberian approach to the analysis of cities, and studies urban institutions and structures, and the actions and aspirations of their inhabitants. To achieve this aim the city is placed in an historical setting and political as well as economic processes are seen as crucial in its development. The book is sociological in its approach and presents a description of urban life including the opportunities for jobs, housing, education and democratic participation.

1A8 ESTRIN, S. and HOLMES, P. (1983) *French Planning in Theory and Practice*. London: George Allen and Unwin.

Economic planning embraces all activities which coordinate economic decisions in a way that would never occur spontaneously. In a market system, coordination is decentralized and choices are left to independent decision-makers; on the other hand, an agency directs the economy to its chosen outcome under central planning. This book is concerned with indicative planning, or planning in a market economy. It explores the scope for an agency to coordinate and disseminate economic information without attempting to direct private choices, considered from the perspective of economic theory and in the light of French planning experience.

1A9 EWERS, H.-J., GODDARD, J.B. and MATZERATH, H. (eds.) (1986) *The Future of the Metropolis: Economic Aspects*. New York: Walter de Gruyter.

In this massive book experiences from four cities are compared – London, New York, Paris and Berlin. Their economic history, present economic problems and political options are discussed, along with descriptions of current trends. The aim is to establish a common research basis so that policy options for industrial metropolises can be assessed. The three sections cover the historical perspective, changes in the spatial structure of economic activity during the last decades in the four cities, and options for economic policy in the metropolis.

1A10 FOOT, D.H.S. (1982) *Operational Urban Models*. London: Methuen.

Urban modelling techniques are an established tool in assessing the possible repercussions of major changes in land use. This book is an introductory guide to the various models that have been developed and to how they can be applied to planning practice, particularly with relation to land-use activities such as residential, industrial and retail development, and changes in the transport network. The focus is on the empirical development of the models and their application.

1A11 FRIEND, J.K. (1983) Reflections on rationalising in strategic choice. *Environment and Planning B*, **10** (1), pp. 63–69.

The author reflects on twenty years of experience in the development of a decision-centred approach to planning – the strategic choice approach – which has found application – both as an aid to the understanding of observed planning processes and as a means of helping planners tackle difficult problems in practice. He first summarizes the view of planning as continuous management of uncertainty, which characterises the strategic choice approach; then looks critically at how far and in what circumstances it is relevant to regard the experience of uncertainty as a meaningful concept at the collective as well as the personal level. This leads to some modest attempts at reformulation of established concepts, which are offered as examples of the kind of progress that can be achieved through pursuing a rationality-seeking, if not a rational, approach to the complexities of planning practice.

1A12 GOLDSMITH, M. (1981) *Politics, Planning and the City*. London: Hutchinson.

This book begins with an analysis of the theoretical context of cities and discusses models of democracy, power and the nature of policy.

Change and the city is a second theme which is presented through a series of case studies on housing, planning and the social services. Discussion then covers the consequences, intended and unintended, for the city of post-war experiences and questions are raised as to whether city governments can cope with the future.

1A13 GRANT, M. (1983) *Urban Planning Law*. London: Sweet and Maxwell.

This is the standard urban planning law text in Britain and it attempts to place the system of controls within a broader functional context. It cites numerous case studies and is explanatory rather than theoretical in its approach. It complements Patrick McAuslan's *The Ideologies of Planning Law* (Oxford: Pergamon, 1982).

1A14 GYFORD, J. (1984) *Local Politics in Britain*. London: Croom Helm.

Local government in Britain has become political in its attitudes and approaches. The reorganization of local government in the 1970s accelerated an already existing trend towards the domination of local councils by party politics. At the same time, the proper role of local government in Britain became the subject of vigorous political argument, especially in the wake of central government attempts to control local authority spending. This book examines the interactions of politicians, officials, political parties, interest groups, the media and the public at local government level. Additionally, the politics of individual local authorities are placed within the wider context of recent debates about the place of local government within the British political system.

1A15 HALL, P. (1980) *Great Planning Disasters*. London: Weidenfeld and Nicolson (also in Pelican).

This book deals with a series of planning decisions and then analyses the central processes involved. The six case studies are taken from Britain, the United States, Australia and the Anglo-French Concorde. The second part of the book analyses the several different actors in the decisions and their own priorities and interests. Finally some tentative suggestions for improved decision-making are presented.

1A16 HALL, P. (1984) Have cities a future? *Futures*, **16** (4), pp. 344–370.

Prospects for the older declining industrial cities may take some reassurances from the example of the US Sunbelt, West Germany and many third world cities. The survival of the city would seem to rely on not only a shift to information processing services but also increasing the ease with which activities, people and ideas are able to move around the urban area. However in the present state of flux and seemingly contradictory indications, prophecy should be approached cautiously.

1A17 HALL, P. and MARKUSEN, A. (eds.) (1985) *Silicon Landscapes*. London: George Allen and Unwin.

The introductory chapter views the process of high-technology growth in terms of long-wave economic development and addresses future issues. The bulk of the book concentrates on US experience, providing insights into the significant contributions of individual innovators, critical commentary on the likelihood of repetitions of innovation, and an analysis of the job creation potential. These developments are contrasted with experience in the UK and the differences in causation and development are examined. Finally, the implications for regional policy are discussed.

1A18 HEALEY, P. (1986) Emerging directions for research on local land-use planning. *Environment and Planning B*, **13** (2), pp. 103–120.

This paper is an exploration of the way the new political economy approaches in the social sciences can be developed to provide a more robust knowledge-base for local land-use planning. Consideration is given to present deficiencies in our understanding and their consequences. There then follows a review of recent developments within political economy and their significance for understanding land-use policy programmes and outcomes. The potential of the approach for addressing methodological issues in the field is then examined, with a particular focus on the importance of a process emphasis, on identifying choices within structural limitations, and on evaluating outcomes.

1A19 HERBERT, J.D. (1979) *Urban Development in the Third World: Policy Guidelines*. New York: Praeger.

1A20 LINN, J.F. (1983) *Cities in the Developing World: Policies for their Equitable and Efficient Growth.* Oxford: Oxford University Press.

The unprecedented rate of urban growth in developing nations created massive new tasks for national and local policy-makers. This book delineates the major policy issues which arise in the efforts to adapt to this growth and it discusses policies designed to increase efficiency and equity of urban development. Particular areas covered include urban employment, income redistribution through the fiscal system, transport, housing and social services. The policy instruments covered include public investment, pricing, taxation and regulation.

1A21 MASSEY, D. and MEEGAN, R. (1982) *The Anatomy of Job Loss.* London: Methuen.

This book examines job loss within the context of economic and political change. The general assumption that the decline in employment is equivalent to the decline in industry is inadequate. Labour's loss is not the same as capital's loss. It is argued that production and location are closely related and that decisions about the latter are crucial. This argument is illustrated with case studies and a comparison of employment decline under monetarist policies with job loss of fifteen years ago.

1A22 MELTZER, J. (1984) *Metropolis to Metroplex: The Social and Spatial Planning of Cities.* Baltimore: Johns Hopkins University Press.

The problems and perspectives of urban planning are reviewed and a viable alternative is suggested for planning and managing the future of American cities. A brief survey of the growth of American cities is provided along with a discussion of the special problems of cities in the twentieth century. The author presents two basic approaches to planning: the social welfare approach, which emphasizes the social needs of the citizen, and the environmental or land-use approach, which is concerned with the utilization and marketing of space. He calls for planners and administrators to take the broad view and to understand that the marketability of land use plans and other programmes ultimately depends on the public's attitudes and behaviour.

1A23 NAKAMURA, R.T. and SMALLWOOD, F. (1980) *The Politics of Policy Implementation*. New York: St Martin's Press.

1A24 OWEN, W. (1987) *Transportation and World Development*. London: Hutchinson.

This book examines the problems and potential of transport on a global scale and includes the movement of people, goods and information. Transport plays a vital role in meeting the world's food requirements, in expanding trade and industry, and in providing access to schools, jobs, services and opportunities for doing business. Many of these issues are common to both the developing and developed world, and the interdependence of the two is being increased through exploitation of resources, trade and travel. The book recommends strategies and proposes specific measures to overcome national and international travel problems.

1A25 OWENS, S. (1987) *Energy Planning and Urban Form*. London: Pion.

The relationship between energy systems and the spatial structure of society has been a subject of growing interest since the energy crisis of the 1970s. It has often been argued that energy considerations should be integrated into the land-use planning process, and some planning authorities – as yet rather few in number – have attempted to put this idea into practice. After a decade of good intention, it is time to take stock. The following issues are explored in detail in the book: the links between energy and spatial structure at the regional, subregional, and local scales; the possible effects of energy constraints on urban and regional trends; and the potential to modify urban form in order to reduce energy requirements for transport and space heating.

1A26 SAUNDERS, P. (1986) *Social Theory and the Urban Question*. London: Hutchinson.

This book begins with a review of the ways in which Weber, Durkheim, Marx and Engels approached the analysis of cities. It then considers four main theoretical approaches which have been developed in twentieth-century urban sociology – those of human ecology, cultural theories, neo-Weberianism and neo-Marxism. Recent ideas and new directions are also discussed and evaluated, and the book concludes by identifying a new sociology of consumption which may now be emerging in the urban studies literature.

1A27 SELF, P. (1980) *Planning the Urban Region*. London: George Allen and Unwin.

About half the populations of Western countries live in huge sprawling urban regions whose planning is done by diverse public bodies such as city governments, new metro governments and various regional planning bodies. The urban region is also the focus of national policies and central government interventions. This book relates the political and organizational factors to the basic elements of planning such as efficiency, environmental conservation, protection of local community life, and the reduction of urban inequalities. Case study material is taken from Britain, the United States, France, Sweden, Canada and Australia.

1A28 SPENCE, N., GILLESPIE, A., GODDARD, J., KENNETT, S., PINCH, S. and WILLIAMS, A. (1982) *British Cities: An Analysis of Urban Change*. Oxford: Pergamon.

The basic objective of this report was to describe the urban change in the United Kingdom since the 1950s, focusing mainly on trends of population and employment change in aggregate. After the basic objective was met, the research continued in order to disaggregate the demographic and economic variables under analysis. It is these disaggregated data which are provided in this book. The information varies widely: employment trends were analysed by birthplace groups and age structure and linked to studies of socio-economic groups. Attention is drawn to the sections of migration and work-travel. The detailed research findings are presented after a brief consideration of worldwide urban change. The book concludes by considering their implications for urban planning.

1A29 TAYLOR, J.C. and WILLIAMS, D.G. (eds.) (1985) *Urban Planning Practice in Developing Countries*. Oxford: Pergamon.

This book presents an overview of planning practice in Asian urban areas through a series of introductory chapters on problems and issues, and criteria for evaluation. The bulk of the volume is taken up by a series of case studies and the conclusions are derived from the practical evidence rather than any theoretical starting point. Good land-use planning is often prevented by lack of knowledge and appropriate skills, not necessarily by a lack of resources or political willpower.

1A30 TROY, P.N. (ed.) (1981) *Equity in the City*. North Sydney: George Allen and Unwin.

1A31 WEBBER, M.M. (1983) The myth of rationality: development planning reconsidered. *Environment and Planning B*, **10** (1), pp. 89–99.

The classical model of rational planning is fundamentally flawed. It assumes widespread consensus on goals, causal theory sufficiently developed as to permit prediction, and effective instrumental knowledge. None of these conditions pertains. As a result, traditional development planning has been proving ineffectual in developed and developing nations alike. That calls for a different style of centralized planning that constrains itself to constituting the rules for deciding and to promoting open debate. In parallel, planning of substantive strategies, designs, and investments should be highly decentralized, thus fostering multiplicities of potential outcomes, compatible with the wants of plural publics.

1A32 WILLIAMS, R.H. (ed.) (1984) *Planning in Europe: Urban and Regional Planning in the EEC*. London: George Allen and Unwin.

This book reviews the operation of the town and country planning system of each of the ten member states of the EEC, and then links this with an outline of the ways in which the policies and institutions of the Commission of the European Communities relate to the activity of planning.

1B The transport context

1B1 ADAMS, J. (1981) *Transport Planning: Vision and Practice*. London: Routledge and Kegan Paul.

The author presents a detailed critique of contemporary transport planning practice and shows how policies have in some cases undermined city, suburban and country lifestyles. The dangers of applying similar methods to other countries are also examined. This very personal view of the transport planning process and its shortcomings has stimulated controversy and debate, and some would argue that it has been influential in changing perceptions of transport issues.

1B2 ALTSHULER, A., WOMACK, J.P. and PUCHER, J.R. (1980) *The Urban Transport System: Politics and Policy Innovation.* Cambridge, Mass: MIT Press.

This book covers the politics and post-war history of urban transport policy, and then advances a series of propositions for ranking potential innovations according to their political feasibility. It also reviews the criteria used in evaluation of the transport system in terms of energy, air pollution, safety, equity, congestion and urban sprawl. Finally, options are discussed in terms of political feasibility and cost effectiveness.

1B3 ALTSHULER, A., ANDERSON, M., JONES, M., ROOS, D. and WOMACK, J. (1984) *The Future of the Automobile.* London: George Allen and Unwin.

This book presents a comprehensive assessment of the world's car industry and analyses the future of the car in terms of environmental and safety challenges, energy imbalance and the dominance of a few producers. The collaborative research team draws on expertise from all the leading producer nations and projects the composition of the industry 20 years hence. Particular emphasis is placed on the growing cooperation between producers on individual models, even though overall competition in the industry has intensified. The authors conclude that in the future there will be even fewer multinational producers competing within an expanding market.

1B4 AMBER, J., SHAW, D.J.B. and SYMONS, L. (1985) (eds.) *Soviet and East European Transport Problems.* London: Croom Helm.

The transport systems of the Soviet Union and Eastern Europe are greatly inferior to those of Western countries. At present there is considerable discussion in the Soviet Union and Eastern Europe concerning their current economic problems and the possibilities of economic reform. This book considers many important aspects of the transport systems in the Eastern block and examines the range of different modes of transport and the problems faced by each. A prospective view is also given of measures which have been taken and their effectiveness.

1B5 BANISTER, D.J. and HALL, P.G. (eds.) (1981) *Transport and Public Policy Planning*. London: Mansell.

This massive tome reviews the current state of transport policy and planning from a broad social science perspective. The first part focuses on a statement of the present position with a series of personal perspectives from researchers with very different experiences. This is followed by sections on resources in transport, alternative technology and the likely impact of the new technology, plus a complementary section on distributional issues. The second major part of the book comprises a comprehensive survey of the methods which have been used in transport analysis. Throughout, certain issues are emphasized, namely the development of methodologies, the variety of techniques which are available, and the links between theory and practice.

1B6 BARAT, J. (1985) Integrated metropolitan transport. Reconciling efficiency, equity and environmental improvement. *Third World Planning Review*, **7** (3), pp. 241–261.

Inter-modal solutions to the problems of congestion in cities should be sought through public transport by the improvement of the operating conditions for buses and existing rail transit facilities. In Third World countries public transport schemes should be planned through the integration of low-cost alternatives with high capacity alternatives in selected corridors.

1B7 BARKER, T. (ed.) (1987) *The Economic and Social Effects of the Spread of Motor Vehicles*. London: Macmillan.

This collection of essays discusses the influence that the car has had over the last century on society. The chapters begin with the origins of the car in Germany, the spread in the United States and further essays on France, Germany and Canada. More recent impacts in Czechoslovakia and Japan contrast with experiences in Zaire and parts of Soviet Central Asia. The general conclusions are similar, namely that the impact is fundamental and that the effects are likely to be with us for at least the next 100 years.

1B8 BAYLISS, D. (1981) One billion new city dwellers – How will they travel? *Transportation*, **10 (4)**, pp. 311–343.

This wide ranging paper tackles the complex issues of how cities can accommodate the predicted levels of growth, and hence travel demand, in the next 20 years. Most of this increase will come in developing countries where existing levels of congestion are among the worst in the world. Alternative strategies for further work are presented.

1B9 BENDIXSON, T. (1977) *Instead of Cars*. Harmondsworth: Penguin.

This classic book examines the alternatives to the ever increasing use of the car. Many different options are considered including buses, trains, pedestrian walkways, taxis and bicycles, as well as the use of new technologies. The approach taken is wide ranging and the interpretation given is also penetrating in that it is not just a question of mobility, but a sensibly integrated system is crucial for safety and to preserve sanity.

1B10 BLACK, J. (1981) *Urban Transport Planning*. London: Croom Helm.

The ways in which transport systems have developed in cities indicates that governments act to meet immediate requirements rather than plan for the future. In an attempt to overcome this problem, a comprehensive approach to planning for future land use and transport facilities has been developed and applied particularly in North America, Britain and Australia, and more recently in developing countries. The book discusses how the systems approach has been applied in the planning of multi-modal transport systems and shows how a city can be represented by land-use zones superimposed with a transport network. By treating the urban area as a system, and recognizing the interactions between land use, traffic and transport, the study shows how it is possible to predict future demand, how transport requirements can be determined, and how alternative plans are formulated and then evaluated. By illustrating the success of the theory when applied to city planning, the book provides a critical and comprehensive state of the art examination.

1B11 BLUNDEN, W.R. and BLACK, J.A. (1984) *The Land-Use/Transport System*. Oxford: Pergamon, Urban and Regional Planning Series 2.

This new edition examines the methods of analysing and treating land use and transport interaction at the local, urban and regional scales. Mathematical concepts are first introduced and then applied at the three distinct scales of analysis. There are also sections on optimization, queueing theory and mathematical programming.

1B12 BLY, P.H. (1985) Technological change and urban form: surface transportation, in Brotchie, J., Hall, P. and Nijkamp, P. (eds.) *The Future of Urban Form: The Impact of New Technology*. London: Croom Helm, pp. 122–141 [1A5].

1B13 BUCHANAN, C. (1983) Buchanan twenty years after: traffic in towns today. *Built Environment*, **9** (2).

A complete issue of *Built Environment* has been devoted to a review of the Buchanan Report on Traffic in Towns from a variety of perspectives. Buchanan himself takes a retrospective view of the significance and relevance of his report today and this is followed by a summary of the changes that have taken place in British cities (overall and in London and Leeds). More critical perspectives are given on the car orientation of the original report and this criticism is contrasted with the view of two Americans where a case of car restraint in California is summarized.

1B14 BUTTON, K.J. (1982) *Transport Economics*. London: Heineman Educational.

The increasingly pressing problems of how to finance local government expenditure, regulate urban land-use patterns, limit traffic congestion and control urban environmental decay, all form central themes of this book. It provides a basic introduction to urban economic theory and attempts to relate theory to practice. Other standard economic texts include Glaister, S. (1981) *Fundamentals of Transport Economics*, Oxford: Basil Blackwell, and Stubbs, P.C., Tyson, W.J. and Dalvi, M.Q. (1980) *Transport Economics*, London: George Allen and Unwin.

1B15 BUTTON, K.J. and PEARMAN, A.D. (1981) *The Economics of Urban Freight Transport*. London: Macmillan.

This volume presents a comprehensive study of the economics of freight transport in Britain and a wide range of other countries. A review section on trends is followed by the main economic theory which covers supply and demand, paying particular attention to environmental and congestion costs as well as costs borne directly by the carrier. Policy options are also included as are the links with public authorities: here, questions of maximizing social welfare are raised. The future of urban freight transport and the impact of national and EEC policy are included in the final chapter.

1B16 BUTTON, K.J. and GILLINGWATER, D. (1986) *Future Transport Policy*. London: Croom Helm.

This book begins with the premise that transport policy is being critically considered and often hotly debated. It presents a comprehensive discussion of the issues involved, examines how transport policies have evolved, what factors have affected present policy-making, and concludes with an assessment of trends likely to prevail in the future. A central theme of the book is the concern for regulation and moves toward deregulation of transport. Relationships between transport and spatial development, and social aspects of transport policy, are also discussed.

1B17 BUTTON, K.J. and PEARMAN, A.D. (1986) *Applied Transport Economics*. London: Gordon and Breach.

A detailed examination of the ways in which economic theory may be applied to transport problems is provided with supporting case studies. Following an introduction, a general overview of transport economics, with highlights of the particular fragments of economic theory that have been drawn on to examine transport problems, is presented. The case studies include an examination of road pricing in Singapore and interurban investment appraisal. The introduction of new technology in an old established transport sector is another focus, and the usefulness of industrial economics is explored.

Other texts by Button, K.J. and Pearman, A.D. include (1985)

Applied Transport Economics: A Practical Case Studies Approach. London: Harwood Academic Publishers, Volume 4 in the Transportation Series; and (eds.) (1983) *The Practice of Transport Investment Appraisal.* Aldershot: Gower.

1B18 DE BOER, E. (ed.) (1986) *Transport Sociology: Social Aspects of Transport Planning.* Oxford: Pergamon.

This edited volume is one of the few collections that synthesizes research on the social aspects of transport. The editor has collected a wide range of good quality, but often dated, papers from well known authors. The papers are grouped into four sections, on the infrastructure, the street, on mobility and ideology; in each case the editor introduces the material.

1B19 DE VORE, P.W. (1983) (ed.) *Introduction to Transportation.* Worcester, Mass: Davis Publications.

The study of transport, its various modes, and the manner in which each mode contributes to the movement of society's resources has been recognized in recent years as a part of overall development in a number of academic disciplines. This text covers the current modes of transport, as well as national and international trends that must be considered by decision-makers in planning future needs. The text is structured to provide information about the relationship of transport to society, the technical and environmental components of the discipline, systems, alternative modes, energy, planning, governmental organizations, research, and future projections.

1B20 DICKEY, J.W., STUART, R.C., DIEWALD, W.J., WALKER, R.D., STEPHENS, N.T., HURST, C.J. and HOBEIKA, A.G. (1983) *Metropolitan Transport Planning.* New York: McGraw-Hill.

The focus of this book is interdisciplinary and covers the transport planning process in a series of modules, which starts with problem identification and ends with project implementation. Coverage is also given to public transport characteristics such as capacity and speed, user costs, air and noise pollution impacts, post-project evaluations, decision-making and community involvement. The volume includes discussion on recent developments in the areas of finance, budgeting and related legislation and organization.

1B21 DUNN, J.A. (1981) *Miles to Go: European and American Transportation Policies*. Cambridge, Mass: MIT Press.

This book systematically compares the American and European policy paradigms with respect to road, rail, urban public transport and the car. The European case studies have been selected to give a comparison and contrast with the different US policies. In this way the benefits and disbenefits of each approach to policy solution can be highlighted. The final part of the book focuses on the great question of what to do with the car. Some changes are suggested that might and, eventually will, have to be made in this realm of American public choice.

1B22 DUPREE, H. (1987) *Urban Transportation: The New Town Solution*. Aldershot: Gower.

The new towns of Great Britain are generally recognized as one of the successes of post-war planning and much has been written about their design concepts and architectural innovations. Less attention has been paid to the towns' transport arrangements. This highly illustrated book traces the history of the 28 new towns and describes in detail how each used its political, professional and financial freedom to develop its own solution to the traffic problem.

1B23 EUROPEAN FOUNDATION FOR THE IMPROVEMENT OF LIVING AND WORKING CONDITIONS (1983) A European study of commuting and its consequences, Report EF/83/26. Shankill, Dublin: European Foundation.

This study looks at commuting from a European perspective. It also includes a selective review of literature, analysis of commuting patterns and policies, and the key issues which are emerging.

1B24 FAULKS, R.W. (1982) *Principles of Transport*. London: Ian Allen.

This book draws together the fundamental issues which are of common importance whatever the branch of transport, considering the basic components, function and characteristics of transport, the structure of the industry and statutory controls over it. Trade organizations, administration, management and industrial relations are all covered, as is the development of the transport system, commercial policies and finance.

1B25 FISHER, R.J. (1984) 'Megatrends' in urban transport. *Transportation Quarterly*, **38** (1), pp. 87–102.

Government involvement in transport markets has undergone considerable change during the last 20 years. Public transport was primarily a private sector business until the 1960s. Now most public transport is publicly owned and operated. However attitudes are again changing with reductions in subsidy levels and a renewed interest in privatization. This paper reviews experience with public ownership and operation of public transport now that it has had a few years to mature.

1B26 FLINK, J.A. (1987) *The Automobile Age*. Cambridge, Mass: MIT Press.

Reviews the history of the car in the US, from the early mass production techniques at the Ford Highland Park plant and the Classic Model T Ford to the present day multiple car owning society. Comment is made on the impact that the car has had on society, life styles, employment, location and the quality of life.

1B27 HALL, P. (1983) Land use change and transport policy. *Habitat International*, **7** (3/4), pp. 67–77.

Following the seminal work of Michael Thomson [1B49], this review classifies the major cities of the world into four groups according to their associated land-use, transport and income-level characteristics. Within limits it is argued that planners can affect the subsequent pattern of development, making a city resemble rather more one archetype than another. This situation is most obvious in the traffic restraint based solution which occurs when the planners impose their most draconian set of options.

1B28 HASS-KLAU, C. (ed.) (1986) New ways of managing traffic. *Built Environment*, **12** (1/2).

This special issue of *Built Environment* covers recent developments in environmental management in European and American cities. Papers discuss pedestrianization and restraint in Britain, *Woonerven* in the Netherlands, pedestrianization, environmental and area wide traffic restraint in Germany, environmental traffic management in Denmark and the redesigning of American residential streets. It seems that similar problems are being experienced in several countries, but that different solutions have been found. Benefits are particularly significant in inner-city areas which suffer from congestion, noise and pollution, together with a shortage of open space.

1B29 HEALEY, P. (1977) The sociology of urban transport planning: a socio-political perspective, in Hensher, D.A. (ed.) *Urban Transport Economics*. Cambridge: Cambridge University Press, pp. 199–227.

This paper argues that transport planning has increasingly experienced a changing social environment, characterized by uncertainty and turbulence. The application of sociology to transport planning in certain specific periods can usefully be seen as a mechanism of adaptation to this environment. First, the various models of social explanation are outlined and then these are placed within the context of transport planning. Secondly, the development of transport planning is seen as a series of stages through acceptance, rejection, response, restudy and an alternative framework. It is concluded that social and environmental evaluation in planning may mean that in the future conflicts will concern explicit choices between goals of a more general significance than those implicit in engineering, economic or narrow impact evaluation.

1B30 HENSHER, D.A. (ed.) (1977) *Urban Transport Economics*. Cambridge: Cambridge University Press.

The essays in this collection were all specially written to provide a systematic and thorough examination of current thinking in urban transport economics. Chapters are included on pricing and investment theory together with applications, demand and supply of passenger and freight transport, interactions between land use and transport, and the relationship between economic theory, sociology [1B29], and institutions.

1B31 KLAASSEN, L.H. (1982) Transportation and societal developments. *International Journal of Transport Economics*, **9** (3), pp. 261–270.

Now that the price of energy and consequently the cost of travelling have risen so steeply, transport will be an important concern in future urban designs, which means that the city planners will have to cooperate more than ever with traffic engineers and transport economists, to arrive at sensible new structures. After the short-term social reorientation, physical reorientation will follow and densities will increase. Physical urban structures may be transformed in the longer run into two stages. The first adjustment could be to prevent current rules for urban design being applied in the future. New constructions could at least be adapted to the present high transport costs. The second adjustment would be to increase existing densities. The philosophy behind the reorientation policy is that we should not, as we have done too often in the past, create physical structures with total disregard for the volume and structure of traffic they generate. The proposal is to design physical structures that implicitly minimize total generalized transport costs for the city as a whole. The less diffuse society, to which we are once more moving, may generate a form of planning which can create new cities that are better to live in.

See also: Klaassen, L.H. (1980) Urban developments and transportation, *International Journal of Transport Economics*, **7** (2), pp. 123–132; and Klaassen, L.H., Bourdrez, J.A. and Volmuller, J. (1981) *Transport and Reurbanisation*. Aldershot: Gower.

1B32 MEYER, J.R. and GOMEZ-IBANEZ, J.A. (1981) *Autos, Transit and Cities*. Cambridge, Mass: Harvard University Press.

The authors recommend that future urban transport must not only be produced by improvement of public transit within clear guidelines but also must give a prominent, although refined, role to the private car. Following a brief review of the way in which urban travel patterns and systems have evolved, the authors continue by describing how government policies were misdirected as they aimed at increasing the effectiveness of mass transport. They discuss not only buses, commuter trains and rapid transit, but the less traditional modes such as van-pooling and dial-a-ride, indicating where public policy went wrong and how to make future public transportation more effective. They then turn to the automobile's impact on land use, energy, air pollution and aesthetics. They discuss safety and transport of the disadvantaged, offering suggestions for dealing with these problems. It is concluded that many transport problems can be solved only by adapting the automobile to meet the increasingly stringent requirements of urban life.

1B33 MEYER, J.R., KAIN, J.F. and WOHL, M. (1965) *The Urban Transportation Problem*, Cambridge, Mass: Harvard University Press.

This seminal book marked the change from traffic being treated as a technical exercise carried out by engineers with some help from economists, to transport planning where all parts of the transport question were covered, in particular the quality of urban transport. The approach used adopts the scientific paradigm where quantifiable relationships between transport and other urban variables (e.g. population, employment and housing) are established. The volume also has a section on the supply side and covers appropriate methods for cost accounting procedures and evaluation. New systems are included in the final section.

1B34 MEYER, M.D. and MILLER, E.J. (1984) *Urban Transportation Planning: A Decision-Oriented Approach*. New York: McGraw-Hill.

The dramatic changes that have taken place in the environment of planning (and this includes the political, fiscal, technological, social, economic, and institutional dimensions) during the last 10 years require a new perception of urban transport planning. This is one of the first textbooks on urban transport planning to reflect the energy crises, municipal finance problems, and major cutbacks in large-scale facility investment that have occurred in recent years. The approach to urban transport planning is different from the traditional transport planning process in which a comprehensive plan is envisioned as a major product of the process. In this new approach it is recognized that, to be effective, urban transport planning must be related to the types of decisions that will be made in a particular problem area and thus to the decision-making process that will produce these decisions. The authors emphasize throughout the link between decision-making and planning, the relationship between techniques and process, and the difference between planning aimed solely at quantitative analysis versus planning oriented toward influencing decisions.

The approach to urban transport planning described is based on the information needs of decision-makers and the recognition that it is equally important to provide decision-makers the information they need as to provide them the information they desire to ensure a more complete understanding of the problem and of the implications of different solutions to the problem. The authors define urban transport planning as the process of understanding the types of decisions to be made; assessing opportunities and limitations of the future; identifying the short- and long-term consequences of alternative choices designed to take advantage of these opportunities or respond to these limitations; relating alternative decisions to the goals and objectives established for an area, agency, or firm; and presenting this information to decision-makers in a readily understandable and useful form.

1B35 MOAVENZADEH, F. and GELTNER, D. (1984) *Transportation Energy and Economic Development: A Dilemma in the Developing World*. New York: Elsevier.

Planners and policy-makers in developing countries are faced with the dilemma of how to provide the transport development necessary for economic growth without increasing petroleum consumption to the detriment of trade balances and economic growth. This book is the first to address this important problem. It is divided into three main parts. Part I contains background information about the most important aspects of the transport-energy-development interaction, including relevant statistics and figures regarding the three underlying binary relationships (transport and development, energy and development, and transport and energy). The relationship between transport and energy consumption is explored in Part II with a particular focus on active or potential ways to save energy in transport. Part III focuses on different aspects of how to save petroleum in the transport sector of developing countries.

See also: Money, L.J. (1984) *Transportation, Energy and the Future*. Englewood Cliffs, NJ: Prentice-Hall.

1B36 MOGRIDGE, M.J.H. (1985) Transport, land use and energy interaction. *Urban Studies* **22** (6), pp. 481–492.

An analysis of data from London and Paris, using directly comparable methods of expressing all results in terms of distance from the centre, is undertaken of the following variables: population density, mean household income, car ownership, median daily travel time per traveller, and energy consumption. It is argued that the results demonstrate that population density and public transport provision are far less important influences on energy consumption than car ownership, and that it follows that economizing energy consumed per car is far more important than policies concerned with decentralization or public transport service levels. The importance of the rail network in setting road network speeds is also noted.

1B37 NASH, C.A. (1982) *Economics of Public Transport*. Harlow: Longman.

The book indicates the manner in which economic analysis can be used as an aid in decision taking in long-range planning and also the daily management of public transport systems. Using detailed applications, the book demonstrates the usefulness of applying economic analyses to problems such as fare structures and level, service planning and investment decisions. Although the emphasis is on road and rail systems, which form the bulk of internal public transport systems, the methods employed can be applied to other transport modes. International comparisons are used to show the relationship between objectives, external circumstances, organizations and policy in the operation of public transport organizations.

1B38 OGDEN, K.W. (1980) Some thoughts on the effects on Australian urban transport of structural economic change. *Environment and Planning A*, **12**, pp. 409–425.

This paper reviews the existing Australian situation in respect of urban person and freight transport. It identifies those aspects likely to be sensitive to structural economic change and related changes. The extent of such sensitivity is discussed using such empirical evidence as is available. In particular the paper examines the possible effects on urban transport of such factors as changes in the demographic structure, changes in energy, institutional and political change, and technological change, as well as structural economic change.

1B39 ORSKI, C.K. (1982) The changing environment of urban transportation. *Journal of the American Planning Association*, **48** (3), pp. 309–314.

A combination of rising operating costs, dwindling federal subsidies, and unfulfilled public expectations about the promise of mass transport are prompting local jurisdictions to question the logic of existing public transport arrangements and to search for less costly and more effective alternatives. The outcome of this reappraisal may be nothing less than a fundamental restructuring and reform of urban public transport. This article discusses the issues that form the backdrop and shape the agenda for the current re-examination of traditional urban transport premises.

See also: *Built Environment* (1983), **8** (3), pp. 157–166.

1B40 OWEN, W. (1985) Transportation and world development. *Transportation Quarterly*, **39** (2), pp. 365–374.

Throughout most of recorded history, humanity has been confined to the narrow geographic limits imposed by poor transport. This paper reviews the current situation and the different sources of aid supplied for Third World transport. It then goes on to outline alternative strategies to overcome the shortage of resources, and the means by which an effective programme can be organized. The present situation in the evolution of transport makes a world that is half mobile and affluent and half immobile and destitute. This is an anomaly which has to be rectified.

See also: *International Journal of Transport Economics*, (1984) **11** (2–3), August.

1B41 PEISER, R.B. (1984) Land use versus road network design in community transport cost evaluation. *Land Economics*, **60** (1), pp. 95–109.

The purpose of this paper is to present the results of an experiment to evaluate the importance of land-use location relative to road network design in determining transport costs within a community. In the trade-off between land-use location and road network design, more attention should be placed on the road design factors; in practice the reverse seems to occur.

1B42 PLOWDEN, S. (1980) *Taming Traffic*. London: Andre Deutsch.

This book follows on from his previous *Towns Against Traffic* and moves away from the critique of the principles and methods of analysis used in land-use transport plans towards the development of a comprehensive alternative approach. Accessibility, not travel, is seen as the key and the book discusses the means by which access for all can be maintained or improved at a minimum environmental cost.

1B43   RALLIS, T. (1987) *City Transport in Developed and Developing Countries*. London: Macmillan.

The introduction gives a view of city transport research and education through the years, and attempts to classify cities in time and space. Evolution factors are covered together with socio-economic characteristics, modes of transport, networks and volumes of traffic. The central part of the book covers models of travel, traffic and land use, and case study material is taken from a wide range of cities as well as on the Megalopolis corridors. The conclusion tries to answer the question as to how much space and time shall be devoted to transport in cities of 50 million inhabitants.

1B44   RIMMER, P.J. (1986) Transport geography. *Progress in Human Geography*, **10** (3), pp. 397–406.

This short paper reviews the contribution of geographers to the study of transport over the last eight years and updates an earlier review by the same author. Much work seems to have been carried out on the land use and transport interactions, the development of analytical techniques and new directions in transport analysis. Policy analysis seems to have lagged behind, but new issues here (e.g. privatization and subsidization) may again bring a further revolution in the types of analytical techniques required.

1B45   SIMPSON, B.J. (1987) *Planning and Public Transport in Great Britain, France and West Germany*. Harlow: Longman.

This book presents detailed information on all forms of public transport in three EEC countries – Great Britain, France and West Germany. Policy differences are outlined together with decision-making processes, legislative contexts and the links between central and local government. Case studies are taken from Birmingham, Frankfurt and Lyon to review the prospects for innovation in public transport.

1B46   STARKIE, D.N.M., (1982) *The Motorway Age*. Oxford: Pergamon.

This book is written around a central theme which expounds the way in which road and traffic policies developed at a national level in the UK after 1945 in response to pressure to provide more road space both within and between towns. The broad structure used is chronological with each chapter focusing on a particular issue or development. The final chapter is speculative in that it assesses the various transport policies implemented in the last 30 years of road building, and it tries to infer reasons and conditions which are necessary before a policy is changed.

1B47 ST CLAIR, D.J. (1986) *The Motorization of American Cities.* Westport, Conn: Greenwood Press.

In the 1920s travel in US cities and towns and across the country most likely would have been by foot, by streetcar or jitney, or perhaps by taxicab. Elevated railways and subways were available in a few of the larger cities. The basic question the author raises here is 'Why did all those streetcars disappear, and how and why did we get all those urban freeways and highways?' Attention is focused primarily on the role of firms in the US automobile industry in motorizing public transit and in influencing highway policy. The economics of public transit, as it relates to the motorization, is explored, along with the factors contributing to the decline of transit.

1B48 STUDNICKI-GIZBERT, K.W. (1986) The changing nature of transport policy and planning. *International Journal of Transport Economics,* **13** (3), pp. 262–291.

This paper reviews how transport analysis has developed in response to changing problems in the transport field, particularly scarcity of resources in recent years. Changing transport sector management and its relationship with macro-economic management is considered. Special reference is made to developing countries.

1B49 THOMSON, J.M. (1977) *Great Cities and Their Traffic.* Harmondsworth: Penguin.

This classic book is a study of one of the most critical problems facing all major cities in the world today – the immense growth of urban traffic and how to deal with it. The urban transport problem has many facets and the same symptoms occur in all cities regardless of wealth, car ownership, the size of the road system or the railway system. After tracing the development of these problems the author devotes the major part of the book to the different approaches used in many cities to tackle the transport question. Five strategies are identified and examined in detail.

1B50 THOMSON, J.M. (1983) Towards Better Urban Transport Planning in Developing Countries. World Bank Staff Working Paper 600, Washington, DC.

The first part of the paper describes the weaknesses of the methods and the difficulties that planners face when trying to use them, particularly in developing countries. The intention is not destructive, but rather to show where the methods need to be improved. The second part of the paper suggests a way forward that builds on the lessons learnt over the last 30 years of applications. Rather than abandoning the whole approach, more care and experience are needed in planning the study process and the structure of the models to be used.

Most important is an appropriate organization with the political, financial and administrative capability to plan; this structure should be supplemented by instruction in the techniques of planning. The approach recommended is based on a two-plan process – a directional plan and a design plan. Directional planning explores the major changes in land use, transport networks and policy. While the design plan goes into specific details of projects on a short-term time scale. Both sets of plans should be amenable to feasibility tests and capable of full costings.

1B51 TRANSPORT AND ROAD RESEARCH LABORATORY (1980) The Demand for Public Transport, Report of the International Collaborative Study of the Factors Affecting Public Transport Patronage. Crowthorne: TRRL.

This major collaborative study brought together individuals from nine countries to examine the factors affecting public transport patronage. This comprehensive summary of the study covers the social context, trends in public transport, methods of analysis and data collection, the sociology of transport planning, the effects of income and car ownership, the effects of fares, quality of service, land use patterns and transport policy, the costs of transit operations and finally the interaction of supply and demand.

Shortened versions of the full document have been published by Webster, F.V. and Bly P.H. (1981 and 1982) in *Transport Reviews* **1** (4), pp. 323-351 and **2** (1), pp. 23-46.

1B52 US DEPARTMENT OF TRANSPORTATION (1983) Urban Transportation Planning in the United States – An Historical Overview. Office of the Assistant Secretary for Policy and International Transportation, Washington, DC.

This report covers 50 years in the evolution of urban transport planning, from early developments in highway planning in the early 1930s to the shift to decentralization of decision-making authority in the 1980s. The key event during this period was the Federal-Aid Highway Act of 1962, which created the federal mandate for a continuing, comprehensive urban transport planning process carried out cooperatively by states and local governments. Planning processes and procedures evolved over the years as new issues and concerns were raised and changes in attitudes and priorities occurred. Planning processes have become more complex and sophisticated but have retained many of the earlier elements and objectives. The evolution is still continuing with the objective of improving procedures and institutions that are adapted to the needs and concerns of today's planners, citizens, and decision makers.

1B53 VAUGHAN, R.J. (1987) *Urban Spatial Traffic Patterns*. London: Pion.

This book is a comprehensive and readable account of continuous models of urban travel, bringing together results which were widely dispersed in the literature. A distinctive feature is the simplicity of the mathematical expressions used, incorporating only a small number of parameters and hence requiring minimal amounts of information and computation. The distribution of homes, workplaces, traffic networks, and traffic over an urban area is represented in terms of distance to the town centre. A simple model is developed for the number of work trips from one suburban area to another. This model and basic representations of traffic networks are used to create a theory of the spatial distribution of traffic over an urban area, and the theory is tested against data from many cities. Thus it is possible for the first time to evaluate quickly and inexpensively the effect on traffic of changes in homes, workplaces, and the transport network.

1B54 VAZIRI, M. and LAM, T.N. (1985) The dynamics of land use/transportation interactions and their planning implications. *Socio-Economic Planning Sciences*, **19** (2), pp. 87–94.

An idealized abstract example of the interactions between two homogeneous regions was studied with respect to a range of policies related to transport and land-use planning. The study took the form of a series of differential equations, each of which represented the rate of change in either the land use or transport parameters.

1B55 VICKERMAN, R.W. (1980) *Spatial Economic Behaviour. The Microeconomic Foundations of Urban and Transport Economics.* London: Macmillan.

The aim of this text is to provide a rigorous introduction to the analysis of various decisions involving a spatial dimension, and to integrate them more closely into a unified theory of spatial economics. There are four parts to the development of the analysis. First, the economics of choice is extended to consider simple decisions about choice of travel mode and destination, residential and other locations and activities with a spatial dimension. Following this, various complications are introduced to cover choice under uncertainty, the theory of search, and conflicts between different groups of decision-makers in local economies. In the third part an attempt is made to relate the various sectors of the local economy together in both equilibrium and disequilibrium adaptive frameworks. Finally the various themes are drawn together with suggestions for future methods of analysis and planning in spatial economies.

1B56 WEBSTER, F.V., PAULLEY, N., BLY, P.H., DASGUPTA, M. and JOHNSTON, R.H. (1985) *Changing Patterns of Urban Travel.* European Conference of Ministers of Transport, Paris.

This report analyses changes in household travel survey data and public transport trends in Europe, North America and Australia. It considers the mechanisms underlying past changes and examines the impact of subsidy and restraint policies upon choice of mode of transport. The impacts of land-use zoning on urban travel patterns are also covered.

See also: *Transport Reviews*, **6** (1), pp. 49–86 and **6** (2), pp. 129–172.

1B57 WERLIN, H.H. (1984) Urban transportation systems in the developing world. *Ekistics*, **51** (306), pp. 192–196.

There is a need for a new approach to the provision of urban transport in developing countries. Alternatives suggested in this short paper include improved safety, making better use of the existing road infrastructure, and low cost traffic management schemes.

1B58 WHITE, P.R. (1986) *Public Transport: Its Planning and Operation*. London: Hutchinson.

Public transport plays an increasing role in our daily life, but knowledge of the way in which it can best be planned to fulfill its crucial role is limited. There is a gap between existing practice and the technical analytical methods used in much research. This book attempts to integrate both parts through a presentation of current British practice in planning, management and operation. The discussion in the central part of the book is then placed in the context of current government policy.

1B59 WHITE, P.R. (1983) Transport, in Pacione M. (ed.) *Progress in Urban Geography*. London: Croom Helm, pp. 168–192.

This review summarizes recent developments in urban transport through trip length changes, the importance of different modes and the effects of city size. Differences in travel behaviour according to person type and household structure are then examined, together with the effect of time on these patterns. Shifting from the demand to supply side, the review then looks at finance and system management. Finally, changes in technology and possible future trip patterns are discussed.

1B60 WHITELEGG, J. (1985) *Urban Transport*. Macmillan Educational: Aspects of Geography Series.

This basic text focuses on social issues in transport in Britain, West Europe and the USA, and how lifestyles in cities are having to accommodate to the imposition of the car. Also covered are the city of the future which may arise through the introduction of telecommunications, and other more radical changes which might occur. There are sections on most modes of transport in urban areas and freight transport is included in the coverage.

1B61 WHITT, J.A. (1982) *Urban Elites and Mass Transportation: The Dialectics of Power*. Princeton, NJ: Princeton University Press.

This study compares three models of political power to see which can best explain the development of the Bay Area Rapid Transit system in San Francisco and the attempts of Los Angeles to build a similar system. Of the pluralist, the elitist, and the class-dialectical models, it is the last which provides the most complete picture of the complex politics of urban transport. Public policy, private planning and the shape of cities are used to serve the interests of those in power. However, when conflict arises within the dominant class, its power is limited by that conflict, as well as by conflict with opposing classes.

1B62 WORLD BANK (1986) *Urban Transport: A World Bank Policy Study*. Washington, DC: The World Bank.

During the last ten years the World Bank has refined its approach to urban transport and has changed its emphasis. Two main tests are now applied to each project. The first ensures that projects are designed to achieve sustained sector-wide benefits, for example projects that improve transport system management or demonstrate replicability, not just those which are targeted at limited sections of the community. Secondly, there is a concern over wider-based transport policies which permit low-cost solutions and include institutional improvements.

The policies put forward in the paper very much reflect current World Bank thinking with the underlying principles of economic viability, financial viability and efficiency in all project assessments. Subsidy inhibits expansion and transport improvements should be self sustaining and replicable. At the heart of this paper is the acceptance of the market as the main determinant of transport provision. Concern is also stated over low-income groups but is not clear how any social priorities can be incorporated into the picture. The World Bank objectives for transport are to: improve efficiency and alleviate poverty in cities by stimulating economic growth and productivity through cost effective installation, operation and management of transport systems.

2 Policy and planning in transport

2A Great Britain

Policy has evolved over the last thirty years without any clear objectives, despite a series of government pronouncements (GB Department of Transport [2A12], Grant [2A16]). Three of the main features in this evolution have been investment priorities (Painter [2A21]), the balance between private and public transport (Robbins [2A23]), and the changes in the role that government itself should play. The 1960s were characterized by road building, accommodating the rapid growth in car ownership and the large-scale redevelopment of town centres. This period of buoyant economic growth was terminated by the energy crisis of 1973–74 with the sharp increases in fuel prices, hyperinflation and a worldwide recession. Policy switched in the 1970s to ensuring the better use of the existing infrastructure through traffic management, junction design modifications, area traffic control and bus priority. It was during this decade that bus and rail services required increased subsidies to maintain existing service levels (Confederation of British Road Passenger Transport [2A7], Gourvish [2A15]).

In the 1980s the principal change has been the replacement of the planned approach to transport provision with the market approach. Public investment is now directed at the basic transport infrastructure through capital investment projects (in roads and railways), whilst the passenger has to pay a market price for the service offered.

This strategy has led to reductions in the overall levels of government expenditure and modifications in the means by which resources have been distributed in transport (Council for Science and Society [2A8], Hibbs [2A18], Plowden [2A22]).

Until about 1980, governments have always played a major interventionist role in transport decisions. The underlying philosophy was that transport should be made available to meet the needs of the population and that everyone could expect a minimum level of mobility, almost as a right. To this end, once the basic road infrastructure had been established, investment was switched to public transport in the form of capital and revenue expenditure. More important in this respect were the roles attached to integration and coordination of services, travelcards and low fares, and a comprehensive network of services which ran throughout the day and on every day of the week (Wistrich [2A26]).

Since 1980 the role of government has been significantly reduced and market forces have been allowed to determine both the quantity and, to a great extent, the quality of urban transport services (Balcombe *et al.* [2A2], Carr [2A6]). All transport should where ever possible be produced by the private sector, services should be determined competitively not in a coordinated fashion, and fares should be market priced. Coupled with these changes is a move towards greater precision in defining the objectives for all public transport enterprises, particularly financial performance measures and the quality of service standards. In practice the reduced role of government is more apparent than real, as it could be argued that central government has become more powerful; it is at the local level that the impacts have really been felt with the abolition of the Greater London Council and the Metropolitan County Councils, the protected expenditure levels and the deregulation legislation. Similarly, where intervention from central government has taken place, it has been targeted towards individual initiatives (e.g. Urban Development Corporations) to correct market distortions (Banister [2A3], Goodwin *et al.* [2A14]).

2B United States of America

Similar trends can be seen in the United States with the search for a national transport policy ever since the Department of Transportation was set up in 1967. Prior to this, the two key events were the Federal-Aid Highway Act of 1962 which created the federal mandate for a continuing comprehensive urban transport planning process carried out cooperatively by states and local governments (Weiner [2B24]), and the Urban Mass Transportation Act of 1964 which provided federal assistance to public transport. Public transport in urban areas had been in decline, and despite cutbacks in services and increases in fares, profitability was only maintained until 1968. Since then it has been operating at a deficit. There are about 1000 public transport operations in the United States, and most are very small bus operations which have gradually moved into public ownership as the financial situation deteriorated (Smerk [2B17]).

During the 1970s actions were taken to reverse a series of public concerns about the inadequate treatment of social and environmental impacts, the focus and preference given to the car, and the almost exclusive interest with long range time horizons. Legislation increased funds for public transport and stressed multi-modal analysis, the importance of budget limitations and the need to improve productivity. Procedures in the US meant new legislation, amended legislation, principally through such measures as transport systems management (Gakenheimer and Meyer [2B4]), a series of National Transportation Studies and several important conferences (Levinson and Weant [2B10]).

In the 1980s the focus has shifted towards the maintenance and improvement of existing facilities, with appropriate roles being defined for national and city governments and for the private sector (Allen [2B1], Gordon and Meyer [2B5], Weiner [2B22]). Transport decisions are principally on a short-term horizon and are guided by the market place rather than by regulation, with decisions being decentralized to state and local governments (McDowell [2B11]). The federal government is reducing its involvement, and the responsibility for local problems is at the local level; it may be difficult for urban transport planning processes to adapt as their development has been controlled by federal requirements. Simpler and short-term planning may be the answer (Wachs [2B21]).

2C Europe

Under Article 3 of the Treaty of Rome (1957) the newly formed EEC stated that 'the activities of the Community shall include . . . the adoption of a common policy in the sphere of transport' (European Community [2C4]). However, progress has been very slow with little agreement between the national and supernational dimensions in transport policy (Gwilliam [2C6]). The Commission's policy has incorporated three main elements: the elimination of discrimination, the integration of international transport, and the organization of the national transport market. As Whitelegg [2C14] has commented, other important supranational issues such as transport and the quality of life, energy, safety and transport and regional development have all been ignored. These shortcomings are now being remedied with a new research programme covering these issues, and the European Conference of Ministers of Transport (ECMT), the broader and political sister organization, has covered some of these topics in its research programme (Ribu [2C12]). The EEC is also moving rapidly towards the liberalization of the market, particularly in the freight sector where regulations will be significantly reduced in 1992, and in civil aviation.

2D Organizational and institutional issues

Coupled with the move towards deregulation of urban transport services has been privatization. The organization of public transport has been radically changed through management buy-outs and the injection of private capital from institutions and banks (Lave [2D2], Mulley and Wright [2D5]). Some of these new practices which are being set up in Europe and North America have been tested in developing countries for many years (Rimmer [2D9], Roth [2D10]). Traditional attitudes to transport have changed, and it is likely that private sector practices, accountability to shareholders and commercial operational criteria will become important determinants of profitability.

Similarly, the institutional framework has changed with the reorganization of the transport planning functions of central and local government (Sections 2A, 2B and 2C: May [2D4], Schmitt *et al.* [2D11]). Studies of institutional structures and decision-making have been limited and often retrospective (Levin [2D3]), or on particular issues such as control and licensing in transport (Glaister and Mulley [2D1]).

2E Management and labour practices

Management issues have emphasized the political nature of many transport decisions, and many decisions are taken not as a result of careful analysis of the problems but for other reasons (Wachs [2E11]). Politicization of transport influences decisions on equity, subsidization and accessibility as well as decisions that effect employment and the location of the car industry, even under the market system (Butler and Schneider [2E1], Ward [2E12]). New management structures are required to accommodate changes in transport organizations and operating practices.

Linked with the organizational changes have been radical innovation with increased part-time labour (Chomitz and Lave [2E2]) and a general lowering of labour costs in public transport (Teal and Giuliano [2E10], Wallis [2D14]). Employment issues are also crucial as transport has historically been a major employer and contributed significantly to the local economy (Altshuler *et al* [1B3]). Changes are also required in methods of training and research to meet these new challenges (Kulash [2E6], Meyer [2E7]).

Changes in transport have to be set against other changes in the economy as a whole; reductions are taking place in the hours in a working week, labour (particularly female) participation rates are higher, and labour is being substituted by technology. World trends indicate that unemployment rates have stabilized at historically high levels and that skilled labour is becoming increasingly mobile.

2A Great Britain

2A1 ADAM SMITH INSTITUTE (1983) *Transport, Omega Report*. Adam Smith Institute, London.

This Conservative 'think tank' regularly produces controversial and radical statements on the scope for free enterprise in all sectors of government activity. This report investigates public transport organization and policy, but goes further and argues for deregulation, decentralization and privatization in varying degrees for roads, road transport and the railways. The most controversial section suggests road pricing so that the car user is aware of the full social costs imposed by him on others.

2A2 BALCOMBE, R.J., HOPKIN, J.M., PERRETT, K.E. and CLOUGH, W.S. (1987) Bus deregulation in Great Britain: A review of the opening stages. Transport and Road Research Laboratory, Research Report 107. Crowthorne: TRRL.

The Transport Act 1985 abolished quantity control of bus services in Great Britain (outside London) and allowed subsidy to be paid for bus services only after competitive tendering. Preparations for the change started in January 1986, and the new regime effectively began on 26 October 1986. Between 70 and 80 per cent of previous bus services were operated commercially, without subsidy, although not always in exactly the same form as before. Local authorities specified subsidized services to supplement commercial ones, attempting to preserve broadly the same overall service levels as before, and invited tenders for them. Tender prices were such that most authorities were able to let contracts for all the services they required, at subsidy levels well within their budgets. Competition between bus services has occurred in only a limited number of cases so far, and has caused few serious traffic congestion problems. There have been random fluctuations in fares, but no systematic trend has yet been detected.

2A3 BANISTER, D. (1984) Central-local relations in Britain: The case of the fares fair policy in London. *Transport Policy and Decision Making*, **2** (3), pp. 275-289.

There is considerable debate over the responsibilities that central and local government should have over the provision of public transport in urban areas. This paper reviews various theoretical frameworks within which this policy dilemma can be investigated, and then analyses the London Fares Fair policy issue (over the period 1981-1982) within a dualist approach advocated by Saunders. The policy context in Britain is outlined together with the particular responsibilities of the Greater London Council in providing public transport services, and this provides an introduction to the case study of low fares policy. The outcomes of the successful implementation of the policy and its subsequent reversal are analysed within an organizational, economic, political and ideological framework. The inevitable conclusion reached is that central control has increased and that this dominance is likely to continue.

2A4 BANISTER, D. and BOTHAM, R. (1985) Joint land use and transport planning: The case of Merseyside, in Harrison, A.J. and Gretton, J. (eds.) *Transport UK 1985: An Economic, Social and Policy Audit*. Newbury: Policy Journals, pp. 95-100.

Transport planning and land-use planning often seem to take place as separate activities with little communication between the professionals concerned. The experience in Liverpool is used to argue this case. It seems that although policy, social conditions and employment have all changed radically over the last thirty years, there has been continuity in planning approaches and policy. The arguments may have changed and the emphasis switched from roads to public transport, but despite the social change land-use and transport policy has remained remarkably robust.

2A5 BUCHANAN, M., BURSEY, N., LEWIS, K., MULLEN, P. and TZEDAKIS, A. (1980) *Transport Planning for Greater London*. Farnborough: Saxon House.

The book reviews transport policies in Greater London and distinguishes between those policies that are effective and those that are not. The authors evaluate issues involved in formulating transport plans for a large metropolitan area and suggest an appraisal of all policy options and a more consistent application of those selected. Policies in all the major fields are reviewed covering road and rail transport improvement, the operation of buses and traffic management. The priorities and improvements suggested are intended as relevant to problems of transport planning in major cities.

2A6 CARR, J.D. (1986) (ed.) *Passenger Transport*: *Planning for Radical Change*. Aldershot: Gower.

This book brings together papers presented at a conference on the major changes which have taken place in Britain over the deregulation of bus services and the abolition of the metropolitan county councils. Four main sections cover the institutional framework, the assessment of needs, competition versus coordination and charting the way ahead.

2A7 CONFEDERATION OF BRITISH ROAD PASSENGER TRANSPORT (1981) *Urban Planning and Design for Road Public Transport*. London: CPT.

For the past 15 years, documents on urban transport have emphasized the need to improve public transport. But few have offered specific advice in Britain: this contrasts with the situation in the rest of Europe. This book explains the need for good public transport in urban areas and develops guidelines for effective services between residential, industrial, commercial and shopping areas. It also looks at ways to encourage organizational integration between the different agencies involved in transport provision and moves towards a positive approach to the improvement of public transport for the benefit of the whole community.

2A8 COUNCIL FOR SCIENCE AND SOCIETY (1986) Access for All? Technology and Urban Movement, Report of a Working Party. London.

The evolution of society can be seen as succeeding waves of technological and social development and associated movement patterns. With the technological revolution fundamental changes are taking place in society and this paper raises the main issues. The demand for movement is likely to increase, particularly by car, and the current approaches to transport planning may be inappropriate. Choices have to be made concerning the allocation of public resources, concerning the types of cities which people live in and concerning the complex social patterns which people are adopting. Certain questions are posed to ensure accessibility is available to all people and to ensure that the environment does not deteriorate as a result of increased mobility. Solutions are not offered, but awareness is raised about the suitability of the current trends in transport policy. Society is changing and the ways in which people are enabled to meet their needs for access must also change. Otherwise the least able to meet their own needs for access will become worse off.

2A9 EVANS, A. (1985) Equalising grants for public transport subsidy. *Journal of Transport Economics and Policy*, **19** (2), pp. 105–135.

In this paper ideas on economic modelling and evaluation have been coupled with ideas on equalization from the field of local government finance. The main conclusion is that if the usual equalization principle were applied to public transport subsidy, almost all central government grant should go to rural areas. Subsidy is directed at urban areas for other reasons.

2A10 FOSTER, C. and GOLAY, J. (1986) Some curious old practices and their relevance to equilibrium in bus competition. *Journal of Transport Economics and Policy*, **20** (2), pp. 191–216.

Many of the bad practices of bus drivers before 1933 will be prevented under the Transport Act 1985, or will be unprofitable. Others which may be revived are not necessarily harmful and may be conducive to competitive equilibrium. The authors make suggestions for policy. Local bus monopolies were created in the 1930s, *inter alia* to overcome dangerous competitive practices. The 1985 Transport Act restored local competition. This paper uses and extends elements of models developed to examine spatial equilibrium, to examine whether equilibrium exists and, if not, whether former dangerous practices will be revived. The answer is that in plausible circumstances, equilibrium exists and the worrying practices would not be rational on routes without appreciable congestion and where demand is reasonably predictable. Otherwise they may occur, but should not be disequilibrating.

2A11 GB DEPARTMENT OF TRANSPORT (1981) *Report of the Inquiry into Lorries, People and the Environment* (chaired by Sir Arthur Armitage). London: HMSO.

The report argues the economic benefits, particularly in the form of reduced transport costs, that accrue from the use of heavier lorries. However, the effects on people and the environment are more complex. Proposals here include the separation of lorries from people through investment in bypasses and the use of local lorry bans, including restrictions on parking. However, the true horizon for these proposals may be 20 years, during which people would suffer unduly from the heaviest lorries. So the lorries themselves have to be improved. Safety proposals relate to brakes and underrun guards, whilst other environment improvements are suggested including reductions in noise and smoke emission. There are also stricter controls over lorry sizes, axle weights and wheel configurations with the vehicle excise duty being related to the road track costs that are imposed. This package of measures has now been accepted by the government.

2A12 GB DEPARTMENT OF TRANSPORT (1984) Buses. House of Commons, Command Paper 9300. London: HMSO.

This Command Paper outlines the government's proposals for major changes to arrangements for the bus industry with a view to giving better service to the passengers at less cost to the ratepayer and the tax payer. The changes concern: abolition of road service licensing throughout the United Kingdom (except for the framework of controls in London which will be retained for the time being); increased supervision of the quality and safety standards of public service vehicles and operators; continued subsidies by local authorities for bus routes which are not viable, but local authorities will be required to seek competitive tenders; continuation of concessionary fare schemes with all operators being enabled to participate in them; additional support by the government for transport in rural areas, and study of the wider use of services run by education, health and social service authorities, the Post Office and others; changes in the structure of the bus industry with a strong tendency towards privatization and competition; licensed taxis and hired cars will be allowed to carry passengers at separate fares in certain circumstances.

2A13 GB HOUSE OF COMMONS (1985) Financing of public transport services: The Buses White Paper. Second report from the Transport Committee Session 1984-85. London: HMSO.

After placing the inquiry and the White Paper in their context, the report outlines the White Paper's diagnosis stating that the problem of the industry is that regulation has kept costs high, has inhibited the development of new services and technologies, and through cross-subsidy, has maintained an archaic pattern of services. A discussion is presented of the effects of the proposed regime as regards competitive practices, safety, minibuses, taxis and shared taxis, congestion, service coordination and integration, coordination with education services, concessionary fares, service loss due to deregulation, and effects on local planning. Possible regimes are considered, and special attention is paid to the evidence of the 1980 Transport Act experiments in evaluating the likely consequences of the government's proposals. Implementation is detailed as regards: proposed registration of services, tendering, restructuring of the bus industry, fair competition, and timing. The last section of the report presents possible solutions to the difficulties encountered and some final conclusions.

2A14 GOODWIN, P.B., BAILEY, J.M., BRISBOURNE, R.H., CLARKE, M.I., DONNISON, J.R., RENDER, T.E. and WHITELEY, G.K. (1983) *Subsidised Public Transport and the Demand for Travel: The South Yorkshire Example.* Farnborough: Gower.

Using both qualitative and quantitative data the report assesses the social and travel changes brought about by the public transport low fares policy in South Yorkshire. Changes in bus service users and effects of the policy on car ownership and extent of car, taxi, rail and motorcycle use and walking are examined as well as its effect on particular groups including shoppers and the unemployed. Future opportunities for marketing public transport and consideration of the balance between fares and service levels are suggested.

2A15 GOURVISH, T.R. (1987) *British Railways 1948-1973: A Business History*. Cambridge: Cambridge University Press.

This is a business history of the first 25 years of publicly-owned railways in Britain. Commissioned by the British Railways Board and based on the Board's extensive archives, it breaks new ground in analysing fully the dynamics of nationalised industry management and, in particular, the complexities of the vital relationship with government.

After exploring the origins of nationalization, the book deals with the organization, financial performance, investment and commercial policies of the British Transport Commission (1948-62), Railway Executive (1948-53) and British Railways Board (1963-73). The special problems of the railway industry, unique in its complexity, are fully explored, and new calculations of profit and loss, investment, and productivity are provided on a consistent basis for 1948-73. The book represents a major contribution not only to the debate about the role of the railways in a modern economy but also to that concerning the nationalized industries, which have proved to be one of the most enduring problems of the British economy since the War.

2A16 GRANT, J. (1977) *The Politics of Urban Transport Planning*. London: Earth Resources Research.

Transport policy and planning in urban areas is reviewed and placed within a range of theories of urban policy making. The author then traces the distinct phases of policy making and uses three case studies – Portsmouth, Southampton and Nottingham – to illustrate the differences in approach. The book includes analysis of the technicians, the community groups and the politicians in the policy-making process.

2A17 GWILLIAM, K.M. and MACKIE, P.J. (1975) *Economics and Transport Policy*. London: Allen and Unwin.

This book discusses the development of transport policy in the UK against a background of economic theory. The historical base and the economic elements of the sector are outlined and the difficulties of applying the theory to the transport situation are discussed. Individual modes of transport are covered and UK policy is compared with EEC transport policy. Finally, the parts of the jigsaw are all put together in a wide review of transport policy and comment is made on the inconsistencies in the policy framework as seen from this economic perspective.

2A18 HIBBS, J. (1982) Transport without politics . . .? A study of the scope for competitive markets in road, rail and air. Institute of Economic Affairs, Hobart Paper 95.

This paper questions whether important parts of the transport industry must necessarily be subject to central administration. The stifling of market mechanisms has led to misallocations of resources and such large and consistent losses as to create the myth that public transport can never be run profitably. Marginal cost pricing should be applied to road users and a national corporation should be given responsibility for the road infrastructure and subsequently for the railways. Cross subsidization should be abandoned and the industry should be decentralized. These proposals are consistent with and are related to Adam Smith Institute [2A1].

2A19 HILLMAN, M. and WHALLEY, A. (1983) Energy and Personal Travel: Obstacles to Conservation. Policy Studies Institute Report No 611.

The 1977 White Paper on Transport Policy described energy conservation as an objective of transport policy to be pursued by all practical and cost-effective means, but the quantity of petroleum used for personal travel continues to rise. The problem is usually discussed in narrow engineering terms; this study shows that there is great scope for saving energy by modifying travel patterns. Among the points discussed are ways of reducing the need for motorized travel by imaginative land-use planning; policies to encourage walking, cycling and public transport; the adverse effects that tax concessions on company cars have on the composition, by engine size, of the car population.

2A20 KEASEY, K. and MULLEY, C. (1986) Deregulation and privatisation of local buses in the United Kingdom. *International Journal of Transport Economics*, **13** (2), pp. 153-175.

The authors review the theoretical arguments and the empirical evidence concerning the likely effects of deregulation and privatization. They conclude that there are good theoretical reasons and some empirical evidence for believing that deregulation will lead to net benefits to society, but no theoretical or empirical support for privatization, unless it is a necessary part of increasing competition.

2A21 PAINTER, M. (1980) Whitehall and roads: A case study of sectoral politics. *Policy and Politics*, **8** (2), pp. 163-186.

Trunk road policy in England is best seen as a case of sectoral policy making, that is the evolution of commitments within narrow conceptual and institutional boundaries. To build trunk roads it was necessary to construct and defend a self-contained world of roads policy and programme implementation. In the 1950s and 1960s an internally accountable set of organizations and routines emerged, with their own logic and a seemingly inexorable momentum. This division of the world into sectoral specialities is a key part of government policy making, and the roads case demonstrates the pressures that exist towards fragmentation within government, while highlighting the artificiality of this fragmentation. Challenges were mounted from the outside world – from local communities and from environmentalists – which could not be contained or co-opted by the roads men. Governments were forced to react and the roads programme declined. However, this occurred as much by internal dissolution – the impossibility of implementation in the face of protest – as from an act of central coordination or reappraisal. It seems that such acts are severely limited by the political and administrative structures and logics of distinct policy sectors.

2A22 PLOWDEN, S. (1985) Transport Reform: Changing the Rules. Policy Studies Institute Report No 642.

This report shows how transport could be made more efficient for users while at the same time the costs in resources, accidents and environmental intrusion would be dramatically reduced. The study is firmly based on a market approach. The role of the State is to set and enforce suitable 'rules of the game': the legal and fiscal framework within which transport users make their decisions. If the State played that role properly, the safety, freedom and opportunity of millions of citizens would be greatly enhanced and the need to spend public money on road construction and on subsidies to public transport would be drastically and permanently cut. The report contains no novelties. All its suggestions are grounded in orthodox economic, political and organizational theory; some have been advocated by transport economists and planners for very many years; at least partial precedents for each of them exist somewhere in the world. But, as the report shows, the cumulative effect of these reforms is much greater than the sum of their individual effects. Individually, they would improve the situation; together, they would transform it.

2A23 ROBBINS, M. (1982) Financing London Transport: A historical review. *Three Banks Review*, December, pp. 19-31.

The operation of public transport in London in the 1890s and 1930s is examined and it is suggested that the two periods exhibit the same characteristics as all succeeding years; strong demand for services coupled with a reluctance on the part of business to invest, leading to patchy and unsatisfactory services. The author looks in more detail at reasons for the decline of the modern public transport system and at the need for a clearer policy on the need for, and scale of, public subsidy.

2A24 STANDING ADVISORY COMMITTEE FOR TRUNK ROAD APPRAISAL (1986) *Urban Road Appraisal*. London: HMSO.

This report reviews the suitability of the Department of Transport's methods for assessing the traffic, environmental, economic and other factors of urban road improvements. The aim has been to advise on any necessary changes in the procedures and techniques used. The historical development of the planning and assessment methods applied to urban transport problems are presented together with current practice. The Committee's suggested approach is then outlined in detail, explaining the changes thought to be necessary, and detailing the principles of assessment, its individual components, and the presentation and use of its results. The final part provides a worked example of a case study to demonstrate the recommended approach.

2A25 WEBSTER, F.V. (1986) Transport in towns, some of the options. *Journal of Transport Economics and Policy*, **20** (2), pp. 129-152.

Increasing use of cars and decentralization of activities will continue. The resulting deterioration in public transport causes hardship to those without access to a car, including some members of car-owning households. The author considers some ways of mitigating or slowing down these trends. In urban areas, current trends in population and employment locations, car ownership, travel speeds and costs for public and private means of transport all favour more private car use at the expense of public transport. Those without easy access to a car, including many members of car-owning households, may experience increasing hardship if these trends continue. The potential of policy options to modify these trends is considered, examining in particular the impacts of public transport subsidy, improved public transport operating efficiency through deregulation, new road and rail investment and private traffic restraint.

2A26 WISTRICH, E. (1983) *The Politics of Transport*. London: Longman.

Transport policy in Britain since 1945 is first reviewed, and this is followed by an analysis of the guiding ideology of the professionals, the politicians, the policy makers and the pressure groups. Key issues are analysed from political and pressure group perspectives; they include the battle of the environment in the 1970s; the conflict over increased lorry weights; and subsidies to public transport in 1981-82.

2B The United States of America

2B1 ALLEN, J.G. (1986) Public-private joint development at rapid transit stations. *Transportation Quarterly*, **40** (3), pp. 317-331.

Location is the most important factor to be considered in planning and encouraging urban development. Location itself, of course, is a product of several variables, but one of the essentials is accessibility.

A parcel of land will not be developed to its full potential unless it is easily reached from other parts of the urban area. Thus, transport can be a major stimulant to metropolitan development. One of the ways that government can encourage private development in urban areas is through joint development at rapid transit stations. This article addresses the essential ingredients of successful joint public-private development at rapid transit stations, and reviews the actual experience several North American cities have had with joint development.

2B2 ANDERSON, S.C. (1983) The effect of government ownership and subsidy on performance: Evidence from the bus transit industry. *Transportation Research*, **17A** (3), pp. 191–200.

Several theories have been advanced to predict the difference in behaviour of government-owned *vs* private firms, such as theories of bureaucratic growth, inefficiency, and concentration on vote-maximizing service with neglect of other important characteristics of service. This study tests the above theories in a declining industry, the US urban bus transit industry of 1960–75. The analysis bridges the period before and during the major federal capital grant programme which was initiated under the Urban Mass Transportation Act of 1964. The empirical results indicate that subsidy at the federal level is associated with higher costs and lower real price and a redistribution of service toward an expanded area, served less frequently. Local and state subsidy is associated with smaller increases in costs and smaller decreases in frequency of service and ridership. The form of public ownership does affect performance, but the unknown size of inter-agency cross-subsidization and tax benefits makes comparison tenuous without case-level investigation. The conclusion is reached that although the bureaucratic growth, inefficiency and vote-maximization theories are supported, inefficiency and bureaucratic growth are associated with passive sponsorship and large size of firm, rather than with public ownership, *per se*.

2B3 DEEN, T.B. (1984) The strategic transportation research study – its origins and purposes. *Transportation*, **12** (3), pp. 195–209.

The highway industry in the United States spends about $35 to $40 billion annually. Management of the industry is almost wholly decentralized. This decentralization plus diminishing fuel tax revenues used to finance road improvements has caused road research efforts to decline to a very low level. Comparisons between funds for highway research and those spent by private firms in similar industries show that private firms spend from 5 to 12 times the rate of highway agencies. The problem of how much to spend on research is difficult both for private-sector and for public-sector enterprises. The level of research spending is shown to correlate well with both profitability and growth in US firms. Four methods used for making research decisions in the private sector are discussed. The goals of the Strategic Transportation Research Study (STRS), which is being conducted by the Transportation Research Board to examine highway and transport needs, are described.

2B4 GAKENHEIMER, R. and MEYER, M. (1979) Urban transportation planning in transition: The sources and prospects of TSM. *Journal of the American Planning Asociation*, **45** (1), pp. 28–35.

A recent federal transport policy initiative has encouraged metropolitan and local transport planners to place increased emphasis on near-term, service-oriented transport problems. This policy, called Transportation System Management (TSM), was designed to affect not only the types of projects to be considered during the planning process, but also the institutional framework established to conduct and guide comprehensive transport planning. This paper describes the emergence of TSM-type planning from a tradition of large-scale, facility-oriented planning. Characteristics of the TSM programme that may significantly affect the process and politics of transport planning are discussed. The paper concludes by identifying some of the characteristics of TSM programme performance and their likely effect on transport planning in general. These include the greater emphasis on short-range actions and the need to resolve apparent conflicts between efficiency and amenity objectives.

2B5 GORDON, S. and MEYER, M.D. (1982) Emerging public-private partnership in urban transportation. *Transportation Research Record*, 877, pp. 132–139.

The private sector has been an important actor in local transport decision-making for many years. However, in recent years, the business community and large employers have begun to take a more aggressive role in identifying transportation problems and implementing programmes to solve them. Joint efforts of the public and private sectors in several urban areas are examined. These cases show that successful public-private action can be directly related to the ability of a small group of people, in both public agencies and private firms, to work together; an understanding of the motivation of private firms; the commitment of top management in both public and private agencies; and careful identification of the expectations of programme operation. It is concluded that increased private-sector involvement in urban transport will significantly influence the politics of transport decision-making, the programme implementation process, the focus of transport planning, and skills required for transport professionals. In addition, a number of questions are raised regarding equity.

2B6 HOEL, L.A., HYMAN, W.A. and KULASH, D.J. (1987) Strategies for managing highway transportation professional needs. *Transportation Research*, **21A** (2), pp. 161–168.

Growth in highway spending and the loss of approximately one-third of the nation's professional engineers in state highway agencies will create significant problems and opportunities over the next decade. Careers in transport will be attractive, rewarding and interesting, with promise for growing responsibility and advancement. This paper describes the dimensions of the problem and suggests approaches that should result in dynamic future-oriented organizations. Recruitment, education and training, compensation, professional satisfaction, skill requirements and other aspects of human resources management must be carefully matched to meet changing needs and skill requirements.

2B7 JOHNSON, G.T. (1987) Review of financing options for highways and transit. *Journal of Transportation Engineering* (ASCE), **113** (1), pp. 72–83.

A review of innovative financing techniques developed by transport agencies in the USA. The techniques fall into four categories: charges on properties that benefit from transport improvements (such as connector fees, negotiated investments, special benefit assessments, the creation of transport corporations and road utility districts, and tax increment financing); joint venture approaches with the private sector (including air rights leasing, donations for capital improvements, and cost sharing); user charges (motor vehicle taxes and fees, tolls, parking taxes and taxes on motor fuels); and marketing and merchandizing approaches (including the provision of advertising space and retail outlets at stations).

2B8 JONES, D.W. (1985) *Urban Transit Policy: An Economic and Political History*. Englewood Cliffs, NJ: Prentice-Hall.

Transit policy in the United States is examined from a historical perspective in this book. Its goal is to provoke a constructive debate about the kind of transit services that would be appropriate for the modern American city. To achieve this goal the author details the growth and decline of transit and assesses the performance of recent policies and programmes designed to preserve and revitalise transit service. He concludes that subsidy has not stabilized the industry and that compound changes in transit's basic way of doing business are necessary if mass transit is to play a significant role in the future of urban transport.

2B9 KIRBY, R.F., BHATT, K.V., KEMP, M.A., MCGILLIVRAY, R.G. and WOHL, M. (1975) *Para-transit: Neglected Options for Urban Mobility*. Washington, DC: The Urban Institute.

2B10 LEVINSON, H.S. and WEANT, R.A. (eds.) (1982) *Urban Transportation Perspectives and Prospects*. Westport, Conn: Eno Foundation for Transportation Inc.

A series of authoritative contributions are included in this review of American urban transport planning. Of particular interest is Hassell's review of the effectiveness of urban transport.

2B11 MCDOWELL, B.D. (1985) Role of metropolitan planning organizations in the 1980s. *Transportation Research Record*, 1045, pp. 41–44.

A new study by the US Advisory Commission on Intergovernmental Relations focuses on the adaptations in transit services, finances, institutions, and policy processes occasioned by current financial stress at all levels of government and by the devolution of national responsibilities to state and local governments. It was found in this study, in part, that most metropolitan transport planning organizations are now locally governed and staffed, their planning is becoming increasingly isolated, less comprehensive, and shorter range, some such organizations are experiencing strong pressure to decentralize or subregionalize, and the desire for these organizations to exercise more effective areawide leadership is not matched by local approval of greater powers for them. It is concluded in the study that informal coordination techniques or new powers granted by state legislatures are the two most likely facilitators of improved metropolitan transport leadership in the 1980s.

2B12 MCKNIGHT, C.E., CHRISTOPHER, E.J. and ZAVATTERO, D.A. (1986) Transportation planning process: the case of the Chicago region. *Transportation Research Record*, 1064, pp. 11-19.

Presented in this paper are the historical background of transport in the Chicago region and a description of the evolution of private involvement in the planning process. Experience in the region indicates that there are several issues that need to be resolved, such as the role that private operators should have in the process, the organization of the private operators to ensure balance and equitable representation, and the organization of efforts to fund the private operators. The paper concludes with recommendations for other regions attempting or contemplating a public or private cooperative planning process.

2B13 PORTER, A.L., REES, L.P., PARK, C.Y., RAO, S. and LARSON, T.D. (1981) Transportation funding structures and policies. *Transportation Research*, **15A** (2), pp. 139-153.

The transport enterprise in the United States relies heavily on federal funding of highways, transit, and airports. Consideration of changes in federal funding policies over the past decade or so, and the effects of those policies, suggests that the way programmes are financially structured can be critically important. The present analysis leads to recommendations concerning the selection of the federal matching ratio, trade-offs between categorical and block programmes and the use of formula or discretionary allocations. It highlights the importance of ascertaining programmatic intent in establishing funding policies, as well as the need for sensitivity to the fiscal climate.

2B14 RODRIGUEZ, C.G. and MCDONNELL, J.J. (1985) *Transportation Planning Data for Urbanized Areas Based on the 1980 Census*. Washington, DC: US Department of Transportation.

2B15 SCHOFER, J.L. (1983) Challenges to the future of urban transportation planning. *Transportation Research Record*, 931, pp. 27–31.

The environment for urban transport planning continues to change. Although a large commitment of resources is being made to this field, the future of the profession and its products may increasingly depend on the perceptions of the cost effectiveness of planning on the part of local decision-makers. Scarce resources and relaxation of federal planning requirements accentuate this challenge. Some key issues and choices facing urban transportation planning and planners in the 1980s are identified. Among these are the selection of the most appropriate role for analytic models, the choice of problems to solve and solutions to test, the relative role of creativity, the need to understand the implementation process, and the choice of an appropriate style for planning. The need for more introspection, self-criticism, methodological variation, and concern about ethical choices among problems, solutions, and tools is emphasized.

2B16 SHAW, P.L. and SIMON, R.B. (1982) Los Angeles urban transportation: who has the power? *Transportation Research Record*, 837, pp. 10–18.

In 1976, the California legislature took a bold step toward untangling the transport planning snarl that has characterized Southern California. Believing that only a new and innovative transport policy planning and coordinating institution could solve the problems, the legislators adopted Assembly Bill 1246, which created transport commissions in four Southern California counties: Los Angeles, Orange, Riverside, and San Bernadino. Of the four, Los Angeles is the largest and faces the most complex and difficult-to-solve transport problems. The development, structure, authority, and operations of the Los Angeles County Transport Commission are described. The Commission is directed by 10 of the principal county and city elected officials and one citizen member. Its powers include short-range planning, policy and programme development, project selection, new system development, and resources generation and allocation (power of the purse). For Southern California, this particular blend of powers and institutional form is innovative and has the potential for making significant public policy impacts. The Commission is fully operational and is involved with a solid schedule of activities. Not all of its major powers are being used, but most are, and the impact is slowly being felt on the decision-making process.

2B17 SMERK, G.M. (1981) A profile of transportation in the United States. *Transport Reviews*, **1** (2), pp. 101–125 and **1** (3), pp. 209–224.

A brief introduction to the geography of the United States is followed by a discussion of the population and economic trends and their possible impact on transport. Each of the major modes of transport is covered briefly in a presentation of current problems and trends, with a special section on urban public transport. The regulation of transport in the US by independent commission is discussed along with a commentary on the recent trends towards deregulation. The difficulty in forming a national transport policy in a nation where private ownership of transport is the principal means of transport provides the background to a debate of the problems associated with the high cost and potential shortage of petroleum-based sources of energy.

2B18 SPIELBERG, F. and ANDRLE, S. (1982) The implications of demographic change on transportation policy. *Journal of the American Planning Association*, **48** (3), pp. 301–308.

This article discusses the relationship between demographics, energy, and transport, recognizing that demographic changes and energy constraints will place pressures on the transport system that must be addressed by policy. The major demographic trends include declining household size and moderate population growth. Also, the labour force will increase more rapidly than the population. Both jobs and households will increasingly be located in the suburbs, where the dominant transport problem in the next two decades will be. Occasional energy shortages and steadily increasing petrol prices will exacerbate the suburban travel problem, but chronic petrol shortages should not be a problem in this century. Transport policy themes will focus on better use and management of existing resources.

2B19 TRANSPORTATION RESEARCH BOARD (1982) *Urban Transportation Planning in the 1980s*, Special Report 196. Washington, DC: Transportation Research Board.

See also: TRANSPORTATION RESEARCH BOARD (1984) *Future Directions of Urban Public Transportation*, Special Report 200. Washington, DC: Transportation Research Board.

2B20 VUCHIC, V.R. (1984) The auto versus transit controversy: towards a rational synthesis for urban transportation policy. *Transportation Research*, **18A** (2), pp. 125-133.

A considerable portion of academic literature on urban transport has been supportive of policies which resulted in extensive urban freeway construction, but highly critical of public investments in transit. This paper challenges these views and points out many flaws in their basic arguments. Criticism of rail transit is particularly emotionally biased and is in direct conflict with real world trends: the number of cities in the United States and other countries which have constructed rail transit as a key element of their viability has steadily increased in the last two decades. For solution of the present serious urban transport problems, there should be a rational policy which recognizes capabilities of different modes and leads to their optimal coordination in a multimodal system.

2B21 WACHS, M. (ed.) (1982) Symposium: emerging themes in transportation policy. *Journal of the American Planning Association*, **48** (3).

This special issue of the Journal summarizes the present situation on urban transport policy, the political role of transport investments, techniques by which planners model and evaluated transport programmes, funding mechanisms for public and private transport, and relationships between accessibility and urban form. All these issues are being reconsidered more seriously today than at any time since the emergence of the car as the major form of transport. The following papers capture the principal features of the debate: Weiner, E. [2B22]; Spielberg, F. and Andrle, S. [2B18]; Orski, C.K. The changing environment of urban transportation, pp. 309-314; Kirby, R.F. Pricing strategies for public transportation, pp. 327-334; Rosenbloom, S. Federal policies to increase the mobility of the elderly and handicapped, pp. 335-351.

2B22 WEINER, E. (1982) New directions for transportation policy. *Journal of the American Planning Association*, **48** (3), pp. 293–300.

There will be a number of major changes in transport policy in the 1980s. These changes have begun to emerge. Concentration is no longer on building and expanding transport facilities. The focus is shifting to maintaining and rehabilitating existing facilities and to improving the use of these facilities for moving goods and people more efficiently and effectively. There is a reassessment underway of the roles of different levels of government and the private sector in the provision of transport services. A reallocation of responsibilities is likely to emerge. These changes indicate a break from the historical direction of expansion to one of preservation and management of resources, and from more centralized control to greater decentralization. Some experimentation with new approaches has occurred which points the way. The transport community will have to learn to adapt to these changes and to develop innovative approaches to the emerging problems.

2B23 WEINER, E. (1984) Devolution of the federal role in urban transportation. *Journal of Advanced Transportation*, **18** (2), pp. 113–124.

During the past few years, the federal role in urban transportation has been changing, and the new federal role is based on two premises. First, state and local governments and the private sector are closer to the problems and issues in urban transport and, therefore, are in a better position to make local transport decisions. Second, transport descisions should be guided by the market place rather than by governmental regulations and requirements. Steps have already been taken to bring about the shift in the federal role. These steps involved changes to policies, legislation, regulations, and programmes. The actions that have been taken are reviewed in this paper, and the dominant trends that are emerging for the coming decade are examined.

See also: Redefinition of roles and responsibilities in US transportation. *Transportation*, **12** (2), pp. 211–224.

2B24 WEINER, E. (1984) Urban transportation planning in the US: a historical overview. *Transport Reviews*, **4** (4), pp. 331–358, and **5** (1), pp. 19–48.

This article provides an overview of approximately 50 years of urban transport planning history. It begins with developments in highway planning in the early 1930s and ends with the shift to decentralization of decision-making authority in the 1980s. The key event during this period was the Federal Aid Highway Act of 1962 which created the federal mandate for a continuing, comprehensive urban transport planning process carried out cooperatively by states and local governments. Planning processes and procedures evolved over the years as new issues and concerns were raised and changes in attitudes and priorities occurred. Planning processes have become more complex and sophisticated but have retained many of the earlier elements and objectives. The evolution is still continuing with the objective of improving procedures and institutions that are adapted to the needs and concerns of today's planners, citizens and decision-makers.

See also: Citation [8.32].

2B25 YAGO, G. (1984) *The Decline of Transit: Urban Transportation in German and US Cities, 1900-1970.* Cambridge: Cambridge University Press.

Cars dominate transport today in most American cities. After World War II, urban planners embraced highway transport as the solution to urban congestion, while mass transit was shunned as outmoded and appropriate only for older, densely populated cities. Yet the prolonged energy crisis, beginning in 1973, shattered most previously held attitudes about the role of mass transit, and it was now promoted as central to energy efficiency and rational land use. If mass transit is now possible and even desirable in new, auto-oriented cities – Los Angeles, Frankfurt, Tokyo – why did it decline in the first place? This book scrutinizes the social, political, and technological forces that shaped our cities and their transport systems. By comparing two of the most powerful twentieth-century economies, the United States and West Germany, it explores the factors – largely those of economic concentration and bureaucratic centralization – that transformed urban life. In examining the historical conditions that led to the current crisis of urban transport, the book offers an explanation of past urban and economic policy failures.

2C Europe

2C1 BUTTON, K.J. (1984) *Road Haulage Licensing and EC Transport Policy*. Aldershot: Gower.

This book provides an introduction to EEC common transport policy, its rationale, development and problems. From this general introduction it then switches to the issue of control of entry into the road haulage sector and discusses the working of the international licensing system at the micro level. The conclusions are not optimistic and a more eclectic approach to policy formulation is suggested with a much enhanced flexibility to problem solving.

2C2 COUSINS, S. and POTTER, S. (1982) Annual vehicle taxation policies in Europe: who gains and who loses from change? *Transportation Research Record*, 858, pp. 1–5.

Annual vehicle taxes can be replaced by taxes on fuel. This may be desirable for energy or transport policy purposes. The effects of this abolition option are examined between interest groups in a single nation and between member nations of the EEC. In the United Kingdom, rural motorists claimed they would be disadvantaged by such a change. Use of the United Kingdom National Travel Survey showed that they would benefit or show no change in total tax paid. In the United Kingdom, 60 per cent of new car purchases are made by companies. The cars purchased by companies are larger than privately purchased new cars and exhibit high annual mileages. Abolition of annual taxes would result in more fuel tax paid by larger vehicles in the United Kingdom and Ireland; about the same level of tax in Denmark, Holland and Germany; and less tax in France, Belgium, and Italy. The different annual automobile taxes provide some non-tariff protection of national car manufacturing industries. A mix of higher fuel taxes, higher initial purchase taxes, and improved consumer information is recommended if annual automobile taxes are abolished in the EEC for reasons of energy and transport policy.

2C3 ERDMENGER, J. (1983) *The European Common Transport Policy*. Aldershot: Gower.

This book describes the efforts of the Community institutions to work towards a common transport policy in the period 1973–82. The emphasis is on the search for an appropriate method of approaching the matters involved and for that which is politically attainable. Railways, roads and inland waterways are covered, but it is air transport and external relations in the transport sector which may become more important.

2C4 EUROPEAN COMMUNITY (1981) *The European Community's Transport Policy*. Luxembourg: Office for Official Publications of the European Communities.

Transport contributes 6 per cent of the gross Community product and thereby holds a larger share than agriculture, which accounts for 5 per cent. Some 6 million people are employed in the transport sector, a million of them in the railways of the Member States. The volume of goods transported throughout the length and breadth of the European Community was 6,500 million tonnes in 1974; the figure is expected to exceed 9,000 million tonnes in 1985. These facts and figures illustrate the importance of transport and the need to integrate it into the European Community. It is no accident that the EEC Treaty specifically states that a common transport policy must be created. Does such a policy exist?

This publication explains the workings of the transport policy in the European Community in terms intelligible to the layman. Some progress has been made but a great deal yet remains to be done. It also gives the reader some idea of the many problems – old and new – which beset the transport sector and must be solved either at Member State or at Community level.

Current problems include: overloading of road infrastructure, structural problems in inland waterways, deficits of the railway companies, problems raised by the explosive increase in energy prices, competition in shipping by some of the State-trading nations, safety of shipping, problems at the frontier crossings, prices charged by the airlines, etc.

2C5 EUROPEAN CONFERENCE OF MINISTERS OF TRANSPORT (1983) Possibilities and limits of regulation in transport policy, Report of the 62nd Round Table. Paris.

This paper argues the case for deregulation of freight transport in Europe and presents a set of proposals to support this process. The headings under which the proposals are made include capacity, prices, market structure, harmonization of costs and choice of investment. If common advances are made in each of these headings then transport policy would ensure that goods transport services can be produced at the lowest cost to the community.

2C6 GWILLIAM, K.M. (1980) Realism and the common transport policy of the EEC, in Polak, J.B. and Van der Kamp, J.B. (eds.) *Changes in the Field of Transport Studies*. The Hague: Martinus Nijhoff, pp. 38–59.

It seems that there is deadlock between the incompatibilities of existing national transport policies and those which the EEC Commission has been attempting to develop. This paper tries to resolve some of these dilemmas. The nature and scope of transport policy is outlined prior to a resumé of UK transport policy and the essential elements of EEC transport policy. The inconsistencies in style, objectives, instruments and administration between the national and EEC policy levels are identified as the basis for the recommendations made for the reconciliation between the two policy levels.

2C7 HALL, P. and HASS-KLAU, C. (1985) *Can Rail Save the City?* Aldershot: Gower.

This book is the result of a 14-month study to assess the impact of rail rapid transit (RRT) investment on urban structure in major cities in the Federal Republic of Germany and Great Britain, with special attention to the cities' economic health. British and German cities that had invested heavily in rail rapid transit were compared with cities that had not invested. The results of the study indicated that increased transit use in the cities in both countries appeared to have no effect on increased urban economic activity.

2C8 HARRIS, D.J. and DAVIES, B.C.L. (1980) European energy policy and planning: the role of the institutions. *National Westminister Bank Quarterly Review*, November, pp. 23–33.

There is a considerable degree of similarity between European organizations on energy policy, and most emphasize the need to conserve energy by using it more efficiently, by reducing the dependence on imported oil and by increasing the use of indigenous coal and nuclear power. However, there is no common EEC energy policy and this paper attempts to establish the reasons for this discontinuity.

2C9 HASS-KLAU, C. (1984) German urban public transport policy. *Cities*, **1** (6), pp. 551–556.

Germany began to invest heavily in new public transport systems after 1960. Car ownership had risen from less than 1 million in 1953 to 6.6 million in 1963, and to 24.1 million by 1982, producing severe congestion in large cities. This paper briefly describes the public transport policies and solutions applied in Germany, with emphasis on the underground, light rail, and rapid transit systems of Munich, Hanover, Nuremburg, Cologne and Frankfurt.

2C10 HEINZE, G.W. (1985) Regional policy and transport in the Federal Republic of Germany. *Environment and Planning C*, **3** (3), pp. 269–284.

In this paper the transport policy aspects of the regional policy presently being pursued in the Federal Republic of Germany is dealt with. The regional policy objectives of resource allocation equity and resource allocation efficiency form the starting point of a discussion outlining the basic relationships between the processes of 'bridging space' (that is, between the totality of all transport and communication processes) and the process of control of regional development. With such relationships can be associated classes of intervention measures affecting supply, adaptation, and conservation. The concept of differentiating transport policy problems according to regional policy problem areas is explained by means of examples taken from the field of passenger transport. In this context, reference is made principally to the results of recent empirical research directed by the author. It will be shown that changes in regional policy occurring within the overall process of structural change can lead to new concepts and strategies ('rationalization' and 'innovation').

2C11 LIJEWSKI, T. (1987) Transport in Warsaw. *Transport Reviews*, **7** (2), pp. 95–118.

The paper is devoted to Warsaw, a city burnt to the ground during World War II and reconstructed from its ruins. This allowed the post-war designers to change the road network and modernize the system of transport. This modernization, however, has turned out not to be far-sighted enough: hence the present transport difficulties. Compared with Western European cities car traffic is less intensive and smoother. The high density of places of work in the central district and of inhabitants in residential districts has resulted in a shortage of parking places. Most people use public transport comprising buses, trams and railways; trolley buses and taxis are less used. Buses are the most frequently used transport within the city; railways play a similar role in the city-suburban zone connections. The first underground line is under construction. The immense amount of daily travel is generated mainly by the inappropriate distribution of residences, places of work and services, and secondly by the low fares on public transport, which is subsidized by the State and works more as a social service than as a branch of the economy.

2C12 RIBU, E. (1985) An overview of European transport policy, Proceedings of the 10th International Symposium on Theory and Practice in Transport Economics, Berlin. Paris: ECMT.

This review is a comparison of the different roles that the EEC and the ECMT have in formulating and influencing national transport policies and international movements. It also comments on individual successes and failures in each organization, and suggests the possibilities for closer future links between both organizations.

2C13 UEBERSCHAER, M. (1987) Transport in the largest industrial region in Western Europe: the Rhine-Ruhr region. *Transport Reviews*, **7** (3), pp. 207-226.

The historical evolution of urban transport in the largest, most densely populated industrial area of Western Europe is shown with special regard to public transport and environmental problems. Facts and figures about the travel patterns are given as well as a description of the transport infrastructure of this region. Finally, governmental objectives and plans for future transport-related development are stated.

2C14 WHITELEGG, J. (1979) The common transport policy: a case of lost direction? *Transportation Science*, **13** (4), pp. 343-357.

While the common transport policy has made significant progress in the regulation, harmonization, change for infrastructure and related areas, it has failed to recognize the wider environment of transport and in particular the ways in which transport policies are inextricably linked with other policies of the EEC. Successive policy statements are examined to illustrate how the EEC's view of transport can be seen as increasingly narrow and unrelated to the central issues of community development in the period immediately preceding economic and monetary union. While very critical of EEC policy, the underlying assumption is that transport is a core policy through and with which one can advance the central issues, as long as the links between policies are understood and the administrative machinery reflects this.

2D Organizational and institutional issues

2D1 GLAISTER, S. and MULLEY, C. (1983) *Public Control of the British Bus Industry*. Farnborough: Gower.

This book reports on research conducted to examine the objects and economic consequences of the licensing provisions for road passenger transport in the Road Traffic Act 1960 and other Acts of Parliament, and considers whether the present degree and nature of public control of the bus and coach industry, and in particular the system of licensing is in the best interests of the consumer, of the industry and of the economy as a whole. It proposes a scheme for replacing current PSV and route licensing procedures.

2D2 LAVE, C.A. (1985) (ed.) *Urban Transit: The Private Challenge to Public Transportation*. Cambridge, Mass: Ballinger.

This book comprises chapters by 15 academics, transit managers, and labour relations experts whose in-depth examination of urban transit focuses on the economics of transit matters, the possible alternative modes of urban transit, and the economic and political problems of implementing changes. Concluding that private free market forms of transit have the only reasonable change of solving urban transit problems, the authors offer policy alternatives that challenge the current public failure of monopolized transit systems. The book contains a comprehensive discussion of the evaluation of public transport problems and policy responses and includes documentation of cases throughout the United States.

2D3 LEVIN, P.H. (1981) Policy-making processes, in Banister, D. and Hall, P. (eds.) *Transport and Public Policy Planning*. London: Mansell, pp. 11–17.

Four main headings are used to investigate policy making processes. Output-based analyses trace outputs in terms of processes and explain them in terms of structures and environment. Process-based studies need to be made at the actual point of policy-making. Input-output studies relate policies to the governmental structure or environment, and structure-based studies ask whether changes in structures have any impact on decision. Applications of each approach are described in terms of actual studies of policy implementation.

2D4 MAY, A. (1982) Transport in London: the case for organisational change. *Public Money*, **2** (3), pp. 31–35.

This paper reviews the background to the development of transport policy in London since the Greater London Development Plan. The generally unsatisfactory arrangements are commented upon and a set of twelve criteria are set up as principles on which any new organization should be based. International experience is used to assess the principles. The paper ends with recommendations for a Metropolitan Transport Authority.

2D5 MULLEY, C. and WRIGHT, M. (1986) Buy-outs and the privatisation of National Bus. *Fiscal Studies*, **7** (3), pp. 1–24.

The authors discuss the rationale behind privatization of the National Bus Company, and analyse the available options. Particular attention is focused on the implications of privatization via the apparently favoured buy-out method. It seems probable that the need for ex-subsidiaries to be viable financially, managerially, economically and organizationally will produce larger rather than smaller buy-outs, with consequent adverse effects on competition since the majority of competitors so created are likely to remain dominant operators over their market territories.

2D6 ORGANISATION FOR ECONOMIC COOPERATION AND DEVELOPMENT (1987) *Toll Financing and Private Sector Involvement in Road Infrastructure Development*. Paris: OECD.

The report presents some historical evidence on toll roads, and construction and financing issues faced by governments. As well as covering the institutional problems the report also reviews the economic theory of toll road pricing and outlines current practice in a number of countries where toll roads are in operation. Recommendations are made in the context of evaluation and regional development; here it is suggested that toll road pricing may accelerate road programmes.

2D7 PAGE, J.H. and DEMETSKY, M.J. (1987) Planning Development with transit projects. *Journal of Transportation Engineering*, **111** (6), pp. 665-678.

This study presents a site-development model which simulates the long- and short-term decision process of developers. Four steps are identified: determination of development demand; analysis of site constraints; analysis of design and marketing opportunities; and financial analysis of the project. The methodology is then applied to three different situations to assess the development potential around a transit station, the alternative project designs and an appropriate marketing strategy.

2D8 PIKARSKY, M. and JOHNSON, C.M. (1983) Trends and options for increasing the role of the private sector in urban transportation. *Journal of Advanced Transportation*, **17** (2), pp. 89-102.

The authors suggest that transport planning should be outside the control of public transport operating agencies and provision should be made to ensure private provider representation in the planning process. On new and heavily subsidized routes, the choice of the transport provider be made on the basis of better serving the region's total transport needs.

2D9 RIMMER, P.J. (1986) Changes in transport organisations within Southeast Asian cities: petty producers to statutory corporations. *Environment and Planning A*, **18**, pp. 1559-1580.

A spate of studies of West European and North American cities have charted and interpreted the remarkable and rapid transformation of public transport since the early nineteenth century. The question arises as to whether the attempts to superimpose metropolitan culture via public transport structures in African, Asian, and Central and South American cities were as spectacular and speedy. Attention, in tackling this question, focuses upon the transfer of public transport technological-organizational structures to Southeast Asia since the 1860s. Rather than accept the transitional process of competition through oligopoly to state monopoly as given, a test is made of whether the basic prerequisites of these phases can be sustained in a Southeast Asian context, from an analysis of core technologies and the structure, conduct, and performance of individual firms. Past corporate growth paths of urban public transport in Southeast Asia can then be mapped out and future directions suggested.

2D10 ROTH, G. (1987) *Private Sector Alternatives in Urban Transportation*. Dallas, Texas: National Centre for Policy Analysis.

2D11 SCHMITT, R.P. (1984) Local organizations of transportation planning activities in the United States. *Transportation Planning and Technology*, **9** (3), pp. 225-236.

Examines alternative methods for organizing transport planning functions using data from a survey of the 100 largest metropolitan areas in America. An in-depth analysis of seven regions shows wide differences between the organization, function and degree of effectiveness of transport planning organizations, differences which result from historical factors and the attitudes of the people involved.

2D12 SCHREFFLER, E. and MEYER, M.D. (1983) Evolving institutional arrangements for employer involvement in transportation: the case of employers associations. *Transportation Research Record*, 914, pp. 42-49.

Many professionals are involved in the urban transport planning process. The characteristics of a relatively new participant in urban transport issues – the employer association – are examined. Five California employer associations, and their role in transport, are described. The analysis emphasizes the factors that influenced the creation of these associations and the characteristics of their operation. Although still in their infancy, these associations have shown some impact on their respective urban areas. The roles played by these associations have ranged from facilitating the resolution of transport controversies to conducting planning studies of critical problems facing employer sites.

2D13 STARKIE, D. (1984) BR privatisation without tears. *Economic Affairs*, 5 (1), pp. 16-19.

A novel approach to the privatization question is proposed in which ownership of the track and other fixed capital remains in public hands while locomotives and rolling stock are privately owned. The author suggests that this is merely an extension of existing practice whereby, for example, a significant proportion of BR freight traffic is carried by private wagons. He outlines how the relationship between a fixed assets BR and a privately owned British Trains sector could operate.

2D14 WALLIS, J.P. (1980) Private bus operations in urban areas – their economics and role. *Traffic Engineering and Control*, 21 (12), pp. 605-610.

The paper is concerned with the role that privately-operated bus services might play in urban areas of Australia, *vis-à-vis* services provided by public operators. It shows that a given level of bus service can be provided substantially more cheaply by private than public operators, and that the majority of the cost savings arise from better utilization of staff and lower wage rates and associated on-costs. Expansion of the role of private services is therefore a possible means of reducing the levels of urban public transport subsidies. The principles which should underlie subsidy schemes for private operators are discussed.

2E Management and labour practices

2E1 BUTLER, S.E. and SCHNEIDER, C.G. (1986) Employment impacts of the Surface Transportation Assistance Act of 1982. *Transportation Research Record*, 1074, pp. 9-15.

This report examines the employment impacts of a legislative change that was designed to improve the road infrastructure and indirectly help reduce unemployment. Analysis proceeds through a series of econometric models and the results indicate that the Act had no significant impact on gross national product but it did have a local impact on employment. Regional differences could be explained by differences in the number of new construction jobs created, differences in wage rates, and the geographic concentration of manufacturing and trade in general and motor vehicle manufacturing in particular.

2E2 CHOMITZ, K.M. and LAVE, C.A. (1984) Part-time labour, work rules and urban transit costs. *Journal of Transport Economics and Policy*, **18** (1), pp.63–73.

The current financial crisis in urban transit has led to suggestions for reform of union work rules. Management has proposed use of part-time labour and flexible assignments, labour has countered with demands for less onerous work schedules and additional compensatory pay. This paper uses extensive computer simulations to quantify the impact of the proposed work rule changes. The work rule changes proposed by management would decrease labour cost by 3–8 percentage points, while changes proposed by labour would increase costs by 3–24 percentage points. That is, the range of changes being discussed has more potential for increasing costs than for reducing them. The potential use of jointly defined labour-management simulations as a tool for exploring trade-offs in the collective bargaining process and for discovering mutually beneficial work rule changes is discussed.

2E3 DIX, M.C. and LAYZELL, A.D. (1983) *Road Users and the Police*. Beckenham, Kent: Croom Helm.

Most people only come into contact with the police as motorists and as road users. Individuals who would never contemplate breaking the law in any other way quite often flout road and traffic regulations. Although the police naturally have to enforce the law in this area, they have long wondered whether the road user experience involving such issues as parking or driving behaviour affects wider attitudes about the role of police in society. Why many drivers break the law, and how and when individual police officers decide to intervene, are questions explored in this book. Actual confrontations between motorists and the police are also examined. By using recordings of interviews conducted with members of the public, police officers, and drivers who had just been stopped for an offence, the authors provide new and valuable insights into the attitudes of road users and the police. How the police and the road user view each other and the way in which each side views the law are described. By maintaining contact with motorists through the various stages of prosecution, it has been possible to monitor changes in their attitudes toward the police and the courts and to consider the likely effects of different sanctions imposed if an offence is repeated. The problems that the police face are emphasized and potential solutions are discussed in terms of their effectiveness and their appearance to the road user.

2E4 DUNLOP, J.T. (1985) Trends and issues in labor relations in the transportation sector. *Transportation Research News*, **118**, pp. 8-15.

This paper examines the impacts of deregulation on labour-management relations in transport. Included in the review is the destabilization caused by such changes, the emphasis from the suppliers on product and market concerns and the general lack of attention given to labour issues.

2E5 EAGLE, D.M. and STEPHANEDES, Y.J. (1985) Dynamic impacts of transport services on unemployment. *Environment and Planning B*, **12** (2), pp. 121-126.

Economic theories of labour supply and demand are modified so that a dynamic unemployment model can be developed. This new model is used to analyse the dynamic impacts of transport policies on unemployment, particularly in rural areas. Transport service is included as an independent variable in four submodels within the labour supply sector. Transport availability, travel time and travel cost are included in the model. The results indicate that transport investment can help alleviate unemployment.

2E6 KULASH, D.J. (1987) Managing transportation research: the highway challenge. *Transportation Research*, **21A** (2), pp. 153-159.

Management specialists have identified numerous principles for keeping companies innovative. Four frequently occurring themes – user orientation, strategic view, management commitment and accountability – appear particularly applicable to highway research, despite their generality and ambiguity. The nation's highway industry is decentralized and relies on rigid standards and procurement processes. These traits pose some barriers to innovation, and research must be carefully structured to overcome them. Although existing research programmes address certain problems well, they are unable to address some key topics. Recently, highway leaders have proposed a largescale Strategic Highway Research Program to fill this gap.

2E7 MEYER, M.D. (1982) Public policy development process. *Transportation Research Record*, 837, pp. 1–10.

In an effort to make transport professionals aware of the process through which public policy is made, the policy development process is described, and concepts that may be useful to transport professionals are identified. Emphasis is given to literature sources on the policy development process. Ambiguities in terminology are clarified, and a distinction is drawn between policy made through legislative action and policy made through administrative and judicial interpretation. The policy development process itself is divided into three major elements – issue identification, policy debate and formulation, and policy implementation – and the importance of each element in the transport context is illustrated by mini case studies of transport issues. It is concluded that there is a need for research in two major areas: the role of analysis in decision-making and how analysis can better inform the policy-making process and how, if at all, the policy-making process can be improved.

2E8 PERRY, J.L. and ANGLE, H.L. (1980) *Labour-Management Relations and Public Agency Effectiveness: A Study of Urban Mass Transit*. New York: Pergamon Press.

2E9 SCHWEITERMAN, J.P. (1985) Labour costs in urban mass transit: a case for regulatory reform. *Transportation Research Record*, 1012, pp. 1–7.

When US airlines, railroads, and motor carriers were deregulated, the incentives for organized labour in collective bargaining changed, causing more active participation in the containment of labour costs. Industrywide improvements in labour utilization and productivity resulted and much of the subsequent savings passed directly to the consumer. In the transit industry, regulatory reform has been largely overlooked as a mechanism to facilitate progress in collective bargaining. However, a unique sequence of events in Chicago – the growth of private transit – provides a clear demonstration of the potential of the private sector in an environment free from regulatory entry barriers. State and local regulatory bodies have not enforced applicable transit regulation and have permitted the private entrepreneurs to enter into direct competition with public transit operators. The implications of regulatory reform for organized labour in the transit industry are explored, focusing on the situation in Chicago.

2E10 TEAL, R.F. and GIULIANO, G. (1982) Increasing the role of the private sector in commuter bus service provision. *Built Environment*, **8** (3), pp. 172-183.

Studies in seven US Metropolitan areas have demonstrated that privately operated commuter bus services can be organized successfully as labour costs are lower and more scheduling flexibility can be introduced. These services seem to operate with no public subsidy in some cases. The paper explores the reasons why some services can operate without a subsidy and assesses the potential for a more general application of this type of service.

2E11 WACHS, M. (1985) Management vs political perspectives on transit policy making. *Journal of Planning Education and Research*, **4** (3), pp. 139-147.

The core of the argument suggests that transit policy has become increasingly politicized over the years. To illustrate this premise, examples are drawn from fares policies that encourage use of public transport in low-density suburbs while penalizing inner-city residents; from service increases to cater for loss making peak hour commuters at the expense of off-peak services; from the emphasis on accessible integrated services for the handicapped rather than cost effective separate services; and from the technical forecasts that are guided by political uses of the predictions rather than their accuracy.

2E12 WARD, M.F. (1982) Political economy, industrial location and the European motor car industry in the post war period. *Regional Studies*, **16** (6), pp. 443-453.

Recent changes in the locational pattern of manufacturing industry in advanced capitalist economies have highlighted the need for new approaches to the study of industrial location. It is argued that analysis must begin at the fundamental level of the nature of the economic system. Locational patterns are the outcome of the interplay of various institutions within the structural framework of the economic system as it is situated in geographical space. The locational development of the European motor industry in the post-war period is used to illustrate the approach. Particular emphasis is placed upon the political interplay between industrial capital, the State and labour.

3 Social issues

3A Land-use patterns

Society is fast changing in both its structure and its tastes and requirements. In contrast urban structure is more permanent and conservative to social changes, mismatches result and the urban transport system is called upon to overcome problems of poor accessibility which arise. At the same time transport is a powerful motivator of urban change itself. (Le Clerq [3A9], Daniels and Warnes [3A4]).

Much of the literature cited in Section 3A deals with the interaction of transport and land use. Two recent emergent trends have been first, the decentralization of homes and jobs from metropolitan centres to peripheral areas (Cervero [3A2]) and surrounding lower order towns in the urban hierarchy; and second, the consequent decay of the economic base within the inner city (May and Patterson [3A10]). Transport systems, via the access they provide, influence land and property markets within urban areas (Nelson [5E24]). The studies cited argue both the case that transport investment can reduce land values (Echenique [3A5]) and that particular large transport investments such as rapid transit systems and new highways could raise local property values. The research tends to suggest that while property prices rise in anticipation of transport investments, the effects are very local Damm *et al*. [3A3]. Following new urban highway construction, local property prices adjacent to the road fell relative to an increase in property prices further away.

3B Technological change

There is a common tension between the scientific development of new technology and society's wish or ability to incorporate the potential it offers. There are more and more rapid developments in Western society toward information economies whereby physical interaction is substituted merely by an exchange of information such as electronic message transfer (Lee and Meyburg [3B5]). Improvements in telecommunications technology in theory could eliminate many existing travel requirements via the development of regimes for remote work locations, home working, improving the opportunities for suburban residents. However, the results of research in this area suggest quite different effects on transport.

Travel to achieve personal contact has a psychological importance in itself, thus the actual transfer of travel to telecommunications may be minimal (Miller [3B7]). Outside the working environment, increased access to telecommunications may actually increase discretionary travel demand (Salomon [3B9]). The impact of improved vehicle technology, telecommunications and information dissemination could potentially have dramatic effects on transport supply and travel requirements. It is clear that the potential to improve vehicle design and introduce new modes could, if implemented, have considerable implications for urban development (Giannopoulos [3B2]). However, in practice it may be that the development of new modes is unlikely to be revolutionary, rather that improved technology will be implemented in a more limited manner through existing modes (Poulton [3B8]).

Shopping travel has been identified as one area where new information technology could radically reshape travel requirements and change the location of retail outlets (Lewis [3B6]). An increase in 'push-button' shopping via television screens could radically change the pattern of retailing in city centres (Guy [3B3], Howard [3B4]). Currently it is the 'out of town' retail outlets which are at the forefront of new technological innovation (Lewis [3B6]). This could produce a greater social polarization in opportunities between inner and outer, and low- and high-income areas. However, the potential of new shopping technology to ease the problems for less mobile persons, such as the elderly and disabled persons, could be considerable (Davies [3B1]).

3C Social groups

On a macro level there have been a number of studies which have emphasized the need to assess the social consequences of transport plans (King [3A8]) and the manner in which transport initiatives have benefited the quality of life of communities (Allsop [5E2]): who benefits from transport investment, by how much and from whom. The problems arise in defining equity and distributional criteria (Studnicki-Gizbert [3C42], Carpenter [3C6], Diandas [3C8]), Gihring [3C11]) and the ways in which these criteria can be incorporated into current evaluation frameworks (Arrowsmith [3C2]) for example, in terms of time allocation and different income levels.

One way in which social criteria have been introduced into transport planning has been through the development of accessibility measures. The concept of accessibility and the use of accessibility indicators have been in use for some years but with diverging interpretations as to their significance. Reviewing the accessibility measures used, Koenig [3C24] concludes that it is a powerful determinant of trip rates. However, comparisons between accessibility and the travel behaviour of different social groups suggest that the relationship is not as strong as might be expected (Hanson and Schwab [3C16], Hall [3C14], Richardson and Young [3C37]). An important paper by Pirie [3C33] stresses that accessibility measures have developed largely independently of the policy-making machine. The possibility of developing an effective social policy based on accessibility suggests that as much attention should be devoted more to a conceptually robust notion of accessibility than to the continual improvement of accessibility measures.

The mid-1970s saw the growth in a concern for the travel needs of disadvantaged groups, specifically those persons living in households not owning cars and persons with limited access to cars. Since 1980 this research effort has continued with an emphasis on specific problem groups and areas, with practical policy suggestions emerging.

Life expectancy in many Western societies is increasing (USDOT [3C44], Bussiere [3C5]). The elderly are constrained in their travel behaviour by frailty, poor health, disability, dependency on others and often low income. Recent years have seen a number of important reports aimed at providing special transport services for elderly and disabled persons. Relative to other social groups, the elderly have less opportunities to use cars (Hopkin [3C18], [3C19]) research has thus concentrated on a comparison of the costs of different types of public transport provision (McKnight et al. [3C30], Jackson, Knapp [3C22]), the institutional framework for providing such services (Noel and Chadda [3C31]) and the implications for subsidy policy (Spear [3C40]).

Many specialized services have been implemented for elderly and disabled persons in recent years (McKnight et al [3C30], Borsay [3C3]), in addition, guidelines have been developed to improve the existing infrastructure for disabled access (Lee [3C26]). One problem has been the definition of disability with regard to eligibility for fare concessions both on normal public transport services and on special disabled services. Mobility handicap extends well beyond the recognized definitions of disability (Hahn [3C13]).

Women are constrained in their travel behaviour not only by their relatively lower level of access to cars than men but also by their gender role. Gender dictates that child care, home work and paid employment often involve women in a complex scheduling of activities in which reliance on public transport can be a limitation (Pickup [3C32], Hanson and Hanson [3C15]). In addition to gender role constraints on their travel behaviour, travel costs may also limit the distance many women are prepared to commute to jobs (Madden [3C29], Andrews [3C1], Fox [3C9]). As the pattern of household life and family structure continues to diversify, planners should be sensitive to the effects of these trends on facility provision and household's use of space (Stimpson [3C41], Singoll and Lillydahl [3C39]).

The world economic recession from the mid-1970s increased unemployment levels in all Western societies. A number of studies have highlighted the role played by the transport system in job mobility, job opportunities and job search. Hedges and Hopkin [3C17] suggest a travel allowance to assist the unemployed looking for work. Other studies suggest the provision of more financial assistance to unemployed persons resident in peripheral housing areas; also to provide more accessible information on job opportunities at locations where high concentrations of unemployed families reside (Quinn [3C35], [3C36]).

The concern for the travel needs of unemployed persons has generated a broader concern to analyse the transport circumstances of low-paid households generally. The travel constraint of low income is a complex area, any change in travel costs could not only affect travel behaviour but other household expenditure and vice versa. Two papers, one by Pucher [3C34] and the other, specifically in the Third World context, by Schuurman [3C38] review past public transport policies. In general public transport developments have not favoured the less well-off which, it could be argued, should be a prime goal of public transport planning.

In addition to studies of the travel problems of different social groups, the 1980s have seen a greater attention being given to conditions and relationships within the transport industry itself. Much of this work has arisen as a consequence of institutional changes in public transport operations and attempts to introduce new working practices. Koutsopoulos [3C25] documents the trend among public transport operators away from expanding services to increasing the efficiency and effectiveness of the workforce. The nature of labour-management relationships and collective bargaining has changed dramatically in recent years and this is fundamentally changing the structure of the industry in many countries. Some work argues that there is the scope for further improvements in workforce efficiency if liaison between different parties were improved (Lieb [3C27]), by reducing operating costs through changing some working practices such as introducing part-time labour, longer shifts, split shifts, changing duties etc. (Chomitz and Lave [3C7], Lieb and Wiseman [3C28]).

3D Impact of transport on lifestyle, commuting and shopping

Sections 3A and 3B have documented the trend toward a greater decentralization of homes and workplaces with consequent increases in commuting distances and in the minority of workers making very long journeys to work. In addition to the development of a 'commuter lifestyle', for many workers of all skills, there is a parallel trend towards a leisure revolution as working hours are slowly reduced and the choice of leisure facilities increases (Theologitis [3D27]). In turn, this has increased the need to assess the travel preferences of different social groups for leisure and recreation (Ergun and Stopher [3D21]). There has been a considerable body of research on the residential mobility of households in relation to their travel requirements for commuting and other facilities. A number of factors have been considered to influence residential choice such as travel costs (Verster [3D29], Vickerman [3D31], Miron [3D20], Dubin [3D9]), new road investment (Mills [3A11]) or rail investments (Nash [4B14]) and the potential use of mortgage subsidy to reverse the decentralization process (Ash and Kornhauser [3D2]). The concensus from this research suggests that households do account for travel requirements when moving residence, but that within their housing cost and accessibility thresholds (which themselves are mode dependent) residences are chosen on the basis of housing and neighbourhood quality (Weisbrod *et al.* [3D33]). In addition, the research suggests that mode changes should be viewed in a longer term perspective when homes or jobs change or when there is a change in the family life cycle (Jones, Clarke and Dix [5A11]).

A large body of research is documented on the characteristics of commuting journeys among different groups of the workforce (Dasgupta [3D7], Cubukgil and Miller [3D4]), between different parts of urban areas (Mogridge [3D21], Fulton [3D13], and to particular work locations such as office complexes (Daniels [3D5]). The main themes to emerge are the growing spatial mismatches between homes and jobs in the inner and outer areas of many cities (Dasgupta [3D6]). Longer duration commuting and the development of a 'commuter lifestyle' can also have adverse effects on family activities undertaken at home, on workplace performance and on worker's health (Pickup [3D24]).

Commuting peaks are a mixed blessing; while they produce some disbenefits, for example through a congested transport system, they have a social benefit which derives from common working hours. Over time, the pattern of peak travel has been changing as more varied working hour regimes have been introduced. Under such regimes, studies have attempted to measure commuters' travel behaviour given that they may have a greater choice of departure on arrival times (Hendrickson and Plank [3D16]) or make multi-stage work journeys (Hanson [3D15]). A variety of working hour regimes have been looked at not only for their travel behaviour and traffic consequences, but also for their environmental consequences: compressed working weeks (Atherton *et al.* [3D3], Transportation Research Board [3D28]), staggered working hours (Wikowski and Taylor [3D34]), and flexible working hours (Daniels [3D5], Ott, Slavin and Ward [3D23], Jovanis [3D18]).

3E Health effects, stress and crime

One of the most pressing social problems has been the increasing crime rate, both theft and physical assaults. A large number of crimes are committed in the travelling environment, particularly in large city centres. In addition, there is the fear of victimization while travelling which can also affect passenger's use of different travel modes and the times at which they travel (Austin and Buzawa [3E1]). In many cases, crime is highest at transport termini (Riley and Dean [3E8]). Bus and rail routes traverse a mix of different urban environments with varied crime rates. The number of physical assaults on bus drivers are often higher than those on passengers (Pearlstein and Wachs [3E6]).

A relatively new though important research area is studying the health and safety implications of urban travel. This is a difficult area in which to trace cause and effect and the research remains exploratory. For example, the health states of travellers depend on the coping ability of the individual and activities undertaken prior to travelling in addition to the conditions which are imposed by the travelling environment *per se* (Pickup [3D24]). The papers in this short section tackle issues of the anxiety and stress induced by different travel modes and the influence of personality on anxiety states; others assess issues such as motion sickness (Reason [3E7]), special public transport initiatives, and the overall well being of urban travellers.

3A Land-use patterns

3A1 BAGBY, D.G. (1980) The effects of traffic flow on residential property values. *Journal of the American Planning Association*, **46** (1), pp. 88–94.

This article presents an empirical study of the effects of traffic flow on residential property values in the community of Grand Rapids,

Michigan. Residential values in two identical neighbourhoods are compared over a 25 year period. One neighbourhood serves as a control for the measurement of the impact of changes in traffic flow upon residential values in the other. The results show that residential property values exhibit a surprisingly high elasticity with respect to reductions in traffic flow. The policy implications of these findings for cities laid out in a gridiron street pattern are explored.

3A2 CERVERO, R. (1984) Managing the traffic impacts of suburban office growth. *Transportation Quarterly*, **38** (4), pp. 533–550.

The growth of major office parks, industrial centres and other large developments on the fringes of many American cities poses significant challenges to transport planners. Trip patterns are becoming more diffuse and the trend toward suburban office development is reinforced by a steady suburbanization of residences and retail activity. While central city congestion might be relieved by office decentralization, commensurate demands for new suburban highway infrastructure will follow. This article therefore examines the transport implications of office growth on the urban fringe. It identifies a number of viable strategies to cope with impending congestion problems.

3A3 DAMM, D., LERMAN, S.R., LERNER-LAM, E. and YOUNG, J. (1980) Response of urban real estate values in anticipation of the Washington Metro. *Journal of Transport Economics and Policy*, **14** (3), pp. 315–336.

The effect of public mass transit systems on the spatial distribution of urban property values is likely to be highly localized. Changes in real estate values may occur both before and after construction of a transit system. This article describes a series of econometric models of real estate values estimated for areas of Washington, DC, over the period of the planning and initial construction of the metro system. Separate models are estimated for single-family dwellings, multi-family structures and retail stores. Access to the metro and its implementation schedule are both found to be significant determinants of property transaction prices.

3A4 DANIELS, P.W. and WARNES, A.M. (1980) *Movement in Cities. Spatial Perspectives on Urban Transport and Travel.* London: Methuen.

This book describes and analyses urban travel in terms of the purpose, distance and frequency of journeys and the modes and routes used. It draws its material from numerous surveys of transport in British towns, with occasional reference to the US, Australia and other countries. The book contains the following chapters: transport revolution and urban growth, the activities of urban populations and their relationship to urban movement, the aspatial characteristics of movement, goods movements within towns, spatial patterns of urban movement: the organising principles, spatial patterns of urban movement: empirical evidence, analysis and prediction of travel patterns, development of legislation concerning urban transport policies and planning, management of urban travel demands, some topical issues in urban transport decision making, geographical perspective in urban movement. An extensive bibliography is appended.

3A5 ECHENIQUE, M. (1981) Transport investment and urban land values. *International Journal of Transport Economics*, **8** (2), pp. 189-215.

In this paper it is argued that investment in transport can reduce urban land values. It is argued that the reduction in land prices has important consequences in terms of increasing efficiency, more equitable distribution of incomes and better environmental conditions. In order to demonstrate the argument, a framework from neoclassical economics is used where land prices are determined by the interaction of supply and demand. Land supply has traditionally been considered fixed. However, in urban areas, supply is increased in the long term by transport investment. Using data from third world cities, it is argued that a similar process is now occurring in Latin American cities.

See also: Button, K.J. (1981) Transport investment and urban land values: A comment. *International Journal of Transport Economics*, **8** (3), and Echenique, M. (1982) Transport investment and urban land values A reply. *International Journal of Transport Economics*, **9** (3), pp. 355-356.

3A6   EVANS, A.W. and BEEN, C. (1986) Transport costs and urban property values in the 1970s. *Urban Studies*, **23** (2), pp. 105–117.

In this paper the authors use data on property values published annually for the 56 local government areas in the Melbourne metropolitan area to investigate the response of the property market to the oil price rises of the 1970s. They show that property values appear to have responded rapidly to the Australian petrol price increase of 1978, more accessible properties gaining in value relative to less accessible. The 1973 increase was not passed on to Australian consumers but the depression in manufacturing industry which started after it, also had an impact on the property market as values in areas where manufacturing workers lived fell relative to others.

3A7   JONES, P.M. (1986) Mobility and the individual in Western industrial society, in Nijkamp, P. and Reichman, S. (eds.) *Transportation Planning in a Changing World*. Aldershot: Gower, pp. 29–47.

The concept of mobility in its various forms is an important feature of Western society, and is reflected in its social, political and economic systems. Travel and transport represent one valued facet of this mobility. This paper discusses the nature and measurement of mobility as seen from the perspective of an individual and the variety of travel problems he or she faces. An activity-based framework is outlined to better analyse these problems.

3A8   KING, R.J. (1983) Some problems in assessing the social effects of transport related plans. *Australian Road Research*, **13** (4), pp. 271–280.

Transport related changes can have direct effects in the form of accessibility changes, changes in barrier effects, changes in local environmental conditions, and/or pricing changes. Behavioural responses to these may take the form of decisions: (1) to change travel behaviour, (2) to change destination(s), (3) to change residential location, (4) to resist direct effects that are judged deleterious, and/or (5) to oppose the changes altogether. Any assessment of longer-term social effects demands some consideration of all five categories of decisions, but especially of the first and the third. Methods are available for the systematic study of all five, although firm prediction presents some problems. It is suggested, however, that 'rough and ready' assessment is possible, based on a knowledge of the relationships currently pertaining between residential location, travel behaviour and social characteristics of the population, and on a perspective of present patterns of residential differentiation and mobility. This approach to assessment is discussed in the context of two case-study areas of Melbourne.

3A9 LE CLERCQ, F. (1984) The effect of spatial factors on the development of mobility. *Transport Policy and Decision Making*, **2**, pp. 501–515.

The last 20 years have seen a tremendous growth in mobility; most of which has been car mobility. Yet the preservation of historic city centres necessitates reducing car traffic and thus restricting mobility. A model of the factors influencing changes in mobility is derived from a time series analysis on data from Amsterdam between 1960 and 1980. In the future the main cause of growth in car mobility will probably be spatial factors stimulated by changes in the demographic structure of society particularly if economic growth and energy supplies stagnate.

3A10 MAY, A.D. and PATTERSON, N.S. (1984) Transport problems as perceived by inner city firms. *Transportation*, **12**, pp. 225–241.

The role of transport policy in assisting inner-city firms is still unclear. This paper raises important policy questions and reviews past research, which suggest that transport problems are a major irritant to inner-city firms but are unlikely to cause them to leave the area; the ability of transport improvements to attract new firms is uncertain. It describes a recent study in Leeds and London designed to determine the effect of transport problems on manufacturing and service industries, whether such problems are more serious in the inner city, and which solutions would be most appropriate. A series of recommendations is provided.

3A11 MILLS, F. (1981) Effects of beltways on the location of residences and selected workplaces. *Transportation Research Record*, **812**, pp. 26–33.

Beltways have been cited as factors that encourage the decentralization of people and jobs from central cities and thereby contribute to inefficient patterns of urban development. This study compared changes in total population, manufacturing employment, retail employment, and commuting in 24 standard metropolitan statistical areas, half of which had a beltway constructed during the study period. When the data are divided into a pre-beltway and either a beltway construction or a post-beltway period, no statistically significant effects on the central cities are found. Comparison with another statistical study by using regression analysis and eight case studies suggests that other forces such as land-use regulation or local opportunities for annexation outweigh the beltway's influence on decentralization.

3A12 PICKETT, M.W. and PERRETT, K.E. (1984) The effects of the Tyne and Wear Metro on residential property values. *Transport and Road Research Laboratory, Supplementary Report* 825. Crowthorne: TRRL.

This report describes a survey of the possible changes in residential property values as a result of the improvement in accessibility for those areas located close to a metro station. The results indicate that properties near to the metro gained on average by £360 over more distant properties.

3A13 RASBASH, D.L. (1983) The use of changes in property values in the evaluation of highway schemes. *Highways and Transportation*, **30** (8/9), pp. 22–25.

Many worthwhile highway schemes such as bypasses, often fail conventional economic criteria. With many similar schemes competing for limited resources the paper argues that it has become necessary to introduce methods for evaluating environmental benefits. Three methods are discussed based on changes in property values brought about by environmental effects. The author concludes that just as compensation for lost amenity or reduced property prices is an accepted cost to a scheme, then the reverse situation should be included as an accepted economic benefit. In conclusion it is suggested that further study be undertaken in conjunction with the development of some environmentally sympathetic schemes to evaluate more fully the proposals put forward.

3A14 STUCKER, J. (1975) Transport improvements, commuting costs, and residential location. *Journal of Urban Economics*, **2** (2), pp. 123-143.

This paper develops a theoretical framework for evaluating one of the long-term or secondary effects of a transport improvement. This is the tendency for such improvements to lead to a change in location of commuter residences in response to the new characteristics of the journey to work. A model of residential location is adapted to provide an equation relating changes in travel costs to changes in preferred location of homes. When applied to a particular situation it was found that journey to work cost was a major locational factor, especially if it also offered substantially increased speed.

3A15 TOWN, S.W. (1980) The social distribution of mobility and travel patterns. Transport and Road Research Laboratory, Laboratory Report 948. Crowthorne: TRRL.

This paper outlines the distribution of mobility between different groups of the UK population using data from National Travel Surveys. Several groups of the population are defined as having below average mobility and the characteristics of their travel patterns are compared with each other and with the overall population. The sources of travel disadvantage among these groups are often factors which constrain them in all areas of their lives not just in their travel behaviour. In addition, there is a need to recognize the influence which non-transport factors can have on travel demand and also the potential for solving transport problems with non-transport solutions.

3B Technological change

3B1 DAVIES, R.L. (1985) The Gateshead Shopping and Information Service. *Environment and Planning B*, **12** (2), pp. 209-220.

The Gateshead Shopping and Information Service (SIS) is an unusual experiment in computerized 'home shopping' in that it is oriented to disadvantaged consumers (mainly the elderly and disabled) rather than to affluent sections of the population. The immediate objectives are to explore the utilities and effectiveness of new information technologies for helping immobile shoppers; but more broadly the organizers are seeking to address the concern that commercial teleshopping developments might prove to be socially divisive unless special complementary services are also provided for the less well-off. This paper is a review of the progress of the experiment to date and a consideration of what problems and prospects lie ahead.

3B2 GIANNOPOULOS, G.A. (1984) Technological innovation in major urban transport systems. *Ekistics*, **51** (305), pp. 139-146.

The author investigates the potential technical innovations in the transport sector and attempts to assess their possible impact on urban form and development. Coverage includes automated guideway systems, dual-mode and demand-actuated buses, electric cars, alternative fuels and increased fuel efficiency. These transport innovations are then contrasted with developments in telecommunications.

3B3 GUY, C.M. (1985) Some speculations on the retailing and planning implications of 'push button shopping' in Britain. *Environment and Planning B*, **12** (2), pp. 193-208.

This paper examines some implications for retail planning of the use of viewdata for the purchase of retail goods. An examination of existing features of retailing and shopping behaviour in Britain indicates that viewdata shopping will probably have the greatest competitive impact on existing methods of 'nonstore retailing' (for example mail order) and unconventional retailing (for example, catalogue sales). The main locational implications are, first, accelerated rates of change in the use of retail and service premises within city centres, and, second, some reduction in recent rates of increase in numbers of suburban 'retail warehouses'. Other policy issues which are likely to confront planners are also discussed, and suggestions for monitoring the growth of remote shopping are made.

3B4 HOWARD, E.B. (1985) Teleshopping in North America. *Environment and Planning B*, **12** (2), pp. 141-150.

North American developments in teleshopping are more numerous than those in Britain. In this paper the experiments that have taken place are reviewed and it is shown that developments of new interactive cabled services provided to the home have not been led by the retail industry. The banking, entertainment, and publishing industries are providing and using the new forms of communication. New forms of retailing have often been seen in North America ahead of those in Britain, but it is suggested that Britain may have a greater potential for the growth of teleshopping than North America.

3B5 LEE, A.M. and MEYBURG, A.H. (1981) Resource implications of electronic message transfer in the letter-post industry. *Transportation Research Record*, 812, pp. 59–64.

As Western societies move more and more rapidly to information economies, the need for face-to-face human interactions and for the exchange of physical goods is being replaced by the need to exchange information. New technologies have been and are being developed that facilitate this flow. Substitution of personal travel and hard-copy communications transport by electronic means is a significant social development with many implications. This paper attempts to illustrate some of the impacts of substituting communication for transport. The use of electronic message transfer technology by the US postal service is examined in the context of current first-class mail shipment patterns.

3B6 LEWIS, J.C. (1985) Technical changes in retailing: its impact on employment and access. *Environment and Planning B*, **12** (2), pp.165–191.

In this paper the major phases of retail investment growth during the post-war period are examined. The effects of this new investment for both the production and the consumption of retail services are also illustrated. In particular, the focus is on the most recent phase of retail investment growth, both in new building and in new production technology, which has been taking place since the late 1970s. This new investment has involved major changes in both the organization and the location of the retail industry. In particular, new types of retail organization such as superstores, hypermarkets, and retail warehouses have emerged, many of which are located away from existing high-street centres in peripheral out-of-town sites. It is these new types of retail outlet which have been at the forefront of new technology applications in the industry. From an examination of recent superstore development in London, it is suggested that a distinct change in the geography of food retailing is emerging, with a growing polarization between inner and outer, and low-income and high-income areas. It is suggested that this emerging polarization in the structure and location of retailing both reflects and reinforces existing trends towards a greater social and spatial polarization of Britain in the 1980s, and that increased inequality of access to new retailing services is an important but frequently ignored consequence of recent developments in the industry.

3B7 MILLER, C.E. (1980) Telecommunications/transportation substitution: some empirical findings. *Socio-economic and Planning Science*, **14** (2), pp. 163–166.

The subsidized provision of telephones is discussed in the context of the substitution of transportation by telecommunications. A study of 'substitution' within the patterns of communication between geographically dispersed members of extended family groups is described. Data on the communication patterns of a sample of New Town families are presented. In this case, no evidence of a substitutive effect is apparent; the policy implications of this result are discussed.

3B8 POULTON, M.C. (1980) Why new technologies cannot radically improve the quality of urban transportation. *Transportation Planning and Technology*, **6**, pp. 75–80.

In recent years effort has been expended on the development of new modes of city transport. It is argued in this paper that this work is unlikely to be very productive because the major remaining flaw in the provision of transportation services – the inability of one mode to provide a good service to concentrated and dispersed trip ends – seems unavoidable. To make the required breakthrough a new mode must be frugal in its demands for space, flexible in its operation and fast. But an analysis of the performance of existing and prototype modes suggest that there is a fundamental technological barrier that precludes any one mode from performing well in more than two out of these three ways. This implies that any further improvements in travel for the urbanite must be made through existing modes and their derivatives and will be quite limited.

3B9 SALOMON, I. (1985) Telecommunications and travel. Substitution or modified mobility? *Journal of Transport Economics and Policy*, **19** (3), pp. 219-235.

The substitution of travel by new telecommunications technologies in other types of interactions between physical and electronic communication modes is considered. It is suggested that enhancement of travel, particularly for discretionary purposes, will offset travel reduction realized through substitution. Were most individuals' needs to be satisfied at home through telecommunications, psychological considerations would suggest that new travel would be generated. Business trips and the avoidance of future travel through use of telecommunications are also analysed. It is argued that the effects on the transport system are dependent not only on the costs of communicating but also on the value of information. In general, the substitution of travel by telecommunications is expected to be minor.

See also: Salomon, I. (1984) Man and his transport behaviour. Telecommuting - promises and reality. *Transport Reviews*, **4** (1), pp. 103-113.

3C Social groups

3C1 ANDREWS, H.F. (1978) Journey to work considerations in the labour force participation of married women. *Regional Studies*, **12**, pp. 11-20.

Both working and non-working married female respondents were asked questions to guage sensitivities to remaining in, withdrawing from or entering the labour force as a result of increasing journey to work times and costs. Similar indications of labour supply elasticity are found for both full-time and part-time workers, though considerable inter-regional variation exists. Associations between elasticity of supply, level of earnings, husband's attitudes and wives' contribution to total household income are also found. Presented with fixed and hypothetical levels of earnings, acceptable journey to work times vary similarly for both current workers and latent workers, though the supply elasticities for those currently working are somewhat higher.

3C2 ARROWSMITH, G. (1984) Equity in transport planning. *The Planner*, **70** (10), pp. 16-17.

The author describes the introduction of considerations of social justice into an economic analysis of transport. Mention is made of the approach adopted by the Department of Transport in its COBA programme for the evaluation of trunk road schemes, where the same value of non-working time was usually assumed for all persons. Another possibility is to devise a radical evaluation model from the assumption that the value of money savings varies with the income. This approach, which may be characterized as social equity (as opposed to the DTP's time equity approach), depends on the difference between the income characteristics of different travel modes. Another suggested approach is the use of taxation policy to change the distribution of wealth so as to choose the policy which best combines welfare with economic efficiency. The advantages and disadvantages of these approaches are discussed and compared.

3C3 BORSAY, A. (1982) Equal opportunities? A review of transport and environmental design for people with physical disabilities. *Town Planning Review*, **53** (2), pp. 153–178.

This article explores ways of offering equal opportunities to the blind and partially sighted, the deaf and the hard of hearing, and all other people with some kind of physical disability or handicap. After outlining the history of policies towards mobility and the built environment, the discussion turns to building usage and the evaluation of design and transport. A final section draws out lessons for future policy.

3C4 BRÖG, W. and RIBBECK, K. (1985) Mobility of handicapped persons: examination of mobility levels of different groups of handicap. *Transportation Research Record*, 1018, pp. 1–13.

A large-scale study of mobility-handicapped persons in the Federal Republic of Germany in 1981 made possible the examination of the mobility of handicapped persons in light of several classifications of handicap. This paper is a report on the mobility of those persons generally defined as handicapped (i.e. with a reduced earning capacity), those defined in the major study as mobility handicapped, and those whose mobility is, officially, considered limited enough to warrant the issue of a free travel pass. The results show the mobility handicap extends well beyond the official definition and that it is particularly evident if movement is possible only with the assistance of a second person. It also appears that free travel passes distributed on the basis of general, not mobility, handicap can result in only those persons who are already most mobile receiving them.

3C5 BUSSIERE, Y. (1984) Population aging and transportation demand: a Montreal case study for 1978-1991. *Ekistics*, **51** (306), pp. 238-242.

The underlying demographic trends suggest that the future demand for transport will diminish the demand for existing public transport services even further. Increases in demand will mainly take place in car passenger trips.

3C6 CARPENTER, S.M. and HEGGIE, I.G. (1981) The distributional effect of transport expenditure, in Banister, D. and Hall, P. (eds) *Transport and Public Policy Planning*. London: Mansell, pp. 159-169.

The main issue discussed in this paper is who benefits from transport expenditure, by how much and at whose expense. It is shown that when differences in household size and levels of employment are taken into account, high-income households spend more on public transport for travel by rail, but not for bus or coach travel. The assumption that the poor benefit from public transport subsidies is not entirely confirmed by the work reported here.

3C7 CHOMITZ, K.M. and LAVE, C.A. (1983) Forecasting the financial effects of work role changes. *Transportation Quarterly*, **37** (3), pp. 453-473.

In 1980 US transit fares covered only 39 per cent of operating costs compared with 52 per cent in 1977. This article examines the possibilities for reducing operating costs by modifying the rules of work. Cost reductions could be made by changing rules in three areas: the use of part-time drivers, allowing existing drivers to work longer shifts, and changing the point at which drivers receive extra pay for working split shifts. Cost savings are calculated from a variety of possible changes across a representative sample of transit districts.

See also: Chomitz, K.M., Giuliano, G. and Lave, C.A. (1985) Part-time public transit operators: experiences and prospects. *Transportation Research Record*, 1013, pp. 32-38.

3C8 DIANDAS, J. (1984) Alternative approaches to transport in Third World cities: issues in equity and accessibility. *Ekistics*, **51** (306), pp. 197–212.

A number of approaches to transport provision are presented individually and as they relate to one another. Included in the list are the range of technological approaches, ownership of transport, operating philosophies, vehicle sizes and traffic management. The evidence used comes from case study material in Colombo (Sri Lanka). Broader issues such as the interface between walking and vehicles and the problems of equity, energy consumption, environment and land use are also considered.

3C9 FOX, M.B. (1983) Working women and travel: the access of women to work and community facilities. *Journal of the American Planning Association*, **49** (2), pp. 156–167.

Because the existing infrastructure no longer fits the travel demands of women with multiple roles at work and in the family, there may be consequences for their access to employment and to community facilities. Although comparisons of travel patterns of women with those of other groups have shown that women take fewer and shorter trips, and use their automobiles less, a newer indicator – travel time over the 24-hour day, reveals that working women with children may have shorter time durations for work, household, and leisure trips. Because travel is traded off as a discretionary activity in favour of obligatory time requirements, compensatory policies should be designed to allow time for travel directly by alteration of work and household organization and indirectly by changes in land-use and transport policies.

3C10 FULLERTON, J., PERRETT, K.E. and COPELAND, D. (1985) Effects of changes in public transport provision on shopping behaviour in Gateshead. Transport and Road Research Laboratory, Research Report 16. Crowthorne: TRRL.

The introduction of Metro in Tyne and Wear has resulted in considerable changes to travel opportunities in the area. This report deals with the effects of the changes on shopping behaviour in Gateshead, one of the major district centres. It is based on surveys conducted in 1979 and 1982. Metro began operation through Gateshead in 1981.

In 1982, Metro was used for 13 per cent of shopping trips to Gateshead. The proportion of shoppers using bus fell by 11 per cent, showing that Metro has primarily attracted people who previously travelled by bus. There has been little change in the total number of public transport passengers crossing the River Tyne to Newcastle. Metro has made it easier for some people to travel into Newcastle and this has lead to a loss of shoppers from Gateshead. However more bus passengers now stay to shop in Gateshead, rather than interchange to Metro. There have been definite shifts in pedestrian flows towards the bus/Metro interchange. There has been a general decline, both in the proportions of people shopping for goods, and in the average expenditure. While expenditure by bus and Metro passengers was similar, car users were spending more and pedestrians less. Durable shopping showed a greater decline than shopping for convenience goods. 21 per cent of Metro based shopping trips to Gateshead were new trips, mostly from Newcastle.

3C11 GIHRING, T. (1982) Accessibility choices and opportunities in Zaria, Nigeria. *Third World Planning Review*, **4** (4), pp. 387–399.

3C12 GUY, C.M. (1985) The food and grocery shopping behaviour of disadvantaged consumers: some results from the Cardiff consumer panel. *Transactions of the Institute of British Geographers*, **10** (2), pp. 181–190.

This paper examines the routine convenience shopping behaviour of two groups of disadvantaged consumers: households containing unemployed adults and households containing retired adults. Evidence from the Cardiff Consumer Panel survey of 1982 shows that these two groups did not generally possess attitudes to shopping consistent with their stereotypes. Their expenditure patterns were similar to the control group, except that superstores were used less and distances travelled to major grocery shopping opportunities were shorter. The retired also travelled shorter distances and were more likely to use independent or affiliated stores than were other groups.

3C13 HAHN, H. (1986) Disability and the urban environment: a perspective on Los Angeles. *Environment and Planning D*, **4** (3), pp. 273–288.

Increasingly, research on disability has been guided by a definition that focuses on the interaction between the individual and the environment and by a minority-group perspective based on the propositions that discriminatory attitudes are the primary source of the problems of disabled citizens, that the environment is shaped by public policy, and that policies reflect prevalent social attitudes and values. The implications of this approach for an analysis of the experience of disabled persons in Los Angeles are examined by assessing major characteristics of this urban area such as geographic dispersion, the absence of a sense of community, and the impact of pervasive standards of personal appearance. The investigation indicates a pressing need to provide increased accessibility for disabled residents to fulfill constitutional principles of freedom and equality.

3C14 HALL, R.W. (1983) Travel outcome and performance: the effect of uncertainty on accessibility. *Transportation Research B*, **17** (4), pp. 275-290.

Traditionally, theorists have based their accessibility models upon deterministic approximations. However, uncertainty in itself can affect whether an activity is accessible, and affect how one measures acessibility. In the first section of this paper, it is shown that travel time randomness interacts with the scheduling of human activities to define the region which is accessible to a traveller. In the second section, a problem is considered where a traveller must search among opportunities to locate a certain activity he desires. It is found that there exists an optimal cluster size which minimizes travel cost, the size being a decreasing function of the probability of locating the activity at any single opportunity.

3C15 HANSON, P. and HANSON, S. (1981) The impact of married women's employment on household travel patterns: a Swedish example. *Transportation*, **10** (2), pp. 165-83.

As the number of married women working outside the home continues to grow, questions arise as to the impact of a wife's employment on household travel patterns. This paper examines the effects of a wife's employment status on her own travel activity pattern and on that of her husband. Using data from Uppsala, the evidence suggests that a woman's full-time employment does bring significant changes to her own travel pattern but has little impact on that of her husband. The paper concludes with a discussion of policy implications and a review of several Swedish programmes that could eventually result in greater similarity in the travel activity patterns of men and women.

3C16 HANSON, S. and SCHWAB, M. (1987) Accessibility and intraurban travel. *Environment and Planning A*, **19**, pp. 735-749.

This paper examines the assumption behind using accessibility indicators: that individual travel behaviour is related to the location of potential activity sites. Following a review of the relationships between accessibility and travel an access measure is tested using data from Uppsala, Sweden. The results show that although travel is related to accessibility to some degree, the relationship is not as strong as deductive models have implied.

3C17 HEDGES, B. and HOPKIN, J.M (1981) Transport and the search for work: a study in Greater Manchester. Transport and Road Research Laboratory, Supplementary Report 639. Crowthorne: TRRL.

A survey of 129 unemployed people was conducted in three areas of Greater Manchester in the autumn of 1978, and a follow-up survey took place in January 1979. The research was a case study which examined access to employment opportunities for unemployed people of similar socio-economic characteristics living near the city centre and in a suburban council housing estate. The results suggest that some form of assistance with the cost of using public transport while travelling to look for work would be beneficial for some unemployed people. In the areas studied, such help could be of particular importance to those living in the suburban council housing estate, unskilled people, and the long-term unemployed.

3C18 HOPKIN, J.M. (1981) The ownership and use of cars by elderly people. Transport and Road Research Laboratory, Laboratory Report 969. Crowthorne: TRRL.

This report describes present patterns of car availability and use among the elderly and the role of different forms of transport in their daily travel. Suggestions about possible future changes in levels of car use and availability among the elderly are also made. The research uses data from a wide variety of sources, but the main surveys used are the 1975/76 British National Travel Survey and a TRRL survey of old people in Guildford, conducted in 1975.

3C19 HOPKIN, J.M. (1986) Concessionary fares and pensioners' travel patterns: an analysis based on the 1978/79 National Travel Survey. Transport and Road Research Laboratory, Research Report 69. Crowthorne: TRRL.

Using data from the British 1978/79 National Travel Survey this report examines the distribution of pensioners with concessionary travel on public transport, and the effect of concessions on travel patterns. Particular attention is paid to estimating the extent to which different types of concessions generate additional bus journeys that would not have been made if pensioners had to pay the full fare.

3C20 HOPKIN, J.M. and PICKUP, L. (1986) The role of the parties involved in planning, financing and running of transport for commuting. Dublin: European Foundation for the Improvement of Living and Working Conditions.

This report summarizes the results of cross-national research to examine the influence which commuters can bring to bear on planning decisions which affect their commuting circumstance. Twenty case studies from five EC member states are reviewed covering a variety of different travel to work situations from worker and employer transport initiatives to area based land-use/transport plans. The report proposes areas where participation processes could be improved to give commuters a larger voice.

3C21 IRCHA, M.C. and GALLAGHER, M.A. (1985) Urban transit: equity aspects. *Journal of Urban Planning and Development*, **111** (1), pp. 1–9.

Evidence from two case studies of urban transit suggests that inequities exist, particularly for those who are dependent on public transport. The needs of the elderly are well known, but no such service exists for young people or low-income travellers as the flat fare system penalizes short journeys. Equity must be considered alongside efficiency.

See also: Ircha, M.C. and Sundararajan, D. (1984) Municipal service distribution: equity concerns. *Journal of Urban Planning and Development*, **110** (1), pp. 34–41.

3C22 JACKSON, R. (1982) The cost and quality of paratransit for the elderly and handicapped. *Transportation Quarterly*, **36** (4), pp. 527–540.

This paper compares the real cost of service provided by two major subsidized paratransit operations in New England, USA with rates currently applicable in the commercial sector. It is concluded that subsidized systems are no more efficient than private enterprise and have serious deficiencies in the quality of service they provide.

3C23 KNAPP, S.F., WOZNY, M.C. and BURKHARDT, J.E. (1985) Estimating the cost of providing transportation services to elderly clients. *Transportation Research Record*, 1018, pp. 22–33.

In this study methodologies were developed for assessing the costs of both transport and in-home services provided to elderly clients under Title III of the Older Americans Act. The study produced (a) a research report summarizing the application of the resource-based cost methodology that was developed for these two studies and (b) a cost assessment manual for use by local service providers. Data used to develop the cost methodology were collected from in-depth interviews with all transport service providers in 16 randomly selected planning and service areas across the United States. A brief overview of the results and of how to use the methodology to construct and analyse the true cost of operating transport services is presented.

3C24 KOENIG, J.G. (1980) Indicators of urban accessibility: theory and application. *Transportation*, **9** (2), pp. 145–172.

The concept of accessibility and its related indicators have been in use for a long time, with still diverging interpretations of their significance and formulation. In this paper, a review is made of various existing theoretical bases, with special emphasis on recent behavioural approaches. It is suggested that this theoretical framework now allows a better appraisal of accessibility indicators and precise recommendations are proposed for their practical formulation and use. Finally, the relations between accessibility and trip rate are examined; from a study made in French cities, it is suggested that accessibility is a powerful determinant of trip rate.

3C25 KOUTSOPOULOS, H.N. and WILSON, N.H.M. (1987) Operator workforce planning in the transit industry. *Transportation Research*, **21** (2), pp. 127–138.

Workforce planning in the transit industry has received increased attention in the last few years as management emphasis has shifted from expanding transit service to increasing service efficiency and effectiveness. This paper builds upon recent work on the optimal level of reserve personnel and extends the analysis approach to incorporate the probabilistic aspects of absenteeism by day of week and season, workforce attrition, and extra, non-scheduled work such as new operator on-street training and special events requiring extra service. It presents an integrated framework for operator workforce planning which includes three inter-related models: strategic, tactical and operational. A case study of workforce planning at the Massachusetts Bay Transportation Authority is used to demonstrate the potential of the general approach proposed in the paper.

3C26 LEE, W. (1986) *Guidelines for Providing for People with a Mobility Handicap*. London: Institution of Highways and Transportation.

The report of a working party set up to review existing guidance on providing for the various forms of disability, to co-ordinate them in one publication, to identify gaps in provision, and to make recommendations. Covers design standards for signing, footways and footpaths, kerbs, ramps, steps, handrails and street furniture, other obstructions, pedestrianized areas, carriageway narrowings, the closing of side streets, seating, lighting, and general and winter maintenance; crossing facilities, including underpasses and footbridges, pedestrian crossings and textured paving; parking; public transport, including vehicles, railway or bus and coach stations, bus stops and shelters and provision of information; and requirements at roadworks. Includes an annotated list of other relevant legislation and a bibliography.

3C27 LIEB, R.C. (1984) The changing nature of labour/management relations in transportation. *Transportation Journal*, **23** (3), pp. 4–14.

The nature of labour/management relations and collective bargaining in transport industries has changed dramatically during the past several years. Unprecedented changes in work rules, compensation patterns, and bargaining format have been prompted by a combination of economic conditions and public policies which have fundamentally altered the structure of the transport industries. While such changes can be viewed with alarm by the participants, there is the opportunity for improving the efficiency of transport companies through mutually beneficial cooperation between management and labour. The productivity changes in airlines, trucking, railroads and mass transit are discussed.

3C28 LIEB, R.C. and WISEMAN, F. (1979) A survey of the use of part-time employees in transit. *Transit Journal*, **5** (2), pp. 3-8.

The purpose of this study was to obtain data to determine the nature and extent of transit industry use of part-time labour. The data indicate that the use of part-time labour is widespread and is more likely to be found in public systems and in those systems not covered by collective bargaining agreements. There has been a significant increase in the number of public systems using part-time labour over the past five years. It would seem that the most likely candidates for new part-time agreements are the larger systems which are subject to collective bargaining agreements. While these systems tend to be troubled by the most significant peak-hour problems, they have tended to be least successful in establishing part-time agreements.

3C29 MADDEN, J.F. (1977) A spatial theory of sex discrimination. *Journal of Regional Science*, **17**, pp. 369-380.

Recent economic publications have contained numerous analytical and empirical treatments of labour market discrimination. This paper proposes to show that in spatially separated markets wage discrimination theoretically can arise as an expected consequence of profit-maximizing decisions by employers, based on sex differences in the spatial elasticity of labour supply to the firm. It is demonstrated that the wage elasticity for female labour supply to the firm is less than that for male labour supply if competing firms are spatially separated, if market-produced goods are not easily substituted with household-produced goods and if spouses' leisure time are complementary.

See also Madden, J.F. (1981) Why women work closer to home. *Urban Studies*, **18** (2), pp. 181-194.

3C30 MCKNIGHT, C., PAGANO, A.M., ROBINS, L. and JOHNSON, C. (1982) Economies of scale in transportation for the elderly and the handicapped. *Transportation Research Record*, 850, pp. 18-25.

The costs of 36 transportation services for the elderly and the handicapped were analysed to determine whether there are economies of scale in the provision of special transportation. A U-shaped cost curve was found for unit costs as ridership is increased by increasing the service area. In the case of increasing ridership by increasing the number of trips within a fixed service area, there are decreasing costs per passenger trip and a U-shaped curve for costs per passenger mile. However, because small agencies receive more unpriced resources in the form of shared overhead and volunteer labour and because of increased management costs and quality of services, coordinated or consolidated services may not lead to lower unit cost.

3C31 NOEL, E.C. and CHADDA, H.S. (1986) Consolidating elderly and handicapped transportation. *Journal of Transportation Engineering (ASCE)*, **112** (2), pp. 131–144.

The attempts of public and private organizations to provide transport services for the elderly and handicapped has led to a proliferation of specialized, independently operated services. This results in fragmentation, waste of resources, inefficiency and duplication. The author considers the consolidation of transport services for these special groups and discusses the associated barriers and constraints.

3C32 PICKUP, L. (1984) Women's gender-role and its influence on travel behaviour. *Built Environment*, **10** (1), pp. 61–68.

Women tend to be more reliant than men on public transport and have lower levels of mobility. However many of their activity patterns are complex as they work both as a wage earner and as a domestic worker. This paper uses travel survey information to present the overall situation and comments on the possible future directions as they affect the travel opportunities for women.

See also: Pickup, L. (1981) Housewives' mobility and travel patterns. Transport and Road Research Laboratory, Laboratory Report 971. Crowthorne: TRRL.

3C33 PIRIE, G.H. (1981) The possibility and potential of public policy on accessibility. *Transportation Research*, **15A** (5), pp. 377–381.

The development of measures of accessibility has proceeded largely independently of concern for the ways in which public policy-makers respond to analytic research. Academic interest in accessibility is not necessarily paralleled by a public interest and the former cannot be expected to have a ready-made market or to promote public policy of its own accord. Public policy on accessibility will only be forthcoming if accessibility is a well politicized issue. Political viability is also vital to the working of accessibility policy. The possibility of formulating and implementing an effective policy on accessibility suggests giving as much attention to the development of a conceptually robust and incisive notion of accessibility as to the improvement of accessibility measures.

3C34 PUCHER, J. (1982) Discrimination in mass transit. *Journal of the American Planning Association*, **48** (3), pp. 315–326.

Helping to offset the mobility deprivations of the poor should be one of the main goals of transit. Yet, in a number of ways, transit systems have implicitly discriminated against this group, which most needs their services. This article examines the nature and extent of various types of inequities in transit finance that harm low-income and minority riders. Through analysis of nationwide, aggregate data for 1978 as well as in-depth studies of individual cities, an assessment is made of the degree to which transit finance inequities represent violations of Title VI of the 1964 Civil Rights Act. Finally, recommendations are made for policy changes that would reverse or at least mitigate these inequities.

3C35 QUINN, D.J. (1986*a*) Understanding accessibility: problems of the unemployed. *The Planner*, **72** (1), pp. 25–27.

This paper addresses the difficult problem of job search patterns for unemployed people in the West Midlands conurbation. Conventional accessibility analysis only covers part of the problem and this research puts forward a familiarity index to supplement accessibility. Local employment initiatives should be concentrated at locations most familiar to residents of high unemployment areas and their location should be accompanied by better support, information and education for job searchers.

3C36 QUINN, D.J. (1986*b*) Accessibility and job search: A study of unemployed school leavers. *Regional Studies*, **20** (2), pp. 163–173.

This paper responds to the urgency underlying recent local authority employment initiatives and focuses on the importance of accessibility in the job search behaviour of one particularly vulnerable group of the unemployed. A two-stage survey investigated unemployed school-leavers' familiarity with Birmingham and decisions made in the process of job search. The results of the survey indicate that there are 'accessible' areas of the city where jobs are not sought. It is concluded that knowledge of the city and perception of travel provides a more sensitive indication of likely job search patterns than conventional measures of accessibility. This clearly has implications for local authority policies on economic regeneration, employment and transport.

3C37 RICHARDSON, A.J. and YOUNG, W. (1982) A measure of linked-trip accessibility. *Transportation Planning and Technology*, **7**, pp. 73–82.

This paper shows that many of the proposed definitions of accessibility form a spectrum of accessibility measures. These measures are shown to be deficient in one major aspect; they assume that for any one measure of accessibility, there is but one origin of trips. In view of the considerable amount of evidence demonstrating the widespread, and increasing, occurrence of trip-linking such a proposition must be viewed as being rather doubtful. In the light of this, the paper proceeds to develop a measure of accessibility which explicitly accounts for the linking of trips. The implications of this measure, compared to a conventional unlinked-trip accessibility measure, are discussed as are some problems which are foreseen in the practical implementation of such a measure.

3C38 SCHUURMAN, F.J. (1985) The access to space for urban low-income groups: the case of public transport. *Third World Planning Review*, **7** (4), pp. 339–349.

Public transport provision poses many problems for urban planners in developing countries, and this paper takes data from a transport study carried out in Arequipa (Peru) in 1982. The analysis examines the problems which low-income groups are faced with in transport terms, and it also comments on the organizational aspects of public transport in Latin American cities.

3C39 SINGELL, L.D. and LILLYDAHL, J.H. (1986) An empirical analysis of the commute to work patterns of males and females in two-earner households. *Urban Studies*, **23** (2), pp. 119–129.

The purpose of this paper is to investigate empirically the proposition that residential decisions are made with reference to the male head of household's job location, disadvantaging females in the labour market. A sample of approximately 50,000 adults in two-earner households in urban areas distributed across the United States is selected from the 1980 census and used to estimate a simultaneous model to explain commute to work behaviour of men and women. The model is estimated separately for households that did and did not change residences in the past year. The impacts of the new residences on the commute times of both male and female workers, holding other variables constant, are compared. We conclude that residential selection does favour males relative to females, although there is evidence that this advantage is eliminated as the ratio of female to male earnings in the same household narrows.

3C40 SPEAR, B.D. (1982) User-side subsidies: delivering special-needs transportation through private providers. *Transportation Research Record*, 850, pp. 13-18.

The user-side subsidy is a method for delivering low-cast transport services to selected groups of travellers. Over the past several years, the Service and Methods Demonstration Program of the Urban Mass Transportation Administration has been exploring various applications of the user-side subsidy concept through a number of demonstrations and case-study evaluations. This paper summarizes and compares the major evaluation findings from these projects to make some general statements about the overall feasibility and cost-effectiveness of providing special needs transportation services through user-side subsidies. It examines the concept from the perspective of three principal groups: the subsidizing agency, the user, and the transport provider. Relevant issues of concern to each of these groups are identified and discussed and those most relevant to policy-makers highlighted.

3C41 STIMPSON, C. (1987) *Women and the American City*. Chicago: University of Chicago Press.

This book presents 23 papers on the ways in which the American city has both enhanced and restricted women's lives. Two chapters deal explicitly with transport related issues, one on women and mobility and the other on women and the urban environment. Both are critical of policies that assume particular gender roles for women and the fact that many women act as chauffeurs to drive children and adults to destinations – this has tended to restrict the opportunities for those women. Often public transport is not directed at women's needs and self-help schemes organized by women offer only a limited service. The general message throughout this edited volume is for more research and action on women's role in the city. There are two useful reviews of current literature on urban issues and women which form an appendix to the book.

3C42 STUDNICKI-GIZBERT, K.W. (1982) Equity and distributional issues in transport policy. *Transport Policy and Decision Making*, **2**, pp. 69–80.

The concepts of 'equity' and different types of distributional concepts are defined and their implications for transport policies indicated. In conclusion it is argued that the proper role of the policy analyst is to identify the prospective losses and benefits and evaluate the costs of alternative solutions as a part of the policy development process.

3C43 US DEPARTMENT OF TRANSPORTATION (1983) Transportation for Older Americans: Issues and Options for the Decade of the 1980s. Technology Sharing Program. Washington, DC: US Department of Transportation.

Demographic and other changes that will influence the design, funding, and implementation of transport services for the elderly are described. Based in part on workshop material from a 1980 mini-conference on transportation for the elderly, and data from the 1970 and 1980 census, this report covers demographic, economic, and social changes among the elderly and the transport implications of these changes. Three major issues that will have particular implications for transport services for the elderly are analysed: inflation, energy and funding.

3C44 US DEPARTMENT OF TRANSPORTATION (1984) *Third International Conference on Mobility and Transport of Elderly and Handicapped Persons* (Bell, W.G. and Ashford N. (eds.)), Conference Proceedings, USDOT report COT-1-85-07. Washington, DC: USDOT.

This report comprises 62 papers of which four are review papers, eight papers review major national developments, five deal with air transport and four discuss the area of micro-computer applications to specialized transport services. The remaining 41 papers report on particular special transport schemes for elderly and handicapped persons around the world. The six main highlights are (i) a strong international policy interest in transport provision for elderly and disabled; (ii) the large scope for modifying and improving existing transport systems for the mobility handicapped; (iii) providing legal rights for disabled travellers such as in Canada; (iv) designing taxis to accept wheelchair users as in London; (v) an interest in improving the conditions of international air travel for the elderly and disabled both while on aircraft and at airports; (vi) a growth in interest among developing countries for providing special transport-services.

3C45 WITKOWSKI, J.M. and BUICK, T.R. (1985) Travel behavior of residents of retirement communities. *Transportation Research Record*, 1018, pp. 13–22.

Urban travel estimation is reviewed in the context of a growing elderly population and the trend towards retirement communities. The life-style characteristics of retirement communities are uniquely different from those of virtually all elderly groups previously studied, and the mobility of the inhabitants appears to be reflected in this lifestyle. Traditional, and newly developed, travel demand models fail to incorporate parameters that account for the significant variation in travel demand of elderly people that exists as a function of life style. An alternative trip generation model is proposed that would estimate travel demand of elderly people on the basis of life style using measures of age, dwelling unit type, employment status, and discretionary or obligatory travel.

3D Impact of transport on life style, commuting and shopping

3D1 ABKOWITZ, M.D. (1981) An analysis of the commuter departure time decision. *Transportation*, **10** (3), pp. 283–297.

Transport planners and transit operators alike have become increasingly aware of the need to diffuse the concentration of peak period travel in an effort to improve petrol economy and reduce peak load requirements. An evaluation of the potential effectiveness of strategies directed to achieve this end requires an understanding of factors which affect commuter trip timing decisions. The research discussed in this article addresses this particular problem through the development and estimation of a commuter departure time (to work) choice model. A number of conclusions were drawn based on the departure time model results and related analyses. The model could potentially be used to study the effect of service and employment policies on transit system peak load requirements.

3D2 ASH, T. and KORNHAUSER, A.L. (1983) Reduction of transportation requirements through home mortgage subsidies. *Journal of Advanced Transportation*, **17** (2), pp. 119–158.

This paper presents the second phase of research examining the potential of mortgage subsidies to encourage people to live closer to work, thus reducing work trip vehicle-miles-travelled (vmt) and automobile-related energy consumption, pollution, and congestion. This paper presents analysis of the effect of a mortgage subsidy programme at Princeton University, which currently (1982) offers a 10.5 per cent home mortgage to eligible university employees who buy a home within an eight-mile radius of the campus. The results suggest that the mortgage subsidy has resulted in shorter work trips, less work trip vmt, and less work trip petrol consumption, compared to similar employees at other nearby firms.

See also: Kornhauser, A.L., Ash, T.M. and Rinderle, C.A. (1982) Reducing work trip lengths through home mortgage subsidy incentives. *Transportation Research Record*, 845, pp. 16–22.

3D3 ATHERTON, T.J., SCHEVERNSTUHL, G.J. and HAWKINS, D. (1982) Transportation related impacts of a compressed workweek: the Denver Experiment. Transportation Research Board, Conference Proceedings 61. Washington, DC: TRB.

This paper summarizes an evaluation of an experiment to compress the working week of 7000 employees in the Denver area to a 4 day week or a 9 day fortnight. Emphasis is placed on transport impacts related to air quality and energy issues, with particular attention to quantifying the indirect effects on household travel patterns. The findings indicate that a compressed working week can lead to a reduction in weekly vehicle use for both commuting and other journey purposes.

3D4 CUBUKGIL, A. and MILLER, E.J. (1982) Occupational status and the journey to work. *Transportation* **11** (3), pp. 251–276.

The importance of occupational status as an explanatory variable in the determination of work trip commuting flows has not been well studied in the literature. This paper addresses this issue by means of an empirical investigation of commuting patterns in the Toronto Census Metropolitan Area (CMA), using 1971 census data. The analysis consists of three parts. First, a descriptive analysis of the work trip characteristics for six relatively homogeneous occupation groups is performed. Second, the employment and residential location distributions for these groups are briefly examined. Third, a series of work trip distribution models are calibrated and compared for each of the six occupation groups. The results of these analyses indicate clear and consistent differences in work trip commuting patterns among the six occupation groups studied.

3D5 DANIELS, P.W. (1981) Transport changes generated by decentralised offices: a second survey. *Regional Studies*, **15** (6), pp. 507–520.

An earlier study of the journey to work to decentralized offices was replicated at the same establishments in 1976. Despite difficulties in comparing two sets of essentially cross-sectional data, the results suggest that replacement staff and new recruits since 1969 have not changed to any significant degree the structure of mode choice for the journey to work anticipated from the earlier findings. Private transport continues to dominate the travel mode changes generated by decentralized offices and although aggregate level use of public transport has continued to fall there have been marginal improvements in the level of utilization particularly in the Greater London Area.

See also: Daniels, P.W. (1980) *Office Location and the Journey to Work: A Comparative Study of Five Urban Areas*. Farnborough: Gower.

3D6 DASGUPTA, M. (1983a) Employment and work travel in an inner area context: background to a Manchester study. Transport and Road Research Laboratory, Supplementary Report 780. Crowthorne: TRRL.

The decentralization of population and employment in urban areas were initiated in past decades and were linked with the advent of modern transport. However, selective redistribution of population is still taking place within towns and cities, and this has resulted in a relative concentration of less skilled workers in inner areas. Manufacturing industries have declined, but service sector industries have expanded. In inner areas there is a mismatch between the skills of the resident labour force and the types of jobs available. Male unemployment levels are twice as high in inner areas as in outer areas of conurbations. The low levels of access to cars means that people are dependent on public transport. But even here distances are shorter and journey times may be longer than in outer areas.

See also: Dasgupta, M. (1982) Mobility and access to employment opportunities: a comparison of inner and outer areas of Greater Manchester. Transport and Road Research Laboratory, Laboratory Report 1054. Crowthorne: TRRL.

3D7 DASGUPTA, M. (1983*b*) Travel to work characteristics of different labour force groups: a survey in Manchester. Transport and Road Research Laboratory, Laboratory Report 1068, Crowthorne: TRRL.

This report examines the employment and travel to work characteristics of different groups such as men and women and part-timers and shift workers. It includes employment characteristics of men and women in different age groups: other socio-economic characteristics such as income, vehicle ownership and license holding and household and residential characteristics: and travel to work characteristics including mode and journey distances and times.

See also: Dasgupta, M. (1982) Young workers' travel to work: a survey in Manchester. Transport and Road Research Laboratory, Supplementary Report 764. Crowthorne: TRRL.

3D8 DASGUPTA, M., FROST, M. and SPENCE, N. (1985) Factors affecting mode choice for the work journey: A Manchester/Sheffield comparison. Transport and Road Research Laboratory, Research Report 38. Crowthorne: TRRL.

This paper presents results of a pilot study of Manchester and Sheffield which have adopted contrasting transport policies in recent years. This report is based on 1971 and 1981 census data and shows that there are a range of factors affecting mode choice: these include spatial distribution of population and employment, the segregation of socio-economic groups, the patterns of residential tenure, the level of female unemployment, and the level of car ownership.

3D9 DUBIN, R.A. (1985) Transportation costs and the residential location decision: a new approach. *Journal of Urban Economics*, **17** (1), pp. 58–72.

This paper presents a general procedure for studying the effects of transport costs (work and non-work related) on the household location decision. The aim is to provide a framework for determining which costs are properly included in full housing cost and which are not. The procedure is based upon the characteristics of the solution set of the Lancastrian consumer demand problem.

3D10 ECMT (1987) *Employment in Transport: Quantitative and Qualitative Evolution, Substitution Possibilities*. Paris: European Conference of Ministers of Transport.

The number of people employed in the transport sector in the EEC countries totals some 10 million. However, there is a trend towards reducing manning levels with increased automation and the use of technology to substitute capital for labour. With deregulation this trend may continue as employment in medium-sized firms contracts – this trend is particularly evident in public transport operations. Transport policy must be directed at increasing productivity as subsidy may lead to higher taxation which in turn curbs consumption. As employment patterns and lifestyles change so will the demand for different forms of transport.

3D11 ERGUN, G. and STOPHER, P.R. (1982) The effects of personality on demand for recreation activities: some preliminary findings. *Transportation Research*, **16A** (1), pp. 55–63.

This paper presents the results of the first stage of a research effort which tries to improve the understanding of travel behaviour to recreation activities through the use of personality variables. A battery of personality scales, containing scales from relevant inventories and some new conceptual constructs, was assembled and some preliminary tests for the usefulness of this battery were carried out. It was postulated that personality variables are related to recreation-participation and this postulate was not rejected by the data collected as part of this study. It was also found that participation in different activities is affected by different personality dimensions to different degrees. Therefore, considerable care is needed in selecting the personality scales for use in a given context.

3D12 FIEGEL, N., KAY, M.A., NAYLOR, M.L. and ZEHNER, R.B. (1981) The journey to work: a comparison of selected suburbs in Sydney and Canberra. National Confederation of Public Transportation, Conference paper 81/10, pp. 103–109. Sydney: University of Sydney.

The study investigates the journey to work in the context of low and medium density housing developments outside the central cities of Sydney and Canberra. Analyses reported are based on 415 interviews from probability samples of households in the study areas. Data on men's and women's journey to work are presented, including information on the length, mode, and direction of the trips. Ratings of the convenience of these trips are related to the respondents overall ratings of convenience in their areas. Also presented are data on automobile ownership, annual mileage, and resident's attitude about the importance of access to community facilities and to work in their choice of a location to live.

3D13 FULTON, P.N. (1983) Public transportation: solving the commuting problem? *Transportation Research Record*, 928, pp. 1–10.

In this paper journey-to-work data from the 1980 census are used to provide a perspective on how well public transport is coping with the increasing spatial complexity of metropolitan communities. The data show that about 6 per cent of all workers in the United States used some form of public transport to commute to work. The decline in commuter use of public transport between 1970 and 1980 is closely associated with the movement of people and jobs to places where public transport is not available or easily accessible. The continued shift of the population from the north to the south and west means that the public transport market is moving from regions that have the most transit service to regions that have the least. Furthermore, the non-metropolitan sector of the country, where public transit is virtually non-existent, is growing faster than metropolitan areas. Finally, in recent years within metropolitan areas, the suburbs have far surpassed the central cities in population growth, many large central cities, where transit is concentrated, have experienced losses of population. In addition, increasing suburbanization of employment and population has resulted in a predominance of lateral commuting in large metropolitan areas – intersuburban work trips for which public transport is not well suited.

3D14 GERA, S. and KUHN, P. (1981) Occupation and the journey-to-work: some further analysis. *Socio-economic Planning Science*, **15** (2), pp. 83–93.

This paper examines the impact of occupation upon commuting distances in the Toronto Census Metropolitan Area. From the residential and job location patterns of each occupational group a minimum distance indicator of the degree of job-residence access of each occupational group is developed through the use of a linear programming algorithm. The distances calculated by the algorithm are compared with actual commuting distances. The analysis suggests that job-residence access is greater for blue collar workers than white collar workers. There was little evidence that occupation influenced the propensity to travel. The main factor here was sex, since female workers exhibited a far lower disposition to commute than did their male counterparts.

See also: Gera, S. and Kuhn, P. (1980*a*) Job location and the journey to work: an empirical analysis. *Socio-economic Planning Science*, **14** (2), pp. 57–65.

Gera, S. and Kuhn, P. (1980*b*) An empirical model of residential location and the journey-to-work in a metropolitan area. *Socio-economic Planning Science*, **14** (2), pp. 67–77.

3D15 HANSON, S. (1980) The importance of the multi-purpose journey to work in urban travel behavior. *Transportation*, **9** (3), pp. 229–248.

This study examines the journey to work as a multiple-purpose trip (home-to-home circuit). Using disaggregate travel diary data collected over 35 consecutive days, the study shows the importance of the multi-purpose work trip in the overall travel pattern of the urban household. A large proportion of many households' total travel is undertaken in conjunction with the journey to and from work. The paper also examines the nature of these work-induced travel linkages and finds that many types of urban establishments depend heavily upon stops made in connection with the work trip. In fact, there is a group of urban functions that have stronger travel links with the workplace than with the home or with any other type or urban establishment. The study examines the implications of the multipurpose journey to work for policies regarding mode use and the viability of centrally-located urban functions.

3D16   HENDRICKSON, C., and PLANK, E. (1984) The flexibility of departure time for work trips. *Transportation Research* **18A** (1), pp. 25–36.

The authors examine the flexibility of departure times for the journey to work making use of data gathered in Pittsburgh, Pennsylvania. Measured travel time peaking is pronounced for trips into the Pittsburgh central business district, although the variation in travel time is low for a particular route, mode and departure time. Estimation of a logit model of simultaneous mode and departure time interval choice is reported. Departure time decisions are found to be much more flexible than are mode choices. Some implications for dynamic or time dependent transport system management strategies are considered.

3D17   JONES, D.W., HARRISON, F.D. and JOVANIS, P. (1980) Work rescheduling and traffic relief: The potential of flexitime. Institute of Governmental Studies Report. Berkeley: University of California.

This report contains results of research conducted in San Francisco concerning the use of flexitime. Correlations are made between flexitime and trip scheduling, between flexitime and choice of transport mode, and between flexitime and traffic congestion. The report also contains a case study of the use of flexitime on metropolitan life, and a comparison of the advantages and disadvantages of flexitime and staggered hours schemes.

3D18   JOVANIS, P. (1981) Flexible work hours and mode change: interpretation of empirical findings from San Francisco. *Transportation Research Record*, 816, pp. 11–19.

A series of surveys was conducted at four San Francisco Bay Area firms in 1979 to study the effect of flexible work hours on choice of mode for the work trip. Analysis of nearly 1200 individual responses showed consistent and statistically significant decreases in solo driving. Although there were diversions from car sharing to transit, the net result was a statistically significant increase in car sharing. The evidence strongly suggests that flexitime is complementary to transit marketing and car sharing promotions, although the change in mode share is likely to be a modest one (less than 5 per cent).

3D19 McCARTHY, P. (1980) Residential location and the journey to work: an empirical analysis. *Journal of Transport Economics and Policy*, **11** (2), pp. 169–184.

There has been a growing trend over the past few years to explore at the microeconomic level, the interrelationship between residential location and transport decisions. This is in contrast to previous urban economic analyses which were concerned primarily with location decisions and paid little attention to individual decisions. The purpose of this study is to formulate and test a behavioural model of transport modal choice. However unlike similar analyses it incorporates residential location decision making and specifically examines its impact upon modal choice for the work trip.

3D20 MIRON, J.R. (1982) Centrifugal relocation and back-commuting from the metropolitan fringe. *Transport Economics and Policy*, **16** (3), pp. 239–258.

This paper focuses on the movement of individuals from inner area residences to ones on the metropolitan fringe. It examines the substantial impact that this pattern of relocation can have on commuting patterns emanating from the metropolitan fringes. The analysis is based on data for the Toronto area from 1964 and 1971. The paper concludes that as the rate of metropolitan growth changes, so will commuting patterns and therefore, a static view of commuting behaviour will become increasingly inappropriate.

3D21 MOGRIDGE, M.J.H. (1981) Some reflections on journey-to-work studies in Sydney, Toronto, New York, London and Paris. *Transportation Research*, **15a** (5), pp. 399–450.

A number of detailed studies of the journey to work in major work conurbations using 1971 census data have now been reported. In some cases, simultaneous surveys of actual travel, rather than the normal travel obtained in censuses, have also been obtained.

Various analysis techniques have been adopted for such studies, according to the type of questions being addressed. It is time to take stock, see what has been achieved, what lessons can be learnt from our successes, and our failures, and whether our understanding of the relationship between travel and city structure has been increased by such studies.

3D22 O'FARRELL, P. and MARKHAM, J. (1980) Commuting costs and residential location: a process of urban sprawl. *Tijdschrift voor Economische en Sociale Geografie*, **66** (2), pp. 66–74.

This paper discusses two types of residential choice theory – one based on transport to work costs, the other based on residential attraction. The residential choices of car and non-car owning households are discussed in the context of both theories in an attempt to explain observed patterns of residential decentralization and urban sprawl.

3D23 OTT, M., SLAVIN, H. and WARD, D. (1980) The behavioural impacts of flexible working hours. US Department of Transportation Report. Washington, DC: US Department of Transportation.

This paper presents new results on the behavioural responses of flexitime, which is a system of flexible working hours under which workers are permitted to select their daily schedules within certain predefined limits. Flexitime has been implemented by an increasing number of firms and institutions in Europe and the United States, and is of particular interest as a transport systems management strategy with potentially significant impacts on work schedules, travel behaviour, traffic congestion, and energy consumption.

3D24 PICKUP, L. (1986) Commuting and its consequences in the European Community: setting the scene, in *Il Pendolarismo; studio del suo impatto sulle condizioni di vita e di lavoro*. Rome: Istituto Italiano di Medicina Sociale.

This paper provides a general background to the key commuting issues facing the member states. The author briefly outlines the patterns of commuting in the EC and related policies. He discusses how these patterns relate to trends in both home and workplace locations, and in transport provision. The commuting problems encountered by workers and the effects of these problems on their living and working situations are outlined. After explaining some of the key issues facing planners in solving these problems, he looks at the degree of choice commuters are able to exert over their commuting circumstances and the extent to which they have a voice in planning decisions which affect their commuting situation.

See also: Pickup, L. and Town, S.W. (1983) Commuting patterns in Europe: an overview of the literature. Transport and Road Research Laboratory, Supplementary Report 796. Crowthorne: TRRL.

3D25 RECKER, W.W. and KOSTYNIUK, L.P. (1978) Factors influencing destination choice for the urban grocery shopping trip. *Transportation*, **7** (1), pp. 19–33.

Destination choice for the urban grocery shopping trip is hypothesized to be determined by three factors: the individual's perception of the destination, the individual's accessibility to the destination and the relative number of opportunities to exercise any particular choice. Results of a multinomial logit model estimation support this hypothesis and provide useful information concerning the role of urban form in this destination choice situation. It is determined that accessibility is the primary aspect influencing destination choice and that its effect is nonlinear.

3D26 SCHULER, H.J. (1981) Grocery shopping choices: individual preferences based on store attractiveness and distance. *Environment and Behaviour*, **13** (3), pp. 331–347.

A conjoint analysis of expressed preferences for experimental levels of supermarket attributes is carried out to forecast spatial behaviour based on how stimulus information is processed by consumers. The aggregate model is tested by means of a behavioural gravity model formulation. The derived utility scales input are measures of attractiveness in the gravity model and these measures are used independently to validate the combination rule of the conjoint analysis. Results of a test support this hypothesis and provide useful information concerning spatial behaviour in the purchase of grocery items.

3D27 THEOLOGITIS, J.M. (1985) Transportation planning and social forces in a changing world environment. *International Journal of Transport Economics*, **12** (1), pp. 31–50.

This paper covers a wide range of issues including the links between transport and planning and the rapidly changing world environment. These changes include the restructuring of economies and activity patterns, and an increasingly dominant role of leisure and recreation. The leisure age is now accepted as a major social development with a powerful influence on a person's daily and seasonal activities. The implications of the leisure revolution for transport planning are discussed.

3D28 TRANSPORTATION RESEARCH BOARD (1980) Alternative work schedules: impacts on transportation. TRB, National Academy of Sciences Report. Washington, DC: Transportation Research Board.

Alternative work schedules can be used to manage transportation demand by shifting commuters away from the peak hours and by reducing the number of days that people need to travel to work. There are three basic forms of alternative work schedules: (a) staggered work hours; (b) flexible work hours; (c) compressed workweeks. The advantages and disadvantages of the three forms of alternative work schedules are discussed, and the following implementation steps are suggested: (a) identify high-priority employment locations; (b) obtain support for feasibility studies; (c) conduct work schedule and transport surveys of employers; (d) design work rescheduling plans; (e) obtain management decisions to implement; (f) provide implementation assistance; (g) evaluate impacts; and (h) refine and extend the programme.

3D29 VERSTER, A.C.P. (1985) Commuting costs and the residential mobility of job changers. *Transportation Planning and Technology*, **10**, pp. 193–207.

In traffic and transport research, attention is given to the relevance of location patterns of activities to moving behaviour, the inverse causality being mostly left out of account. This paper considers what influence (changes in) travel costs have on moving behaviour and residential choice. The analysis has been carried out for employed people who change jobs. The residential choice has been split into a marginal probability of moving and a conditional destination choice. Both choices appear to be influenced significantly by travel-cost variables.

3D30 VERSTER, A.C.P. (1986) Towards an information system for interregional relations between living and working. *Transportation Planning and Technology*, **11**, pp. 1-17.

Medium-term changes in the pattern of commuter flows are caused on the one side by spatial changes in housing and job supply, and on the other by the behaviour of workers, especially their starting or leaving jobs, or changing residential and/or job addresses. The dynamic spatial interrelations between residential and work activities are systematically described for regions in a large urban area – Randstad, Holland and its surroundings. The possible uses of this type of information for analysis and planning are indicated.

See also: De Langen, M. and Verster, A.C.P. (1979) View on location behaviour, moving behaviour and accessibility, in Jansen, G.R.M. *et al.* (eds.) *New Developments in Modelling Travel Demand and Urban Systems*. Farnborough: Saxon House, pp. 161-199.

3D31 VICKERMAN, R.W. (1984) Urban and regional change, migration and commuting – the dynamics of workplace, residence and transport choice. *Urban Studies*, **21** (1), pp. 15-29.

A key factor in the spatial structure of metropolitan areas is the relationship between workplace and residential location. This is particularly critical in any attempt to model the changes in structure which result from intra-metropolitan moves of employment and households. This paper attempts to provide a more satsifactory framework for understanding the dynamics of these changes. Empirical evidence is presented for the London region based on both aggregate data from unpublished Census material and the Greater London Transportation Study and disaggregate survey material from a specially commissioned household interview survey.

3D32 VICTORIA MINISTRY OF TRANSPORT (1980) *Victoria Transport Study: Staggered Working Hours*. Melbourne: Victoria Ministry of Transport.

The full utilization of the transport system is very low indeed, possibly less than 25 hours per week and the need for its availability and use for peak hour traffic represents a very severe financial impact on the business of public transport in Victoria. Relevant submissions made to the study are summarized, and a recent report by the Victorian division of the Australian Institute of Urban Studies is discussed in some detail. The potential benefits of implementing further staggered working hours and flexitime work schemes are significant enough to warrant positive encouragement of them. Recommended initiatives that the government could take to encourage further staggered working hours and flexitime schemes are included in the report.

3D33 WEISBROD, G.E., LERMAN, S.R. and BEN AKIVA, M. (1980) Trade offs in residential location decisions: transportation versus other factors. *Transport Policy and Decision Making*, **1**, pp. 13–26.

There has been a substantial discussion among planners in North America concerning the role that transportation can play in affecting the residential development patterns of urban areas. The purpose of this paper is to analyse consumers' trade offs in the decision to move and the selection among alternative residential locations. The study is based on an analysis of the actual moving decisions and residential choices of individual households. The empirical results suggest that households make significant trade offs between transportation services and other public service factors in evaluating potential residences, but that the role of both in determining where people choose to live is small compared with socio-economic and demographic factors.

3D34 WITKOWSKI, J.M. and TAYLOR, W.C. (1982) Energy conservation potential of staggered work hours. *Transportation Research Record*, 870, pp. 1–9.

This research evaluates the potential of staggered work hours to reduce work-trip fuel consumption and to assess the relationship between the size of the participating workforce and the level of fuel savings. A simulation programme was designed to distribute population and employment throughout an urban area. Several alternative temporal distributions of work travel were used to simulate the effects of staggered work-hour programmes. The results indicate that staggered hours can significantly reduce car petrol consumption; they also have a strong negative effect on bus use for work journeys.

3E Health effects, stress and crime

3E1 AUSTIN, T.L. and BUZAWA, E.S. (1984) Citizens' perceptions of mass transit crime and its deterrence: a case study. *Transportation Quarterly*, **38** (1), pp. 103-120.

Crime against patrons of transit systems has become a major concern to transit administrators, government, the press and the public. Perceptions of crime, along with increasing fares and decreasing subsidies, are recognized as dramatically affecting the viability of mass transit in many urban areas. Reported in this article are the level of fear of transit crime in Detroit, rates of victimization, and the extent to which such fears adversely affect ridership. The level of public knowledge and acceptance of the use of undercover police officers and various alternatives is determined. A survey instrument is developed and a data base is established to allow consistent future studies.

3E2 BEXLER, A., GARELIK, S. and COOPER, S. (1980) Sex crimes in the subway. *Criminology*, **18** (1), pp. 35-52.

3E3 EUROPEAN FOUNDATION FOR THE IMPROVEMENT OF LIVING AND WORKING CONDITIONS (1984) The journey between home and work: the effects of commuting on the health and safety of workers - consolidated report. European Foundation Report EF/84/72. Dublin: European Foundation

This study analyses the effect of commuting on workers' health and safety. The analysis was carried out on study cases in industrial sectors purposely chosen for being significant and comparable. The research clearly shows the negative effect of commuting on commuters' psychological state (stress, insomnia, etc) and stresses the possible consequences for physical well-being and for the quality of social and family life. The negative impact appears to be strengthened in particularly heavy work situations and in combination with other negative factors.

3E4 LEVINE, N. and WACHS, M. (1986) Bus crime in Los Angeles. 1. Measuring the incidence. *Transportation Research A*, **20** (4), pp. 273-284; and 2. Victims and public impact. *Transportation Research A*, **20** (4), pp. 285-293.

Based on a large study of bus crime in Los Angeles these two articles estimate the number and characteristics of bus crime, and the effect of such crime on the victims and the public generally. During 1983, it is estimated that 23,000 bus and bus-related crimes occurred which account for between 20 and 30 per cent of all crimes experienced by the central city population. These overall statistics are examined in greater detail. The second paper examines the extent to which fear and personal security affect bus ridership. Victimization was most clearly related to the frequency of service and more frequent among certain social groups. Fear of victimization did affect bus use at certain times and places but this was secondary to car access, the convenience of bus services and age.

3E5 NOVACO, R.W., STOKOLS, D. and CAMPBELL, J. (1979) Transportation stress and community psychology. *American Journal of Community Psychology*, **7** (4), pp. 361–380.

Conditions of transport were investigated as sources of psychological stress as they effect the physiology, task performance and mood of commuters. Participants in the study were 100 employees of industrial firms. Traffic congestion was construed in terms of the concept of impedance which itself is defined by the parameters of distance and time. It was expected that the effects of impedance would be mediated by personality factors, such as locus of control. In multiple regression analyses, the distance and speed of the commute to work were found to account for significant proportions of variation in blood pressure, while several indices of personal control had significant regression effects on the task measures. The implications of the results for research in community psychology are discussed.

3E6 PEARLSTEIN, A. and WACHS, M. (1982) Crime in public transit systems: an environmental design perspective. *Transportation*, **11** (3), pp. 277–297.

Crime on public transit is receiving increasing attention in the United States. This paper reviews security precautions taken in the planning of bus operations. Also included is a statistical analysis of criminal incidents occurring over a ten-year period on the Southern California Rapid Transit District of Los Angeles. The analysis shows that crime on transit has increased about in proportion to transit ridership, and that it is concentrated in both space and time. Crimes occur mostly on routes which traverse areas having high crime rates in general. Although most transit crimes occur at hours when ridership is high, the rates of occurrence are disproportionately high during the evening hours. Bus drivers experience much higher rates of exposure to criminal incidents than transit passengers. The transport environment is really a complex of many dissimilar environments, and a variety of strategies is required to meet the needs posed by diverse environments.

3E7 REASON, J. (1978) Motion sickness: some theoretical and practical considerations. *Applied Ergonomics*, **9** (3), pp. 163–167.

This paper reviews some of the more important theoretical and practical considerations relating to the widespread problem of motion sickness. A brief outline is given of the sensory rearrangement theory which seeks to define the essential nature of the nauseogenic stimulus. A wide range of provocative situations is classified as involving either a visual-inertial conflict, or a canal-otolith conflict or both. A number of behavioural measures by which the passenger can minimize the risk of motion sickness are described. Also considered are quantitative studies of vertical oscillatory motion, factors influencing motion sickness susceptibility (sex, age, exposure-history, receptivity and adaptability and personality characteristics), and the paper concludes with recommendations regarding the most effective use of anti-motion sickness drugs.

3E8 RILEY, N.E. and DEAN, D.L. (1985) Bus station security: crime at intercity bus stations. *Transportation Research Record*, 1012, pp. 56–64.

The issue of crime at California's intercity bus stations is examined through a review of records maintained by public and private carriers and by law enforcement agencies at the federal, state, and local levels. None of these sources provides complete information on crime at intercity bus stations. Crimes reported during 1983 at California bus stations are reviewed, and the legal implications of crime for bus station operators and specific countermeasures to station crime are also discussed. To overcome the current deficiencies in transport security, a uniform transport crime-reporting (UTCR) system is proposed.

4 Travel modes

The references cited in this chapter review the literature on the different modes of urban transport. Evidence on the policies, trends and use of different transport modes are provided from countries of both the developed and developing worlds.

4A Bus services

A wealth of literature has been published since 1980 on local bus services. Three main themes emerge: firstly, papers reporting trends in bus service provision, patronage and the changing market structure for buses. Secondly, papers discussing the increasing costs of bus services, possible ways of reducing these costs and the effectiveness of subsidies provided to bus operators. Thirdly, studies focusing on the possible alternative forms of financing bus services particularly through deregulation and the encouragement of competition between operators.

While bus patronage has been undergoing continual decline in many countries, this pattern is not universal. The factors which influence changes in bus use are summarized in the references by Button [4A10], Lago et al. [4A35], Webster [4A52], Webster et al. [1B56] and Weisman [4A53]. The social structure of the bus market has been changing. In showing this trend, Mitchell [4A37] also demonstrates that the pattern of destinations and journeys for which buses are used have also been changing.

The demand for and supply of buses varies with the social, economic and geographical characteristics of different urban areas. Several important references have sought to find similarities between urban structure and public transport provision: Webster and Bly [1B51] for European countries; Pucher [4A42] and Bechdolt and Williams [4A3] for the USA; and Jacobs *et al.* [4A32] for developing countries. Vijayakumar and Jacobs [4A49] also provide a comparison of bus operations between cities of both the developing and developed worlds. While bus operations in Third World cities are generally characterized by a surplus of demand over supply, the opposite is true of bus services operating in many cities of the developed world.

The increasing geographical dispersal of activities and the rise in car use which has accompanied it, have produced financial problems for bus operators. Costs have risen and, since the mid-1960s, subsidies have become increasingly necessary to bridge the gap between costs and revenue. Up to the mid-1980s, subsidies were increasing rapidly in most developed countries (Webster and Bly [1B51]). A number of the references cited review the policies, and priorities adopted for allocation (for example Button [4A10], Stern [4A46], Obeng [4A39], Kirby [4A34] and Williams [4A58]), and their effectiveness in improving the bus services provided to the public. The social benefits which can accrue from bus subsidies are exemplified by Hay's study [4A28] in one UK metropolitan area. Pucher [4A43], Morris [4A38] and Dodgson and Topham [4A20] generally assess the costs and benefits of bus subsidies; who gains and who loses.

In contrast to those who argue for the retention of bus subsidies on the basis that they achieve a net social benefit, other authors argue that they have not produced the maximum benefits to passengers that was potentially possible. The papers by Cervero [4A15], the European Conference of Ministers of Transport [4A22] and Bly and Oldfield [4A7] argue that while subsidies have reduced fares, increased services and increased patronage; they have also leaked into higher wages and lower output. Anjomani and Amico [4A2], Cervero [4A13], Forkenbrock and Stoner [4A24] and Rock [4A45] suggest possible alternative ways of funding public transport and the objectives on which such funding should be allocated to operators.

A number of the references cited above assess the potential for reducing subsidies by increasing fares and/or reducing services. Keppleman and Rose [4A33] argue that such strategies are negative ones. More positive policies are required to encourage a growth in the bus market by offering novel ticketing regimes, selective fares and by placing a greater emphasis on premium services, better quality services and more efficient operations. In terms of improving efficiency, references by Hovell and Moran [4A31], Cherwony *et al.* [4A17] and the United States Transportation Research Board [4A48] provide guidelines on the better management, route costing and scheduling of bus services. Bladikas and Crowell [4A5], Cervero [4A16], Daskin [4A18], Mayworm [4A36] and White [4A56] report the experiences of operators introducing differential fare schemes to better target subsidy. White [4A55] also assesses the growth in popularity of network and zone ticketing schemes to enhance customer loyalty and retain patronage.

The other important way in which subsidies could be reduced is through cutting the unit costs of bus operations. Higginson and White [4A29], Cervero [4A14], Pickrell [4A41] and Button and O'Donnell [4A11] analyse the effectiveness of different sizes of bus operator. Their results suggest that costs have risen less rapidly in small and medium sized operators although this may be a reflection of the different types of services operated by these companies. Webster [4A52] stresses the urgent need for operators to reduce their costs rather than simply increasing their subsidy requirements, particularly by reducing their labour costs. In this context the implications of the recent increase in part-time staff, one-person operated buses and automatic fare collection are discussed by Wells *et al.* [4A54], Boyd [4A9] and Abkowitz [4A1], respectively.

Some studies report that private bus operators are generally more efficient than are those under public control (Talvitie and Heinila [4A47], Perry [4A40], Viton [4A50]). The recent deregulation and privatization of local bus services in Great Britain has prompted a series of articles comparing the advantages and disadvantages of open competition between operators for the bus market. The two key papers arguing the cases for and against deregulating the bus market are those of Gwilliam, Nash and Mackie [4A27] and Beesley and Glaister [4A4]. Other papers by Glaister [4A26] and Emmerson and Bly [4A21] simulate the potential effects of a loss of cross-subsidy on urban bus routes in favour of competition between operators. Bly and Oldfield [4A8] suggest that high frequency minibus services have important advantages in a deregulated bus market.

4B Urban rail

Since the 1960s, there has been a substantial development of urban rail networks in cities of both the developing and developed world. Investment has included the introduction or upgrading of light rail systems, the development of existing suburban railway systems and the construction of new rapid transit systems. The 1980s have seen the costs of urban rail investment rise sharply. Despite the escalation in costs, city authorities in all five continents continue to place heavy emphasis on urban rail development to help to solve the urban transport problem. Argument now centres on which form of system is most appropriate and most affordable.

Giannopoulos [4B6] compares the operational and planning characteristics of the world's metro systems; Smith [4B16] compares American and Asian cities. Both reviews underline the future potential of rail for serving high demand corridors within cities. In similar fashion to Giannopoulos, the Transportation Research Board [4B18] and Gordon and Wilson [4B9] review the factors determining the demand for light rail transit in urban areas, comparing current American systems with those in European countries. These two papers favour the further development of light rail systems and underline the potential for economy in designing such systems, for example by using available infrastructure. In contrast, Gomez-Ibanez [4B8] using the American experience, cites examples where light rail systems were 'oversold' at greater cost than bus services yet with only marginal improvements in patronage. Cervero [4B2] also stresses that if it is possible to plan new light rail systems and new urban development jointly, the policy of re-using existing infrastructure may not necessarily be the most efficient option to adopt. The comparative financial performances of different urban rail systems are also discussed by Kettle and Beesley [4B11] and Nash [4B14]. The particular potential for guided bus ways is discussed by Vuchic [4C15].

A number of important studies have emerged in recent years which evaluate the overall impact of new urban rail investments. The report by the European Conference of Ministers of Transport

[4B4] compares the detailed experience of urban rail investment in a variety of European cities and the role played by rail within the overall urban transport system. A particular issue has been the potential of urban rail systems to influence the process of urban development itself. Knight and Trygg [4B12] and Stringham [4B17] in the USA and Walmsley [4B19] in the UK analyse the impact of different types of rail investment on land use and travel behaviour around new rail stations. The broad conclusion is that new rail systems can act as a focus for growth but only if other factors are also present and if station areas are commercially developed when the system is implemented (Cervero [4B2]).

In addition to improving access within the urban centre itself, one of the main uses of urban rail is for commuter traffic both from the city suburbs and from the wider city region. Adiv [4B1] assesses the potential of rail as a commuting mode, based on the experience of the San Francisco BART system. He concludes that suburban rapid transit is not a viable commuting mode due to the dispersed nature of living and working areas in many modern cities; most workers will continue to commute by car. For a smaller UK city, Pickett *et al.* [4B15] note the negligible effect which new rail park and ride facilities had on peak congestion levels following the introduction of a metro system. In contrast to Adiv [4B1], Ghoneim and Wirasinghe [4B5] feel that suburban rail systems can better serve commuting needs providing that realistic travel to work zones are used in designing networks. Kanarek and Truncellito [4B10] discuss a number of criteria which could be used to evaluate which stations to improve within a commuter rail network to best serve demand. The cost of rail commuting is also an important factor in addition to station access. Papers by Glaister [4B7] and Yamada [4B20] assess the pricing strategies used both on commuter rail services and city centre metro services.

4C Unconventional public transport and taxis

Recent years have witnessed a rapid increase in research into unconventional public transport modes in the developed world. This has also raised the awareness of the forms of unconventional public transport which have been operating in cities of the Third World for many years. Unconventional public transport is an umbrella term: it includes the use of vehicles from private cars, taxis and eight seat microbuses to mini and larger buses (Vijayakumar [4C14]). Services operate outside the conventional regulated system of fixed routes and timetables in favour of hail and ride, dial-a-ride (Oxley [4C7], Sutton [4C10]), shared taxis and the organized 'ridesharing' of private cars or minibuses. Many of the services operating in urban areas of the developed world have been implemented for specific population groups with restricted mobility such as the elderly or disabled persons (see section 3C). The community and voluntary sectors have become increasingly important in providing these services.

The references cited in this section provide a detailed review and evaluation of unconventional public transport schemes from many cities. Silcock [4C9] stresses the way in which 'paratransit' schemes in the developing world have just grown up to suit specific local conditions and needs. While these private operations have attracted commercial success, there are doubts about their safety standards. From the developed world, reports by the European Conference of Ministers of Transport [4C3] and the US Department of Transportation [4C11] provide both a typology and detailed examples of the range of paratransit schemes operating in Europe and the United States and discuss future directions for this form of transport in urban areas.

Taxis

A majority of the literature on taxi services focuses on the issue of their regulation and licensing; other research has evaluated their potential use for transporting elderly and handicapped persons (Teal and Berglund [4C11]).

Two main issues emerge: firstly, the implications of deregulating taxi operations in urban areas and secondly, the potential for shared taxi operations already happening in countries such as Turkey or Greece (Greening and Jackson [4C5], European Conference of Ministers of Transport [4C3]). Britton [4C1] reviews the current state of the taxi industry from the World Taxi Survey undertaken by the OECD and forecasts trends in the supply of and the demand for taxis up to 1990. Several studies report the US experiment to deregulate taxi operations in selected cities. The US Department of Transport report [4C13] reviewed the taxi regulation policy operating in 120 US cities. Most cities regulated the entry of taxi operators into the industry and the fares they could charge; few urban areas had deregulated taxi operations. Where taxis had been deregulated, Teal and Berglund's comparison [4C11] concludes that the change in legislation had failed to produce benefits. Under deregulation, the industry made a rapid change to more smaller companies with drivers employed on contract only (Gilbert [4C4]). For the UK, Coe [4C2] reviews the structure of the taxi industry and trends in taxi demand and fares charged, in the light of possible deregulation.

4D Cars

The most important influence on urban travel behaviour over the past 35 years has been the fivefold increase in car ownership and use (ECMT [4D5]). Economic recession has had little adverse effect on the growth in car ownership outside congested city centres. When a private car is available, it is generally used in preference to public transport; society provides more space for car travel and is becoming more and more reliant on it. Car users are rarely aware of the full costs of using their vehicles (Adiv [4D1]).

The papers listed in this section review the factors influencing patterns and changes in car ownership and use. Reviewing such changes in one particular metropolitan area, Goodwin [4A25] stresses that the factors and effects of increasing and decreasing car ownership are not a mirror image of each other but are indeed quite different. In developed countries, one of the most important trends has been the growth in households owning two or more cars (Mannering [4D19], Goodwin and Mogridge [4D9]). In some countries, company car acquisition has also radically altered the pattern of car use by different household members both as car drivers or passengers (McCoomb and Stewart [4D16], Schou [4D25], Whitelegg [4D30]). Several references discuss the future use of cars with reference to examples from Australia (Hensher [4D12]), the Third World (Khan and Willumsen [4D13]) and Europe (European Conference of Ministers of Transport [4D5]). One key issue for the future of car use could be finite energy resources and the uncertainty of supplies from the OPEC nations (Hensher [4D11]). While advances in telecommunications technology could potentially reduce car use,

Suiden [4D27] argues that such a transfer would be minimal as car use is more suited to serving dispersed living and working environments. The Organization for Economic Cooperation and Development [5F8] reviews the potential for improving the use made of cars.

An increasing amount of research has emerged on ways in which car users could be additionally charged for the external costs of their car use for reasons of social equity, energy conservation and to combat the urban transport problem. The full social costs of car use are identified by Wachs [4D29] who argues that by not charging motorists the full social costs of car use in the past, suburban sprawl has resulted.

Other references explore a variety of ways in which such an objective might be achieved and their advantages and disadvantages (general review in Organisation for Economic Cooperation and Development [4D21]): ideas include the restructuring of fuel taxes (Forkenbrook and Hoefer [4D7]), introducing road taxes (Ralston and Barber [4D23]), tolls and severance charges (Gaj *et al.* [4D8]) or by taxing congestion (Levinson *et al.* [4D15], Else [4D4]). One current road pricing scheme already in operation is the electronically operated system in Hong Kong. Fong [4D6] reviews the traffic, social, environmental, economic and political considerations when introducing the Hong Kong scheme and its broad impacts. The literature suggests that no single system of car use charges is best for all towns and cities; unique financing philosophies most appropriate to local conditions are likely to emerge. However, whereas the technical constraints of road pricing schemes are now less of a problem, strong political constraints remain against introducing further charges on private motoring. The national policies toward car use in four countries are contrasted to show the different views on regulation (Mace [4D17], Spencer and Chia [4D26], McShane *et al.* [4D18]).

As a response to the fuel crisis of the mid-1970s, a wealth of literature emerged on the potential and practice of 'ridersharing' in private cars or minibuses; where one driver either 'shared' his car with other travellers or where several drivers 'pooled' their cars and took turns to give lifts to the other drivers in the 'car pool'. In either sharing or pooling, drivers could receive payment for their efforts. Reviews of the experience and comparative costs of ridesharing in the United States are given by Teal [4D28] and Owens [4D22], in the UK by Bonsall *et al.* [4D3], Greening and Jackson [4D10] and

Bailey [4D2], and in Australia by Richardson and Young [4D24]. With the exception of some American schemes, ridesharing has not lived up to its early potential. In addition to the problems of organizing and maintaining schemes, studies revealed considerable driver resistance to participating in them.

4E Freight transport

The transport of goods within urban areas has become an increasingly complex issue. How to improve the efficiency of the urban goods distribution system while minimizing the negative external costs of urban goods movements (GB Department of Transport [5E10]).

The literature concentrates on the issues of goods access to city centre sites; whether restrictions ought to be applied to the size of vehicles operating into city centres, whether limits should be set on delivery times, routes, areas or vehicle types which can and cannot be used. The series of papers on urban freight movement edited by Leutzbach [4E3] indicates the volume of goods movement within city centres and stresses that recent policies are now avoiding large-scale technical solutions in favour of lower cost planning measures which can be gradually implemented. Problems remain, however, for planning agencies who are often different bodies to those who control urban goods movement; often private agencies working within government guidelines Hedges [5E11]. Urban freight policy needs to be given a higher profile than in the past, and a range of potential policy instruments are outlined in the references. Ogden [4E4], [4E5] provides a review of the directions in urban freight policy and a planning framework within which freight issues can be assessed based on studies undertaken in Australia. The significant urban freight component of shipping costs receives particular emphasis with suggestions as to how savings might be achieved by reducing the conflicts between freight and passenger transport. Freight is one sector where the impact of road investment and technological change are having a significant effect on distribution systems through changes in operational practices, new management and organizational structures and the growth in warehouse based networks for distribution.

The reports by the European Conference of Ministers of Transport and by Button and Pearman [1B15], [4E2], [5E8] provide a discussion of the key issues with reference to experience from many European cities. Industrial restructuring and changes in the siting of activities are changing freight modal split in favour of road transport. Rather than the comparative costs of different transport modes, shippers are more sensitive to the overall costs of manufacture, warehousing and packaging whereby seemingly high transport costs can be offset by savings elsewhere in the chain. Both the papers by the European Conference of Ministers of Transport [4E2] and by Bohlander and Farris [4E1] argue for the need for freight transport modes to be more flexible to market needs by the easing of current regulations. However deregulation has potential drawbacks for employees in the industry and could lead to greater instability.

4F Walking and cycling

Perhaps surprisingly, it is only in the last ten years or so, that walking has been seriously analysed by transport planners. In their review paper, 'Walking as a mode of transport', Mitchell and Stokes [4F5] provide a comprehensive appraisal of patterns of travel on foot by different population groups, both as a main mode and for access to other modes (in terms of travel distances, times, journey purposes etc.). This review updates the seminal book by Hillman and Whalley *Walking is Transport* (Policy Studies Institute, 1979). For some journeys such as routine shopping, the large majority of journeys are made on foot, indeed it is the chief way in which most shops obtain their trade. Guy and Wrigley [4F1] discuss the implications of 'individual's' walking behaviour for the distribution of shops, particularly the location of 'convenience' shopping facilities. The provision of conveniently located facilities within acceptable walking distances can potentially reduce the demand for motorised travel. For example, Stewart and Mihalcin [4F10] document the impact of a policy to build more apartments within easy walking access of city centre workplaces as part of a broader initiative to reduce peak travel requirements.

The literature cited also reviews the difficulties which can arise for travellers while walking and the implications of such difficulties for city centre planning strategies. Mitchell and Stokes [4F5] discuss the categories of the population who have difficulty walking.

Seneviratne and Morrall [4F7], [4F8] report studies to ascertain critical walking distances and route choices among different groups of pedestrians, stressing the need for planners to consider seriously the characteristics of travel on foot in the design of car parking and urban public transport termini. This feeling is underlined by the National Consumer Council [4F6] reviewing the maintenance and safety standards of footways, arguing for the formation of 'Pedestrian Units' within planning agencies to prepare 'movement plans' for the pedestrian environment within city and neighbourhood centres. Pedestrian-only areas have grown rapidly in town and city centres in recent years. Their implementation have been the source of some controversy with local traders, a topic several papers address (Smith [4F9], Seneviratne and Morrall [4F7], [4F8]), Guy and Wrigley [4F1]. A review of policies on pedestrian precincts is given by Hass-Klau [1B28].

In many countries, the potential use of bicycles as an urban transport mode is seldom realized. In contrast, countries such as the Netherlands and Denmark and many cities in the Third World witness extensive cycle use. The few cycling references which are cited provide a general grounding on the characteristics of bicycle use and the planning issues involved in providing safe road space for them. Hudson *et al*. [4F4] provide a cross-national comparison of cycle use. Specifically for the UK case there is a discussion of cycle policy issues relating to planning and safety plus directions for further research. For West Germany, Herz [4F3] describes the factors influencing bicycle use, and policies which might increase it. In addition to a minority of regular cyclists, it should be recognized that there are also large numbers of occasional bicycle users. In Australia, Wigan [4F11] discusses the rates of cycle use within different types of households and the pattern of trips made.

4A Bus services

4A1   ABKOWITZ, M.D. (1987) Automatic fare collection in transit: a synthesis of current practice. *Transport Reviews*, **7** (1), pp. 56–63.

This article brings together information on the operation of automatic fare collection systems, drawing on the experience of public transport operators. It includes a discussion of the equipment required, and the advantages and disadvantages of automatic systems. Performance measures of reliability and maintainability are defined, and used to evaluate some systems in use in America.

4A2 ANJOMANI, A. and AMICO, L.T. (1986) The use of tax incentives for public transit as a subsidy alternative. *Policy Studies Review*, **5** (3), pp. 536-545.

One means by which use of public transport could be increased would be through the use of incentives to stimulate demand. A tax incentive is proposed and examined as a form of revenue source subsidy which can be coupled with a congestion toll or petrol tax policy to stimulate demand. The implications of such an approach are presented.

4A3 BECHDOLT, B.V. and WILLIAMS, M. (1980) Demand for bus transit in US urbanized areas. *Regional Science Perspectives*, **10** (1), pp. 3-14.

Regression analyses show that the determinants of demand for bus services in large, medium and small urbanized areas in the US are significantly different. This suggests that appropriate policies should also be designed for specific situations rather than general application.

4A4 BEESLEY, M.E. and GLAISTER, S. (1985) Deregulating the bus industry - a response. *Transport Reviews*, **5** (2), pp. 133-42 and **5** (3), pp. 223-224.

This paper takes issue with the proposition put forward by Gwilliam *et al.* [4A27] that free competition in buses reduces welfare. In reality the paper is a defence of the proposition that planning for buses is good for the industry, bus consumers and society at large. In their response Beesley and Glaister argue that competition and innovation will be encouraged with deregulation and that any defence of existing systems should be based on real outcomes not theoretical arguments. The proposals put forward in the 'White Paper' offer an alternative to the decline in patronage, rises in costs and subsidy levels, and decreases in efficiency which have characterized the bus industry over the last twenty-five years.

4A5 BLADIKAS, A.K. and CROWELL, W.H. (1985) Pricing options for urban transportation modes. *Transportation Research Record*, 1012, pp. 23-30.

Urban public transport has often been in serious financial trouble and fares increases are often difficult to implement for political reasons. Normally fares should be related to the marginal costs of the services and elasticities of demand so that costs can be covered and an acceptable level of profits generated. The pricing analyses presented follow a similar approach; the Metropolitan Transportation Authority in New York City is used as a case study. Net benefit changes were shown to be greater for efficiently set peak and off peak fares than for flat fares. The fares levels set had low elasticities of demand with respect to price. The paper demonstrates which transport pricing options maximize public welfare within given budgetary constraints.

4A6 BLY, P.H. (1987) Managing public transport: Commercial profitability and social service. *Transportation Research*, **21A** (2), pp. 109-125.

In the past 20 years emphasis on the social role of public transport has grown more subject to the direct intervention and financial support of external authorities. It is rare for the social objectives to be specified in a way which translates clearly into quantifiable targets, and the public transport operator is left to tread an ill-defined path between commercial objectives and the wider social requirements. This paper examines the range of objectives of public transport policy, and the difficulties of ensuring maximum efficiency and effectiveness when much of the revenue comes from subsidies and when the goals are poorly specified. It discusses management information and operating strategies in relation both to commercial considerations and to satisfying social objectives. Particular reference is made to the changes which may follow the deregulation of bus services in the UK.

4A7 BLY, P.H. and OLDFIELD, R.H. (1986) The effects of public transport subsidies on demand and supply. *Transportation Research*, **20A** (6), pp. 415-427.

The authors report the results of statistical analysis of cross-sectional and longitudinal public transport operating statistics from 16 countries aimed at identifying the relationships between subsidy on the one hand, and fares, service, passengers, unit costs and output per employee on the other. The study updates earlier work carried out in 1979 for the European Conference of Ministers of Transport. It shows that subsidy has reduced fares, increased the amount of service operated and increased passenger numbers. There is also a significant relationship between increases in subsidy and increases in unit costs and wages, and reductions in ouput per employee.

See also: Bly, P.H. and Oldfield, R.H. (1983) Future use of stage bus services. *Transportation*, **12** (1), pp. 45-59.

4A8 BLY, P.H. and OLDFIELD, R.H. (1986) Competition between minibuses and regular bus services. *Journal of Transport Economics*, **20** (1), pp. 49-68.

Results reached in this paper indicate that services run entirely by minibuses are unlikely to cover their costs. But minibuses running on the same routes as existing big bus services in London may do well, and may produce some net social benefit.

See also: Oldfield, R.H. and Bly, P.H. (1985) using smaller buses in Central London. Transport and Road Research Laboratory, Research Report 31. Crowthorne: TRRL.

4A9 BOYD, C.W. (1981) The impact of reduced service quality on demand for bus travel. *Journal of Transport Economics and Policy*, **15** (2), pp. 167-178.

This paper describes the analysis of the effects on passenger demand and operators' revenue of one-man operation of urban bus routes in Great Britain. It attempts to cover all aspects of one-man operation and concludes that the net effect is one of a welfare cost: the benefits appear small by comparison with the increased generalized costs of travel for other passengers, diversion of passengers to other modes and congestion costs imposed by buses halting longer at bus stops.

See also, Boyd, C.W. (1981) Cost savings from one-man operation of buses. *Journal of Transport Economics and Policy*, **15** (1), pp. 59-67.

4A10 BUTTON, K.J. (1985) Subsidies, political control, and costs of UK urban bus provision. *Transportation Research Record*, 1012, pp. 8-13.

In this paper the impact of three aspects of public policy on the costs of providing urban bus service in the United Kingdom is examined;

subsidy levels, policy objectives and scale of operations. A cross section of operations is surveyed by using standard econometric procedures and data for the financial year 1979-1980. The general conclusions are that public policies of the kind examined do, to differing degrees, exert an influence over the costs of public bus service provision.

See also: Button, K.J. (1984) Subsidies and the provision of urban public transport. *International Journal of Transport Economics*, **11** (2/3), pp. 177-188.

4A11 BUTTON, K.J. and O'DONNELL, K.J. (1985) An examination of cost structures associated with providing urban bus services in Britain. *Scottish Journal of Political Economy*, **32** (1), pp. 67-81.

There is evidence of diseconomies of scale which could lead to the questioning of the current size of some of the bigger district bus undertakings. Equally many of the smaller concerns seem to be enjoying increased returns. The results differ markedly from those of earlier UK studies which relied upon more restrictive assumptions and the paper also questions some of the traditional views on the costs of urban bus provision.

4A12 BUTTON, K.J., PEARMAN, A.D. and FOWKES, A.S. (1982) *Car Ownership Modelling and Forecasting*. Aldershot: Gower.

Interest in forecasting car ownership levels has grown considerably in recent years. It has become a serious area of study resulting in a diversity of models being developed. In addition to reviewing the models developed, this book considers trends in ownership and the socio-economic influences on car ownership such as income, household composition, fuel prices and accessibility. The methods covered include extrapolation methods, causal models and forecasting car ownership at the local level.

4A13 CERVERO, R. (1983) Tax equity and the finance of transit. *Transportation Quarterly*, **37** (3), pp. 379-394.

This article examines the incidence of various public transport tax sources. Who contributes to these revenue sources has some bearing on how public transport costs might be allocated among population groups and government levels. The article suggests which sources are most appropriate for financing American public transport services.

4A14 CERVERO, R. (1984a) The anatomy of transit operating deficits. *Urban Law and Policy*, **6** (4/5), pp. 477–497.

Public transit systems in the US have been faced with spiralling deficits over the past decade due to a combination of factors. The paper outlines the reasons for the ever-increasing deficits and suggests how local authorities could respond to control costs and expand transit's revenue base. Proposals include the controlling of input costs, changing service and fares policies, revising assistance programmes, and deregulating entry requirements for other competitive modes.

4A15 CERVERO, R. (1984b) Effects of operating subsidies and dedicated funding on transit costs and performance. *Journal of Transportation Engineering–ASCE*, **110** (5), pp. 467–480.

The empirical evidence of operating subsidies impacts are reviewed together with a recent study in California. Evidence strongly suggests that subsidies have had a degrading effect on transit performance over time, in particular contributing to high unit costs and low labour productivity. Although subsidy increases patronage, evidence suggests that the additional costs incurred are excessive. A combination of user-side subsidies and producer-side subsidies which are distributed on the basis of performance criteria might offer the best compromise.

See also *Journal of Urban Analysis*, **8** (1), pp. 37–53, 1984.

4A16 CERVERO, R. (1985a) Examining recent transit fare innovations in the United States. *Transport Policy and Decision Making*, **3** (1), pp. 23–41.

This paper discusses a variety of public transport fare innovations, particularly those involving time of day differentials. Four case studies covering Columbus, Ohio; Portland, Oregon; Cincinnati, Ohio; and Bridgeport, Connecticut are presented and the impact of fare innovations on ridership and revenue is discussed. So far this has been rather modest.

See also: Cervero, R. (1982a) Examining likely consequences of a new transit fare policy. *Transportation Research Record*, 877, pp. 79–84.

Cervero, R. (1982b) Peak load transit pricing: Theory and practice. *Journal of Advanced Transportation*, **16** (3), pp. 209-230.

Cervero, R. (1985b) Normative framework for transit fare policy making. *Journal of Advanced Transportation*, **19** (2), pp. 115-131.

4A17 CHERWONY, W., GLEICHMAN, G. and PORTER, B. (1981) *Bus Route Costing Procedures: A Review*. Philadelphia: Booz Allen and Hamilton.

Many public transport systems currently develop cost estimates as part of their bus service planning process. The systems use a wide variety of cost estimation techniques, and no single technique is accepted as more accurate or reliable than others. To assist these systems, the office of planning assistance of the Urban Mass Transportation Administration has initiated a study of cost estimation techniques for bus service planning. The purpose of this study is to develop a manual of costing procedures that will enable public transport systems to estimate accurately the incremental cost of planned service changes. This document is the first interim report from the study and it includes a review of existing cost estimation techniques and an evaluation of applicability of these techniques to the service planning process.

4A18 DASKIN, M.S. (1983) A review of transit service and pricing options. *Journal of Advanced Transportation*, **17** (3), pp. 219-251.

The author proposes a conceptual structure for evaluating service and pricing changes on public transport and suggests market differentiated pricing and service. Three classes of pricing options are examined: distance based fares; time of day pricing; and service based fares. He reviews the use of passes and other implementation issues. Finally, he discusses and evaluates options designed to improve service reliability.

4A19 DAWSON, J.A. (1983) Segmentation of the transit market. *Transportation Quarterly*, **37** (1), pp. 73-84.

Various methods of segmenting public transport fare structures to maximize revenue and maintain demand are discussed. They include off peak discounts, distance-based fares, surcharging of premium services, season tickets and discretionary fares. Details of the use of such systems in the United States are included and a hypothetical fare structure is outlined.

4A20 DODGSON, J.S. and TOPHAM, N. (1987) Benefit-cost rules for urban transit subsidies. *Journal of Transport Economics and Policy*, **21** (1), pp. 57-72.

The paper considers rules for assessing the benefits and costs of urban transit subsidies, taking account both of the allocational and of the income-distributional implications of public transport services.

4A21 EMMERSON, P. and BLY, P.H. (1987) The effects of cross-subsidy in an urban bus network. Transport and Road Research Laboratory, Research Report 94. Crowthorne: TRRL.

The 1985 Transport Act in the UK will open up the provision of bus services to competition and most of the cross-subsidy which presently exists between individual services in an operator's network will disappear. In this radical reorganization there will be both gains and losses. This report examines the likely outcome in an urban bus network, using a computer model.

4A22 EUROPEAN CONFERENCE OF MINISTERS OF TRANSPORT (1984) Aims and effects of public financial support for passenger transport. Report of the 67th Round Table. Paris: ECMT.

This Round Table discussion is based on a keynote paper by K. Gwilliam analysing the aims and effects of public transport subsidies. Discussion centres on the role of subsidy in maximizing social welfare, the values of a regulated system and cross-subsidization, and the extent of contestability within the bus market in the light of possible deregulation. The discussion draws on the policies and experiences of many European countries.

4A23 EVANS, A. (1987) A theoretical comparison of competition with other economic regimes for bus services. *Journal of Transport Economics and Policy*, **21** (1), pp. 7-36.

If a bus route is open to any number of operators, and they must operate without any form of collusion or co-operation, will there be a stable pattern of services? If so, what sort of pattern will it be, and how will it compare with services operated under other regimes? The paper considers a theoretical model to deal with these questions and makes theoretical estimates of the order of magnitude of important features.

4A24 FORKENBROCK, D.J. and STONER, J.W. (1983) Support for a local transit tax. *Transportation Research A*, **18A** (3), pp. 243–252.

Survey data from a small, blue collar, mid-Western US city are analysed to identify the factors that influence support for a local tax earmarked for transit. In Council Bluffs, Iowa, a telephone survey was carried out to measure willingness to pay a proposed two million dollar property tax to fund public transport. The benefits affecting support for the tax most strongly proved to be those accruing to non-users specifically, the beliefs that public transport contributes to cleaner air, stimulates business within the city, and helps the poor to find or keep jobs. The belief that urban government is performing well also strongly affects support. Personal use of public transport, use by other members of one's household, and the view that public transport is a back-up transportation mode have a very minor effect on support. The conclusion is reached that public transport planning should take into consideration social objectives as well as performance measures to ensure continued support.

4A25 GLAISTER, S. (1986) Bus deregulation, competition and vehicle size. *Journal of Transport Economics and Policy*, **20** (2), pp. 217–244.

Simulation of open competition on the network of bus routes in a medium size British town is presented. Pricing product differentiation and level of service are discussed. Service frequencies and patronage will be substantially increased on the densest route. Some routes previously in receipt of cross-subsidy might be capable of modest expansion and the weakest routes will contract somewhat. Small vehicles will often have a competitive advantage over the traditional size. On dense routes they may operate in competition with larger vehicles offering a faster service at a premium price. There might be significant adverse effects on traffic congestion.

See also: *Journal of Transport Economics and Policy*, **19** (1), pp. 65–81, and subsequent comment and rejoinder to that paper in **19** (3), pp. 313–317.

4A26 GOODWIN, P.B. (1986) A panel analysis of changes in car ownership and bus use. *Traffic Engineering and Control*, **27** (10), pp. 519–525.

The object of this paper is to analyse changes in travel patterns, especially bus use, in South Yorkshire between 1981 and 1984. The study forms part of an assessment of the cheap fares policy initiated in 1976 and abandoned with the abolition of the county council in 1986.

4A27 GWILLIAM, K.M., NASH, C.A. and MACKIE, P.J. (1985) Deregulating the bus industry in Britain – the case against. *Transport Reviews*, **5** (2), pp. 105–132 and **5** (3), pp. 215–222.

In its White Paper 'Buses', the British Government sets out its proposals for creation of a freer local bus service sector than exists in any developed industrial economy in the world. The purpose of this paper is to examine the basis and nature of the proposals, and particularly to assess the validity of the analysis that has been presented in support of them.

The White Paper diagnosis of the bus industry is that a potentially virile sector is being stifled to such an extent by regulation that the variety and quality of service is poor, demand is unnecessarily low, and costs unnecessarily high. The prescription is for a heavy dose of free competition on the road between commercially motivated, financially autonomous companies, supported (lest the cure be worse than the disease) by tighter quality regulation, fair competition protections, and direct support of socially desirable unremunerative services. The prognosis is the elimination of cross-subsidy, the introduction of new types of service, and the establishment, essentially through market pressures, of the best attainable price/frequency/quality combination consistent with the external finances available.

The essence of the White Paper can be reduced to four propositions: (1) deregulation will produce a competitive market; (2) competition will substantially reduce costs; (3) a competitive market will improve resource allocation; (4) a competitive market will not cause any significant undesirable spin off effects. Each of these propositions is examined in turn.

4A28 HAY, A. (1986) The impact of subsidised low-fare public transport on travel behaviour. *Environment and Planning C*, **4** (3), pp. 233–246.

In this paper, changes in travel behaviour in Sheffield–Rotherham (1972–1981) and Manchester–Salford (1976–1982) are compared with special reference to the effect of bus fare levels in real terms, which fell by about 70 per cent in Sheffield-Rotherham but remained constant in Manchester-Salford. The analysis is directed to seven distinct household types, and overall changes in bus trip rates, estimated elasticities, effects on traffic congestion, city centre use, mobility of low mobility groups, and income redistribution are examined. The conclusion is made that although reducing real fares resulted in highest levels of bus patronage, evidence for the other beneficial effects was absent.

4A29 HIGGINSON, M.P. and WHITE, P.R. (1982) The efficiency of British urban bus operators. Polytechnic of Central London Research Report 8, London: PCL.

This substantial report (320 pages) provides a detailed analysis of the experience of urban bus operations during the 1970s. In the 1970s urban bus operators in Britain lost 25 per cent of their patronage; rising car ownership is not accredited with the dominant role. The other major problem for the industry has been rising costs. Operating costs per bus mile rose by 28 per cent in real terms over the decade despite the fact that the spread of one person operations more than offset the rise in real wages for crews. The main cause of this increase was the rapid rise in maintenance costs due partly to the switch to rear engined vehicles and partly due to the failure to achieve productivity increases in this area to off-set rising real wages. The authors draw conclusions for the future of the industry and the optimal size of operators.

4A30 HOROWITZ, A.J. and ZLOSEL, D.J. (1981) Transfer penalties: Another look at transit riders' reluctance to transfer. *Transportation*, **10** (3), pp. 279-282.

Two on-board surveys were conducted to determine how public transport riders perceive transfers. The surveys were conducted before and after the imposition of a transfer in the middle of an existing bus route. Results of the surveys showed that riders perceive bus public transport trips as significantly worse when the trip requires a transfer, even if transfer time is neglible.

4A31 HOVELL, P.J. and MORAN, A.J. (1985) *The Management of Urban Public Transport: A Marketing Perspective*. Aldershot: Gower.

This book is divided into three parts. The first provides an environmental framework for the analysis of public transport management. The second demonstrates how the five English Transport Executives and 28 North American and continental West European undertakings have responded to environmental pressures in their marketing and operations. The final section focuses on the way in which the industry can develop more competitive and profitable services by reviewing the different approaches to marketing and the implementation of controlled programmes of research in the cities studied. It is argued that if the principles established through the assessment of management ideas are implemented, they would pay for themselves through increases in patronage.

4A32 JACOBS, G.D., MAUNDER, D.A.C. and FOURACRE, P.R. (1986) Characteristics of conventional public transport services in Third World Cities. *Traffic Engineering and Control*, **27** (1), pp. 6-11.

The urban public transport sector in developing countries is broadly characterized by its high growth rate, its diversity and in many cases its poor financial performance. This paper reviews conventional bus operations in cities of the Third World using data obtained from a postal survey implemented in 1984 by the Transport and Road Research Laboratory. Results indicate a growing demand for public transport over recent years and an increase in ridership on minibuses and shared taxis. There is evidence of broad correlation between a city's characteristics, its transport system and the demand and supply for public transport. However, greater understanding is needed to avoid the problems of creating long-term problems through solving immediate problems of travel demand.

4A33 KEPPLEMAN, F.S. and ROSE, G. (1983) Supply factors and transit demand. *Journal of Advanced Transportation*, **17** (3), pp. 201-217.

The paper investigates the effects of fares and service characteristics on public transport demand to show that fare increases and service reductions may not be the best strategy to reduce subsidy levels. It identifies the factors likely to affect travel decisions. It also identifies three strategies likely to be effective in retaining or attracting patronage: selective fares increases; implementation of what the authors call premium services; and improvements in the quality of service.

4A34 KIRBY, R.F. (1982) Pricing strategies for public transportation. *Journal of the American Planning Association*, **48** (3), pp. 327–334.

Pricing of most public transport services in urban areas is the responsibility of local governments, acting either individually or jointly through metropolitan agencies. To date, local government decisions on public transport fares typically have been shaped primarily by short-term political, fiscal, and administrative expediency. Recently, however, growing transit deficits and stringency in public subsidy budgets have demanded a more comprehensive view of public transport pricing. This article reviews the public policy objectives commonly stated for public transport programmes, and uses them to formulate some general guidelines for pricing. The article then discusses some pricing strategies which appear from recent research and experimentation to have promise for responding to the challenges currently faced by public transport systems.

4A35 LAGO, A.M., MAYWORM, P. and MCENROE, J.M. (1981) Transit service elasticities. *Journal of Transport Economics and Policy*, **15** (2), pp. 99–120.

This paper presents the current state of knowledge on the size of public transport service elasticities compiled from demonstrations and demand models. The review of public transport services focuses on passenger responses to changes in headways, aggregate vehicle miles, and components of travel time. Other service attributes, such as reliability and comfort, which appear to be important to decisions on travel but for which no demand elasticities are available, are reviewed in terms of their impact on ridership. The paper concludes with a summary of ridership responsiveness to public transport service adjustments.

4A36 MAYWORM, P.D. (1982) Transit fare elasticity: Role in fare policy and planning. *Transportation Research Record*, 862, pp. 29–35.

Fare elasticity of demand and its role in patronage and revenue planning and in developing fare policy are discussed. The fare elasticity is a useful concept because it provides information on how riders respond to fare changes. Since fare elasticities usually vary significantly by trip distance, time of day, and quality of service, public transport managers can take advantage of these differences by differentially pricing their services in order to increase revenues and ridership. Differential pricing, however, does have its political and monetary cost, and these issues are discussed within the American context where federal operating subsidies are being phased out over five years.

4A37 MITCHELL, C.G.B. (1980) The use of local bus services. Transport and Road Research Laboratory, Laboratory Report LR923. Crowthorne: TRRL.

Patronage of local bus services has been falling since at least 1952. This report uses the National Travel Surveys of 1965, 1972-73 and 1975-76 to examine how the use of local bus services has changed since 1965. A declining proportion of bus trips are made to and from work, and an increasing proportion for shopping. Characteristics of bus users with respect to age, sex, area of residence, car ownership, income and the socio-economic group of the user's household are studied. Variation of bus use with time of day and with season is shown. It is found that demand for bus travel by adults has become less peaked, and that by 1975-76 most of the additional peak demand was due to children.

4A38 MORRIS, P. (1983) Should we subsidise public transport? *Political Quarterly*, **54** (4), pp. 392-398.

Three economic arguments in favour of subsidies are presented: the accruing of a consumer surplus, or extra benefits to users over and above those represented by fares paid; benefits to non-consumers such as traders in a city centre; and the benefits to all potential consumers of having a service available when needed. However, despite these apparent benefits the economic argument does not support the Greater London Council Fares Fair Policy because it effectively redistributes income from the poorer to richer sectors of society by financing subsidies from highly regressive rates.

4A39 OBENG, K. (1983) Fare subsidies to achieve Pareto optimality – a benefit cost approach. *Logistics and Transportation Review*, **19** (4), pp. 367-384.

Studies on optimal fare subsidy generally have been based on welfare analyses, and deficits have not been considered explicitly in the objective function. A different method of deriving Pareto optimal subsidies in deficit situations is presented. Deficits are treated explicitly in the objective function and the resulting subsidy is demonstrated to be sufficient to yield Pareto optimal outcome. From the models developed and the numerical example, it has been concluded that the rule is to make the subsidies inversely proportional to transit average cost elasticity. Providing subsidies that depend jointly on fare elasticity and on average cost elasticity could yield outcomes that are consistent with federal policies. The analysis further indicates that marginal cost pricing defines the efficiency frontier where user benefits equal increased loss to the operator. Furthermore, transit fare subsidy is demonstrated to be efficient so long as it is calculated by using the optimal subsidy formula developed in this paper.

See also: Obeng, K. (1981) Pricing and transit subsidies. *Journal of Advanced Transportation*, **15** (3), pp. 231–246.

4A40 PERRY, J.L. (1986) Comparative performance in urban bus transit: assessing privatization strategies. *Public Administration Review*, **46** (1), pp. 57–66.

Five ownership-management structures were compared for urban bus services on a series of performance indicators. The results indicate that privately owned and operated systems produced more output per dollar and generated more revenues than other types of systems. Publicly owned systems managed by contractors performed no more efficiently and effectively than publicly owned, publicly managed systems.

4A41 PICKRELL, D.H. (1983) Sources of rising operating deficits in urban bus transit. *Transportation Research Record*, 915, pp. 18–25.

Annual operating expenses incurred by US urban public transport systems rose more than $5 billion from 1960 to 1980, of which a rapidly declining fraction was covered by farebox receipts. As a result, the industrywide operating deficit approached $4 billion by the end of this period. Although urban rail systems first incurred large operating losses, by 1980 the motor bus segment of the US public transport industry accounted for three-quarters of its aggregate deficit. Recent growth in bus operating deficits can be traced to escalating costs per unit of service, rapid service expansion despite declining utilization of existing service levels, and decisions to simplify and reduce fare structures. A detailed examination of each of these sources of rising operating losses is presented, and attempts are made to assess both their individual contributions to deficit growth and their respective underlying causes. Following this examination, an illustration of how these developments interacted to produce the explosive growth in bus operating deficits that occurred during the 1970s is given. Specific recommendations are made for bringing growing losses under control.

4A42 PUCHER, J. (1982a) Who benefits from transit subsidies? Recent evidence from six metropolitan areas. *Transportation Research*, **17A** (1), pp. 39-50.

On the basis of detailed case studies of six US metropolitan areas, this paper examines variations among cities in the income-redistributive impact of public transport subsidies in 1980. The distribution of subsidies in each city is estimated through analysis of the socio-economic characteristics of riders on each type of public transport service and the degree to which each type of service was subsidized. The estimated distribution of the public transport tax burden reflects the tax mix used for transit finance in each city as well as the composition of funding by level of government. The subsidy and tax cost distributions are compared to calculate the distribution of net subsidies in each area. Causes of the variation among cities in redistributive impact are discussed, and recommendations are made for increasing the progressivity of public transport finance.

See also: Pucher, J. (1982b) Effects of subsidies on transit costs. *Transportation Quarterly*, **36** (4), pp. 549-562.
Pucher, J. (1981) Equity in transit finance: distribution of transit subsidy benefits and costs among income classes. *Journal of the American Planning Association*, **47** (4), pp. 387-407.
Pucher, J. and Hirschman, I. (1982) Distribution of the transit tax burden in five US metropolitan areas. *Transportation*, **11** (1), pp. 3-28.

4A43 PUCHER, J. (1982c) A decade of change for mass transit. *Transportation Research Record*, 858, pp. 48-57.

The public transport industry in the United States was transformed during the decade of the 1970s. This transformation consisted of changes in institutional structure; changes in the amount, type, and location of public transport service; and changes in cost levels and in the means by which costs were financed. The purpose of this paper is to examine the nature and extent of these changes, with particular emphasis on changes in levels of service, costs, and financing. Variations in these trends among different public transport systems are highlighted, and causes of the variations are analysed by a range of statistical methods. Although the econometric results are not entirely conclusive, they suggest that various aspects of the current public transport programme may encourage cost escalation and thus hamper the effectiveness of government subsidies to public transport.

4A44 QUARMBY, D.A. (1984) Public transport operations. *Highways and Transportation*, **31** (4), pp. 22–27.

The author identifies briefly the role and objectives of conurbation public transport, with particular reference to buses; then discusses the road traffic environment for the operator and highlights issues which affect the quality of service and what the operator can do about it: he then deals with the institutional framework and competition. Finally, a marketing perspective on the public transport operator illustrates a number of issues which fall largely within the operator's own responsibility, and where operators themselves need to take the initiative to improve the service they provide.

4A45 ROCK, S.M. (1983) New funding sources for public transit: who pays? *Transportation Research Record*, 900, pp. 35–38.

As financial crises have increasingly plagued public transport systems, new and/or additional sources of funding have been sought. One issue that has not been well documented in this area is the question of who pays for each source. A number of potential household-based funding sources and their general impact on families at different income levels can be analysed by using data published by the US Bureau of Labor Statistics. Sixteen options including fares were examined and compared as to their relative regressivity (burdens). The results can be used to compare the impact of one source versus another or to choose a source to minimize negative distributional impacts. Subject to certain qualifications, it was found that most household-based sources were regressive. The most regressive were household (head) tax, cigarette tax, and public transport fares. Progressive alternatives include parking, income, and stock-transfer taxes. It is suggested that decreased federal funding will lead to the tapping of more regressive sources as well as to increasing reliance on business-based taxes, service cutbacks, and fare increases.

4A46 STERN, E. (1984) Delineating regions for transit assistance allocation: a geographical approach. *Applied Geography*, **4** (4), pp. 267-281.

A priority allocation index based on principles such as rank-size distribution, gravitation and spatial equity has been used as a national experiment in Israel. It involves cluster analysis to generate several alternative allocation regions from which planners may select an appropriate policy. This paper reviews the experiment and discusses the implications of the results for allocation of transport subsidies.

4A47 TALVITIE, A. and HEINILA, A. (1986) A comparison of privately and publicly owned bus companies and a public bus transit agency. *Transportation Research Record*, 1051, pp. 35-42.

An examination is made of the level of service provided to patrons, the cost structure, the productivity, and the profitability of the companies that offer regularly scheduled bus service in the metropolitan area of Helsinki, Finland, which includes the cities of Espoo and Vantaa. Data are given on the following types of bus companies: city-owned, private, and a public bus transit agency, Helsingin Kaupungin Liikennelaitos, in Helsinki. The data are averages, and they conceal a variance that is often substantial. It is believed that this variance is due more to management and managerial skills than to economies of scale or operating environment. Unit costs of bus transportation in the Helsinki region and the composition of these unit costs are presented. A discussion of productivity concludes the paper.

4A48 TRANSPORTATION RESEARCH BOARD (1985) Bus Route and Schedule Planning Guidelines. National Cooperative Highway Research Programme Synthesis of Highway Practice. Washington, DC: TRB.

Bus transit service planning in most urban areas is largely an outgrowth of historic and geographic circumstances. Planning should reflect the specific needs and operating requirements of each urban area. Relevant planning factors include: past operating practices and procedures; the current operating authority and system extent; revenue requirements (i.e. reliance on fares); land-use, population density, and employment features; street patterns; and the availability of off-street rail transit. These factors, singly and in combination, influence the pattern of bus services and the opportunities for change and expansion. The best possible service should be provided to the greatest number of people within the governing economic constraints. Planning must balance the amount and type of services provided with the net costs of providing the service. This trade-off underlies all service planning decisions. Bus services should be carefully related to existing and potential markets and concentrated in heavy travel corridors with the greatest service frequency and route coverage in the approaches to the city centre. Route structure should be clear and understandable, and service duplication should be avoided. Changes in transit service must be coordinated with planning and traffic agencies to expedite bus flow and to assure that streets in nearby developing suburban areas are able to accommodate buses. All these issues are presented as a synthesis of current practice in the United States with respect to bus route and schedule planning.

4A49 VIJAYAKUMAR, S. and JACOBS, G.D. (1983) Factors affecting the use of public transport in cities in developed and developing countries. *Traffic Engineering and Control*, **24** (5), pp. 258–268.

This paper presents an analysis of some of the factors which influence stage-carriage bus operations in urban centres. In this analysis a broad distinction is made between operators in cities of the developed world and those in Third World cities. The aim has been to identify and explain why urban public transport is a growth industry in the Third World, while it has been in decline in the developed world. Distinction between the two sets of cities was based on national per capita income. Cities in countries with a GNP per capita of less than US $1000 per annum were classified as developing and those above as developed. The analysis demonstrated the different effect of increasing prosperity in cities of the Third World and of the developed world. It was also apparent from the study that there is a much greater demand for public transport in Third World cities than in the developed world and that it is generally accompanied, and influenced, by a lack of supply. Conversely, there is some evidence in cities of the developed world that supply has not declined at the same rate as the decline in patronage.

4A50 VITON, P.A. (1982) Privately provided urban transport services. *Journal of Transport Economics and Policy*, **16** (1), pp. 85-94.

In another paper, Viton (1980), the author examined a model of the urban transport market, designed to determine when a profit-maximizing operator could enter the market. The results showed that entry is possible under a wide variety of circumstances. This paper extends that research. It suggests that the scarcity of market entry by private operators is due to the deterrent effect of services operated by incumbents. The social welfare implications of entry are also explored.

See also: Viton, P.A. (1980) The possibility of profitable bus service. *Journal of Transport Economics and Policy*, **14** (3), pp. 295-314.

4A51 WALTERS, A.A. (1982) Externalities in urban buses. *Journal of Urban Economics*, **11** (1), pp. 60-72.

This paper develops a simple model to determine the optimum size of a bus within a competitive market. Plausible values for the model parameters suggest that the size would be considerably smaller than the typical bus currently operating in cities of Western Europe and America. However, the individual operator has no incentive to provide the minibus service unless competitors do so as well, or unless the increased frequency and speed attract new passengers to the service. It is also argued that small buses could help reduce waiting time, increase load factors, reduce congestion, raise fare levels, reduce wage costs and have most impact at peak periods. Many of these arguments may seem counterintuitive but a strong case for a greater number of minibuses for all operators is put forward.

4A52 WEBSTER, F.V. (1983) The importance of cost minimisation in public transport operations. Transport and Road Research Laboratory, Supplementary Report 766. Crowthorne: TRRL.

This paper looks at the consequences of rising costs on the scope for setting fares and service levels, on car ownership and modal split and on the location of activities. It examines the likely effects of both higher and lower levels of productivity on future bus use and concludes that even with rising wages improved productivity would have a significant effect on ridership by the end of the century. In many countries the reaction to rising costs in the past has been to increase subsidy levels. Alternative strategies are considered in this paper. The combined effect of such measures could well reduce overall operating costs by some 15 to 20 per cent and the paper assembles what evidence there is in support of this. The move to less labour intensive systems such as rail, however, appears to be a feasible proposition only when the demand along a corridor is exceptionally heavy, unless the infrastructure is already in existence.

4A53 WEISMAN, M. (1981) Variables influencing transit use. *Traffic Quarterly*, **35** (3), pp. 371–383.

Planners have relied on selected criteria of public transport service quality to evaluate levels of demand on public transport systems. The criterion of service quality can be operationally measured by a range of variables that influence the public's response to public transport. These variables have been defined in several studies but they have rarely been analysed to determine the degree of influence each one has on public transport patronage. This study analyses statistical data to test the relationship of different aspects of public transport systems – speed, frequency, express services, route coverage, services outside the city centre and transfers between services.

4A54 WELLS, M.J., MCCOLLOM, B. and DOOLEY, T. (1985) Review of the use of part-time transit operators and methods for assigning part-time work. *Transportation Research Record*, 1013, pp. 39–48.

The use of part-time transit operators is a subject of increasing attention as a means of controlling labour costs and improving transit productivity. Part-time operators can significantly reduce the cost of providing peak-period service because they are subject to less restrictive work rules than are their full-time counterparts; they typically receive no spread or overtime premiums, they almost always receive lower fringe benefits, and they may earn lower wages. Three out of four labour contracts permit the use of part-time operators, and one in every twenty operators nationwide is a part-timer. A national perspective on the range and norms of contractual provisions affecting the use of part-time operators is offered. The methodologies used by three transit agencies to assign part-time operators on the basis of existing run cuts, in accordance with the different work rules that govern the use of part-timers at each agency, are presented. The methodologies used by two systems to incorporate part-time operators into automated run-cutting procedures are also presented.

4A55 WHITE, P.R. (1981) 'Travelcard' tickets in urban public transport. *Journal of Transport Economics and Policy*, **18** (1), pp. 17–33.

Travelcard tickets may be distinguished from traditional season and multiple-ride tickets because they offer use of an entire network, or substantial zones within a network rather than of selected routes and/or fare stages only. Travelcards have grown rapidly in importance, and their holders now account for well over half the trips made on some European urban public transport networks. In Britain their importance is less marked, partly because of the graduated fare scales, and market penetration reaches a maximum of about 20 per cent in the West Midlands. Pricing policies have often been arbitrary, and so have the reasons for their initial introduction, but a more rational framework can be outlined, based on the concept of a threshold level up to which the price may be raised with very little loss of sales, enabling a realistic revenue to be obtained without loss of operational benefits. Time-series analysis of data from West Midlands PTE and Lothian Region Transport in Britain suggests a negligible elasticity by price for moderate increases in price of travelcards from a low initial level. This is corroborated by the work of Brög in West Germany, in which user response to price increases is shown to differ by ticket type. The British results suggest that the lower end of the range of Brög's estimates is most likely to be found in practice (that is, a reduction closer to 0 than 3 per cent in travelcard sales after a real price increase of up to 10 per cent).

4A56 WHITE, P.R. (1983) Further developments in the pricing of local public transport services. *Transport Reviews*, **3** (4), pp. 329-340.

The article supplements and updates earlier work by the author which described the situation concerning public transport services in Britain for 1980, with examples from other countries. This article updates the position regarding four main issues: (a) impact of the Transport Act 1980 in Britain, which has virtually removed fares control from stage carriage services, and removed all price and quantity control from express services by road; (b) further development of zonal pricing, travelcards and off-bus fare collection on urban systems, and the effects of price reductions (and subsequent increases) in London, West Midlands, and Merseyside; (c) problems concerning the legality of financial support for fares policies in British cities; (d) following a presentation of work arising from the earlier paper at the meeting of the Transportation Research Board in Washington, DC, in January 1983, the contrast between British and American policy is reviewed, with the writer's personal view on current policy there. In addition, evidence on certain other points in the text is updated.

4A57 WILLIAMS, H.C.W.L. and SANDERSON, I.R. (1985) Cross subsidy in urban bus operations: analysis and planning implications. *Transportation Research*, **19B**, pp. 73-79.

Summary of a joint study by the University of Leeds Institute for Transport Studies and the National Bus Company which examined alternative definitions of cross subsidy in bus operations, identified the role played by subsidies in the provision of bus services and related infrastructure, and developed a model to consider the likely outcome of various operating strategies.

4A58 WILLIAMS, M. (1980) The economic justification for local bus transport subsidies. *International Journal of Transport Economics*, **8** (1), pp. 79-88.

The primary argument used for government intervention in the transportation market is usually made in terms of economic efficiency and other broad social objectives. This paper deals with aspects of federal, state and local intervention through subsidies payments to local bus transportation systems in Illinois. The paper begins with a review of the essential economic and social arguments for subsidies, followed by a discussion of the special transport subsidy programme instituted in the State of Illinois to aid its smaller urban communities. Some empirical results are provided in an attempt to evaluate the justification for subsidies to these systems, and to assess the extent to which federal and subfederal aid commitments are expected in the future.

4B Urban rail

4B1 ADIV, A. (1986) The limitations of commuting to work by rail: analysis from the potential users' viewpoint. *Transport Policy and Decision Making*, **3**, pp. 357–373.

This paper evaluates the ability of an urban rail system to provide an alternative mode of commuting. The specific data were derived from analysis of the Bay Area Rapid Transit (BART). The analysis is based on two sources: first, objective manual trip path assignments from home to work; and second subjective judgements by the potential users who stated why they did not ride BART to work. It also shows that in spite of growth in BART patronage over the last decade, urban rail transit will probably continue to be an impractical alternative for most commuters, because of its spatial incompatibility with patterns of living and working in American Metropolitan areas.

4B2 CERVERO, R. (1984) Light rail transit and urban redevelopment. *Journal of the American Planning Association*, **50** (2), pp. 133–147.

Recent construction of light rail transit systems in a number of North American cities raises crucial questions about their possible effects on land use and urban development. Although serving passengers and keeping construction costs down have been the primary aims of new rail investments, the possibilities for joint development and land use are numerous. This paper explores light rail transit's potential influence on urban growth and revitalizing central city areas. Some cities are integrating light rail transit with pedestrian malls as part of downtown redevelopment. A significant number of others, however, are downplaying the development potential of light rail transit by aligning their systems principally along abandoned railroad rights-of-way and industrial belts in order to cut costs. For most cities in the preconstruction stages of their projects, policy-makers need to recognize the trade-offs involved when the lowest-cost corridor and alignment are chosen. On the whole, the land-use potential of light rail is moderately high, where there are pro-development policy environments and other complementary forces.

4B3 CERVERO, R. (1985) A tale of two cities: light rail transit in Canada. *Journal of Transportation Engineering*, **111** (6), pp. 633–650.

Toronto and Montreal are often cited for having effectively tied together rail transit and land-used planning. This paper focuses on two other Canadian cities (Calgary and Edmonton), and examines the impacts of LRT on densities, residential construction and mixed use development. Costs per passenger have risen steadily, but patronage levels have remained stable. There is some doubt about the long-term impacts on urban form or travel behaviour.

4B4 EUROPEAN CONFERENCE OF MINISTERS OF TRANSPORT (1980) Scope for railway transport in urban areas. Round Table 47. Paris: ECMT.

This report presents studies from a number of European towns and cities. For each town there is a description of the characteristic geographical and social features, the nature of urban rail provision relative to other transport modes and a financial analysis of rail operations. In conclusion, a synthesis is presented based on a questionnaire supplied by each case study author. It summarizes the possibilities for rail within the urban environment and outlines possible areas of policy to develop further.

4B5 GHONEIM, N.S.A. and WIRASINGHE, S.C. (1987) Optimum zone configuration for planned urban commuter rail lines. *Transportation Science*, **21** (2), pp. 106–115.

The optimum zone structure for a planned urban commuter rail line with one to many or many to one type demand during peak periods is analysed. The objective is to minimize the passenger time costs as well as the relevant system operating and capital costs. The analysis is based on the interaction of a range of variables such as the number of zones, zone boundaries, uniform station spacings, fleet size and train headway. The approximately optimum values of the decision variables are determined mostly in closed form. A numerical application and sensitivity analyses are presented.

4B6 GIANNOPOULOS, G.A. (1981) Metropolitan railways: present characteristics and future prospects. *Transport Reviews*, **1** (1), pp. 45-74.

The paper reviews the main technical, operational and economic characteristics of metro systems in operation or planned around the world and attempts to arrive at some conclusions about their future prospects. First, metros are examined in their town planning context and their basic characteristics are correlated with some basic town planning elements such as population size and density. Secondly, a detailed presentation is made of collective statistics showing trends and tendencies around the world on network characteristics, rolling stock, 'degree of sophistication', various operational characteristics, as well as fare structures and economic performance of metro systems worldwide. Finally, prospects for the future of metros are reviewed and it is stated that today these prospects are encouraging despite escalating costs of construction and operation.

See also: Giannopoulos, G.A. (1984) Urban metropolitan railways. *Ekistics*, **51** (305), pp. 123-130.

4B7 GLAISTER, S. (1983) Some characteristics of rail commuter demand. *Journal of Transport Economics and Policy*, **17** (2), pp. 115-132.

In the article a method is proposed for explaining variations in the market shares of different ticket types (annual, monthly and weekly seasons, full fare and cheap dailies) as relative fares and external factors vary. Results suggest that annual season ticket fares are too low and low-cost, off-peak tickets are too expensive. It is considered that revenue could be increased by price discrimination against season ticket holders so that costs could be reduced by helping to spread peak load. The loss of traffic resulting from the opening of a competing motorway was predominantly from cheap day travel. No effect was detected from changes in service frequencies.

4B8 GOMEZ-IBANEZ, J.A. (1985) A dark side to light rail? The experience of three new transit systems. *Journal of the American Planning Association*, **51** (2), pp. 337-351.

Many medium-size cities are planning or building new light rail transit (LRT) systems, the modern equivalents of streetcars or trolleys. Proponents argue not only that light rail is far less expensive to build than heavy rail, or subway, systems but also that it costs no more to operate than conventional bus transit and offers much improved service. Although it is too early to draw definitive conclusions, the first several years of experience of the new light rail systems in San Diego, Calgary, and Edmonton suggests that proponents have oversold LRT. In all three cities the LRT costs more than the conventional bus service it replaced. Public transit ridership increased modestly in two of the three cities, but the costs per added rider were high.

4B9 GORDON, P. and WILLSON, R. (1984) The determinants of light-rail transit demand - an international cross-sectional comparison. *Transportation Research*, **18A** (2), pp. 135-140.

An international cross-section of light-rail public transport (LRT) systems is examined. Demand is tested as a function of transport system, city, and population attributes. All tests confirm the standard hypotheses at high levels of significance. High levels of explanatory power support the notion of model transferability. The models developed in this paper are used to predict demand for new LRT systems now being installed in North American cities. Model outputs suggest that the official forecasts are very optimistic.

4B10 KANAREK, J.M. and TRUNCELLITO, V.J. (1982) Determination of priorities for station improvements on a commuter rail system. *Transportation Research Record*, 838, pp. 64-67.

There are numerous criteria that cover a wide range of concerns that could be used to evaluate the relative importance of rail station rehabilitation needs among the many stations of a large commuter rail network. Consideration of policy factors and other elements of the economic and political environment inherent to New Jersey allowed the selection of a smaller and simpler set of priority factors, such as degree of unsatisfactory conditions, level of ridership, degree of community interest, potential for ridership growth, and potential for urban redevelopment. Application of these factors yielded a priority ranking for each station of the New Jersey commuter rail system, which facilitated for programming of a statewide multi-year station-modernization project in an equitable manner.

4B11   KETTLE, P.B. and BEESLEY, M.E. (1985) *Improving Railway Financial Performance*. Aldershot: Gower.

This work presents a case study of an approach to tackling a general problem for railway management, namely the formulation of a strategy to improve business financial performance. The study, of VicRail's system in Australia, was undertaken in 1980, and its purpose was to investigate the current and potential relationships between costs and pricing options associated with VicRail's main passenger and freight markets, including the likely impact on cost functions of changes in rail operating practices. To draw conclusions for the business as a whole, this meant giving attention to all of the railway's business activities, including ancillary functions such as property management and station trading represented in its accounts.

4B12   KNIGHT, R.L. and TRYGG, L.L. (1977) Evidence of land use impacts of rapid transit systems. *Transportation*, **6** (3), pp. 231-247.

This paper draws from the findings of published empirical studies and observations of the impacts of rapid transit systems on urban development. Analysis is based on comparisons of impact findings by different researchers and for different cities. An initial set of key issues is proposed, against which available information is arrayed and compared. It is concluded that rapid transit can have substantial growth-focusing impacts, but only if other supporting factors are present.

4B13   MARKOWITZ, J.E. (1985) BART impact update. *Transportation Research Record*, 1036, pp. 69-78.

This paper contains documentation as to what has happened with Bay Area Rapid Transit (San Francisco-BART) use and travel in the primary BART service corridor since 1978, and an illustration showing that many of the earlier constraints on BART patronage and, thus, its impact, have been relieved. BART's service reliability has improved dramatically, attracting many new patrons, and population and employment in BART's market area have grown. As a result, BART carries a large share of trips in its intended market – long-distance commute trips to the urban core.

4B14 NASH, C.A. (1985) Policies towards suburban rail services in Britain and the Federal Republic of Germany – a comparison. *Transport Reviews*, **5** (3), pp. 269–282.

This paper compares the major role played by suburban rail (S-Bahn) systems in West German cities with the much more limited role of rail in the British conurbations. Clearly, the difference owes much to the institutional and financial arrangements in the two countries. In West Germany, large amounts of funds have been available for rail investment, whilst the Federal government has been willing to shoulder much of the burden of operating subsidies. The Verkehrsverbund has emerged as a highly effective way of coordinating fares and services without direct ownership of any mode of transport. By contrast, in Britain funds for rail investment have been much more limited. Progress with integration has been far slower, and is threatened by current government policies regarding both bus deregulation and the abolition of the Metropolitan county councils. Whilst rail is firmly established in German cities, its future in Britain looks bleak.

4B15 PICKETT, M.W., PERRETT, K.E. and CHARLTON, J.W. (1986) Park and ride at Tyne and Wear Metro stations. Transport and Road Research Laboratory, Research Report 40. Crowthorne: TRRL.

Substantial improvements in public transport provision have been achieved in Tyne and Wear through the investment in the Metro. To encourage travellers to transfer from their cars to the Metro system, Tyne and Wear County Council built or improved car parks at a number of Metro stations. This report describes the combined effect of that car parking provision and the Metro in attracting park and ride trips. The number of cars parked by Metro passengers has increased by six times compared with the number of cars parked by BR passengers previously, from about 200 to about 1200, about one-third of the total capacity. Fares paid by passengers using park and ride generated approximately £0.8m per annum in fares revenue in 1984. There has been no actual significant reduction in traffic congestion.

4B16 SMITH, W.S. (1984) Mass transport for high rise high density living. *Journal of Transportation Engineering ASCE*, **110** (6), pp. 521–535.

A review of the relationship between mass transportation and urban form in American and Asian cities indicates that, historically, transport has done much to shape urban development. The author looks particularly at rail transport and finds that in countries where governments foster high-density residential development, transport planners can make an important contribution to that development. Public transport and high-density living can be mutually supportive if carefully planned.

4B17 STRINGHAM, M.G.P. (1982) Travel behaviour associated with land users adjacent to rapid transit stations. *Proceedings of the Roads and Transportation Association of Canada Conference*. Halifax: RTAC.

Although it is estimated that trips to and from employment or school account for less than 20 per cent of total urban travel, these trip types are commonly identified as being the least efficient and as contributing most directly to the chronic peak hour transportation congestion problems. Many major urban centres in North America are moving towards the development of sophisticated rapid transit systems as one solution to the inefficient movement of people. The research conducted in this study was focused on a preliminary examination of the travel behaviour, specifically related to transit, associated with land uses and adjacent to rapid transit stations.

4B18 TRANSPORTATION RESEARCH BOARD (1985) Light rail transit: System design and cost effectiveness. National Research Council State of the Art Report 2. Washington, DC: TRB.

This state of the art report contains most of the papers that were presented at the 1985 LRT Conference as well as some that were presented at the TRB 1985 Annual Meeting. The emergence of light rail transit (LRT) as a cost-effective component of the urban-suburban transportation environment has reinforced the need to examine current issues of design, construction, and operation of

LRT systems in a variety of settings and in comparison with other alternatives. The framework of the 1985 LRT Conference was structured to report on innovative solutions and alternative strategies in a wide variety of site-specific situations. Because the cost of constructing all varieties of fixed-guideway systems has increased in recent years, emphasis is being placed on justifying, constructing, and operating these systems in the most economical fashion. Because of its flexibility of design, operational characteristics, and physical placement, LRT has much potential to achieve cost-effectiveness. At the 1985 LRT Conference issues that arise when LRT is compared with other modal alternatives were explored and discussed. Systems design, technology application, and implementation planning, as they relate to the overall efficiency and effectiveness of LRT, were also considered.

4B19 WALMSLEY, D.A. (1982) The Glasgow rail impact study: the effects of urban rail investment in Scotland. *Transport Policy and Decision Making*, **2**, pp .353–372.

This paper summarizes the results of the study into the effects of the Argyle rail link connecting the northern and southern rail networks, and the complete modernization of the underground railway system. They cover changes in passenger numbers and types of trip, the impact on activities, and the impact on the physical and social environment. Comments on the financial performance of the new services are included, the results of the study are compared with those of other cities in Britain and France.

4B20 YAMADA, T. (1985) The probable effects of introducing a sectional fare system into the New York city subway. *International Journal of Transport Economics*, **12** (3), pp. 315–331.

This paper examines the likely effects of increasing the existing flat fare in terms of improving the financial position of the subway. The present fares structure would be replaced by a sectional approach based on mileage travelled. The conclusion reached is that such a policy would be more equitable, would not lead to a decline in ridership and would produce an 11 per cent increase in revenue.

4C Unconventional public transport and taxis

4C1 BRITTON, F.E.K. (1986) Taxicab transportation: International structures, trends and prospects to 1990. *Transport Policy and Decision Making*, **3**, pp. 341–356.

EcoPlan International has launched a three-year survey of taxi industry structures, practices, policies, trends and innovations in the OECD region. In this article, some of the preliminary findings are presented. The first part of the article sketches the broad outlines of the situation of the taxi industry as it exists today in the OECD region, with specific reference to several public policy considerations which the author believes warrant attention. The second briefly describes the World Taxi Survey, which has been launched to provide an improved basis for policy decisions with respect to such issues as industry structure and organization, the array of services offered, technology advances, and, more generally, in support of more cogent public policy in the sector. The third looks briefly at the considerable range of variations of countries that exist in terms of the taxi industry's presence and coverage within the region, and goes on to comment on some of the social implications of these differences. The closing section sets out a certain number of tentative conclusions stimulated by the survey, which are intended to guide those concerned with policy in the sector.

4C2 COE, G.A. (1986) The taxi and hire car industry in Great Britain. Transport and Road Research Laboratory, Research Report 68, Crowthorne: TRRL.

A TRRL study undertaken in 1980 showed taxis and hire cars to be an increasingly important element in public transport provision in recent years. In late spring 1985 TRRL repeated the survey of all district councils in England and Wales (the regulating authorities for taxis and hire cars outside London), and also conducted a survey of Scottish districts. Comparisons were made with the situation in the capital using data supplied by the Public Carriage Office. The study was undertaken to update the previous work, and to provide a basis for the assessment of the effects on the taxi and hire car industry of the Transport Act 1985. The results of the work are given in the report and clearly indicate that the importance of taxis and hire cars in providing public transport is continuing to increase. Since 1980 their numbers have increased while the number of buses has remained broadly unchanged. However in recent years taxi fares, in real terms, have been tending to rise more quickly than bus fares.

See also: Coe, G.A. and Jackson, R.L. (1983) Some new evidence relating to quantity control in the taxi industry. Transport and Road Research Laboratory, Supplementary Report 797. Crowthorne: TRRL.

4C3 EUROPEAN CONFERENCE OF MINISTERS OF TRANSPORT (1979) *Paratransit*, Report of the 40th Round Table on Transport Economics. Paris: ECMT.

This ECMT round table report contains a background paper on paratransit by Bovy and Krayenbuhl which covers the typology of paratransit systems, the characteristics of paratransit and the development of the sector. Supplementary papers are included on extending the use of taxis as a part of urban passenger transport, dial-a-ride schemes in Great Britain, the dolmus, car pools and transport services provided by employers in France. The report ends with a summary of the main issues under the headings of organization, institutional constraints and financial problems, with certain recommendations for further research.

4C4 GILBERT, G., BURBY, R.J. and FEIBEL, C.E. (1984) Taxicab operating characteristics in the United States. *Transportation*, **12** (2), pp. 173–182.

In 1982, a national survey of US taxicab operators was conducted. This survey sought to assess the economic, operational and organizational status of the industry and to determine how these characteristics have been changing in response to rising costs and an economic recession. Two results of this survey are reported in this paper; the size structure and the organization of the industry. Both of these characteristics show that it has recently been undergoing two fundamental changes. These are the rapid switch away from employees as drivers to independent contractor drivers and decreasing average company size.

4C5 GREENING, P.A.K. and JACKSON, R.L. (1983) Shared taxi operation: cost considerations. Transport and Road Research Laboratory, Supplementary Report 793. Crowthorne: TRRL.

This report gives the results of work carried out to investigate, in broad terms, when and where the use of shared taxi services might be justified in light of cost considerations. Comparisons have been made in financial, resource and fuel terms. The findings indicate that when public transport demands are low it may be more cost effective to provide a service with up to three shared taxis than with a bus. When demands are higher, and greater substitution ratios would be required to accommodate them, a bus represents the cheaper option.

4C6 LAWRENCE, D.S. (1985) Helicopters and urban communities. *Transportation Quarterly*, **39** (1), pp. 5-16.

Examines the social costs and benefits of helicopter operations in urban areas from the point of view of the helicopter industry. Covers the financial and environmental costs and benefits of heliports, financial and other benefits to local business, and the land-use implications of heliport location.

4C7 OXLEY, P.R. (1980) Dial-a-ride: a review. *Transportation Planning and Technology*, **6**, pp. 141-148.

It is now almost 10 years since the first dial-a-ride bus service started operation in Mansfield, Ohio. This paper reviews 10 years experience and considers future prospects. Three generations of dial-a-ride system in the UK are discussed in detail (i) small scale, specialized demand; (ii) more ambitious systems, (iii) special systems in deeper rural areas providing access to higher order settlements.

4C8 SILCOCK, D.T. (1981) Urban paratransit in the developing world. *Transport Reviews*, **1** (2), pp. 151-168.

Many Western transport planners seem not to be aware, or choose to ignore, the fact that most developing countries have a variety of public transport systems, some carrying passengers numbered in millions per day. Generally these systems have 'just grown', rather than resulting from sophisticated transport plans. Whilst such evolution does not guarantee desirability in a social context, or ensure 'adequate' standards of safety, the transport systems which have evolved do seem to perform well with respect to local conditions and needs: it may well be that useful conclusions which will have implications for public transport in Western cities can be drawn from examining the 'unconventional' operations of the developing world. Many are privately owned and operated and almost all are commercially successful for their owners; the 'Jeepney' in the Philippines and the 'Public Light Bus' (PLB) in Hong Kong are well-known examples. This paper discusses such systems, attempts to identify their characteristics and compares these with more 'conventional' passenger transport modes.

4C9 SILCOCK, D.T. (1986) Bus or paratransit? The issues involved. *Transportation Planning and Technology*, **10** (6), pp. 305-322.

In many cities of the developing world substantial paratransit systems provide an important part of the transport infrastructure. Often these are seen as being in competition with bus services and proponents of one or other mode seek to demonstrate their advantages and to make a case for their sole use. This paper reviews the more important issues in the 'bus or paratransit?' debate, arguing that it is by no means clearcut. The pros and cons of each mode are discussed under the headings: economics and finance; management and productivity; regulation and control; operations; and the use of infrastructure. Evidence from a number of developing world cities is used to point to circumstances which appear to favour one mode or the other.

4C10 SUTTON, J.C. (1987a) Community transport service in the United Kingdom: a state-of-the-art review. *Journal of Specialised Transportation*, **2** (4), pp. 325-350.

The paper explores the development of community transport in the post-war era to the present day and examines their role within the hierarchy of passenger transport systems, focusing in particular on rural voluntary car services, urban community minibus projects and dial-a-ride schemes.
 See also: Sutton, J.C. (1988) *Transport Coordination and Social Policy*. Aldershot: Avebury.
Sutton J.C. (1987b) Transport innovation and passenger needs-changing perspectives on the role of Dial-a-Ride systems. *Transport Reviews*, **7** (2), pp. 167-182.

4C11 TEAL, R.F. and BERGLUND, M. (1987) The impacts of taxicab deregulation in the USA. *Journal of Transport Economics and Policy*, **21** (1), pp. 37–56.

Several large cities in the USA have deregulated their taxi industries. This paper analyses the results of deregulation and offers explanations, based on industrial organisation concepts, of why deregulation has largely failed to produce benefits for either consumers or providers.

See also: Teal, R.F., Goohve, R.E., Rooney, S.B. and Mortazavi, K. (1982) Taxi-based public transportation for the elderly and the handicapped. *Transportation Research Record*, 863, pp. 26–32.

4C12 US DEPARTMENT OF TRANSPORTATION (1982) *Paratransit: Options for the Future. The Overview Report*. Washington, DC: Technology Sharing Programme.

A synthesis of five earlier paratransit reports, this report includes an overview of the nature of paratransit services, the current experiences and state of the art of various paratransit alternatives, and possible future directions for these various service concepts. The evolution of various commuter ridersharing concepts, services for the elderly and handicapped, rural services, and suburban and community-scale systems are covered along with a brief contrast with the European experience. Providers of paratransit are discussed with special emphasis on the role of federal, state, and local governments. The report also includes some speculation on the future of paratransit, including factors that will influence the direction that paratransit will take, barriers to paratransit development, and future directions in providing paratransit services.

4C13 US DEPARTMENT OF TRANSPORTATION (1983) *Taxicab Regulation in U.S. Cities*. Washington, DC: Urban Mass Transportation Administration.

This two-volume publication is a detailed overview of the regulatory practices of cities around the country regarding taxicabs. It includes data from a telephone survey of some 120 cities, stratified by size, as well as a set of 10 case studies of cities that have enacted substantive taxicab regulatory changes. In the first volume changes in entry control, fare regulation, and administrative procedures for taxicabs are explored and the process of regulatory change in cities where taxicab regulation has been attempted is characterized. The second volume contains detailed case studies of Sacramento and Fresno, California; Tampa and St. Petersburg, Florida; Des Plaines, Illinios; Fayetteville and Charlotte, North Carolina; Dayton and Springfield, Ohio; and Madison, Wisconsin. The study revealed that most cities regulate both entry into the industry and fare levels and that relatively few cities have changed to deregulated environments.

4C14 VIJAYAKUMAR, S. (1986) Optimal vehicle size for road based urban public transport in developing countries. *Transport Reviews*, **6** (2), pp. 193–212.

The purpose of this paper is to review and critically assess current research work on urban public transport with particular reference to vehicle size in the context of Third World conditions. Road-based public transport in the cities of developing countries comes in a variety of physical and organizational forms. Many of these cities have a large component of unconventional or intermediate public transport (IPT). IPT often fills the gaps in service that cannot be provided by the operators of conventional public transport. The contrast in institutional framework between the operators of conventional vehicles and IPT is sharpened by the profitability of the two types; conventional buses, usually organized in large fleets and often run by the government, are seemingly difficult to maintain as a commercial enterprise whereas IPT which is usually privately owned in small fleets is profitable. A considerable debate has arisen over which type of public transport system (conventional or IPT) to encourage. The debate has often been confused because it involves two quite separate issues: whether the provision of public transport should be left entirely to private enterprise, and, the technical and economic benefits of different bus sizes. Size of vehicle is a particularly important issue in the developing world because vehicles of different size are in common use and are frequently in competition with one another.

4C15 VUCHIC, V.R. (1985) O-Bahn: description and evaluation of a new concept. *Transportation Research Record*, 1011, pp. 8–15.

The O-Bahn system, developed in the Federal Republic of Germany in recent years, consists of conventional diesel buses equipped with a special guidance mechanism that can be extended or retracted. The vehicles can thus run on regular streets or on special guideways that have two simple vertical guidance surfaces. The O-Bahn concept is intended to combine the advantages of low-investment bus operation on streets in low-density areas with the advantages of narrower right-of-way and greater highway safety of guided-mode operation on higher-density route sections. However, because the basic vehicle is the standard (or articulated) diesel bus, the most important advantages of guided modes – high-capacity vehicles, ability to form trains, electric traction with a number of superior aspects, and fail-safe running – are not captured. A systematic analysis of all characteristics shows that the O-Bahn is much more similar to semi-rapid bus (bus lines that use busways and other separated ways on individual sections) than to light rail transit (LRT). In comparison with the semi-rapid bus, the O-Bahn offers the advantages of narrower right-of-way, somewhat greater comfort and safety, guaranteed permanent retention of the exclusive right-of-way for buses only, and greater suitability (O-Bahn with dual-traction vehicles) for operation in tunnels. These advantages must be weighed against the higher investment cost and lower capacity and operating flexibility of the O-Bahn, which is due to the inability of O-Bahn vehicles to overtake or bypass each other on the guideway. The O-Bahn represents a higher cost, higher quality system than the semi-rapid bus, which may be advantageous for use in such special cases as areas with narrow rights-of-way. It is not suited for lines that require high-capacity, low-cost transit systems, which are typical of cities in developing countries.

4C16 WILLIAMS, D.J. (1981) Peak-load pricing: an urban transport case study. *Australian Road Research*, **11** (3), pp. 19-27.

The regulatory structure which exists for taxicab operation is similar throughout the major cities of the world. The periodic pricing framework is no exception with most cities using one of two systems: (a) the same fare structure operates whatever the time of day: or (b) users pay a surcharge when the cab is used in what can generally be described as the off-peak hours. This paper examines the taxicab industry as it exists in Melbourne, which has recently switched from the former to the latter system. The intuitively anomalous situation of higher off-peak fares is examined in the light of the difficulty in hiring cabs during peak hours in many major cities. Recourse to peak load pricing theory, and to the limited data available suggest that the decision to introduce higher off-peak tariffs may not have been well founded. The surcharge is unlikely to have improved the public's chances of hiring a taxicab during peak periods but has probably increased taxi supply at times when service was already satisfactory.

4D Cars

4D1 ADIV, A. (1982) Commuter's versus analyst's perception of automobile travel cost. *Transportation Research Record*, 980, pp. 18–24.

A study that attempts to narrow the gap between objective and perceptual measures of travel costs is discussed. The study is based on telephone interviews of working people in the San Francisco Bay Area, who reported at length their perception of automobile cost. In turn, their reports were compared with objective measures used in the calibration of travel demand models. The conclusion reached is that people perceive their costs of travel by car to be lower than that estimated in the analysis.

4D2 BAILEY, J.M. (1982) Comparative commuting costs: vanpooling, carpooling and driving alone. *Transportation Research Record*, 876, pp. 33–38.

The costs of alternative commuting modes are compared by developing and using models that recognize both time and travel costs. Vanpool survey data from the Baltimore region are used to calculate costs and find an equal-cost commuting distance beyond which vanpooling is cheaper than carpooling or driving alone. The distance is found to be approximately 18.5 miles for leased vanpools that provide front-door service and 30 miles for leased vanpools that pick up passengers at a few central places. However, front-door vanpools seem less workable for commuting distances beyond 30 miles. Equal-cost distance is shown to decrease, which makes vanpooling cost-effective for smaller commuting distances, as the result of various changes. These include increased fuel cost, and increase in the perceived cost of operating an automobile, employer subsidy, provision of tax rebates or free loans for purchases of vans, and elimination of free commuter parking. High-occupancy-vehicle lanes would encourage vanpooling but no more than other, less costly strategies. Lighter 7-passenger vans do not appear to be as cost-effective as 13-passenger vans. The decrease in equal-cost commuting distance with perceived value of time suggests that vanpooling should be attractive to lower-income workers if they were given an opportunity to join a vanpool.

4D3 BONSALL, P.W., SPENCER, A. and TANG, W.S. (1983) Ridesharing in Great Britain: performance and impact of the Yorkshare schemes. *Transportation Research*, **17A** (3), pp. 169–181.

Four organized car sharing schemes (the YORKSHARE schemes) were established and monitored in West Yorkshire between 1979 and 1981. Three of the schemes were based on employment sites and one on a residential suburb. Differences in site characteristics and in procedures allowed conclusions to be drawn as to the determinants of scheme performance and impact on the transport system. The proportion of the target population participating in new car sharing arrangements as a result of the YORKSHARE promotion varied from 2 per cent to less than 0.5 per cent. Impacts on car use for the work journey were minor and the main result was an abstraction of public transport users. The article also includes a detailed analysis of costs and benefits and comments on the proper role of ridesharing promotion within transport policy.

See also: Bonsall, P.W. (1981) Car sharing in the United Kingdom – a policy appraisal. *Journal of Transport Economics and Policy*, **15** (1), pp. 35–44.

Bonsall, P.W., Spencer, A.H. and Tang, W.S. (1984) What makes a car sharer? *Transportation*, **12** (2), pp. 117–145.

4D4 ELSE, P.K. (1984) Road pricing: some further comments. *Transportation Planning Technology*, **8** (4), pp. 295–300.

The author argues that the government's apparent lack of enthusiasm for road pricing systems stems as much from political considerations as the more technical problems of applying it. He shows that the value of time varies between different groups of traffic using the same congested road, bringing optimal road pricing problems. Also he suggests that queueing may have a role to play alongside conventional pricing.

See also: Else, P.K. (1981) A reformulation of the theory of optimal congestion taxes. *Journal of Transport Economics and Policy*, **15** (3), pp. 217-232.

4D5 EUROPEAN CONFERENCE OF MINISTERS OF TRANSPORT (1982) The future of the use of the car. Round Tables Report 55/56/57. Paris: ECMT.

This report is a compilation of three Round Tables on (i) the costs of using a car; (ii) forecasts of car ownership and use; and (iii) the relationships of changing car use to changing activity patterns in space and time. In the first Round Table analysis of the demand elasticities, generalized costs and travel budgets of car use are related to perceived costs. The effects of increasing petrol tax at the expense of vehicle tax is simulated. In the second Round Table there is a review of the methods used for predicting car ownership and use, a general approach to forecasting is suggested in addition to data comparability between countries. The third Round Table includes both a theoretical discussion of the factors operating within households and companies that influence spatial interaction; and a practical analysis of the spatial structures of urban areas. In the discussion in each of the three Round Tables it is concluded that the car has had a permissive role in the changes that have taken place in urban structure. Policies should now be developed to limit urban growth and certain proposals are made to achieve this aim.

4D6 FONG, P.K.W. (1985) Issues of the electronic road pricing system in Hong Kong. *Transportation Planning and Technology*, **10** (1), pp. 29-41.

This paper attempts to examine the issues relating to the experiment of the world's first pilot scheme of Electronic Road Pricing System in Hong Kong. A brief review of theories of road pricing and a description of the technical components as well as an analysis on the social, economic, political and environmental impacts of the system are given. It intended to generate further research and analysis of the system's applicability in tackling urban traffic congestion problems.

4D7 FORKENBROCK, D.J. and HOEFER, C.A. (1983) Variable motor fuel taxes: problems and prospects. *Transportation Quarterly*, **31** (1), pp. 23-40.

A variety of ways of restructuring motor fuel taxation and a means of providing finance for the road system are examined. The authors look in particular at methods of indexing such taxes and assess each method using data from Iowa.

4D8 GAJ, S., POLITANO, A. and GOLDBERG, L. (1983) Local financing opportunities for urban highway transportation improvements. *Transportation Research Record*, 900, pp. 39-42.

Highways in the United States are at a turning point because of their condition and the cost to repair or replace them. Local public funds for highway construction and repair are not keeping pace with inflation due to reduced purchases of fuel and in some cases constraints on state and local funding, i.e. property tax limits. This paper addresses the funding dilemma by focusing on local financing, including sources of funding, the use of such funds, the range of opportunities for additional sources, and an evaluation of their merits. Based on a review of funding sources and their advantages and disadvantages, the authors conclude that while there are newly emerging sources such as toll financing, private financing, severance taxes, and others, the suitability of a specific source will necessarily vary. This is because each area has a unique financing philosophy and unique physical characteristics.

4D9 GOODWIN, P.B. and MOGRIDGE, M.J.H. (1982) The distance travelled by second cars. *Traffic Engineering and Control* **23** (12), pp. 600-604.

This paper discusses qualitative and quantitative evidence on the nature of second car ownership and use and how this varies with the ownership and use of first household cars. Differences emerging between first and second household cars are related to the method presently used for estimating kilometres per car by the Department of Transport.

4D10 GREENING, P.A.K. and JACKSON, R.L. (1984) Pooling for the journey to work: the outlook in Great Britain. *Transportation*, **12** (1), pp. 97-116.

This paper considers the potential for bus, minibus and car pooling in Great Britain, drawing both on relevant theoretical and economic studies, and on practical operational experience. It concludes that under reasonable assumptions about the transport situation in the next decade or so, pooling could become increasingly useful for solving the travel problems of individual local groups, but that it is unlikely to become a major mode in terms of the numbers of trips carried. The effects of recent legislative changes are discussed, and the justification for further change assessed. Relevant comparisons are made with the United States.

4D11 HENSHER, D.A. (1984) The automobile and the future: some issues. *Transport Policy and Decision-Making*, **2** (2), pp. 123–128.

The automobile has been central to debates on the future of oil-based societies in which economic progress is believed to be heavily dependent on a healthy industrial base, with the state of the auto industry an indicator of the overall condition of this sector. The effect of the OPEC cartel and the successful implant of Japanese cars in the domestic markets of North America, Europe, Britain and Australasia have transformed a highly predictable transport sector into one of great uncertainties and great potential. Nine years have elapsed since the initial OPEC price rises, sufficient time to begin to assess the influence of energy and other factors on the auto industry and on the demands by households and businesses for types of vehicles and the use thereof. This article discusses the future of the automobile in the light of the special emphasis being directed to the auto industry, fuel options, and consumer energy conservation.

4D12 HENSHER, D.A. (1986) Dimensions of automobile demand: an overview of an Australian research project. *Environment and Planning A*, **18**, pp. 1339–1374.

The major objective of the study of the dimensions of automobile demand (1981–1988) is to obtain reliable forecasts of the variables which drive the fundamental energy equation: energy consumed (litres) equals efficiency of technology (litres per 100 kilometres) times utilization rate (kilometres per period). Since the level of utilization is unlikely to be independent of the state of technology, and since both dimensions are conditioned by the state of the economy and the nature of households as well as by the extent of corporate-sector support to the household sector, it is necessary to view the levels of vehicle usage and vehicle fuel efficiency as outputs of the broader household decision process. This paper provides an overview of the theoretical, methodological, and empirical dimensions of the project including the broader context in which household decisions are made. The analysis is dynamic in that it examines the process of household vehicle acquisition and use over a five-year period (1981-85).

4D13 KHAN, M.A. and WILLUMSEN, L.G. (1986) Modelling car ownership and use in developing countries. *Traffic Engineering and Control*, **27** (11), pp. 554-560.

This paper explores the car ownership modelling needs for transport planning in developing countries and argues that these needs are essentially different from those of the developed world. The difference lies in the fact that in many developing countries car ownership is seen not only as a factor affecting the demand for roads, but also as a policy variable in itself. Car ownership should not be seen as an exogenous planning variable, but as part of the transport planning process - it should be a policy option.

4D14 LEE, L.W. (1984) The economics of car pools. *Economic Inquiry*, **22** (1), pp. 128-135.

This paper presents a theory of car pooling which shows how the separate parts of a work trip enter into the decision to participate. It examines how the size of the car pool is related to petrol prices, wage rates, speed limits and other factors. Proposals designed to promote car pools may also have unforeseen effects on overall fuel consumption.

4D15 LEVINSON, H.S., REGAN, E.J. and LESSIEU, E.J. (1980) Estimating behavioural response to peak period pricing. *Transportation Research Record*, 767, pp. 21-26.

The concept of applying peak-period pricing policies to highways and other urban transportation facilities has been proposed as one means of reducing rush-hour congestion and compensating for the social costs of travel. This research was designed to assess the potential impacts of rush-hour pricing on the six toll bridges and tunnels between New York City and New Jersey that are operated by the Port Authority of New York and New Jersey. Several options were identified, including ridesharing, transit, and time-of-day shift. To avoid higher toll charges, the average motorist would react in the following order of preference: (a) switch to another crossing; (b) switch time of travel; (c) switch to transit; (d) travel less often or not at all; and (e) join a car pool.

4D16 MCCOOMB, L.A. and STEUART, G.N. (1981) The automobile passenger – a forgotten mode. *Transportation Research*, **15A**, pp. 257–261.

Current practices in urban transportation planning tend to neglect the automobile passenger. This study shows that a large number of urban trips are made as an automobile passenger and that the general characteristics of these passengers are similar to transit passengers rather than automobile drivers. The significance of these findings are discussed in terms of modelling the use of various urban travel modes.

4D17 MACE, S. (1986) National policy towards cars: Hong Kong, *Transport Reviews*, **6** (2), pp. 173–191.

The Hong Kong transport policy objective is simply mobility. With this the automobile must conform. A confined land area, difficult to develop, has absorbed excessive immigration and must now service a dynamic entrepreneurial economy. Transport infrastructure based on major planning studies is created through government capital and is backed by careful legislation, effective administration and private sector participation. The problem is that overall expansion is even faster: widespread urban renewal – roads cannot equally expand; enormous New Territories New Towns – people still want to move in and out so the need for more transport accelerates. Over ten million trips daily are made by 5.5 million people. The answers cannot be more and more private cars: it must be promoting the most effective use of major transport investments, where possible off roads, and the mass carriers on roads. The need to curb congestion by containing escalating car numbers (especially as so far only 17 per cent of households have access to an automobile) led in May 1982 to imposition of severe taxes on ownership. The ultimate and equitable objective is to control usage. Road pricing may be the answer. In

Hong Kong the private car is part only of a complex strategy including metro, rail, bus, minibus, ferry, taxi and tram. The car cannot take precedence.

4D18 MCSHANE, M.P., KOSHI, M. and LUNDIN, O. (1984) Public policy towards the automobile: a comparative look at Japan and Sweden. *Transportation Research A*, **18** (2), pp. 97–109.

This article compares two different national approaches to regulation and promotion of the automobile. It examines how the problem was perceived, what styles of intervention developed, and how implementation of seemingly standardized solutions differed. Japan tended to view the private automobile as a socially expensive luxury until quite recently. Some features of its policy response, e.g. low spending on roads, high motor vehicle taxes, flow from this outlook. Other aspects, such as the effective mass public safety campaigns, and the coordination between industrial and regulatory policies flow from Japan's social and cultural patterns. Sweden's policies are aimed at 'civilizing' the car, not restricting it. They tended to develop in a relatively straightforward manner on the basis of an underlying social consensus, as contrasted with the adversarial approach common in the US.

4D19 MANNERING, F.L. (1983) An econometric analysis of vehicle use in multi-vehicle households. *Transportation Research*, **17A** (3), pp. 183–189.

The significance of the multi-vehicle household in the US has increased substantially in recent years to the point where over 80 per cent of household vehicles holdings are owned by multi-vehicle households. Despite this fact, traditional travel demand models have not explored the determinants of individual vehicle use in such households, even though knowledge of vehicle usage allocations within household fleets is critical to subsequent fuel consumption forecasts. This paper presents a discussion of vehicle use in multi-vehicle households and then develops an appropriate modelling specification. The specification consists of a simultaneous equation system which is estimated using a sample of two-vehicle households from a recently conducted national survey.

4D20 NEWELL, J. (1987) The morning commute for nonidentical travellers. *Transportation Science*, **21** (2), pp. 74–88.

In previous theories of the morning rush hour, travellers with different work starting times are assumed to attach certain values to queueing delay and schedule delay (deviations from their work starting times), the same values for all travellers. The goal was to establish and evaluate a stable assignment of trip starting times such that no individual traveller can find a more desirable time than the one assigned. This theory is extended here to situations in which different travellers may attach different values to these delays. For a certain class of cost models it is shown that there is still a stable assignment but it is dictated by only a certain fraction of travellers who are most willing to be early or late for work. Other travellers will choose to be at work on time. The queueing pattern is significantly different from that of the previous theories.

4D21 ORGANISATION FOR ECONOMIC COOPERATION AND DEVELOPMENT (1985) *Coordinated Urban Transport Pricing*. Paris: OECD.

The study reviews member countries' urban transport goals and then presents trends in the structure, use and financial performance of urban transport systems. Theoretical approaches to pricing are covered and related to actual pricing practices in public and private transport, and pricing coordination.

4D22 OWENS, D.D. (1981) Ridesharing programmes: governmental response to urban transportation problems. *Environment and Behaviour*, **13** (3), pp. 311–330.

The objective of this paper is to summarize the development of the government sponsored series of community based ridersharing schemes introduced after the fuel crisis in 1974. It attempts to assess the characteristics of successful schemes so that suggestions can be made to improve the effectiveness of new schemes.

4D23 RALSTON, B.A. and BARBER, G.M. (1984) Taxation and optimal road penetration. *Geographical Analysis*, **16** (4), pp. 313–330.

Three road financing methods that could be used by an authority faced with specifying an optimal road penetration policy are examined. Each taxation scheme leads to differing levels of benefits and patterns of spatial development. The optimal tax type and rate are dependent on the level of road penetration, the stability and spatial structure of the market, and the degree of technological change.

4D24 RICHARDSON, A.J. and YOUNG, W. (1981) Spatial relationship between carpool members' trip ends. *Transportation Research Record*, 823, pp. 1-7.

The potential for carpool formation is a function of the density of common trip ends, both spatially and temporally. It is also a direct function of the deviation from a direct route that carpool drivers will tolerate in order to pick up and deliver carpool passengers. This paper examines the spatial relationships between the origins and destinations of carpool trip lengths, passenger pickup and delivery radii and deviations, total deviations from a direct route, and deviations as a function of the direct route distance for the carpool driver. Data for this study were obtained by means of roadside questionnaire surveys at 20 sites in the metropolitan area of Melbourne, Australia.

4D25 SCHOU, K. (1980) Company cars: characteristics and energy conservation potential. *Transport Policy and Decision Making*, **1** (4), pp. 349-360.

This paper reports on a study of the characteristics of company cars in Australia, and the possible impacts of selective energy conservation policies on company car fleets. The fundamental proposition is that the company car sector offers a considerable potential for energy conservation through changes to smaller, more fuel-efficient cars. Company cars constitute a very important share of the new car market, and they tend to be larger, less fuel-efficient types of cars, travel longer distances, and be of more recent vintage than private cars. Responses of companies to a range of policy scenarios indicate that the policies considered would have negligible impacts on the overall demand for company cars, but that the shift to smaller cars would be substantial. The characteristics of companies and fleets were found to have very significant effects on the policy responses.

4D26 SPENCER, A.H. and CHIA, L.S. (1985) National policy towards cars: Singapore. *Transport Reviews*, **5** (4) pp. 301-323.

Singapore has experienced rapid growth in car ownership, and private transport accounts for just under half of motorized trips in

Singapore. Yet only since 1970 have determined efforts been made to curtail this increase. Simultaneously with this growth, Singapore's land-use planners had called for the diversion of population growth into outlying residential estates while maintaining the central area's importance as an employment centre. The resulting anticipated concentration of commuter movement suggested a need for controls to restrain car ownership, reduce central-area congestion and divert road users on to public transport. The policies followed are described. Those against ownership have included heavy road taxes and registration fees, with a system of discounts on the latter to discourage new purchasers except when replacing scrapped cars. Policies against car use include fuel taxes and the Area Licensing Scheme in the city centre, while parking space is also closely regulated. The measures adopted imply a goal of efficiency in promoting Singapore's planning objectives rather than environmental, safety or equity considerations, although the first two of these have lately received much more attention than formerly. The policies' effect has been a temporary reversal in the growth of car ownership, but this growth has since resumed and recent further fee increases suggest a panic reaction rather than a coordinated strategy. Such coordination appears at present to be hampered by the fragmented administration of matters relating to transport. Other measures relating to car ownership and use in Singapore are also described.

4D27 SVIDEN, O. (1983) Automobile usage in a future information society. *Futures*, **15** (6), pp. 478–490.

The information society provides a challenge for the future of the automobile. This article, based on a two-year Swedish study as part of the Massachusetts Institute of Technology Future of the Automobile Programme, used four scenarios against which to predict the future of the car in Sweden. It concludes that, overall, information technologies will not substitute for travel, only for the information carried on paper; rather, future moves towards increasingly dispersed living will keep car usage high.

4D28 TEAL, R.F. (1987) Carpooling: who, how and why? *Transportation Research*, **21A** (3), pp. 203–214.

Carpooling is the commuting mode of 18 to 20 per cent of American workers, but relatively little definitive information has been available on who carpools, how and why. Based on data from the 1977-78 Nationwide Personal Transportation Survey, this paper analyses the characteristics of carpoolers, distinguishes among different types of carpoolers, identifies the key differences between carpoolers and drive alone and transit commuters, describes how commuters carpool, and offers explanations of why commuters carpool. The paper also addresses the issue of the feasibility of a substantial increase in carpool mode share.

4D29 WACHS, M. (1981) Pricing urban transportation: a critique of current policy. *Journal of the American Planning Association*, **47** (3), pp. 243-251.

Recent increases in the price of petrol have influenced urban travel, but have reduced car travel volumes only slightly. This has occurred because the price of petrol is only a small part of the total price of car travel. Incentives to car use, such as free parking at the work place, still make it an attractive option for most commuters. Pricing policy can be used to influence urban travel patterns, but uncoordinated pricing of transit and car alternatives merely corrects for inefficient and inequitable subsidies to one mode by adding inequitable and inefficient subsidies to others. As a result, all urban transport modes are underpriced, and together they continue to encourage suburbanisation and increasing travel volumes.

4D30 WHITELEGG, J. (1984) The company car in the United Kingdom as an instrument of transport policy. *Transport Policy and Decision Making*, **2** (3), pp. 219-230.

A company car in the UK is a fringe benefit conferring great advantages on employer and employee alike. Approximately 70 per cent of all new cars sold in the UK are purchased by companies under very advantageous taxation arrangements. The system of support for the company car, it is argued, is a major transport policy in its own right and one which confounds policy in other areas and contributes to problems of energy resource depletion and social inequalities in the distribution of transport resources. The paper examines the context of company car support in the UK and argues that a study of the company car demonstrates that a transport analysis must be based on an understanding of the wider social and economic environment.

4D31 WHITELEGG, J. (1987) A geography of road traffic accidents. *Transactions of the Institute of British Geographers New Series*, **12** (2), pp. 161–176.

There is a limit to the effectiveness of traditional measures for reducing accidents, particularly as those that reduce accidents among car occupants sometimes seem to increase them among children and other pedestrians. The author argues that since the movement of vehicles and pedestrians is a function of the land-use pattern, a geographical analysis of accidents might identify some novel approaches to their prevention. He looks at the spatial distribution of accidents in the UK, including variations between counties and between urban and rural areas, and considers the need for more study of accident rates in housing layouts of different types, and in towns which have adopted low-fare policies for public transport. He highlights the problem of child casualties.

4E Freight transport

4E1 BOHLANDER, G.W. and FARRIS, M.T. (1984) Collective bargaining in trucking – the effects of deregulation. *Logistics and Transportation Review*, **20** (3), pp. 223–238.

This paper discusses the labour-management structure, concessionary bargaining, and the Teamsters union. The structure of negotiations has moved away from a predominantly national pattern to an emphasis on regional and local bargaining and there have been substantial modifications in labour agreements. Contract changes have also caused a new relationship between labour and management, and this has lead to some instability in the freight industry.

4E2 EUROPEAN CONFERENCE OF MINISTERS OF TRANSPORT (1985) Changes in transport users' motivations for modal choice: Freight transport. Report of the 69th Round Table, Paris: ECMT.

This report includes four background papers from Austria, West Germany, the Netherlands and Sweden in addition to a report of the discussions held. The papers set out the factors that determine overall choice, especially from a logistics point of view. Modal choice is only relevant to a limited sector of goods transport demand. Industrial restructuring and changes in the siting of activities are changing the freight modal split in favour of road transport or combined road/rail transport. Shippers are now taking increasing account of qualitative factors in addition to comparative costs when choosing transport modes. Modal choice is sensitive to the overall cycle of manufacture, warehousing and packaging; the optimal transport system may include several modes. Where transport costs are high, these may be offset by productivity gains elsewhere in the production/distribution cycle.

The Round Table studied the respective capabilities of road and rail to meet logistic requirements. Past policies for influencing modal split have not led to conclusive results; modes must better respond to market needs by easing regulations on road transport and by concentrating the supply of rail services on links with high traffic potential and with improved operational flexibility.

4E3 LEUTZBACH, W. (ed.) (1987) Urban goods movement. *Transport Policy and Decision Making*, **3** (2).

This journal issue contains seven papers on urban freight movement. Papers discuss the variety of ways in which the conflicts between urban freight and other aspects of urban travel can be resolved. Eckstein discusses the role of goods distribution centres on the urban fringe. Stienstra outlines Dutch experiences of handling goods deliveries to city centres. Other papers by Hedges, Pernica and Sonntag discuss a number of transport system models to assist with the development of urban freight policies.

4E4 OGDEN, K.W. (1984) A framework for urban freight policy analysis. *Transportation Planning and Technology*, **8** (4), pp. 253-265.

A framework for the supply and demand analysis of urban freight is developed, and within that structure particular aspects are analysed. Seven main instruments related to public policy are described together with their application – taxes and subsidies, regulations, investment, operational instruments, planning, public ownership and research. A higher profile for urban freight transport is required and there are a range of relevant policy instruments available.

See also: Ogden, K.W. and Bowyer, D.P. (1985) Directions for urban freight transport research in Australia. *Transportation Research Record*, 1038, pp. 51-58.

4E5 OGDEN, K.W. (1985) Shore based shipping costs: the urban freight component. *Transport Policy and Decision Making*, **3** (2), pp. 181-198.

Shore-based shipping costs are an important factor in overall freight transport costs for an island continent such as Australia. The author examines in detail the problems of moving freight in Australian cities, particularly in port areas, with comment on potential conflicts between freight and passenger transport. He concludes with suggestions for traffic management, road construction and other strategies to reduce freight costs.

4F Walking and cycling

4F1 GUY, C.M. and WRIGLEY, N. (1987) Walking trips to shops in British cities: an empirical review and policy re-examination. *Town Planning Review*, **58** (1), pp. 63-79.

This paper examines the behaviour and needs of the large majority of British shoppers who regularly, or occasionally, carry out walking trips for convenience shopping. Characteristics of walking trips to shops are summarized from previously published sources and from a major survey carried out in Cardiff in 1982. These analyses indicate that walking trips play a dominant role in the routine shopping behaviour of many households and that many shops gain most of their trade from such trips. The implications for local planning, particularly concerning the role of district shopping centres and 'convenience stores', are discussed.

4F2 HARLAND, D.G., JACOBY, R.G. and PICKERING, D. (1986) Footways used by cyclists and pedestrians. *Traffic Engineering and Control*, **27** (5), pp. 283-287.

This paper describes a study of 10 footways converted to shared use. The study included an examination of the process of conversion, user counts, an analysis of user behaviour and interview surveys of users. Cyclists using the carriageway instead of the converted footways and the occupiers of adjoining properties were also interviewed. While only a third of all the cyclists counted used the converted footways, about three-quarters of the child cyclists (the most vulnerable cyclists) did use them. No serious conflicts between pedestrians and cyclists were observed and the majority of footway-users thought that the sharing arrangements were satisfactory. An analysis of the flows on these footways and other shared facilities suggested that footways separated from the carriageway by a barrier or wide verge can carry combined flows of 180 persons per hour per metre width.

4F3 HERZ, R.K. (1985) The use of the bicycle. *Transportation Planning Technology*, **9** (4), pp. 311–328.

The author reports research in West Germany to investigate the influence upon bicycle use of such factors as age, education, car availability, residential density, size of town, topography and time of year. He identifies those groups of people with the greatest cycle usage potential and suggests policies which could activate that potential.

4F4 HUDSON, M., LEVY, C., NICHOLSON, A.J., MACRORY, R. and SNELSON, P. (1982) *Bicycle Planning Policy and Practice*. London: Architectural Press.

Transport planners have an increasing requirement for information detailing the planning and implementation of cycle policy which this book provides. The initial chapters are concerned with the development of policies and plans for bicycle networks. This is followed by an examination of current bicycle use and how bicycle surveys should be carried out. The next section deals with the question of the safety of bicycling, arguably the most important disincentive to bicycle use, since this is the factor that can most easily be influenced by the efforts of engineers and planners. This is followed by sections dealing with the actual layout of bicycle routes from an engineering point of view, including aspects such as road signs and bicycle parking facilities. Education and enforcement are two areas of bicycle planning that tend to be overlooked and these are covered in the next sections. The penultimate chapter deals with monitoring and evaluation questions pointing out the criteria, particularly those unique to cycle schemes, that need to be included in an evaluation exercise. The final chapter deals with legal aspects in the United Kingdom and the United States and attempts to give answers to such important questions as: is a bicycle to be regarded as a vehicle?

4F5 MITCHELL, C.G.B. and STOKES, R.G.F. (1982) Walking as a mode of transport. Transport and Road Research Laboratory, Report 1064. Crowthorne: TRRL.

Walking as a mode of transport differs from all other transport modes. Less than 3 per cent of the population cannot go out on foot. Furthermore, virtually all travel by any mode involves some walking at the beginning and end of the journey. This report uses data from the National Travel Survey and many other sources to examine patterns of travel on foot, both as a main mode and for access to other modes, and reviews those aspects of the environment that cause difficulties for pedestrians. There has been relatively little previous study of walkers and of the purposes of walk journeys, and this report is intended to provide as complete a picture of the use of this mode as can be done at the present time. The report provides information on the frequency, length and purpose of walk trips, on the social characteristics of walkers, and on walking access to other modes. Such information assists those planning for pedestrians and for access to transport systems.

4F6 NATIONAL CONSUMER COUNCIL (1987) *What's Wrong with Walking?* London: HMSO.

This report is on the maintenance and safety of footways, and among its recommendations are proposals for new national standards, pedestrian units in local authorities which would prepare 'movement' plans, enforcement of bans on pavement parking and a comprehensive system of cycleways created from road space, not the pavement.

4F7 SENEVIRATNE, P.N. (1985) Acceptable walking distances in central areas. *Journal of Transportation Engineering*, **111** (4), pp. 365-376.

Pedestrian walking distances in a central business district are mostly dependent on the arrival mode in that central district and the layout of the transport network. A set of characteristics that influence the distribution of walking distances are identified and the 'critical' distance is determined. This distance is related to an individual's propensity to walk.

4F8 SENEVIRATNE, P.N. and MORRALL, J.F. (1985*a*) Analysis of factors affecting the choice of route of pedestrians. *Transportation Planning and Technology*, **10**, pp. 147-159.

Pedestrians as compared to vehicular traffic enjoy a high degree freedom of movement even in heavily congested areas. Consequently, there are more alternative links available to pedestrians between a given origin-destination (O-D) pair. This paper describes a study done by the University of Calgary to evaluate the factors affecting the choice of route on intra-CBD trips or trips within the Central Business District (CBD). An origin destination survey conducted in downtown Calgary, Alberta enabled the identification of the most significant factors influencing the choice. These factors were analysed in relation to the physical characteristics of the location, personal characteristics of the trip maker and the type of the trip. It appears that most people chose the shortest link and factors such as the level of congestion, safety or visual attractions were only secondary. This suggests that the length should be made a major consideration when planning and designing pedestrian links.

See also: Seneviratne, P.N. and Morrall, J.P. (1985*b*) Level of service on pedestrian facilities. *Transportation Quarterly*, **39** (1), pp. 109–123.

4F9 SMITH, J. (1985) Pedestrianisation – shopping streets in Scotland. *The Planner*, **72** (5), pp. 12–16.

A review of the range and extent of pedestrianized shopping streets in Scotland is presented. Details of each scheme is given for the pre implementation to the post implementation stages and each type is classified along with comments on the environmental after effects.

4F10 STEWART, G. and MIHALCIN, E. (1983) The walk to work trip in downtown Toronto. *Transportation Quarterly*, **37** (4), 623–633.

Generally, little attention has been given to the walk to work component of peak-period commuter travel. This, perhaps, reflects the fact that in most large North American cities walk to work trips represent only a small fraction of total commuter trips. However, the Council of the City of Toronto approved, as part of its 1976 Central Area Plan, a policy of promoting more housing development in the Central Area in order to achieve, among other things, the provision of more homes closer to the growing Downtown office employment sector. It was hoped this strategy would contribute to a reduction in trip lengths and travel times, an increase in walk to work trips, and a more balanced, two-way use of transportation facilities. This article presents the results of that policy to date and possible extensions to it.

4F11 WIGAN, M.R. (1984) Bicycle ownership, use and exposure: participation and activity patterns in Melbourne, Australia. *Transportation Research*, **18A** (5/6), pp. 379-398.

The users of bicycles are usually assumed to be children. The data collected in transportation studies are, therefore, of great value as they are sufficiently extensive to be used for a broader analysis of this question than would ever be possible in a special bicycle survey. Most bicycle surveys are aimed closely at schools, so that the concentrated traffic known to move to and from schools can be used to pinpoint other origins and destinations of these journeys. This paper reports a systematic analysis of bicycle access, usage and exposure for households of different compositions and people of different ages, based on transport survey home interview data from Melbourne (Australia) in 1978. Time profiles of involvement in cycling and other modes are presented for Melbourne, and comparisons are drawn with similar results from Adelaide. A key feature of this analysis is the decomposition of 'trip rates' into participation rates and the corresponding activity rates (i.e. trips) of those who participate at all in the specified mode or activity. This technique is shown to have considerable potential.

4F12 YANG, J.M. (1985) Bicycle traffic in China. *Transportation Quarterly*, **39** (1), pp. 93-107.

China not only houses the largest population, but also the world's largest fleet of bicycles. Bicycles are the principal and most often used means of private transport in this eastern Asian nation. In fact, the bicycle plays an important transport role in all developing countries. Bikes have many advantages: low initial cost, low operating expense, small space needs for operating and storing, and flexibility to go where other vehicles cannot. Bicycles are especially advantageous in China where city mass transit systems are often inadequate for meeting urban travel demands. Used as a primary means of transport by large numbers of urban inhabitants, bicycles are a mixed blessing, having advantages as well as serious disadvantages. Like some of the adverse impacts of motor vehicle traffic, bicycles contribute to street congestion and noise (bicycle bells), interfere with pedestrian and other vehicular movements, and are the cause of many street accidents. If urban transportation in China is to be improved, the best place to start is with the use and misuse of bicycles. This article describes bicycle traffic in China and suggests measures to improve bicycle use in the overall transport mix.

See also: Ying, L.J. (1987) Management of bicycling in urban areas. *Transportation Quarterly*, **41** (4), pp. 619–629.

5 Methods and evaluation

5A Theoretical frameworks

Transport planning has evolved over the last thirty years, but with no clear theoretical foundations. Everyone is aware of the problems created by increased demand for transport and most effort has been directed at finding methods of analysis with a practical, usually quantitative output. This has meant that analysis has been empirical and positivist in its approach.

Initial developments were concerned with aggregate analysis and the efficiency of overall movement of people and goods (Hutchinson [5A10]). The central problem tackled in the classic four-stage modelling process was the analysis of the current situation and prediction of future demand so the obstacles to the free flow of traffic could be eliminated. When resources became more limited, evaluation methods ensured that value for money was obtained (Allen [5A1]). These analysis methods tended to be reactive and their output tended to specify the well known and even reinforce the present system.

In the 1970s there was an increased concern over the distribution of costs and benefits from transport decisions, and the realization that the objectives of transport policy cannot be summarized by selected performance criteria, but that there are different and often competing objectives. Economic based theory became more important with the application of the notions of supply and demand, pricing and costs, and cost benefit analysis to transport issues. These methods together with those 'borrowed' from other disciplines have formed the basis of transport policy and planning analysis. The individual choice decision is conceptualized as a utility maximization procedure where the individual maximizes his own utility given the availability of a set of alternatives and a series of personal and system constraints.

Other approaches to analysis have been explored, but have not replaced the established methods, and there seems to be a certain reluctance to using them (Jones et al. [5A11]). Included here are approaches based on the notions of constraint rather than choice. The two best known are the activity based approaches and those based on time geography. Each considers travel as a derived demand, as a means to gain accessibility, and not an end in itself. Consequently, the complexities of travel are recognized, and constraints operating on the individual, the household and the destination are all included. Travel is seen as one part of a complex set of activities which are in turn moderated by differences in lifestyle. Conceptualization of travel is based on accessibility and not mobility.

Recently, debates have been initiated on a range of potentially interesting theoretical issues. Dynamic and longitudinal frameworks for analysis (Layzell et al. [5A16]) may have much to offer to our understanding of travel and transport; concepts of time budgets and the temporal stability in travel again raise basic questions on the way travel should be analysed (Kostyniuk and Kitamura [5A13], Huff and Hanson [5A9], Wigan and Morris [5A24], Zahavi [5A25]); the choices of route and the mode for commuting journeys and the trade off between alternatives (Mogridge and Holden [5A17]); and the increasing number of critiques of current practice (Atkins [5A2], Heggie [5A7], Supernak [5A22]). However, this critique is primarily methodological and not theoretical. Transport researchers have tended to avoid a fundamental theoretical self-analysis in favour of improving existing methods.

5B Analysis methods

A tremendous amount of effort has been expended on the analysis of travel demand, and much of this work has been haphazard with a variety of inputs but little assessment or review of the output. The vast array of research can be grouped into three blocks.

The first is concerned with establishing empirical relationships within data sets and between data sets. It also covers the range of survey methods available and the use of statistical packages, many based on analysis of variance techniques. Most traditional studies have involved the collection and analysis of cross sectional data, and this is still the most commonly used survey tool (Ampt et al. [5B2]). Much of the categorical data analysis has been carried out through the use of linear models and a variety of means for the segmentation of the population into groups with a common set of characteristics. Example of work include car ownership models (Ben-Akiva et al. [5B8]), car use models (Horowitz and Daganzo [5B37]) and time use studies (Neale and Hutchinson [5B52]). More recently, methods have been developed to update available data, to allow for the transfer of parameters from one data set to another, and to expand data sets with partial information. The best example here is the work of Willumsen [5B76] in deriving origin destination matrices from traffic counts. Other types of data sets include before and after surveys and a whole battery of longitudinal data collection methods including panel and diary survey. Longitudinal data allows change to be examined over time with many of the sources of variation being controlled (Hensher [5B34]).

The second group includes the extensive literature on models of travel demand and behaviour. Travel demand has traditionally been examined through statistical methods or analogies (such as the gravity model). More recent work has placed demand analysis firmly on an economic base through the concepts of discrete choice and random utility theory (Barnard [5B7], Kanafani [5B39], Williams [5B75]). Choice based analysis has recently been extended through the debate over models based on revealed preference or on stated preference, and the use of micro simulation to represent particular situations (Gensch [5B32], Mannering and Hensher [5B48]).

As a complement to the notions of choice, some research has focused on constraints as the means to determine behaviour. Here it is realized that not everyone has unconstrained choice and that constraints vary between individuals, between modes of transport and by time of day. Activity frameworks have been used for analysis, and much of the research is qualitative in approach (Forer and Kivell [5B31], Pas [5B57], Jones et al. [5A11]). To complete the picture on modelling behaviour, there is also an increasing literature on industrial and retail location decisions, organizational linkages between firms, the impact of technological innovation on production and distribution methods, and marketing strategies (Horowitz [5B36]).

The final group is the macro-level analysis of transport, urban structure and economic development. This research includes traditional studies of the links between land use and transport, but it is now being extended to include the examination of the impact of transport on the local economy, land values, employment and the economic base of an urban area (Anas [5B4], Berechman and Paaswell [5B10], Bland [5B12], Mackett [5B45], Putman [5B59], Wilson et al. [5B77]). Economic models are being used to examine both the supply of and demand for public transport, and how systems should operate within a deregulated market. Studies have also been carried out on methods of subsidy allocation, the effects of fares and service level changes on demand, and the likely impact of technological change on the demand for travel (Evans [5B30], Koppelman [5B43], Obeng [5B54], and Section 4A). Other city wide analysis has applied equilibrium models to particular aspects of the urban system such as trip generation, travel speeds and trip timings (Ardekani and Herman [5B5], Boyce and Kim [5B16]).

As noted at the outset, the range of methods is vast and new ones are continually being added to the list as researchers explore new issues or search other disciplines for appropriate methods. However, compared with other fields of urban analysis, the level of critical appraisal is limited even though many examples of poor analysis and implementation come from the transport sector. Analysis has concentrated on the product and not the process.

5C Investment appraisal and evaluation

Choices have to be made about what projects should be financed. Economic evaluation (Standing Advisory Committee on Trunk Road Assessment [2A24]) is only a partial assessment, and requires traffic forecasts and assumptions on the value of time (Atkins [5C1]). Decisions are based on net present values and the first year rate of return. Each particular problem should have a statement of objectives, the identification of road and public transport problems, the development of a series of feasible options, and an economic evaluation with an assessment of environmental and social impacts.

Evaluation should include both road and public transport solutions, and analysis should take place together. In the past this has often been undertaken separately (Beesley *et al*. [5C2], Dodgson and Topham [5C5]) even though cost benefit criteria have been used in both cases. In urban public transport, cost benefit criteria have been used to appraise both the level of bus service provision and to justify public transport subsidy.

Slightly different approaches have been adopted in developing countries where the main savings are in vehicle operating costs, not time savings, and the reduction in accident levels are often significant (Dickey and Miller [5C4], Hills and Jones-Lee [5C7]). However, in the urban context the development impacts are minor when compared with those associated with rural roads.

A range of non-economic evaluation methods have been used, and these include multi-criteria analysis (Janarthanan and Schneider [5C8]), matrix approaches (Standing Advisory Committee on Trunk Road Appraisal [2A24]), social impact analysis (Wilson and Neff [5C24]), and dynamic programming (Schnuerer [5C18]). Other research has focused on particular issues where there are no established procedures; for example the notion of uncertainty in evaluation (Pearman [5C14]), and appropriate pricing mechanisms for charging for congested urban road space (Niskanen [5C11], Sharp *et al*. [5C20]).

5D Energy

Transport is the only sector where there has been an increase in oil consumption (Banister and Banister [5D1]). Short-term savings have been made through a variety of measures, but pricing and taxation are still the principal means by which demand is controlled (Horowitz [5D9]). In real terms the price of petrol has been reduced, and this is despite the significant increases in the costs of oil from the producers in 1973 and 1979 (Dunkerley and Hoch [5D5]) and the short-term contingency plans which were produced to respond to any disruptions in supply (Meyer and Belobaba [5D14], Sullivan [5D19]).

It is in the longer term that the most significant savings are made as technological innovations and more efficient engines become readily available (Greene *et al*. [5D8], Khan [5D11], Lam [5D12], OECD [5D16]). Land use control and integrated urban development can also have an impact if journey distances are reduced with the local availability of facilities (Keyes [5D10], Newman and

Kenworthy [5D15]). However, the trends here seem to be in the opposite direction, and with the increase in leisure time and disposable income, more travel (and energy) will be consumed. Alternative fuels have also been considered so that the dependence on imported oil can be reduced (Geltner [5D7]). Included here are alcohols, vegetable oil, methane and hydrogen (Bloch and Pignataro [5D3], Lucas and Richards [5D13]), and some of these fuels are already used in transport in some countries.

5E Environment and safety

Environmental factors are again high on the political agenda, whether it is a question of the transport of irradiated fuel (Surrey [5E31]) or of the movement of heavy goods vehicles in urban areas (Cooper [5E6], Eckstein [5E7], ECMT [5E8]). A considerable volume of research is still being undertaken on pollution and air quality (Horowitz [5E13]), noise (Kamerud and Von Buseck [5E16], Smith and Stansfeld [5E30]), and community severance (Burkhardt and Wozny [5E4]. Some papers have focused on the legal and regulatory framework, and have tested various policies within this context (Cohn and Harris [5E5], Plowden [5E28]).

Transport safety has also been at the forefront of policy-makers' and planners' attention with the debate over the risk compensation hypothesis. The issue here is whether safety measures such as seat belt wearing and compulsory use of helmets by motorcyclists do result in a net benefit in terms of a reduction in the number and severity of accidents. Some researchers have argued that the evidence is not conclusive and it has been suggested that road users are prepared to take greater risks when they perceive that they are safer (Adams [5E1], Bragg and Finn [5E3], Jonah and Lawson [5E15], Shannon [5E29], Svenson and Fischhoff [5E32]). Other policy research has investigated the impact of public transport fares levels on road casualties. The argument here is that cheap fares encourage more use of public transport and hence reduce demand for road space, and the net result is a reduction in accidents (Allsop and Turner [5E2]). There has also been widespread interest in area wide safety measures, and the links between road safety and factors related to urban development in both developed (Henning and Hager [5E12]) and developing countries (Jacobs and Cutting [5E14], Mohan and Bawa [5E23]).

5F Engineering

The literature relevant to this section would merit a bibliography in its own right, and so comment is restricted to a few key publications. Engineers have the task of improving performance of all modes of transport and to reducing their operating costs through effective construction and management schemes (Chatterjee and Hendrickson [5F1]), and the current state of the art is comprehensively summarized in the Transportation Research Board's Highway Capacity Manual [5F11].

Recent technological advances have allowed engineers to make significant progress in the computerization of traffic systems through Area Traffic Control (Clelland [5F2]), SCOOT and electronic road pricing (Dawson [5F3]). In addition to real time information being used to control traffic signals, it can also be used to give accurate information to passengers on what is actually happening. The most recent advances are being used to set up expert systems (Yeh *et al.* [5F13]), in goods transport and logistics (Waters [5F12]), and in other sectors (Strobel [5F10]).

Parking is a second important area that overlaps between engineering and planning. Here policy is aimed at maximizing the use of space, and novel management systems have been devised (Higgins [5F4], Meyer and McShane [5F6]), as well as the overriding necessity for more rigorous enforcement (May [5F5]). Good summaries and review papers have been produced by the OECD on management [5F9], parking [5F7], and traffic [5F8.]

5A Theoretical frameworks

5A1 ALLEN, J.G. (1985) Post-classical transportation studies. *Transportation Quarterly*, **39** (3), pp. 451–463.

In the 1950s and 1960s transport planning was largely synonymous with highway planning and little attention was paid to public transit. The late 1960s and 1970s were marked by a departure from this classic approach with four new aspects: less reliance on computer models; more public participation; wider range of criteria for evaluation; increased interest in transit alternatives. This post-classical approach is helpful for cities with controversial transport issues because it allows an outside agency to make one-time, clear-cut recommendations having credibility that is not influenced by existing institutions. Its approach can be more constructive and less recriminatory than that of a regional planning commission which has watched its reports gather dust or of a transport agency that wants to eliminate interference and get on with the job. The applicability of the post-classical style that marked planning in Boston and Toronto is well on its way to becoming part of the accepted North American planning process.

5A2 ATKINS, S.R. (1987) The crisis for urban transportation planning modelling. *Transport Reviews*, **7** (4), pp. 307–325.

The paper considers the performance of land-use transportation study techniques over the past ten years. Although primarily viewed from a UK perspective the paper reviews matters of principle which are of international relevance. The changing context and tasks for modelling are reviewed and the current role and applications of such models considered. The capability of established models to meet these changing requirements is examined. Attention is drawn to model specification and the ability of models both to represent new policies and to predict traveller responses to them. Also relevant is the 'behavioural' theme and the way in which survey technique conditions the data obtained. Particular emphasis is placed on the accuracy of modelling, both in the representation of base year travel patterns and in the forecast mode. The inherent uncertainty concerning input data is discussed and the frequent failures to establish model validity are noted. Three crises for UK transportation planning practice are identified: the ageing of data bases, the accuracy and validity of models and the current changes to the institutional context of transport planning in the UK. Some potential remedies for the first two difficulties are proposed. It is concluded that only the last 'crisis' represents a real threat to the application of rational methods in transportation planning.

5A3 BAILEY, J. (1984) The meaning of car availability in mode choice decisions. *Transportation Planning and Technology*, **9** (2), pp. 125–134.

The paper examines various definitions of car availability that have been used in the literature and compares the results when applied to a common data set. It argues that car availability means different things to different people depending on their licence holding/car owning status. Using in-depth interview data, the factors determining car allocation and transferability within a household, and subsequently mode choice, are discussed. An attempt is made to draw some general conclusions for research and modelling. This suggests that different approaches are required depending on whether or not there is competition for use of the car within a household. Also that in cases of competition, mode choice is not a two-stage process depending on car availability and trip characteristics, but a concurrent decision based on both of these factors.

5A4 BURNETT, P. and HANSON, S. (1982) The analysis of travel as an example of complex human behaviour in spatially-constrained situations: definition and measurement issues. *Transportation Research*, **16A** (2), pp. 87-102.

This paper argues for greater attention to the definition, measurement and causal modelling of travel behaviours in cities of 'advanced' economies. Greater discrimination and flexibility in definition and measurement is required to distinguish between 'trips' and 'trip chains', as choices, and 'travel patterns' as deeply ingrained habits, for example. In addition, trips, trip chains or travel patterns may be the outcome of environmental constraints on behaviours, or of avoidance or other strategies, and not the usual choices or decisions, for many, at all. Thus, current models and modelling strategies based on classical choice theories may be badly misspecified and produce unacceptable results in the transportation and energy policy arenas. The paper outlines a 'revised' choice theory to handle this situation, and feasible empirical research methods to begin judiciously to develop it.

5A5 GOODWIN, P.B. (1981) The usefulness of travel budgets. *Transportation Research*, **15A**, pp. 97-106.

Many researchers have found the idea of a 'constant outlay' on travel a magnetic hypothesis. If true, it would proviede a useful touchstone to test the reliability of existing transport models and a constraint to improve them. This paper has five parts. First, a number of ways are investigated in which a known travel budget could be incorporated into the generation, mode choice or distribution parts of current models. Secondly, there is a discussion of some implications of doing this on policy evaluation. Thirdly, consideration is given to some of the difficulties in interpreting empirical work on this subject, to judge whether inferences that have been drawn on stability of travel budgets are supported. Fourthly, some theoretical problems are raised, particularly relating to the behavioural implications of stable budget assumptions. Lastly, some general conclusions are drawn. It is suggested that we are likely to learn most about travel behaviour, mobility and the effect of alternative policies if the time and money allocated to travel are treated as variables, not behavioural constants. These outlays are likely to be influenced, in particular, by travel opportunities and costs, as well as various socio-economic and personal characteristics.

5A6 GOODWIN, P.B., DIX, M.C. and LAYZELL, A.D. (1987) The case for heterodoxy in longitudinal analysis. *Transportation Research*, **21A** (4/5), pp. 363–376.

Longitudinal analysis should be developed with the prime objective of discovering the characteristics of dynamic, disequilibrium processes. This will require a range of different research methods, including qualitative social research, repeated cross-section surveys, panel surveys, aggregate time series analysis, and simulation models. In each case it is essential that models should be formulated in a dynamic way (e.g. with lags, inertia and asymmetry). Examples are given of work using each of these methods, applied to the analysis of habit, aging, market volatility, turnover, long-term demand elasticities, and forecasting using demographic information.

5A7 HEGGIE, I.G. (1978) Putting behaviour into behavioural models of travel choice. *Journal of the Operational Research Society*, **29** (6), pp. 541–550.

This article argues that disaggregate behavioural travel models are not, as their authors claim, 'behaviourally sound and policy relevant'. They merely caricature behaviour and produce predictions in conflict with the available evidence. The article sets out to provide a description of household travel behaviour and asks how it can be realistically modelled. It suggests three ways of doing so, using models which are either pragmatic, mathematical, or interactive. The latter is developed in response to the query 'if one cannot capture the individuals' decision-making process within a finite set of mathematical equations, then why not use the individual himself as a surrogate for this part of the model? The article concludes that models of behaviour may have to become more human and less mathematical if they are to give realistic insights into the way in which individuals arrange their activities in time and space.

5A8 HEGGIE, I.G. and JONES, P.M. (1978) Defining domains for models of travel demand. *Transportation*, **7** (2), pp. 119–135.

Travel demand models implicitly assume that people respond to changes in a continuous way. This is in contrast to the physical sciences, where discontinuous response is a common phenomenon and is embodied in such concepts as sub-critical and super-critical states. Recent studies have shown that responses to transport policies differ in degree and kind according to the nature and severity of the stimulus and the types of people affected. Response patterns may be categorized by the extent to which they involve adjustments to spatio-temporal or inter-personal linkages. This paper identifies four response domains, with a further distinction between permissive and forced changes. Most travel demand models are designed to operate within an independent, forced (and to a lesser extent independent permissive) domain and their forecasts become unreliable when responses lie outside that domain. Conversely, a model designed for a more complex domain is unnecessarily cumbersome where simpler responses apply. This paper describes the types of model which are appropriate for each domain and discusses how the effects of a policy may be assigned to the correct domains(s).

5A9 HUFF, J.O. and HANSON, S. (1986) Repetition and variability in urban travel. *Geographical Analysis*, **18** (2), pp. 97–114.

Most travel models and theories assume the existence of habitual behaviour, yet few empirical studies have examined the question of how much repetition or variability characterizes daily travel. This paper reviews the arguments and presents an empirical study over a five-week period. The results show that, whereas many behaviours that make up the daily pattern are highly repetitious, the similarity between daily travel patterns on different days in an individual's longitudinal record is quite low. Even the day that is the most typical of the individual's travel is a poor indicator of that person's overall travel pattern.

5A10 HUTCHINSON, B.G. (1981) Urban transport policy and policy analysis methods. *Transport Reviews*, **1** (2), pp. 169–188.

The change in emphasis of urban transport policy during the past 25 years is described. The concentration on identifying opportunities for investments in new transport capacity has given way to policies which emphasize the better management of existing facilities and the more equitable provision of transport services. The evolution of transport systems analysis tools is also briefly reviewed and the capabilities of these techniques as policy analysis aids are discussed. Four groups of techniques are discussed: land use-activity allocation models; multi-stage aggregate demand models; disaggregate demand models; and household-based activity models. It is concluded that while available analysis techniques can assist in evaluating a limited range of policy options their relevance is decreasing as the urban transport environment changes rapidly.

See also: Hutchinson, B.G. (1974) *Principles of Urban Transport Systems Planning*. New York: McGraw Hill.

5A11 JONES, P.M., CLARKE, M.I. and DIX, M.C. (1980) *Understanding Travel Behaviour*. Aldershot: Gower.

The main objective of this five-year study was been to obtain a better understanding of household travel behaviour, and to develop an analytical and modelling capability that would enable this knowledge to be applied in transport research and planning. In the process it proved necessary to develop new survey methodology and to provide an alternative conceptual framework for the study of travel behaviour. The project comprised four main phases: diagnostic studies (an exploratory phase) in which travel was examined in a very general way, through a combination of loosely structured depth interviews and the careful formulation of concepts; understanding daily behaviour, a qualitative and quantitative examination of daily patterns of household behaviour, and their variation by type of household; household adaptation (a further phase of survey and analysis) concerned more specifically with the dynamics of response to change; model development, a final phase in which the role of models is considered in the light of project findings, and a new form of activity-based travel demand model is developed.

5A12 KHISTY, C.J. (1985) Research on appropriate planning methodology in developing countries. *Transportation Research Record*, 1028, pp. 18-25.

Developing countries have generally adopted the planning methodology conventionally practiced by developed countries. The results have not been encouraging. There is a dire need to evolve inexpensive appropriate methodology especially applicable to developing countries, which will help policy-makers reduce the inefficiencies in transport, correct misguided priorities, promote equity, and enhance the quality of life. The following topics connected with appropriate planning methodology are examined in this paper: development and diffusion of planning methods; basic problems of land-use and transport planning; the meaning of need as compared with demand; distributional effects of current planning methods; appropriate planning methodology; and the ethics of methodology assessment. The issues concerning appropriate planning methodology are clarified and areas where further research is needed to improve the planning process are identified. An agenda for action is included.

5A13 KOSTYNIUK, L.P. and KITAMURA, R. (1984) Temporal stability of urban travel patterns. *Transport Policy and Decision Making*, 2 (4), pp. 481-500.

This study examines the temporal stability in several indicators of travel patterns of urban residents using 1965 and 1980 origin-destination survey results from a metropolitan area in the United States. The analysis examines trip chaining, sequencing of activities, transition between activity types, and time-of-day dependencies of activity choice, as well as trip rates and trip durations. The results show that, in spite of the qualitative similarities in activity scheduling, many aspects of travel patterns including trip rates do not possess quantitative stability over time. This is also the case for sample sub-groups defined in terms of such commonly used factors as auto ownership. The study points out the instability in travel patterns as an additional element of uncertainty in long-range policy development, demand forecasting, and evaluation of user benefit.

5A14 LANDROCK, J.N. (1981) Spatial stability of average daily travel times and trip rates within Great Britain. *Transportation Research*, **15A** (1), pp. 55–62.

Average daily travel times and trip rates are calculated for individuals resident in areas of differing population size and population density using data for the whole of Great Britain. Contrary to recent suggestions there is no indication from this study that daily travel time is more stable than daily trip rate. For example when the data are categorized by population size the maximum average daily travel time is 21 per cent higher than the minimum average daily travel time while the maximum trip rate is only 14 per cent greater than the minimum trip rate. Cross tabulations of daily travel time and daily trip rate by population size and ward population density showed no systematic variation except for higher travel times and trip rates in wards with low population density in large cities.

5A15 LANDAU, U., PRASHKER, J.N. and HIRSH, M. (1981) The effect of temporal constraints on household travel behaviour. *Environment and Planning A*, **13**, pp. 435–448.

Recent theoretical works dealing with space-time modelling of individuals' behaviour indicate that temporal constraints are extremely important in the proper representation of this behaviour. In this paper, the authors define and test empirically a framework for trip-generation models which is sensitive to temporal constraints. A sequential choice process is assumed where at the first stage the household decides whether or not to perform a trip for a specific purpose during the day, and in the second stage a decision is taken as to which period. These types of models are sensitive to important policy issues such as evaluating the changes in activity patterns of individuals that result from changes in working hours, the opening and closing times of stores and businesses, and changes in the number of working days in a week.

5A16 LAYZELL, A.D., GOODWIN, P.B. and DIX, M.C. (1987) (eds.) *Transport Policy and the Dynamics of Travel Demand*. Farnborough: Gower.

This book argues that the effects of transport policy on travel behaviour cannot be correctly discovered by static methods of analyses, and that it is necessary to rely on methods which can detect a process of change. Using a range of available methods, changes in individual, household and aggregate travel behaviour are analysed in a number of different policy contexts, including increasing fares and declining services, changes in petrol prices and car costs and increasing and reducing incomes.

5A17 MOGRIDGE, M.J.H. and HOLDEN, D.J. (1987) A panacea for road congestion? A riposte. *Traffic Engineering and Control*, **28** (1), pp. 13-22.

A recent conjecture by Mogridge claims that if Wardrop's Principle, which concerns choice of route on a road network, is extended to choice of private car or rail for commuting journeys into the centres of large cities, it leads to the conclusion that average door-to-door speeds by the two modes must be equal. A consequence of this conclusion is that road improvements in congested areas where demand is suppressed will ultimately be counterproductive, lowering journey speeds by both road and rail. Commuter speeds by road and rail are surprisingly similar to the city centre, but the explanations for this phenomenon have led to debate, both on theoretical and technical issues.

For the counter argument see Bly, P.H., Johnston, R.H. and Webster, F.V. (1987) A panacea for road congestion? *Traffic Engineering and Control*, **28** (1), pp. 8-12.

5A18 ROTH, G.J. and ZAHAVI, Y. (1981) Travel time 'budgets' in developing countries. *Transportation Research*, **15A** (1), pp.87-95.

As part of continuing efforts to develop new tools for modelling and forecasting urban travel, World Bank staff tabulated urban travel data in order to identify regularities in the allocation of time to travel in cities of developing countries. A major motivation in this approach is to investigate the daily mean expenditures on travel, in time and money terms, which are regarded as 'budgets', allocated to travel if they display predictable regularities. The paper summarizes the results relating to travel time obtained from four cities: Bogota, Singapore, Salvador and Santiago. Average travel times are stratified by income in all four cities, and further stratified by household size, vehicle availability, sex, age and occupation for some cities. In all cities examined, the daily travel time per traveller appeared to exhibit regular trends associated with income, household size and other socio-economic characteristics.

5A19 RUSCH, G. (1984) Is the crisis of urban transport (also) a crisis of transport planning? *International Journal of Transport Economics*, **9** (1), pp. 7-21.

In this article an assumption is made according to which the expanding of road networks not only improves, but also reduces the individual possibilities of acting in time and space, above all for pedestrians and cyclists. As a consequence, they are often 'forced' to use a motorized vehicle. Thus major road projects may have traffic producing effects, which sometimes reinforce instead of solving urban transport problems. In showing these negative effects and the measures to avoid them, the Hagerstrand's time-space model is employed. In the time-space diagram the spatial distribution of land uses and facilities, and the time controls of activities in a planning area are shown. In this diagram the daily routines of the individuals living in this area, and the time-space coordination requirements to realize these routines can be examined as well as the question of how they are affected by major road projects. Finally, the possible use of the time-space model in transport planning is demonstrated by a case study.

5A20 SCHOFER, J.O. and STOPHER, P.R. (1979) Specifications for a new long-range urban transportation planning process. *Transportation*, **8** (3), pp. 199-218.

This paper asserts the continuing need for a long-range component to urban transport planning, citing particularly the relationships between short- and long-range planning and the dangers of a single-minded concentration on short-range planning. However, the nature of the long-range planning procedure that is required is substantively different from that of most extant approaches. Some of the specific requirements and capabilities of a new procedure are described, and existing procedures are compared against these. In the latter part of the paper, some of the elements of a new long-range planning procedure are characterized. It is suggested that the procedure be built around a scenario approach to confronting and bounding future uncertainty. Second, the need to incorporate financial forecasting in the process is laid out and related to the scenario concept. Third, the need for travel- and impact-forecasting procedures is recognized and a set of input, output and operating requirements for such procedures is specified. It is suggested that improved sketch-planning tools may fit the requirements to a large extent. It is also suggested that some procedures or models in the process should be 'synthetic' models, not needing calibration for each new application. Finally, a number of requirements are specified for the display and evaluation of planning proposals from this procedure. A major emphasis is placed here on transparency of the process and responsiveness to direct intervention by the decision-maker.

5A21 STOPHER, P.R. (1985) Travel forecasting methodology: transfer of research into practice, *Australian Road Research*, **15** (3), pp. 157–162.

This paper examines the extent to which results from transport planning research have been transferred into practice. It is concluded that the current rate of transfer is low. Possible reasons for the low transference rates are examined and suggestions made on how the situation may be improved. The paper focuses on research and practice into travel forecasting methods in the United States. However, it is argued that the research/practice interface pertaining to travel forecasting methods is not too different from other areas of transport planning and the situation existent in the United States tends to only differ in degree from that in Western Europe and Australia.

5A22 SUPERNAK, J. (1983) Transportation modelling: lessons from the past and tasks for the future. *Transportation*, **12** (1), pp. 79–90.

In spite of the recent progress made in household activity analysis and travel budget studies, urban transport modelling still remains a 'not-too-well developed' research field. There are conflicting theories, analysis units are not uniform, terms are not precisely defined, basic studies of sub-systems involved are not yet completed, and many models lack behavioural background as well as basic attributes such as simplicity, sensitivity, compatibility, transferability and forecasting ability. Gaps in methodology may be partially responsible for this situation. There is an urgent need for simple, yet not primitive, easily applicable urban transport models which can respond to the technical needs of planners and engineers. Lessons from the past, as well as experiences from other disciplines, suggest that future research should concentrate on: new, 'unconventional' approaches based on systematic, basic studies of all sub-systems involved; proper definition and stratification of an analysis unit; revision and unification of definitions, classifications, etc., in order to improve the behavioural background of the models; dynamic rather than static approaches, able to describe feedbacks between transportation and land use as well as between transportation demand and supply; interrelations between subsequent sub-models, particularly between car availability, trip generation and modal split; developing models which are not only sensitive to transportation policies but also to other local policies (e.g. land use, city development, social, etc.).

See the debate on this original paper. Polak, J. (1987) A comment on Supernak's critique of transport modelling. *Transportation*, **14** (1), pp. 63-72, and Supernak, J. and Stevens, W.S. (1987) Urban transportation modelling: The discussion continues. *Transportation*, **14** (1), pp. 73-82.

5A23 TANNER, J.C. (1981) Expenditure of time and money on travel. *Transportation Research*, **15A** (1), pp. 25-38.

The report examines the suggestion that the total amount of time, money or generalized cost spent on personal travel may be constant over time, in cross-section or under changes of travel costs or policies. Invariant expenditure of either time or money on travel is inconsistent with rational economic behaviour and with conventional transport modelling. A theoretical analysis concludes that generalized expenditure on travel might be invariant. Data from the National Travel Survey indicate that generalized expenditure is much the same in urban as in rural areas, despite the wide variation in modes available and distances to destinations. In comparisons of households at different income levels, generalized expenditure per person is almost directly proportional to gross income per person; in other words, consumption of 'generalized time' is constant. Time series data from 1953 to 1976 are also examined and, though the data are poor, they indicate that generalized travel expenditure per person has increased over the years appreciably faster than has real income per person. Caution is therefore needed in using constant budget concepts in forecasting models.

5A24 WIGAN, M.R. and MORRIS, J.M. (1981) The transport implications of activity and time budget constraints. *Transportation Research*, **15A** (1), pp. 63-86.

Time budget and activity analysis ideas from sociological and geographical disciplines are reviewed in a transport context. A systematic examination of international data sources shows a regular structure, which applies only at a fairly aggregated level. The modelling structures so far used include stochastic models and entropy maximization approaches: both appear to be able to replicate certain aspects of the linkage between and the duration spent in different activities, although from contradictory bases. The competition for travel time is shown as a function of stage in family lifecycle, with the pressure on trip combination, destination substitution, and on other activities such as sleep and leisure. The different forms of time expenditures at different locations are related to different appraisal purposes, including environmental exposure. Data from over 14 countries including Australia show broadly similar trends in travel time budgets, but little advance has yet been made in proving an effective model of the elasticity and cross-elasticity of demands for time for different activities. Moreover, the variations in personal budgets which show up at almost any level of disaggregation suggest that analysis by market segments will be essential. The first order variations in travel time budgets, income and vehicle licence holding, and detailed analyses of household interview data should first be carried out to establish the links between time and financial budgets in satisfying the activity programmes which transport sustains. The implications of an activity programme approach for the valuation of time savings are considered.

5A25 ZAHAVI, Y. (1982) Travel transferability between four cities. *Traffic Engineering and Control*, **23** (4), pp. 203-208.

Models calibrated on one city could be used to represent travel conditions in another city at the same time. However, model transferability can only be assured by basing the model on travel characteristics which are themselves transferable. The most transferable characteristic seems to be daily travel time expenditures per traveller, as developed in the UMOT travel model (Unified Mechanism of Travel). The question of transferability is tested with data taken from Baltimore, Washington, London and Reading.

5B Analysis methods

5B1 ABELSON, P. and BAKER, S. (1982) Household car ownership in Sydney and Australia. *Transportation Policy and Decision Making*, **2** (2), pp. 129-144.

This article briefly reviews time-series and cross-section models of car ownership, as an introduction to two empirical studies. The first is a cross-section study of car ownership in Sydney, with special reference to household incomes, household size, distance to rail, and residential density. The second is a time-series model of car ownership in Australia since 1960, in which income, capital and operating costs of cars and interest rates are the independent variables. it is argued that the results are complementary and may be used separately or jointly according to the type of forecast required.

5B2 AMPT, E.S., RICHARDSON, A.J. and BROG, W. (1985) *New Survey Methods in Transport*. Utrecht: VNU Press.

This book was the first comprehensive compilation of survey techniques used in the broad field of transport planning. It provides state-of-the-art reviews in several areas of survey methodology, including cross-sectional, longitudinal, and interactive surveys. Papers cover various aspects of the design, execution, and analysis of cross-sectional and longitudinal surveys and highlight the use of in-depth and interactive surveys. Attention is given to the emerging issue of systematic biases inherent in various survey methods. Briefer introductions to the main themes discussed in the book plus the keynote addresses are summarized in *Transport Reviews*, **6** (1), pp. 113-124.

5B3 ANAS, A. (1984) Discrete choice theory and general equilibrium of employment, housing and travel networks in a Lowry-type model of the urban economy. *Environment and Planning A*, **16**, pp. 1489-1502.

Five influential paradigms established by Beckmann, Lowry, Wilson, Mills, and McFadden are unified by developing a long-run economic general equilibrium model of urban land use based on probabilistic discrete choice theory. The model takes into account the interdependence of export-oriented and service employment with population. Households' choices of employment type, employment location, type and location of housing, shopping destination, and choice of travel routes in the journey to work and journey to shop are determined simultaneously by means of stochastic utility maximization. Firms' choices of building type and location and landowners' choices of land-use type and density are determined by means of stochastic profit maximization. Travel occurs on a congestible link-node network. The model determines the wage rate for each employment type in each zone, the price of floor space for each building type in each zone, the price of land in each zone, the price of the locally traded composite commodity in each zone, and the peak and off-peak congested travel-cost and travel-time for each link of the network. The quantity of land which remains undeveloped is also determined.

See also: Anas, A. (1985) The combined equilibrium of travel networks and residential location markets. *Regional Science and Urban Economics*, **15** (1), pp. 1–21.

5B4 ANAS, A. (1982) *Residential Location Markets and Urban Transportation: Economic Theory, Econometrics and Policy Analysis with Discrete Choice Models*. London: Academic Press.

As part of a discussion on urban economics, the book reviews the development of economic equilibrium theory concerning the housing market and incorporating stochastic utility maximization models of discrete choice. Chapters discuss empirical estimation, policy application and extensions of an urban simulation model. Census data from the Chicago Standard Metropolitan Statistical Area (SMSA) is used to estimate the demand- and supply-side models which represent households choosing a residential location and mode of travel for the journey to work. This formulation of demand integrates the methodology of travel demand measurement with the comparable measurement of residential location demand. The models are combined into an equilibrium simulation model which determines travel and residential choices, and is intended for the examination of business district transport investment and policies.

5B5 ARDEKANI, S. and HERMAN, R. (1987) Urban network-wide traffic variables and their relations. *Transportation Science*, **21** (1), pp. 1–16.

Time-lapse aerial photography over the Central Business Districts (CBD) of Austin and Dallas, Texas, has been employed to determine the averages of concentration, speed and fraction of vehicles stopped and to examine the relations among such network-wide averages including the flow which was measured on the ground simultaneously. The results have indicated that the average flow in a street network may indeed be expressed as the product of the space mean speed and concentration. Simultaneous ground experiments have also been conducted in the Austin CBD to investigate the reasonableness of the assumption of the 'two-fluid model', a curvilinear relation between the trip time and stop time per unit distance, which may be used in characterizing the quality of traffic service in urban street networks. As a result of these simultaneous ground experiments and aerial observations, the assumptions of the model have been verified. Moreover, relations between the fraction of vehicles stopped and concentration as well as between speed and concentration have allowed the two-fluid model to be used to compare the quality of traffic service in various street networks under the same level of concentration. The two-fluid model may then be used to predict, for a given change in vehicular concentration in a street network, the resulting changes in the averages of speed, fraction of vehicles stopped, flow, etc. This is particularly useful as a performance model in urban planning where for a given concentration it is desirable to predict the resulting traffic conditions.

See also: Ardekani, S. and Herman, R. (1984) Characterizing traffic conditions in urban areas. *Transportation Science*, **18** (2), pp. 101–140.

5B6 BANISTER, C.E. (1981) Car ownership and modal use – an analysis of some census data for a metropolitan area. *Traffic Engineering and Control*, **22** (7), pp. 396–397.

In an attempt to evaluate the reasons for modal split, the author attempts to extend the scope of investigations through an examination of different modes. In particular, a differentiation is made between rail and bus as public transport modes. A study is made of significant relationships between levels of car ownership and the use of particular transport modes for the journey to work: the possible reasons for such relationships are discussed. The data set used is the 1971 census of population, the work being restricted to commuting in the Greater Manchester area. The study is intended as a pilot study for a larger, similar, study that might be carried out on the 1981 census of population. Conclusions discuss the effect of car ownership levels on the demand for bus services.

5B7 BARNARD, P.O. (1987) Modelling shopping destination choice behaviour using the basic multinomial logic model and some of its extensions. *Transport Reviews*, **7** (1), pp. 17–51.

This paper reviews basic multinomial logit (MNL) models of shopping destination choice and some extensions to the basic MNL model. Issues include the identification and form of inclusion of measures of destination attractiveness, identification of the appropriate destination choice set, modelling multi-destination tours and choices over time, and linking destination choice models with activity measures. The paper begins with a discussion of modelling philosophy and forecasting-related informational needs and concludes with a summary of areas requiring further research.

5B8 BEN-AKIVA, M., MANSKI, C.F. and SHERMAN, L. (1981) A behavioural approach to modelling household motor vehicle ownership and applications to aggregate policy analysis. *Environment and Planning A*, **13**, pp. 399–411.

A unified approach to the modelling of household motor vehicle ownership level, vehicle demand levels, and vehicle use is described. The model system is founded on a utility theory of household behaviour, and is implemented through probabilistic discrete choice models estimated from cross-sectional samples of households. Following the introduction of the model, an application involving forecasts of US motor vehicle sales through the mid-1980s is presented.

5B9 BENJAMIN, J. and SEN, L. (1981) An evaluation of public transportation using market segmentation techniques. *Journal of Advanced Transportation*, **15** (2), pp. 143–161.

The continuing emphasis on fuel-efficient public transport has led to a need to design transit services to attract all population segments. This paper presents a method of evaluating public transport. The method derives groups of residents based on current transit usage and common viewpoints towards existing public transport service characteristics. As a part of this approach, the residential location of each group member is compared with bus routes and service levels.

From this comparison, recommendations are made for service improvements.

5B10 BERECHMAN, J. and PAASWELL, R.E. (1983) Rail rapid transit investment and CBD revitalization: methodology and results. *Urban Studies*, **20** (4), pp. 471-486.

A $450 million light rapid rail transit (LRRT) system is currently under contruction in Buffalo, New York. This project represents a large public investment for a transport system for which user benefits are not the sole or even a major consideration. Anticipated increases in service employment, retail activity and land development, mainly in the declining CBD area, are viewed as the major benefits. This paper describes the methodological framework used for the analysis of these impacts. Based on the empirical results from this methodology, the paper then evaluates the overall potential of the project to promote CBD revitalization.

5B11 VAN DEN BERG, L. (1983) Spatial dynamics and urban transport. *International Journal of Transport Economics*, **10** (3), pp. 577-592.

In conventional transport research the starting point for network design is an exogenously determined future spatial structure of the area under consideration. Workplaces, housing, shopping facilities, etc, are all introduced as basic data. Two objections can be raised to such an approach. First, the development of the spatial structure of an (urban) area is not independent of the way the transport infrastructure is designed; there is an obvious interaction. Second, urban areas tend to show an internal dynamic development according to a rather fixed pattern affecting the location and relocation of households, firms, and facilities. The present paper sets out to show that in any analysis of the interrelation among the spatial structure of urban areas, their transport infrastructure, and the pattern of daily movements, these two points should be taken into account.

5B12 BLAND, B.H. (1983) Land-use patterns and travel. Transport and Road Research Laboratory, Laboratory Report 1092. Crowthorne: TRRL.

The LUTE model of travel by car, bus and on foot has been used to predict travel in a set of hypothetical towns with a wide range of sizes, shapes and population densities, subject to the average time spent travelling per day and the number of trips being held constant, the fares revenue covering a specified proportion of the operating cost, and allowing for the finite seating capacity of the buses. The results are intended to be of interest to bus operators concerned about future levels of service, fares, patronage and profitability as car ownership increases and residential densities decline, to transport planners interested in the behaviour of the transport system as a whole, and to planners who wish to assess the travel and accessibility consequences of alternative development patterns.

See also: Bland, B.H. (1982) The 'LUTE' land use and transportation model. Transport and Road Research Laboratory, Supplementary Report 716. Crowthorne: TRRL.

5B13 BLY, P.H. and WEBSTER, F.V. (1984) Land use/transport models: how effective are they? *Ekistics*, **51** (305), pp. 147–154.

This paper examines techniques used up to the present and what has been done to assess their performance. It describes a current international study designed to compare a number of predictive techniques and the likely impacts on a range of transport and land-use policies. Several of the models embody Lowry's central mechanism that assumes the location of employment in basic industry is given and then estimates the total population that employment can support. This population is then located in the various zones of the area in proportion to its accessibility. Models intended as general purpose tools for study of particular urban regions use some flexible versions of Lowry's allocation mechanism. Other models use a different starting point but the desirability of a location still depends upon accessibility to employment and services amongst other things.

5B14 BOYCE, D.E. (1980) A framework for constructing network equilibrium models of urban location. *Transportation Science*, **14** (1), pp. 77–96.

Recent advances in network equilibrium modelling provide efficient algorithms for solving the urban trip assignment problem. These models can be extended to incorporate the trip distribution problem with two types of variable demand functions. By reinterpreting the zone-to-zone trip variable, these models can be viewed as urban location models. This paper synthesizes these results, and shows how several urban location models can be derived from the mathematical framework based on the network equilibrium problem.

5B15 BOYCE, D.E. (1986) Integration of supply and demand models in transportation and location: problem formulations and research questions. *Environment and Planning A*, **18** (6), pp. 485–489.

The first part of the paper provides an introduction to integrated supply and demand models so that a classification of problem types can be given. Then the basic mathematical formulation of these models is examined and solution algorithms from economics and mathematics are presented. The implications for solving problems involving network-equilibrium travel and location choices are discussed in the final section.

See also a special issue of *Transportation Research* (1985, **19A** (5/6)) edited by David Boyce on 'Transportation research: The state of the art and research opportunities'.

5B16 BOYCE, D.E. and KIM, T.J. (1987) The role of congestion of transportation networks in urban location and travel choices. *Transportation*, **14** (1), pp. 53–62.

Congestion of urban transport systems results from an equilibrium of location and travel choices with generalized travel costs which increase with vehicle flows as well as other factors. The use of network equilibrium concepts in analysing urban policies and evaluating alternative plans is examined. Issues arising in the use of network equilibrium models are described, and formulations of urban network prediction and design models are explored.

5B17 BRACKEN, I. (1984) An integrated policy-based forecasting framework for land-use planning. *Environment and Planning B*, **11** (4), pp. 455–475.

Forecasting is essential in all planning activity; yet there are serious conceptual and methodological issues to be faced, particularly where public policymaking is involved. Forecasting methods in planning have varied widely from unsystematic and highly subjective scenario writing to the unimaginative extrapolation of trends. In practice, some blend of these methodologies is often employed. In this paper, it is argued that an effective approach may lie in the development of explicitly hybrid methodology which can blend perspectives on futures and provide a proper integration of policy expectations into policy planning forecasts. In the paper a framework is described which offers the possibility of overcoming some limitations of existing approaches.

5B18 BROUGHTON, J. and TANNER, J.C. (1983) Distribution models for the journey to work. *Environment and Planning A*, **15** (1), pp. 37–53.

The paper describes a model, based on random utility theory, for simulating the choices of home and workplace made by individual workers in a region. Each worker chooses the home and job which maximizes his utility (comprising rent, salary, cost of the journey to work, and a random personal element); rents and salaries are adjusted iteratively until the distribution of workers' choices of home and work place matches the existing distribution of homes and workplaces. The model is applied first to several idealized urban geometries; it is then applied to 1971 Census data for the Manchester area, where the model reproduces satisfactorily the observed pattern of choices. Some of the effects of changed travel costs and of alternative policies for redistributing homes or jobs are then simulated.

5B19 BURNS, L.D. (1979) Consumer preferences relative to the price and network capability of small urban vehicles. *Transportation*, **8** (3), pp. 219–236.

Preferences of consumers for small urban vehicle concepts differing only with respect to their hypothetical purchase prices and network capabilities (i.e. whether they are capable of operating on expressways, major arterials or local streets) are analysed using statistical techniques based on psychological scaling theories. Results from these analyses indicate that a vast majority of consumers are not readily willing to give up the accessibility provided by conventional automobiles. More specifically, over the range of hypothetical prices considered here, network capability dominates as a determinant of preferences for vehicle concepts. Also, the ability to operate vehicles on expressways is of utmost importance to consumers.

5B20 CAVALLI-SFORZA, V. and ORTOLANO, L. (1984) Delphi forecasts of land use-transporation interactions. *Journal of Transportation Engineering*, **110** (3), pp. 324–339.

The delphi method is used to predict the impacts of three alternative transport programmes in San Jose, California. Variables projected concern both land use (e.g. number of single-family housing units) and choice of transit mode. Forecasts are made for 1990 and 2000 for four spatial zones within San Jose. Delphi panelists are individuals familiar with land-use and transport issues in the San Jose area. A preliminary questionnaire survey is used to set general economic conditions and land-use policies that serve as a context for specific forecasts of land-use – transport interactions. Strengths and weaknesses of the delphi method in forecasting land use are assessed.

5B21 CHANG, Y.B. and STOPHER, P.R. (1981) Defining perceived attributes of travel modes for urban work journeys. *Transportation Planning and Technology*, **7** (1), pp. 55–65.

Whereas psychological measurement procedures have been used frequently to enrich the variable set for mode choice models, most uses have lacked either methodological rigour or adequate range and definition of concepts (attributes). Here, a rigorous procedure from psychology was applied and defined nine concepts, measured by 68 items. These were used in a survey of Boston commuters and the results factor-analysed to recover eight of the nine original concepts, five of which have good reliability scores. Subsequently, the item sets were reduced to four for each concept, which increased the reliability of four concepts and decreased slightly that of the other four. The concepts identified are labelled as comfort, convenience, reliability, safety, cost, time, privacy and opportunity.

5B22 COSHALL, J.T. (1985) Urban consumers' cognitions of distance. *Geografiska Annaler*, **67B** (2), pp. 107–120.

This paper examines the relationship between consumers' cognitions of distances and the physical distances that separate shops in the micro-spatial retail environment. Literature and methods are reviewed prior to the selection of one approach (ratio estimations) and its application to Maidstone in Kent. Estimates are regressed against true distances for a range of different consumer groupings and the results suggest that distance is overestimated. However the extent of overestimation varies between groups and the variance cannot be explained by physical distance alone. The results suggest that time estimates may be a component of micro-spatial cognition of distance, especially for the elderly.

5B23 DALY, A. (1982) Applicability of disaggregate models of behaviour: a question of methodology. *Transportation Research*, **16A** (5/6), pp. 363–370.

The paper considers the possibility of quantitative analysis of behaviour, with particular reference to travel behaviour, from a methodological standpoint. The chief conclusion is that the nature of the subject implies that disaggregate statistical analysis is the most useful technique. The relationship of this methodology to theoretical issues is discussed, concluding that general theoretical issues are not susceptible to empirical resolution. The theoretical framework essential to analysis or forecasting of behaviour must therefore be established *a priori*. The paper concludes with a discussion of the practical problems and achievements of disaggregate analysis.

5B24 DAMM, D. and LERMAN, S.R. (1981) A theory of activity scheduling behaviour. *Environment and Planning A*, **13**, pp. 703–718.

Recognizing that travel is a demand derived from individuals' desires to undertake out-of-home activities, researchers in the area of travel demand have become increasingly interested in analysing and predicting individuals' decisions about activity participation. This paper formulates a theory of activity scheduling for urban workers. In this theory, each worker chooses whether or not to participate in an out-of-home, non-work activity in each of five blocks of time defined around their obligatory trip to work. In addition, conditional on the decision to participate in any particular time block, the chosen duration of participation is analysed. The econometric problems of operationalizing the theory are resolved, and the resulting model is applied to analyse the scheduling behaviour of a sample of workers in the Minneapolis-St Paul metropolitan area. This case study suggests some significant directions for further research on activity analysis.

See also: Damm, D. (1982) Parameters of activity behaviour for use in travel analysis. *Transportation Research*, **16A** (2), pp. 135–148.

5B25 DASGUPTA, M., FROST, M. and SPENCE, N. (1985) Interaction between urban form and mode choice for the work journey: Manchester/Sheffield. *Regional Studies*, **19** (4), pp. 315-328.

This paper analyses the intra-city, inter-city and temporal variations in the mode used for the work journey in Manchester and Sheffield. The research examines the interaction between mode choice and urban-structure by establishing associations between mode choice and residential location (as measured by distance from the city centre), socio-economic factors, and land-use attributes. Temporal changes are affected by factors operating externally, such as the growth of car ownership. Intra-city variations may be explained by the spatial ordering of socio-economic and land-use attributes. Intercity differences could arise from differing urban structure, the relative distribution of homes and jobs, as well as contrasting transport policies.

5B26 DAVIES, R.B. and PICKLES, A.R. (1987) A joint trip timing storetype choice model for grocery shopping, including inventory effects and nonparametric control for omitted variables. *Transportation Research*, **21A** (4/5), pp. 345-361.

In principle, stochastic modelling methods are ideally suited to the analysis and forecasting of discretionary travel; they formalize both the capriciousness and continuity which are empirically typical of recurrent choice. In practice, the development of theoretically justifiable but tractable stochastic models has appeared to be an illusive goal in transport research and stochastic models have found little favour. Recent statistical results on the non-parametric characterisation of mixing distributions now enable stochastic models to simultaneously represent a much greater variety of behaviour while, at the same time, actually reducing problems over tractability. The consequent case for reappraisal is illustrated by the development and calibration of a new joint timing/choice model for shopping travel. This model has sound theoretical underpinnings, permits complex variation in the frequency and regularity of shopping due to both observed and unobserved characteristics and constraints, and yet is readily calibrated from diary data.

5B27 D'ESTE, G. (1985) The effect of staggered working hours on commuter trip durations. *Transportation Research A*, **19A** (2), pp. 109–117.

Staggered working hours have the potential to alleviate the excessive demands made on the transport infrastructure during the morning and afternoon 'peak hours'. A more uniform demand profile would lead to a decrease in peak traffic densities and a resultant increase in traffic speed. This paper uses a traffic speed model sensitive to changes in traffic activity to calculate the effect of staggered working hours on the average duration of commuter trips. The cases of discrete and continuous distributions of departure times are considered and an optimization process is outlined.

5B28 DOWNES, J.D. and EMMERSON, P. (1985) Urban transport modelling with flexible travel budgets. Transport and Road Research Laboratory, Research Report 5. Crowthorne: TRRL.

Travel budget models measure travel in terms of distance and, unlike other types of urban transport model where travel is mentioned in terms of trips, are able to take account of known regularities in the amounts of time and money spent on travel. The model examined here differs from the Zahavi UMOT model in that the total amount of time and money spent on travel by people living in different categories of income and car ownership is estimated by maximizing the utility of travel subject only to upper limits of 24 hours per person per day and the national average expenditure per household per day.

5B29 DUNCAN, G.J., JUSTER, F.T. and MORGAN, J.N. (1987) The role of panel studies in research on economic behaviour. *Transportation Research*, **21A** (4/5), pp. 249–263.

The analytic and monetary costs and benefits of panel surveys are assessed in light of experiences from the Panel Study of Income Dynamics, an 18-year panel survey on the economic status and behaviour of the US population. The analytic benefits of panel are formidable, ranging from description of gross change to various analytic advantages of continuous and discrete time modelling. Analytic costs such as the conditioning of responses in subsequent participation or non-response bias are possible in panel surveys, but their effects can be minimized with proper data collection procedures and analytic adjustments. Surprisingly, the monetary costs of panel surveys are less than the costs of comparable repeated cross-sectional surveys.

5B30 EVANS, A. (1987) A theoretical comparison of competition with other economic regimes for bus services. *Journal of Transport Economics and Policy*, **21** (1), pp. 7–36.

This paper uses a theoretical model to compare the economics of bus service operation under four different regimes: competition, maximization of net economic benefit subject to a requirement to break even, unregulated monopoly, and unconstrained maximization of net economic benefit. Competition is generally found to lead to higher fares and higher frequencies than a regime of maximum net economic benefit subject to a requirement to break even.

5B31 FORER, P.C. and KIVELL, H. (1981) Space-time budgets, public transport, and spatial choice. *Environment and Planning A*, **13**, pp. 497–509.

This paper addresses the problem of access to urban facilities for housewives without cars, and the methodology of the Lund School is used to investigate the spatial constraints affecting access to and choice between a selected group of urban facilities in the city of Christchurch, New Zealand. To do this, the characteristics of the public transport system are investigated, and time-budget data used to specify typical windows of free time during a housespouse's day. From there the potential action and activity spaces of individuals in four suburbs are delimited, and these are used in assessing the variations in access to and choice between facilities in these suburbs. Finally, the social impact of the current bus provision in the context of the social structure of the city is raised as a policy issue.

5B32 GENSCH, D.H. (1980) Choice model calibrated on current behaviour predicts public response to new policies. *Transportation Research*, **14A** (2), pp. 137–142.

The standard approach to predicting public response to possible changes in transport policy is to describe the changed environmental conditions in a scenario and ask individuals what their choice would be. These stated intentions tend to mislead policy-makers in the absolute sense because of the varying degrees of overestimation. Sophisticated attribute choice models which are calibrated in terms of the stated intentions also tend to be weak predictors of actual public response to new policies. A logit model is calibrated using the attribute ratings of the alternatives under the new policy conditions described in the scenario in relation to current behaviour not stated intentions. This empirical approach provides highly accurate predictions of the actual public reaction to new policies.

5B33 GUNN, H.F. (1981) Travel budgets – a review of evidence and modelling implications. *Transportation Research*, **15A** (1), pp. 7–23.

This paper reviews the empirical data that have been put forward as evidence for the feasibility of direct forecasts of the average amounts of time and money allocated to travel, and the alternative model frameworks which have been designed to exploit such forecasts. It is concluded that the evidence for the stability of aggregate travel behaviour from analyses of cross-sectional data has not yet been reconciled with the varations shown over time. At an individual level, there are large, and apparently random, variations in the amounts of travel undertaken in a day. The hypothesis that an overall 'budget mechanism' governs individual travel decisions is discussed; it is concluded that this hypothesis remains unproven, but raises interesting questions about current methods of forecasting travel demand.

5B34 HENSHER, D.A. (1987) Issues in the pre-analysis of panel data. *Transportation Research*, **21A** (4/5), pp. 265–285.

An important phase of longitudinal data research is the pre-analysis of the data to determine the nature and extent of biases attributable to missing data. Loss of information takes many forms, but can be classified into the broad categories of loss of item data (i.e. a specific variable for some units of observation) and loss of unit data (i.e. the loss of an entire observation due to refusal or movement out of the sampled population). In this paper the author discusses various ways of correcting for identified bias. The methods outlined are separated into those statistical procedures which are suitable in testing and correcting at the aggregate level, those relevant at the individual unit level, and non-statistical procedures such as unit tracing. Since correction at the unit level is especially important for household panel data that are to be used in econometric modelling, the author looks in detail at the relationship between imputation and weighting methods of correcting for bias due to attrition.

5B35 HIRSH, M., PRASHKER, J.N. and BEN-AKIVA, M. (1986) Dynamic model of weekly activity pattern. *Transportation Science*, **20** (1), pp. 24-36.

This paper presents a model of weekly activity pattern, based on a theory of individual behaviour. The week is divided into time periods, and the following dynamic decision-making process is suggested. At the beginning of the first period, the individual selects his/her activity pattern for the entire week. At the beginning of the second period, the individual updates his/her plans for the remaining periods of the week on the basis of the actual behaviour and the additional information that was acquired during the first time periods. In this way, the individual proceeds from period to period and the observed weekly activity pattern is the outcome of successive decisions. Based on utility maximizing principles, a parametric model of this dynamic decision-making process that can be estimated with revealed preferences data is formulated. A version of the model for weekly shopping activity behaviour is estimated with survey data from Israel. The model is then applied to predict the effects of shortening the workweek. The empirical results support the dynamic behaviour hypothesis and demonstrate the potential biases that may arise from the omission in a travel demand model of the interdependencies among the days of the week.

5B36 HOROWITZ, J.L. (1985) Travel and location behaviour: state of the art and research opportunities. *Transportation Research*, **19A** (5/6), pp. 441-453.

This review is divided into two main sections. The first section reviews the theoretical and methodological basis of current travel-demand analysis, with particular emphasis on the role of utility theory. The main concepts and techniques associated with utility-theoretic travel demand models are summarized, important outstanding questions concerning the utility-theoretic approach are identified, and the relations between utility-based and alternative approaches to travel demand analysis are discussed. The second section treats substantive problems in travel demand analysis. The success that has been achieved so far in solving substantive problems is summarized, and a variety of important unsolved problems are identified.

5B37 HOROWITZ, A.D. and DAGANZO, C.F. (1986) Extrapolating automobile wage data to long time periods. *Transportation Science*, **20** (1), pp. 48–51.

This study illustrates a statistical procedure that can be used to estimate the fraction of a given population experiencing a 'rare' event during a long time period, given a few days of observation. In an automobile usage context, the rare event could be the occurrence of an automobile occupancy of four or more persons and/or a travel distance of 100 miles or more on any given day. The technique, which can be important for the design of durable goods, is illustrated with four numerical examples.

5B38 JANSEN, G.R.M., NIJKAMP, P. and RUIJGROK, C.J. (eds.) (1985) *Transportation and Mobility in an Era of Transition*. Amsterdam: North Holland.

Conference proceedings and revised papers are grouped in three sections. The first covers recent trends in transport and mobility, the second with new models and techniques of analysis, and the third with planning and policy issues.

5B39 KANAFANI, A. (1983) *Transportation Demand Analysis*. New York: McGraw-Hill.

This book offers thorough coverage of microeconomic demand theory and its application to transport, ranging from urban to regional transport and including both passenger and commodity flows. Quantitative material is supplemented by extensive discussion to demonstrate that traffic estimation is not an exact science, even though traveller or shipper behaviour can be represented by mathematical formulation. The first four chapters cover microeconomic demand theory, transport supply, and the conceptual and quantitative framework of transport demand analysis. The remaining chapters cover recent developments in travel behaviour analysis and in stochastic modelling of traveller choice, references for computer programmes available for applications, and an updated review of various computer models.

5B40 KEYS, E.C. and BENNETT, D.W. (1987) An analytical approach to sketch planning in suburban railways. *Transportation Planning and Technology*, **11** (4), pp. 289–298.

This paper presents a sketch planning model to assist operational planners in suburban railways. Its two component sub-models allow quick but approximate estimations to be made of various parameters. The fleet performance model estimates such parameters as fleet distance, fleet time and fleet size while line capacity is estimated in the second model. An analytical approach is adopted to provide insight into some of the fundamental relationships in rail operations. This makes the models useful not only for quick estimates but also as an aid to understanding the interactions within the system.

5B41 KITAMURA, R. (1981) A stratification analysis of taste variations in work-trip mode choice. *Transportation Research*, **15A** (6), pp. 473–485.

This study develops and applies a heuristic stratification procedure to the exploration of variation in tastes in tripmakers' choice of travel mode. The stratification procedure systematically identifies a set of socio-economic sub-groups that effectively accounts for the variation. Empirical results indicate that a limited number of socio-economic variables are associated with the taste variation, that the entire sample can be stratified into a few socio-economic sub-groups with distinctive tastes, and that choice models can be relevantly specified for respective sub-groups using exclusively level-of-service variables of travel modes as the model's independent variables.

5B42 KITAMURA, R. (1984) A model of daily time allocation to discretionary out-of-home activities and trips, *Transportation Research*, **18B** (3), pp. 255–266.

This paper presents a model of discrete activity choice and continuous resource allocation which is based on the premise of random utility maximization and which can be conveniently estimated using existing statistical software packages. The model derivation involves virtually no approximations and adheres strictly to the utility maximization concept. The empirical analysis applies the model to the participation choice and resource (time) allocation to non-work, out-of-home activities by workers. The statistical results show that activity choice and time allocation are governed by the same mechanism as the utilitarian assumptions indicate and support the theoretical framework employed in the model development.

5B43 KOPPELMAN, F.S. (1980) Consumer analysis of travel choice behaviour. *Journal of Advanced Transportation*, **14** (1), pp. 133–159.

This paper presents a conceptual framework for inclusion of psychological measures in the analysis of travel choice behaviour. This framework integrates and extends existing models of consumer choice based on consumer behaviour theory, marketing research, and transport demand theory. The model is illustrated by application to two distinct analyses of travel choice behaviour: selection of a destination for non-grocery shopping trips and choice of travel mode for non-work/school travel. Benefits of including psychological measures in travel choice analysis are related to improved understanding and predictive utility.

5B44 KOPPELMAN, F.S. (1983) Predicting transit ridership in response to transit service changes. *Journal of Transportation Engineering*, **109** (4), pp. 548–564.

The development of a simplified form of the multinomial logit model and its application to the prediction of travel mode shares for a range of transit service changes is reported in this article. Equations for predicting transit share for a new or improved service are presented. Procedures are described that can be employed to use the proposed equations to estimate transit ridership in a specific corridor if different levels of public transport service are established.

5B45 MACKETT, R.L. (1981) Modelling the impact of alternative transport strategies upon social groups. *Transportation Planning and Technology*, **6** (4), pp. 233–247.

In this paper, the application of a model representing the impact of interaction between transport costs and the location of housing, population, job employment, shopping and land is described. Two particular uses of the model are considered. Firstly, the effects of changing transport costs upon people of different social status in terms of money and time spent on travelling are examined and compared with results based upon the assumption that the location of population and employment are not responsive to changes in transport cost, as in the conventional transport demand model. Secondly, the effects of six land-use–transport policy sets are examined in terms of the impact upon urban morphology, and the opportunities and travel behaviour of the three social groups. The effects are also compared with the objectives of the strategies.

See also: Mackett, R.L. (1980) The relationship between transport and the viability of central and inner urban areas. *Journal of Transport Economics and Policy*, **14** (3), pp. 267–294.

5B46 MACKETT, R.L. and JOHNSON, I. (1985a) Residential search behaviour: the implications for survey and analytical design. *Tijdschrift Voor Economische en Sociale Geografie*, **76** (3), pp. 173–179.

This article focuses on the residential search process and the role of accessibility to work in that process. Case material is taken from a survey of the location behaviour of rail commuters in South-East England. Among the findings were that access to work was the single most important reason for the choice of a particular dwelling, that the search process is rarely as well-defined as implied by researchers, and that many people revise their ideas while searching as a result of an implicit learning process.

See also: Mackett, R.L. and Johnson, I. (1985b) Modelling the impact of rail fare increases. *Transportation*, **12** (4), pp. 293–312.

5B47 MADDALA, G.S. (1987) Recent developments in the econometrics of panel data analysis. *Transportation Research*, **21A** (4/5), pp. 303–326.

The present paper surveys different issues related to the econometric analysis of panel data. It discusses the controversy over fixed effects vs. random effects models, specification error tests with panel data, the problem of specification of the distribution of initial values in dynamic models, maximum-likelihood estimation of dynamic models, tests for serial correlation with panel data, serial correlation vs. state dependence, multiple equation models with panel data, and errors in variables in panel data. References are also given for certain other miscellaneous problems involving panel data.

5B48 MANNERING, F. and HENSHER, D.A. (1987) Discrete/continuous econometric models and their application to transport analysis. *Transport Reviews*, **7** (3), pp. 227-244.

A wide range of transport-related decisions involve the linking of discrete choices (e.g. of vehicle choice) and continuous choices (e.g. of vehicle use). In recent years econometricians have developed procedures for integrating such choices into a framework that is both economically and statistically sound. The literature is however somewhat technical. The objective of this paper is to provide a general overview of the basic elements of discrete/continuous econometric modelling with an emphasis on transport applications. It is hoped that such an introduction will demonstrate that the essence of the approach for the practitioner is quite straightforward and can be implemented with widely available computer software.

5B49 MATSOUKIS, E.C. (1986) Road traffic assignment: Non equilibrium methods. *Transportation Planning and Technology*, **11** (1), pp. 69-79; and Equilibrium methods. *Transportation Planning and Technology*, **11** (2), pp. 117-135.

This study reviews, in two parts, the formulation, interpretation and solution methodology of the traffic assignment problem. An extensive literature exists on this subject, and in the study an attempt is made to classify it. The first paper is devoted to non-equilibrium assignment models. The accompanying paper examines algorithmic approaches which are based on or make use of the Wardropian principle of equal travel times and which are thereafter characterized as equilibrium assignments. Non-equilibrium models are classified into: all-or-nothing assignments; capacity-restraint assignments; diversion models; multipath assignments; and combined models. In each category the operating principles are described in brief, together with other details such as advantages-disadvantages, validation efforts and applications of these models. For the equilibrium methods a similar approach is adopted to cover assignments with fixed demand, assignments with elastic demand, and combined models. Examples are given, and an assessment is made of the advantages and disadvantages of both types of assignment methods.

5B50 MORRIS, J.M. and WIGAN, M.R. (1979) A family expenditure perspective on transport planning: Australian evidence in context. *Transportation Research*, **13A**, pp. 249–285.

Australian family expenditure survey data are used to develop an appraisal perspective on transport planning issues from this social viewpoint. Comparisons are also made with data from other countries where these are available. Issues covered include: basic organizational features of family expenditure surveys; general limitations in using this source of data; the practical value of family expenditure data in the appraisal of transport needs and demands; complementary sources of data and/or refinements to family expenditure surveys which are needed for transport planning purposes; and key research areas presently left untouched by family expenditure surveys. The family expenditure perspective is peculiarly appropriate to the examination of the social impacts of transport changes from both operational and construction standpoints: transport is a derived demand, and the examination of the patterns of constraints and revealed preferences for transport in competition with other goods in a household budget has been shown to have a clear and helpful relevance to questions of access, mobility and differential impacts of transport changes. There are also indications that such a viewpoint may lead to greater consistency with international findings in these areas.

See also: Morris, J.M. and Lane, J.E. (1980) Variations in household transport expenditure within major Australian cities. *Transportation Planning and Technology*, **6** (2), pp. 189–202.

5B51 NAROFF, J.L., MADDEN, T.J. and DILLON, W.R. (1984) Neighbourhood influences on travel behaviour and availability constraints. *Environment and Planning A*, **16** (1), pp. 33–47.

Traditionally, transport demand studies have, for the most part, viewed modal choice in terms of an aggregate system-wide function. However, it seems reasonable to expect that the travel decision may be influenced by a composite of factors that include not only availability conditions, but determinants relating to neighbourhood characteristics and peer-group pressures. In this paper, supply-side constraints on availability were used to segment the market, and logit probabilistic choice models were fitted to each segment. It was found that inducements to individuals to alter their modal choice must consider not only cost factors and standard demographics, but also peer-group (class) constraints. System-wide approaches will fail to consider these important demand considerations.

5B52 NEALE, J.L. and HUTCHINSON, B.G. (1981) Analysis of household travel activities by information statistics. *Transportation Research*, **15A** (2), pp. 163-171.

The travel times of various types of activities by a sample of Vancouver households are analysed using a mutual information statistic. The basic objective of these analyses was to isolate those household factors influencing the consumption of travel. The advantage of the mutual information statistic over the normally used parametric statistics is that nominal variables such as stage in life-cycle and marital status may be analysed along with ordinal and ratio scale variables. The variables describing households are first analysed and the information redundancy between the various variables is displayed through the use of a maximally weighted tree. Cluster analysis is used to develop clusters of households with similar travel time consumption profiles and the information statistic is used to identify the most important household descriptor variables. The method of analysis described in the paper is particularly useful for transport systems analysis where nominal and ordinal variables are frequently encountered.

5B53 NICHOLSON, A.J. and LIM, Y.H. (1987) Household expenditure on transport in New Zealand. *Australian Road Research*, **17** (1), pp. 28-39.

This paper describes the results of an analysis of data from the annual New Zealand Household Expenditure Survey, for the period 1975-83. Several alternative forms of model relating expenditure to income are described and their relative merits are discussed. The temporal stability of expenditure patterns is discussed, as are the effects on transport expenditure of factors other than income (e.g. household size and household type).

5B54 OBENG, K. (1985) Constrained welfare maximization – application to transit fare determination. *Transport Policy and Decision Making*, **3** (1), pp. 61-80.

This paper determines optimal transit fares based on constrained net welfare maximization. The methodology is an extension of the

Baumol-Bradford pricing rule which is shown to be inapplicable to transit systems if net benefit is considered. The major conclusions of the paper are: for unconstrained net welfare maximization, the ratio of fare to its corresponding elasticity of demand is constant; consistent deviation of marginal revenue from marginal cost is required for constrained net welfare maximization. The application of the methods to a transit system shows that the Baumol-Bradford rule will generally result in higher fare compared to the method developed in this paper.

5B55 OGDEN, K.W. and YOUNG, W. (1984) A model of managers' preferences for location of freight facilities. *Transportation Planning and Technology*, **8** (4), pp. 283-294.

An elimination by aspects model is developed to analyse a range of location decisions by managers of freight firms. Results are comparable to those obtained with a logit model. The most important factors in structuring preferences are closeness to existing customers, closeness to arterial roads, availability of suitable sites, costs of operation and labour availability.

5B56 ORTUZAR, J. de D. (1983) Nested logit models for mixed mode travel in urban corridors. *Transportation Research*, **17A** (4), pp. 283-299.

The nested logit (NL) model is a generalization of the well-known multinomial logit (MNL) model which copes with its 'independence from irrelevant alternatives' problem at the expense of more difficult calibration and use. Mixed-mode movements (i.e. park-and-ride) are by nature not independent of competing single-mode options and have, therefore, traditionally been inadequately modelled in most empirical applications. This paper reports on the specification, estimation, testing and comparison of MNL and NL models using disaggregate data of work trips in an urban corridor, where choice was among several alternatives including mixed-mode options. It was found that the more general NL model was more adequate, not only in theory but in practice. The paper concludes by comparing the disaggregate NL model with previously calibrated aggregate NL models for the same corridor using a different data set.

5B57 PAS, E.I. (1985) State of the art and research opportunities in travel demand: another perspective. *Transportation Research*, **19A** (5/6), pp. 460–464.

This paper presents a brief overview of the state of the art in one stream of travel demand research, namely the activity-based approach. A number of research opportunities and needs in travel demand analysis are identified and discussed. Finally, data needs are examined.

See also: Pas, E.I. (1983) A flexible and integrated methodology for analytical classification of daily travel-activity behaviour. *Transportation Science*, **17** (4), pp. 405–429.

5B58 PAS, E.I. and KOPPELMAN, F.S. (1987) An examination of the determinants of day-to-day variability in individuals' urban travel behaviour. *Transportation*, **14** (1), pp. 3–20.

Day-to-day variability in individuals' travel behaviour (intra-personal variability) has been recognized in conceptual discussions, yet the analysis and modelling or urban travel are typically based on a single-day record of each individual's travel. This paper develops and examines hypotheses regarding the determinants of intra-personal variability in urban travel behaviour. Two general hypotheses are formulated to describe the effects of motivations for travel and related behaviour and of travel and related constraints on intra-personal variability in weekday urban travel behaviour. Specific hypotheses concerning the effect of various socio-demographic characteristics on intra-personal variability are derived from these general hypotheses. These specific hypotheses are tested empirically in the context of daily trip frequency using a five-day record of travel in Reading, England. The empirical results support the two general hypotheses. First, individuals who have fewer economic and role-related constraints have higher levels of intra-personal variability in their daily trip frequency. Second, individuals who fulfil personal and household needs that do not require daily participation in out-of-home activities have higher levels of intra-personal variability in their daily trip frequency.

5B59 PUTMAN, S.H. (1975) Urban land use and transportation models: a state-of-the-art summary. *Transportation Research*, **9** (2), pp. 187–202.

The paper assumes that the general relationship between transport and land-use may be defined in terms of three primary components: economic activity (i.e. employment), demographic activity, and transport facilities. After a brief introductory section, the second section of the paper contains a review of the state of the art of models of economic activity location i.e. intra-urban employment forecasting. The third section of the paper contains a review of the state of the art of models of demographic activity location, i.e. intra-urban population forecasting. The final section of the paper begins with a brief description of urban transport network models. The section and paper are then concluded with a discussion of possible integrated land-use and transport model packages.

5B60 PUTMAN, S.H. (1983) *Integrated Urban Models: Policy Analysis of Transportation and Land Use.* London: Pion.

This book presents the results of more than a decade of investigation of the interrelationships between transport and land use in metropolitan regions. Theoretical and empirical analyses are described. The theoretical work begins with a simple models of transport and land use, while the empirical work begins with attempts to fit these models into an observed reality. The development of the first integrated transport and land-use model is then described, together with the results of prototype applications. The author then traces a series of theoretical developments, empirical verifications and subsequent policy analyses, as well as their effects on one another.

See also: Putman, S.H. (1979) *Urban Residential Location Models.* Studies in Applied Regional Science No. 13. The Hague: Martinus Nijhoff.

5B61 PUTMAN, S.H. (1984) Dynamic properties of static-recursive model systems of transportation and location. *Environment and Planning A*, **16**, pp. 1503–1519.

In the past decade there have been a number of efforts aimed at the development of more-complete representations of urban transport and land-use interactions. In this paper, it is suggested that there is a great deal to be learned from experimentation with existing as well as emerging techniques. Systems of models are discussed in general terms with particular reference to the implications of selecting one system over another. A report is given of some empirical work with an integrated transport and land-use model structure and the consequences of the model-system structure for the empirical work are discussed.

5B62 RICHARDS, M. (1982) Disaggregate demand models – promises and prospects. *Transportation Research*, **16A** (5/6), pp. 339–344.

For nearly two decades it has been recognized that there are serious deficiencies in the traditional aggregate modelling approach to travel demand analysis. It was hoped that many, if not all, of these deficiencies would be overcome through the development of disaggregate models. Yet nearly 10 years after some of the first major research projects, it has been suggested that they have not yet been successfully applied in any major planning study. There can be little doubt that disaggregate model techniques do offer the scope for major improvements over aggregate models, yet there would seem to be a growing groundswell of doubt about their ability to live up to the expectations which were cultivated during the early 1970s. The crucial question to most of those concerned with planning and policy development is, even if disaggregate models are not the panacea they were hoped to be, whether they can still improve our forecasting ability, or not.

5B63 ROONEY, S. and TEAL, R. (1986) Developing a cost model for privately contracted commuter bus services. *Transportation Research Record*, 1051, pp. 48–56.

Provision of public transport services by the private sector is often cited as a strategy for reducing transit costs and required subsidies. Attempts to compare public agency and private contractor service costs for transit operations of a significant size are complicated, however, by the small number of comparable services now being provided and by the difficulty of comparing estimates of public and private costs when only a portion of the service delivery system is being contracted. An approach is presented in this paper to remedy one aspect of this cost comparison problem by developing a cost model for privately contracted commuter bus service. This model permits the full service costs of a privately contracted commuter bus operation to be estimated. The model utilizes a fixed-variable expense approach to estimate cost, and is based on information obtained from actual commuter bus contractors for two large transit systems. Capital charges, which depend on vehicle use as well as vehicle cost and contract length, represent a major portion of service costs. The model was applied to three situations and the results were satisfactory; it estimated route costs within 2 to 12 per cent of average actual values in each case. The model performed much better than two previously developed models and appears satisfactory for its intended purpose.

5B64 SIKDAR, P.K. and HUTCHINSON, B.G. (1981) Empirical studies of work trip distribution models. *Transportation Research*, **15A** (3), pp. 233-243.

The goodness of fit characteristics of three members of the Wilson-family of gravity models in explaining observed work trip interchanges are examined using an almost 100 per cent sample of journey to work trips in Edmonton, Alberta. Model parameters of the three model types and several variants are estimated for four zone systems ranging in numbers from 22 to 234 zones. Changes in parameter magnitudes and model performance are examined across model types and spatial scales. It is concluded that current gravity models calibrated to cross-sectional data and using only trip end and aggregate travel cost constraints have inadequate explanatory power to justify their use in planning studies. Additional trip end constraints, such as socio-economic stratification, do not yield significant improvements and trip interchange constraints appear to offer the most productive improvement possibilities. The most important factor which is not captured by current cross-sectional models is the timing of urban development which can only reasonably be captured through trip interchange constraints.

5B65 SONNTAG, H. (1985) A computer model for urban commercial traffic-analysis, basic concept and application. *Transport Policy and Decision Making*, **3** (2), pp. 171-180.

A model for computing the extent and variety of urban commercial traffic has been developed and put into operation as a programme system. This model is capable of calculating trip generations, the structural relationships between traffic producers and receivers as well as presenting trip distribution as a source-destination matrix. The results are now available, logically organized into categories of time and space. Commercial groups and trip purposes can be identified, in addition to basic traffic zones and hourly intervals. The model has been designed as a behaviour-oriented simulation model and derives its basic information on structural data of traffic production and the long-term behaviour patterns of traffic users on contemporary planning case histories. The model can, therefore, basically be used for planning purposes involving different areas and different periods of time.

5B66 STEPHANEDES, Y.J. and EAGLE, D.M. (1986) Time-series analysis of interactions between transportation and manufacturing and retail employment. *Transportation Research Record*, 1074, pp. 16–24.

Using data on state highway expenditures and employment from 30 Minnesota non-metropolitan counties over a 25-year period, possible interactions between transportation and employment are investigated. Although cross-sectional analysis suggests no significant interactions, causality tests and time-series analysis indicate that highway expenditures affect manufacturing and retail employment, and employment influences expenditure. Although increases in expenditures cause employment improvements in the short term, long-term effects are less favourable. Highway expenditures respond quickly to increased needs caused by retail improvements.

5B67 STOPHER, P.R. and ERGUN, G. (1982) The effect of location and demand for urban recreation trips. *Transportation Research*, **16A** (1), pp. 25–34.

This paper is concerned with the development of models for forecasting and predicting the choices of urban residents for urban recreational and cultural activities and, hence, the travel for such activities. In earlier work, reported elsewhere, some preliminary choice models, using the multinomial logit model, were reported with one-way segmentations for each geographic location, perceived attractiveness, and stage in the family lifecycle. Geographic segmentation was found to be statistically the most significant segmentation scheme which is an undesirable result. It was postulated subsequently, that geographic segmentation was a proxy for social and economic differences in the populations of the geographic units used. This paper reports on the results of two-way segmentations using location as one dimension and various socio-demographic variables as the second dimension. In all cases, it was still found that the effects of location were significant, although seemingly less so than in the one-way segmentation schemes.

See also: Stopher [5A21].

5B68 SWAIT, J. and BEN-AKIVA, M. (1987) Empirical test of a constrained choice discrete model: mode choice in Sao Paulo, Brazil. *Transportation Research*, **21A** (2), pp. 103–109.

This paper examines the properties and empirically tests a model of discrete choice which incorporates probabilistic choice set generation. Denominated the Parametrized Logit Captivity (PLC) model, it is a generalization of the well-known 'dogit' specification. The PLC model is shown to be theoretically and empirically more flexible than the latter. Work mode choice data collected in a 1977 origin/destination (O/D) survey in Sao Paulo, Brazil, is used to obtain parameter estimates, as well as to evaluate consumer reaction to a series of perturbations in travel time, travel cost and income, for both the PLC and Multinomial Logit models. Comparisons between the two specifications are made in terms of statistical fit, reasonableness of predictions and differences in predictions across models.

5B69 TEODOROVIC, D. (1986) *Transportation Networks: A Quantitative Treatment*. Transportation Studies Series Volume 6. London: Harwood Academic Publishers.

This book provides detailed coverage of the theory of transport networks as a general traffic and transport discipline. The author examines some of the daily difficulties encountered by traffic and transport experts, uncovering the intricacies of vehicle routing and scheduling, crew planning and facilities placement. This problem-solving approach uses many numerical examples and simple mathematical methods to enable newcomers to apply the book's solutions to the situations they encounter on the job.

5B70 TIMMERMANS, H. (1982) Consumer choice of shopping centre: an information integration approach. *Regional Studies*, **16** (3), pp. 171–182.

This paper is concerned with the relationships between the physical attributes of the retailing system, consumer decision-making and overt behaviour. The appropriateness of an approach, which is based on information integration theory and functional measurement, as a means of predicting consumer response to changes in physical attributes of shopping centres, is considered, both from an empirical and methodological point of view. The results of the empirical study tend to provide general support for the approach. Several methodological issues are raised which deserve further investigation in order to refine the approach.

5B71 TIMMERMANS, H., VAN DER HEIJDEN, R. and WESTERVELD, H. (1982) The identification of factors influencing destination choice: an application of the repertory grid methodology. *Transportation*, 11 (2), pp. 189-203.

A common problem of all cognitive-behavioural models of destination choice is that of the identification of factors influencing the behaviour of interest. This paper considers the applicability of Kelly's repertory grid methodology to identify the factors influencing consumer choice of shopping centres. Firstly, some methodological issues in the assessment of the relative importance people attach to certain variables in deciding where to shop are discussed. Secondly, the main findings of an application of the repertory grid methodology are presented. The paper concludes by discussing some implications of the measurement of the determinants of choice behaviour and the construction of mathematical models of destination choice.

5B72 TRAIN, K. (1986) *Qualitative Choice Analysis*. Cambridge, Mass: MIT Press.

The recently developed methods of qualitative choice analysis and their application to the analysis of consumer demand for automobiles are presented in this book. The author develops the general principles that underlie qualitative choice models that are now being applied to numerous fields in addition to transport, such as housing, labour, energy, communications, and criminology. The general form, derivation, and estimation of qualitative choice models are explained, and the major models – logit, probit, and GEV – are discussed in detail.

5B73 TURNER, G.E. (1984) Simulation of pedestrian movement in means of egress. *Journal of Architectural and Planning Research*, **1** (3), pp. 181–189.

A general modelling approach to pedestrian movement is presented at the scale of specific building circulation system components. Empirically derived descriptions of individual human walking are used in a computer simulation of aggregate movement. Different patterns of movement can be generated so that alternative design layouts can be tested.

5B74 WEGENER, M. (1986) **Transport network equilibrium and regional deconcentration.** *Environment and Planning A*, **18** (4), pp. 437–456.

Processes of urban and regional change can be classified in terms of their temporal characteristics as fast-adjusting, medium-response, or inert. Based on this classification, a modelling approach is presented that combines a fast-adjusting equilibrium-type transport model, a medium-response residential occupation (housing-market) model, and a strongly lagged residential location (housing-construction) model. It is suggested that such a model structure takes better account of the range of temporal behaviour observed in metropolitan regions than modelling approaches directed at determining a simultaneous equilibrium of transport and location. With data of the Dortmund, West Germany, metropolitan region, the model is employed to demonstrate the role of the transport system in the process of regional deconcentration observed in that region.

5B75 WILLIAMS, H.C.W.L. (1981) Travel demand forecasting: an overview of theoretical developments, in Banister, D.J. and Hall, P.G. (eds.) *Transport and Public Policy Planning*. London: Mansell, pp. 283–306.

The purpose of this paper is to review the theoretical development of travel forecasting models, with particular emphasis on British experiences, to examine the problems which have been overcome and those which currently confront us, and finally to offer some views on future prospects. Aspects relating to the aggregation issue are discussed along with dispersion theories and the accommodation of choice contexts. Further theoretical topics such as the requirements of internal consistency and the 'goodness-of-fit' of models are covered, and these issues are then related to the more practical evaluations of transport/land use strategies. In a final section a general overview is given of issues relating to the state of the art, and problems and prospects are discussed.

See also Williams, H.C.W.L. and Ortuzar, J de D. (1982) Travel demand and response analysis – some integrating themes, *Transportation Research*, **16A** (5/6), pp. 345–362.

5B76 WILLUMSEN, L.G. (1980) Simplified transport models based on traffic counts. *Transportation*, **10** (3), pp. 257–278.

Having accepted the need for the development of simpler and less cumbersome transport demand models, the paper concentrates on one possible line for simplification: estimation of trip matrices from link volume counts. Traffic counts are particularly attractive as a data basis for modelling because of their availability, low-cost and non-disruptive character. It is first established that in normal conditions it may be possible to find more than one trip matrix which, when loaded onto a network, reproduces the observed link volumes. The paper then identifies three approaches to reduce this underspecification problem and produce a unique trip matrix consistent with the counts. The first approach consists of assuming that trip-making behaviour can be explained by a gravity model whose parameters can be calibrated from the traffic counts. The second approach uses mathematical programming techniques associated to equilibrium assignment problems to estimate a trip matrix in congested areas. This method can also be supplemented by a special distribution model developed for small areas. The third approach relies on entropy and information theory considerations to estimate the most likely trip matrix consistent with the observed flows. A particular feature of this group is that they can include prior, perhaps outdated, information about the matrix.

5B77 WILSON, A.G., COELHO, J.D., MACGILL, S.M. and WILLIAMS, H.C.W.L. (1981) *Optimisation in Locational and Transport Analysis.* Chichester: John Wiley.

In a review of urban and regional modelling the authors discuss aspects of the subject based on optimization techniques. A range of applications of these techniques in the field of locational and transport analysis is covered. Chapters of the book detail mathematical programming methods, the use of random utility theory and programming approaches to spatial interaction and activity location. Regional account-based models are generated using entropy maximizing methods and it is shown how the Lowry model can be presented as an input-output model. Current perspectives of dynamical systems theory are outlined. A range of applications of the methods covered is discussed including some systematic studies of design procedures in transport planning.

5B78 WILSON, F.R., STEVENS, A.M. and ROBINSON, J.B. (1984) Identifying mode choice constrained urban travel market segments. *Canadian Journal of Civil Engineering*, **11** (4), pp. 924–932.

Using a case study approach based on workplace surveys taken in the downtown core of Ottawa and involving only choosers and captives to given modes, this paper successfully models these two market segments. Trip-related and traveller-related data provided by the respondent are examined using analysis of variance techniques and significant differences are found between the two segmentations.

5B79 YOUNG, W. and RICHARDSON, A.J. (1983) The application of an elimination-by-aspects model to residential location choice. *Australian Road Research*, **13** (2), pp. 100–111.

The choice of residential location is characterized by the existence of many multi-attribute alternatives. In such a complex choice situation, a decision-maker may attempt to simplify the choice such that a decision is made before all attributes have been considered. This paper describes the development of a model which explicitly accounts for this type of behaviour. The theory behind the model, known as an Elimination-by-Aspects model, is discussed and its extension to allow for use of maximum likelihood estimation procedures is described. The model is then calibrated using a data set of 716 observations of residential location behaviour in Melbourne. Statistical testing of the model and its estimated tolerances shows that the model explains a high proportion of variance in the data set. Split sample model calibration and cross-prediction demonstrates high stability in the calibrated models and tolerances. Finally, choice elasticities are calculated and are shown to yield highly non-linear effects with different percentage changes in attribute satisfaction. It is concluded that the model should, with continued development, provide a useful input to informed policy advice in the area of residential location choice.

See also: Young, W. and Richardson, A.J. (1979) Residential area location preference surfaces. *Transportation Research Record*, 707, pp. 39–47.

5C Investment appraisal and evaluation

5C1 ATKINS, S.R. (1984) Why value travel time? The case against. *Highways and Transportation*, **31** (7), pp. 2–7.

Changes, usually savings, in travel time are a major output of most highway schemes. For the purpose of project evaluation these changes must be compared with other impacts, including those to which a definite cost can be allocated. It has been conventional practice, therefore, to attempt to place a monetary value on travel time savings in order to improve perception of the trade-off implied by an evaluation decision. This paper seeks to present an alternative case, that the valuation of travel time is unnecessary, that it is inconsistent with current evaluation procedures and that in many cases it can even be unhelpful. First, it is argued that the current framework approach to highway appraisal accepts that both multi-attribute considerations and the distributional aspects of these impacts are relevant, and that this necessarily implies that 'political' values must be used. In this context, the retention of fixed rates of trade-off between travel time and money remains an anachronism. If the valuation of travel time could be easily and uncontroversially accomplished there would, perhaps, be little to gain from abandoning the practice. Secondly, however, it is shown that adequate measurement of appropriate travel time values is extremely difficult from a practical perspective. Thirdly, it is argued that valuation of travel time is undesirable from a philosophical, even moral, standpoint. In concluding it is suggested that by obscuring the distinction between political and technical matters, travel time valuation may bring professionalism into disrepute.

5C2 BEESLEY, M.E., GIST, P. and GLAISTER, S. (1983) Cost benefit analysis and London Transport's policies. *Progress in Planning*, **19** (3), pp. 173–269.

This study selects certain changes in London Transport's policies to provide insights into the significance of social cost benefit analysis in justifying different levels of output achieved by the operator. The four changes tested are service level provisions on specific bus routes, closure of tube stations, service level reductions on the underground and a global evaluation of fare and service changes in buses and underground, viewing these activities as a whole. Full discussion is included on objective measures used and assumptions in the analysis.

5C3 CADY, P.D. (1983) Inflation and highway economy analysis. *Journal of Transportation Engineering*, **109** (5), pp. 631-639.

The methodology for incorporating the effects of inflation in economic analyses within the current highway funding scenario is developed in this paper. The consequences of ignoring the effects of inflation are significant. The situations most affected are evaluation of replacement alternatives versus maintenance of existing facilities and the deferring of needed capital expenditures.

5C4 DICKEY, J.W. and MILLER, L.H. (1984) *Road Project Appraisal for Developing Countries*. London: Wiley.

This book is concerned with the appraisal of road projects in developing countries using World Bank experiences and data from a range of West African and Latin American countries. The stages in analysis are presented from the development of objectives and alternatives, the principle of economic analysis, cost analysis, user costs and benefits, price analysis and non-user impact analysis. Included here are the broader development effects, multipliers and the impact on agricultural output. The coverage is extensive with further discussion on organizational issues, financial analysis and budgeting, and training requirements. Finally, the overall evaluation is placed in an economic framework and issues such as risk and uncertainty, and monitoring are commented on.

5C5 DODGSON, J.S. and TOPHAM, N. (1986) Cost-benefit criteria for urban public transport subsidies. *Environment and Planning C*, **4** (2), pp. 177-185.

In this paper cost-benefit rules for public transport subsidies are considered. Recent applications of cost-benefit analysis to the appraisal of bus service provision are surveyed, and justifications for public transport subsidy considered. The authors derive the cost-benefit ratio appropriate for considering the benefits to public transport users of a fare reduction financed through increased local taxation on housing services. The cost-benefit rules are then extended to allow for the impact of central government assistance through grants-in-aid, and to incorporate allowances for external benefits in the form of reduced road traffic congestion and for income distributional considerations. A cost-benefit rule appropriate for assessing the case for service-level improvements which reduce passenger waiting times is also noted.

See also Dodgson, J.S. (1986) Benefits of changes in urban public transport subsidies in the major Australian cities. *Economic Record*, **62**, pp. 224–235 and [4A20].

5C6 GORDON, P. and MURETTA, P. (1983) The benefits and costs of the San Bernadino busway: implications for planning. *Transportation Research*, **17A** (2), pp. 89–94.

This paper presents an economic evaluation of Los Angeles' San Bernardino Freeway express busway. The potential for efficiency of this mode in a highly dispersed metropolitan area is demonstrated. Findings indicate that the mixed-mode operations allowed on the facility generate a good part of the benefits. It is also suggested that a lane flow reversal design would have increased efficiency beyond that of the existing facility. Finally, the wisdom of recently enacted (California) legislation, requiring convertibility to rail transit on all future busway construction, is questioned.

5C7 HILLS, P.J. and JONES-LEE, M.W. (1983) The role of safety in highway investment appraisal for developing countries. *Accident Analysis and Prevention*, **15** (5), pp. 355–369.

The high and rising toll of death, injury and material damage caused by traffic accidents has become a matter of serious concern both to politicians and to professionals involved in transport planning and project appraisal in developing countries. As a consequence, transport planners are showing an increasing awareness of the need to evolve rational, systematic procedures for taking account of safety effects in highway investment appraisal for such countries. The systematic analysis of safety in highway investment appraisal has two fundamental aspects: (a) estimation of the effects of different projects and design features on accident rates; (b) the specification of a decision criterion or procedure which will allow the effects estimated in (a) to be incorporated in project appraisal. This paper considers the various different ways in which safety effects, once estimated, might be evaluated in the course of project appraisal. It is argued that if inconsistency and allocative inefficiency are to be avoided, then explicit monetary costs of accidents and values of accident prevention are required. The paper then proceeds to examine the way in which such costs and values might be defined and estimated.

5C8 JANARTHANAN, N. and SCHNEIDER, J. (1986)Multicriteria evaluation of alternative transit system designs. *Transportation Research Record*, 1064, pp. 26–34.

One of the most important but underdeveloped parts of the transit planning process is the evaluation of alternative designs. The results from evaluation studies provide a basis for decision making. Evaluation of alternative transit system designs is now even more important because of reduced public funds. A computer-based multicriteria method using concordance analysis is described and applied to evaluate alternative transit system designs. Development of objectives and criteria, normalization methods, and the use of relative important weights are presented. A non-linear method of normalization technique that uses a logistic curve is introduced. The shape of this curve can be varied by the user. An application of the multicriteria evaluation methodology to five alternative transit system designs is presented to illustrate how the best design can be identified.

5C9 JARA-DIAZ, S.R. (1986) On the relation between users' benefits and the economic effects of transportation activities. *Journal of Regional Science*, **26** (2), pp. 379–391.

It is shown that a competitive productive environment makes consumers' surplus exactly equal to the net economic benefits provoked in the producers' markets. However, when monopolistic production prevails, the users' surplus may not reflect the benefits to the economy with accuracy.

5C10 LIMA, P.M. (1985) An economic analysis computer package for urban highway improvements. *Transportation Research Record*, 1012, pp. 14–22.

The structure and operation of an interactive FORTRAN computer package to perform economic analyses on highway improvements are described. The computational methodology of the program is discussed; this includes defining the broad range of alternatives, computing highway segment costs, computing intersection delay costs, computing intersection accident costs, and performing an economic analysis of the alternatives. Next, the overall design and operation of the program are outlined along with descriptions of the inputs and outputs of each program within the package. The various program options available to the user are also presented. In addition, the data file structure within the package and the programs provided to update existing files are discussed. A comparison of a four-way stop sign control with a fully actuated traffic signal is then presented to illustrate one application of the package.

5C11 NISKANEN, E. (1987) Congestion tolls and consumer welfare. *Transportation Research*, **21B** (2), pp. 171–174.

This short paper outlines the theory of congestion tolls when the time valuations by different users are not identical. It also investigates the conditions for an improvement in the aggregate consumers' surplus under a rise in the user charge.

5C12 ORGANISATION FOR ECONOMIC COOPERATION AND DEVELOPMENT (1985) *Coordinated Urban Transport Pricing*. Paris: OECD, Road Transport Research Group.

This report reviews member countries' urban transport policies. Analysis then considers the trends in structure, use and financial performance of urban transport systems, alternative theoretical approaches to transport pricing, and the practice of pricing and coordination. Recommendations are made as to where further research should be directed.

5C13 ORGANISATION FOR ECONOMIC COOPERATION AND DEVELOPMENT (1987) *Toll Financing and Private Sector Involvement in Road Infrastructure Development*. Paris: OECD, Road Transport Research Group.

After an introductory section on the historical developments on toll roads, road financing and construction issues, the bulk of the report is concerned with a presentation and assessment of the options available. It covers the institutional provisions available, the risks and their allocation, and other elements of the legal and/or contractual framework such as design standards, pricing controls and conditions related to concessions. The economic theory of toll roads is presented, and the advantages are discussed through a series of case studies. Finally, recommendations to governments are made on the benefits of road tolling in terms of accelerated road programmes, the stricter application of economic criteria and the benefits for general economic and regional development.

5C14 PEARMAN, A.D. (1985) Uncertainty in planning. Characterisation, evaluation and feedback. *Environment and Planning B*, 12 (3), pp. 313–320.

Uncertainty is a double-edged sword for the planner. Without it, society's need for strategic planning would be much reduced, but its existence is often at the root of much of the criticism which public perceptions of the planning profession induce. In this paper it is argued that not only is the need to take proper account of uncertainty greater than ever before, but so too are the opportunities to do so in practice. Three aspects of the uncertainty question are analysed. How should uncertainty be characterized within the planning process? What influence should the presence of uncertainty have on evaluation procedures? How should plan design respond to the presencce of uncertainty? It is concluded that increasingly the required formal techniques and computational capacity are available: planners must be sure to use them to good effect.

5C15 PEARMAN, A.D. and BUTTON, K.J. (1982) Some conventional and not-so-conventional views of congestion. *Transportation Research Record*, 887, pp. 29–34.

The purpose of this paper is to explore the extent to which the conventional treatment of highway congestion, as developed in the economic analysis of road pricing, provides an acceptable theoretical or practical foundation for policy. The conventional theory is first outlined, and it is emphasized that, although it is probably technically sound, it relates to highly abstract circumstances. The main body of the paper then develops two themes. First, a number of arguments are put forward that imply that, in quantitative if not qualitative terms, the conventional analysis of congestion seems unlikely to provide an adequate basis for the proper formulation of policy. Second, some reasons for regarding congestion as an effective allocative mechanism in its own right are given. Although the arguments in the paper are not developed sufficiently far to reach firm conclusions of an operational kind, there are clear indications that traffic management and related policies aimed at securing efficient use of existing highway facilities should proceed with care when valuing congestion savings and when assessing optimal congestion levels.

5C16 POOLE, M.R. and CRIBBINS, P.D. (1983) Development and application of the benefit matrix model for transportation project evaluation. *Journal of Advanced Transportation*, **17** (3), pp. 253–277.

The development and application of a procedure for evaluating proposed urban highway projects that can serve as a framework for establishing statewide construction priorities are described. Guidelines are provided for local officials who need to select and rank urban area projects in order of priority. The research methodology included the following sequential steps: evaluating previously developed priority models, specifying criteria for the model, model building, and testing the model by using candidate urban highway projects from three North Carolina test cities. A benefits matrix model for transport project evaluation was developed. The model consisted of five elements designed to provide the decision maker with relevant project evaluation information that directly relates to transport planning objectives.

5C17 SACCOMANNO, F.F. (1980) Transport policy analysis through site value transfer. *Journal of Transport Economics and Policy*, **14** (2), pp. 169–184.

The transfer of investment impacts into a modified site value pattern on urban land suggests a tool for policy analysis empirically more manageable than a traditional welfare economics approach. The use of site value transfer (changes in the value of land attributable solely to relative locational advantage) reduces the problems associated with the valuation of intangibles and consumer surplus for a complex investment programme. An empirical model of site value transfer for the residential sector, based on data from Toronto, employs an iterative algorithm that inter-relates reductions in commuting expenditures, changes in site value, land development adjustments, population-employment allocation and transport planning.

5C18 SCHNUERER, H. (1984) Optimisation of road investments based on accessibility criteria using dynamic programming model. *Transportation Planning and Technology*, **9** (3), pp. 237-246.

The use of the dynamic programming concept to determine road construction needs using accessibility criteria is discussed. An attempt is made to specify political and social goals, such as quality of life and equal opportunity, as parameters of road dimensioning. The objective of the method, which is illustrated by a case study, is to determine minimum total costs for various threshold values of conceivable accessibility standards.

5C19 SHALLAL, L.A.Y. and KHAN, A.M. (1982) A decision-theoretic framework for urban transport design and investment decisions. *Transportation Quarterly*, **36** (2), pp. 283-299.

This paper examines transport decision making through a structured and sequential process, and suggests ways in which established procedures could be improved. Different frameworks are incorporated into the approach, including those from decision theory, evaluation of design, and expected values of information. These approaches are then applied to data from the Regional Municipality of Ottawa-Carleton in Canada. It is suggested that the application of the decision-theoretic framework is useful in examining planning and management decisions with optimal design decisions being different from those made as a result of conventional planning methodology. The cost effectiveness of the approach is enhanced if the investment is great with a high degree of uncertainty.

5C20 SHARP, C., BUTTON, K. and DEADMAN, D. (1986) The economics of tolled road crossings. *Journal of Transport Economics and Policy*, **20** (2), pp. 255-274.

This paper examines the nature and problems of tolling crossings in the USA and the UK. It outlines the basic economic theory upon which tolls could be based, and considers the divergence of current practices from this theory. It pays particular attention to the difference in approach adopted by the central authorities of the two countries, and examines reasons for these differences and the implications for the pursuit of an efficient transport policy. Some estimates are provided of the long-term debt problems which are likely to be encountered on certain crossings in the UK if current policies are continued.

5C21 SICKING, D.L. and ROSS, H.E. (1986) Benefit-cost analysis of roadside safety alternatives. *Transportation Research Record*, 1065, pp. 98–105.

In recent years, benefit-cost analysis procedures have been widely accepted as a rational method for evaluating safety treatment alternatives. Most methods of analysis employed to date have significant limitations, overstate the severity of accidents, and are cumbersome to use. An advanced benefit-cost analysis model that incorporates numerous modifications to enhance versatility and improve determination of accident severity is described. Basic encroachment data on which the model is based are presented, and the applications and limitations of the model are discussed. An example of the use of the model to develop general barrier use guidelines is also included.

5C22 TYSON, W. (1985) Appraising transport policy options: performance mixed and likely to get worse, in Harrison, A.J. and Gretton, J. (eds.) *Transport Policy UK: An Economic Social and Policy Audit*. Newbury: Policy Journals, pp. 51–58.

This review starts by examining current practice in transport appraisal as it effects the road sector, railways and buses, so that the obstacles to the use of a consistent set of appraisal methods can be identified. Two main categories are highlighted, the technical (where not enough is known to apply a particular appraisal method) and the organizational (where the knowledge is available, but is not used). The paper ends with a set of proposals to overcome these two obstacles.

5C23 WATTERSON, W.T. (1985) Estimating economic and development impacts of transit investment. *Transportation Research Record*, 1045, pp. 1–9.

Although economic and development impacts are frequently included as positive objectives of major transit investments, the issues, methods, and results of actual impact analysis remain rather crude and are sometimes misleading. Reported in this paper is an empirical analysis of economic and development impacts from a study of major transit investment for the Seattle area, using state-of-the-art econometric and spatial interaction models. Economic impacts are found to be quite sensitive to assumptions on financing local shares of transit investment, although project financial planning and economic impact analysis have rarely been considered together. Development impacts, in terms of both job and household locations, are modest overall and are concentrated in the vicinity of the central business district that was to be the focus of the transit service, despite the magnitude of the investment involved. The research findings are somewhat tentative, but do suggest directions for applied research in quantitative analysis with operational models to the end of clarifying for policy purposes the potential impacts of major investment projects.

5C24   WILSON, T. and NEFF, C. (1983) *The Social Dimension in Transportation Assessment.* Aldershot: Gower.

This book begins by describing the inadequacies in the evaluative frame of reference adopted by transport planners on both sides of the Atlantic which has led to the expenditure of vast sums of money without the proper assessment of social implications, thus creating enormous problems. Potential sources and the generation of social information are then discussed, and some specific British and Canadian transport studies are compared. The final section of the book discusses the decision-making implications of social information generation.

5C25   YU, J.C. and PANG, L.M.G. (1985) A quick-response technique for impact assessment of highway improvement projects. *Transportation Research Record*, 1026, pp. 66–72.

To help master the complexity involved in the evaluation of highway improvement projects, this study was intended to develop a procedural framework for identifying a general set of significant impact measures and to further suggest a quick-response technique for assessing potential impacts of project alternatives. The impact identification procedure is in three stages: search, screening, and consolidation. The project impacts are assessed by consideration of the level, scope, and number of potential impacts and are rated on a numerical scale employing a linear utility function. Although many highway impact evaluation methods have been developed in the past, this study has suggested a quick and inexpensive tool for preliminary project evaluation that requires little detailed data and reasonable staff time yet should provide adequate estimates of whether further planning and development of a project or projects are worthwhile.

5D Energy

5D1 BANISTER, C. and BANISTER, D. (1983) Transport, travel and energy in the UK: trend analysis of published statistics. *Energy Policy*, 11 (1), pp. 39–51.

Transport is the only major sector where there has been an increase in energy consumption over the last 10 years. This article concentrates on the road and rail sectors and presents for the first time an intermodal comparison of the trends on a time-series basis. The underlying reasons are explored and some of the complex interactions between individual factors highlighted. Several options for reducing energy consumption in the transport sector are proposed. Given the efficacy of oil for transport, there is only a limited opportunity for improvements in the existing stock of vehicles (through measures such as increases in car occupancy) and technological improvements offer the best alternative.

5D2 BEAUMONT, J.R. and KEYS, P. (1982) *Future Cities: Spatial Analysis of Energy Issues*. Chichester: John Wiley.

The book presents a general outline of contemporary energy policy issues as a background for discussion. A number of topics relating to the supply and demand of energy at the urban level are considered highlighting relationships and approaches that could be adopted. Particular attention is given to the planning context and the operation of analyses. The discussion is broadly based as the fundamental issue concerns the desirability of alternative types of future society and the development of wider social and economic policies. The chapters discuss energy in the United Kingdom; consumer choice and domestic energy consumption; combined heat and electrical power generation schemes; land-use transportation systems and energy conservation; and, telecommunications-transport trade-off.

5D3 BLOCH, A.J. and PIGNATARO, L.J. (1985) Alternative fuels for buses: current assessment and future perspectives. *Transportation Research Record*, 1049, pp. 79–86.

The issue of alternative fuels for transit buses is examined from the perspective of the 1980s and beyond. At a time when federal involvement in alternative fuel development is of lesser significance and marketplace actions appear to be of greater value than government intervention or investment, it is relevant to examine the objectives of developing diesel fuel alternatives for public transport vehicle use. Four fuel groups are evaluated: alcohols, vegetable oils, methane (or natural gas), and hydrogen. An assessment is made of current development status and conclusions are presented regarding future research efforts.

5D4 CURTIS, F.A., NEILSEN, L. and BJORNSON, A. (1984) Impact of residential street design on fuel consumption. *Journal of Urban Planning and Development (ASCE)*, **110** (1), pp. 1–8.

Potential fuel savings offered by conventional, solar superblock, and grid street patterns using a subdivision in Regina (Saskatchewan) are compared. A modelling procedure is used to simulate commuter and mode travel for the portion of the work and non-work trip within the subdivision. Fuel budgets are compared for the alternative street patterns. Conclusions are reached on which design of residential street is likely to use least fuel.

5D5 DUNKERLEY, J. and HOCH, I. (1986) The pricing of transport fuels. *Energy Policy*, **14** (4), pp. 307–317.

There is now widespread agreement on the need for correct pricing as a necessary, if not sufficient, condition for securing optimal efficiency in road transport energy use. Despite the fact that road transport is invariably the largest single market for liquid fuels, empirical work on transport energy pricing has been confined largely to industrial countries. This paper attempts to fill the gap by examining within a comparative framework the structure of transport energy pricing in both developing and industrial countries.

5D6 FERREIRA, L.J.A. (1984) The potential for fuel savings from urban transport management (UTM) in the UK.. *Transportation Planning and Technology*, **9** (2) and **9** (3).

These papers provide the background and an assessment of urban transport management schemes in terms of their energy saving potential. The proportion of total UK road transport fuel consumption which is likely to be affected by such measures is estimated and the amount of travel by motorized modes is disaggregated by urban area size and by time of day – peak and off-peak periods. Estimates of the additional consumption directly attributable to peak period congestion are obtained and the fuel savings achieveable through congestion easing measures are assessed. In the UK approximately 50 per cent of total annual travel on all roads is undertaken in built-up areas, with 43 per cent of this urban travel taking place in towns and cities with more than 100,000 population. Around 10 per cent of the annual fuel consumed by road vehicles is used by passenger cars during the two 2-hour peak periods of the day.

5D7 GELTNER, D. (1985) Transport and energy in developing countries. *Energy Policy*, **13** (4), pp. 340–344.

A comparison of energy consumption in the transport sector in developing and developed countries suggests considerable scope for savings. Four broad policy approaches which affect transport energy consumption are identified – information and training programmes; subsidies; pricing and tax policies; and administrative regulations. The impact of prices over the last decade has not resulted in savings and there is still a need to improve efficiency.

5D8 GREENE, D.L., HU, P.S. and TILL, L. (1985) An analysis of trends in automotive fuel economy from 1978 to 1984. *Transportation Research Record*, 1049, pp. 51–56.

Between 1978 and 1984, the fuel economy of new automobiles increased by an estimated 6.7 miles per gallon. Previous analyses have shown that fuel economy improvements have been primarily achieved by lowering the average weight of the automobile and reducing the size of the engine. Detailed sales data were used to analyse the contributions of consumer sales shifts and engineering and design improvements to the 1978 to 1984 gain in fuel economy.

Most of the gain (70 per cent) was found to have resulted from changes in vehicle offerings by manufacturers, whereas only 30 per cent of the gain was attributed to sales shifts. The lack of improvement in fuel economy of new automobiles since 1982 is attributed to both consumer selections and manufacturer decisions.

See also Greene, D.L., Meddeb, N. and Liu, J.T. (1986) Vehicle stock modelling of highway energy use. *Energy Policy*, **14** (5), pp. 437-446.

5D9 HOROWITZ, J. (1982) Modelling traveller responses to alternative gasoline allocation plans. *Transportation Research*, **16A** (2), pp. 117-133.

This paper describes a modelling technique for estimating responses of urban travellers to petrol shortages under three different procedures for allocating scarce petrol supplies. The allocation procedures are: allow the price of petrol to rise to a market clearing level; allocate petrol by means of white-market coupons; and allocate petrol by means of traditional rationing. The modelling technique is based on a system of disaggregate travel demand models and provides for representation of non-price restraints on petrol consumption (e.g. traditional rationing) and for changes in multi-destination travel, as well as for changes in petrol prices and in modes, destinations and frequencies of travel. The application of the modelling technique is illustrated by using it to estimate the effects of a petrol shortage in the Washington, DC, area.

5D10 KEYES, D.L. (1982) Energy for travel: the influence of urban development patterns. *Transportation Research*, **16A** (1), pp. 65-70.

Rising energy prices and supply shortfalls have underscored the need to improve the energy efficiency of urban travel. Long-run solutions may involve rearranging development patterns in urban areas, or at least locating new growth in ways which reduce the need to travel. To test the degree to which altering development patterns may effect transport energy savings, relationships between petrol consumption and urban development characteristics were investigated in 49 US metropolitan areas. The results suggest that cities of medium size with clusters of high residential densities are associated with lower levels of per capita petrol consumption. However, it is unlikely that changes in current development patterns during the next two decades would be substantial enough to cause a significant reduction in US energy consumption.

5D11 KHAN, A.M. (1981) Urban public transit efficiency: economic and energy factors. *Journal of Advanced Transportation*, **15** (3), pp. 213–230.

This paper describes a micro-level treatment of the efficiency of urban transit in terms of economic and energy factors. Measures of efficiency are discussed and selected statistics about the Canadian transit industry are examined. Results obtained from an investigation of the Ottawa area (Canada) case study are discussed and frequent comparisons are made with findings of other investigations. Economic and energy efficiency gains achieved through such means as: petroleum price increase, transit system innovations and automobile disincentives are illustrated.

See also a parallel paper by Khan, A.M. in the same journal (**15** (3), pp. 195–211).

5D12 LAM, T.N. (1985) Estimating fuel consumption from engine size. *Journal of Transportation Engineering*, **111** (4), pp. 339–357.

Previous studies have shown relationships between fuel consumption, journey speed, vehicle weight, and idling fuel rate under urban driving conditions. The results of a statistical analysis of these known relationships with published data are presented. The objective is to establish equations for estimating fuel consumption from travel survey data such as journey speed and engine size. Two equations were found to give good estimates of journey fuel consumption.

See also Biggs, D.C. and Akcelik, R. (1987) Estimating effect of vehicle characteristics on fuel consumption. *Journal of Transportation Engineering*, **113** (1), pp. 101–106.

5D13 LUCAS, G.G. and RICHARDS, W.L. (1982) Alternative fuels for transportation. *Transportation Planning and Technology*, **7** (3), pp. 167–170.

The alternatives to oil based fuels for transport are considered and analysed. There are the synthetic fuels made from coal, the liquid petroleum gases of propane and butane, compressed natural gas and methane. The problems associated with electric vehicles are discussed, the main one being that of range. The possible use of hydrogen as a fuel is analysed in some detail.

5D14 MEYER, M.D. and BELOBABA, P. (1982) Contingency planning for response to urban transportation system disruptions. *Journal of the American Planning Association*, **48** (4), pp. 454–465.

When public transport service is interrupted, or when a fuel shortage occurs, the routine travel behaviour of millions of individuals can be affected, particularly within congested metropolitan areas. When no advance preparations are made, uncoordinated government responses can combine with tremendous public confusion and uncertainty to leave the urban transportation system in a state of near paralysis. This article examines contingency planning processes used in three different situations, identifies important characteristics of a contingency planning process, and presents a model for contingency planning, emphasizing the establishment of a management structure in concert with a crisis management strategy; the formulation of specific plans for activities common to most crises; and the development of a draft implementation plan for specific types of crises.

5D15 NEWMAN, P. and KENWORTHY, J. (1980) Public and private transport in Australian cities. The potential for energy conservation through land use change. *Transport Policy and Decision Making*, **1** (2/3), pp. 149–167.

An attempt has been made to explain observed difference in public and private transport and per capita energy consumption in five Australian cities by reference to a number of non-land-use and land-use variables. Non-land-use variables were considered inadequate to explain the differences in transport and energy patterns. However, numerous significant correlations were found between the seven key transport parameters and various land-use indicators representing density, centralization and traffic restraint characteristics. The correlations suggest a key role for these three factors in giving a competitive edge to public transport and increasing the feasibility of cycling and walking. A policy combining densification, centralization and traffic restraint measures is recommended as an effective way of promoting transport energy conservation in the short and long terms.

5D16 ORGANISATION FOR ECONOMIC COOPERATION AND DEVELOPMENT *Energy Savings and Road Traffic Management.* Paris: OECD.

This study was conducted to assess the potential impact of various traffic management schemes on motor vehicle fuel consumption in OECD member countries. The focus of the report is on management measures as tools for energy savings, including street-use strategies, traffic control at junctions (isolated or signalized), speed limits, parking policies, motorway traffic control, management of incidents, and promotion of public transport. The role and potential of computer traffic simulation models are highlighted and issues relating to their practical application are addressed.

5D17 OWENS, S. (1985) Energy demand: links to land-use and forward planning. *Built Environment*, **11** (1), pp. 33–44.

It has long been accepted that energy and land-use are closely interrelated. Energy systems influence spatial structure and land-use patterns in part determine levels of energy consumption. Three questions are examined in this paper: first, could planners realistically expect to achieve anything in terms of energy efficiency; secondly, what have been the successes and problems in the past; finally, why do planners in Britain still ignore the energy issue. The pessimistic conclusions on each of these questions suggests that energy considerations should be made a constituent part of strategic land-use planning.

See also Owens, S. (1981) Energy: why planners must be involved. *International Journal of Environmental Studies*, **16** (2), pp. 197–206.

5D18 SHARPE, R. (1980) Improving energy efficiency in community land-use transportation systems. *Environment and Planning A*, **12** (2), pp. 203–216.

The form of our cities is a major determinant of energy consumption, especially that related to the oil-consuming transport sector. This is particularly so in Australia, which is one of the most highly urbanized nations in the world with a high degree of dependence on automotive transport. The paper discusses planning changes to cope with future oil shortages in terms of modifying urban form, community hardware (buildings, infrastructure, and rolling stock), and community software (life-styles, rules and regulations, fuel economics, etc). Energy savings of at least 40 per cent are possible in the larger cities through changes such as increasing vehicle operating costs, increasing vehicle occupancy, higher-density development, and shorter-trip behaviour. Subcentre development within the urban area is found to be less energy expensive than fringe or satellite development.

See also Sharpe, R. (1978) The effect of urban form on transport energy patterns. *Urban Ecology*, **3** (2), pp. 125-135.

5D19 SULLIVAN, E.C. (1982) Perspectives on urban transportation energy contingency planning in the United States. *Transportation Planning and Technology*, **7** (4), pp. 217-229.

This paper is a review and gentle critique of existing transport energy contingency plans for the local and metropolitan levels. For the most part, these documents were prepared either by regional planning bodies (councils of government) or public transport operating agencies. While contingency plans developed by public transport operators naturally tend to be narrower than those developed by councils of government, their similarities are more numerous than their differences; and this combination provides an interrelated body of ideas upon which to focus this discussion.

5D20 TOMAZINIS, A.R. (1982) Patterns of urbanization and energy requirements: recent regulation changes and simulation studies concerning American urban areas. *Transportation Planning and Technology*, **7** (3), pp. 171-175.

This paper focuses on the experience gained within the American framework in the various attempts to facilitate changes or to study the impact of such changes. The motive of energy efficiency has proven quite instrumental in introducing change and fostering its implementation. The paper is divided into two parts. The first part reviews the experience gained in handling aspects of site development, and mixes of land use, density, and grain within the overall framework of metropolitan areas. The second part focuses on several simulation studies that explored the relationships between urban patterns and networks on the one hand and energy consumption quotients on the other.

5D21 VAN DER TOUW, J.W., JARRETT, R.G., TRAYFORD, R.S. and JOHNSTON, R.R.M. (1983) Fuel consumption in urban traffic – a guide to planning experiments. *Transportation Research*, **17A** (3), pp. 219–231.

A linear mathematical model to describe the fuel consumption of cars traversing a stretch of road is given, and the parameters of this model are estimated using data from a designed experiment carried out in Sydney, Australia. It is shown how these parameter estimates can be used in planning future traffic experiments. Travel time is also considered, both as an end in itself, and as a means of improving accuracy in a fuel consumption experiment.

5D22 WADHWA, L.C. (1980) Simulation and analysis of energy demand for passenger automobiles in Australia. *Transportation Research*, **14A** (3), pp. 235–240.

The demand for gasoline for auto passenger travel has been identified to be the most crucial aspect of energy policy in Australia. Qualitative as well as quantitative analysis has been presented to explore the energy saving potential of various measures in reducing travel demand and in making travel more energy efficient. A computer simulation model has also been developed to assess future fuel demand for automobiles in Australia in response to a variety of assumptions about social, economic, technological and policy variables. On the basis of the present analysis it is concluded that the passenger travel demand is less likely to be contained but a combination of conservation and efficiency measures can significantly reduce the energy intensity, thereby controlling the gasoline demand in the next 25 years to present consumption levels.

5D23 WANG, G.H.K. and SKINNER, D. (1984) The impact of fare and gasoline price changes on monthly transit ridership: Empirical evidence from seven US transit authorities. *Transportation Research*, **18B** (1), pp. 29–41.

This paper presents eight empirical models of monthly ridership for seven US Transit Authorities. Within the framework of these models, the impacts upon monthly ridership from changes in the real fare and gasoline prices are examined. Important findings are: the elasticities of monthly transit ridership with respect to the real fare

are negative and inelastic, ranging from 0.042 to 0.62; and the elasticities of monthly transit ridership with respect to the real gasoline price are positive and inelastic, ranging from 0.08 to 0.80. Such results have important policy implications for decisions based on the relationships of price, revenue, and ridership; and for assessing the impacts of changing gasoline prices upon urban modal choice.

5D24 WHITE, P.R. (1982) Energy conservation in urban public transport. *Transportation Planning and Technology*, **7** (2), pp. 143-152.

Urban public transport energy use is determined largely by the weight of the vehicle, and frequency of intermediate stops, imposing repeated acceleration/steady running/braking cycles, in which most of the kinetic energy is dissipated. Energy consumed for the same capacity and vehicle performance may be reduced by coasting, cutting vehicle weight, and use of regenerative braking, on electrically-powered systems, to convert the otherwise wasted braking energy into useful form. Particular attention is paid to the last-named, identifying results of past experience and recent simulations. Practical constraints limiting the amount of energy actually recovered are discussed, including proportion of vehicle weight braked electrically, receptivity of the supply system, stop spacing and number of vehicles operated simultaneously. Reference is also made to battery vehicles and flywheel energy storage. It is suggested that considerable scope exists in urban electric rail operation for reduced energy consumption, as existing fleets are replaced by lighter weight vehicles, fitted for regenerative braking, but other methods produce less immediate benefits.

5E Environment and safety

5E1 ADAMS, J.G.U. (1983) Public safety legislation and the risk compensation hypothesis: the example of motorcycle helmet legislation. *Environment and Planning C*, **1** (2), pp. 193-203.

The 'experiment' in the United States in which 28 states in the latter half of the 1970s repealed their laws which made the wearing of motorcycle helmets compulsory is widely believed to have proved conclusively that helmet legislation is a highly effective public health measure. The principal statistical foundations of this belief are found in a report to Congress by the National Highway Traffic Safety Administration (1979, *The Effect of Helmet Usage on Head Injuries and the Effect of Usage Laws on Helmet Wearing Rates – A Preliminary Report*. Washington, DC: US Department of Transportation) and in a study by Watson, G.S., Zador, P.L. and Wilks, A. (1981, Helmet use, helmet use laws and motorcyclist fatalities. *American Journal of Public Health*, **71**, pp. 297–300). These foundations are examined and found to be open to criticism. The evidence surveyed here suggests that the effect, if any, of helmet legislation on motorcycling facilities is perverse. The 'risk compensation theory' is proffered as a possible explanation of the available evidence.

5E2 ALLSOP, R.E. and TURNER, E.D. (1986) Road casualties and public transport fares in London. *Accident Analysis and Prevention*, **18** (2), pp. 147–156.

The specific objective of this project was to estimate the size and statistical significance of such recent changes in numbers of road casualties in London as may have been associated with the large changes in London Transport fares which took place in October 1981 and March 1982. Log-linear regression models were fitted to casualty data for different classes of road user, and were used to estimate numbers of casualties that would have been expected, according to the fitted models, in the year May 1982–April 1983 if a near-doubling of fares that took place in March 1982 had not occurred, but instead the relatively low fares resulting from a reduction of about one-third in October 1981 had continued. The results indicated that several thousands fewer casualties would have been expected than actually occurred, most of the difference being among pedal cyclists and users of cars or taxis. A further fares reduction took place in May 1983, and data for the subsequent year are being used in a further study, which is also investigating various ways of improving and extending the models.

5E3 BRAGG, B.W.E. and FINN, P. (1985) Influence of safety belt usage on perception of the risk of an accident. *Accident Analysis and Prevention*, **17** (1), pp. 15–23.

Does the use of a safety belt increase or decrease the perception of the risk of an accident? Young and older male drivers were asked to drive an urban route and rate their perceptions of the risk of an accident.

On the first driving trip all subjects were unbelted, while on the second driving trip half of the subjects wore a safety belt while half did not. Results indicated that young male drivers decrease their perception of the risk of an accident as they become familiar with a driving route if they are not wearing a safety belt. Young male drivers asked to wear a safety belt sustained their perception of the risk of an accident as they became familiar with the test route. Older drivers' perception of the risk of an accident was not affected by familiarity or safety belt usage.

5E4 BURKHARDT, J.E. and WOZNY, M.C. (1984) Comparative assessment of selected models of community cohesion. *Transportation Quarterly*, **8** (3), pp. 375-392.

There are numerous models of community cohesion including the mobility index, stability index, social feasibility model and neighbourhood social interaction index. This paper reviews them all and applies them within a case study of a corridor in Delaware. The numerical values of the models generally indicate the levels of cohesion before and after the scheme, and compares the range of models. The conclusions suggest that the concept of cohesion is imprecise, that data are limited and that impacts can only be inferred not predicted.

5E5 COHN, L.F. and HARRIS, R.A. (1987) Environmental planning in urban transportation. *Journal of Transportation Engineering*, **113** (3), pp. 229-247.

The importance of environmental analysis in transport is outlined together with a review of the procedures used in the USA. The focus is restricted to the impacts of roads and airports, and the issues covered include noise, air quality, and water resources. The paper is essentially an overview of current practice as it relates to the law and regulations, within the context of the available analytical methods for the prediction of impacts.

5E6 COOPER, J.C. (1986) Operator responses to area lorry bans: the unit load contribution. *Transportation Planning and Technology*, **11** (3), pp. 227-239.

Area lorry bans are often proposed as a way of relieving the environmental nuisance of heavy vehicles. If a ban was implemented, operators would need to adopt new distribution strategies for their goods. The main purpose of this paper is to develop the cost analysis of unit load operation and to examine the role unit loads might play in a lorry ban area.

See also: Cooper, J.C. (1983) Complying with area lorry bans. An evaluation of some operating alternatives. *Transportation Planning and Technology*, **8** (2), pp. 117-26.

Cooper, J.C. and Walker, M. (1986) Planning the amenity control of lorries. *Traffic Engineering and Control*, **27** (9), pp. 452-454.

5E7 ECKSTEIN, W.E. (1985) Goods distribution centres: a contribution to the systematizing of local goods traffic in towns. *Transport Policy and Decision Making*, **3** (2), pp. 135-148.

This paper discusses the potential from reducing levels of goods traffic on the regional road system by the use of improved management and organizational techniques. The theoretical evidence has been combined with practical experience to establish appropriate structures for goods distributional centres. Procedures to improve good distribution practice are discussed.

5E8 EUROPEAN CONFERENCE OF MINISTERS OF TRANSPORT (1984) Goods distribution systems in urban areas. Round Table 61. Paris: ECMT.

The resource paper outlines economic approaches to urban freight transport and various measures likely to improve it. It also proposes that an integrated long-term strategy be worked out so that, when infrastructure projects are being planned, account can be taken of forecasts for the development of urban economic structures and transport requirements. Discussion was based on the main problems and the impact of current economic and social changes on goods distribution, the limitations of economic models, and the possibility of organising a system of logistics for urban goods transport.

5E9 EVANS, L. (1986) The effectiveness of safety belts in preventing fatalities. *Accident Analysis and Prevention*, **18** (3), pp. 229-241.

The effectiveness of safety belts in preventing fatalities to drivers and right front passengers is estimated by applying the double pair comparison method to 1974 or later model year cars coded in the Fatal

Accident Reporting System. The method focuses on 'subject' occupants (drivers or right front passengers) and 'other' occupants (any except the subject occupant). Fatality risks to belted and unbelted subject occupants are compared using the other occupant to estimate exposure. In this study, drivers and right front passengers are subject occupants; choosing other occupants differing in age, seating positions, and belt use, generated 46 essentially independent estimates of safety belt effectiveness.

5E10 GB DEPARTMENT OF TRANSPORT (1983) *Manual of Environmental Appraisal*. London: HMSO.

The growing number of passenger and goods vehicles in use on the roads implies more intense, as well as widespread, environmental effects. Transport plans therefore need to be evaluated on environmental as well as economic and operational grounds. This manual outlines appropriate procedures at both the strategic and local level, and examines the nature of environmental costs, their measurement and their impact.

See also GB Department of Transport (1982) *Lorries, People and the Environment* (Chairman Sir Arthur Armitage). London: HMSO [2A11].

5E11 HEDGES, C.A. (1985) Improving urban goods movement: the transportation system management approach. *Transport Policy and Decision Making*, **3** (2), pp. 113–133.

Transport Systems Management consists of the application of general management techniques to transportation. It attempts to make the most efficient use of existing resources, particularly street and highway capacity in downtown areas. TSM can provide improved performance in the short-term, and frequently is superior to ambitious capital improvement programmes with respect to the costs required to achieve improved levels of service and other goals. In many situations, but particularly in congested downtown areas and at other major activity centres, the success of TSM strategies to improve the movement of people will depend on how well the freight activities are taken into account. Trucks are part of the system, and compete with passenger vehicles for street and curb space. Because their operating characteristics differ from those of automobiles, trucks may frustrate TSM strategies if the strategies ignore them.

This paper reviews the options for TSM as appropriate to the goods sector and discusses where there might be conflicts with other sectors, thus reducing the overall gains.

5E12 HENNING-HAGER, U. (1986) Urban development and road safety. *Accident Analysis and Prevention*, **18** (2), pp. 135–145.

The present study aims at increasing the level of knowledge of the relationship between factors that influence urban and transport planning and road safety. The empirical evidence is taken from 21 typical residential areas for which a total of 56 variables has been collected on urban and transport planning factors and safety issues. Regression and correlation analysis are used to establish relationships and elasticities.

5E13 HOROWITZ, J. (1982) *Air Quality Analysis for Urban Transportation Planning*. Cambridge, Mass: MIT Press.

This book integrates and presents the results of research as it applies to a major source of air pollution – petroleum – and diesel-powered motor vehicles in cities. It includes discussions of the transport-related air pollutants (mainly carbon monoxide, ozone, and nitrogen dioxide) and their effects on human health and welfare; motor vehicle emissions measurements, standards, and control devices; the effects on air pollution of traffic engineering measures (such as widening streets or creating vehicle-free zones), transit improvements, carpool incentives, pricing and restraint measures, and land use measures; and the modelling of atmospheric dispersion.

5E14 JACOBS, G.D. and CUTTING, C.A. (1986) Further research on accident rates in developing countries. *Accident Analysis and Prevention*, **18** (2), pp. 119–127.

Earlier studies have shown that by using cross-sectional data for a group of developing countries, a significant relationship can be established between fatality rates and vehicle ownership levels. This paper updates relationships established in earlier years and identifies whether or not the slope of the regression line has continued to increase (and suggests that for the group of countries as a whole, there is a worsening in the safety situation). Similar relationships are also established for casualty rates. A detailed analysis is made of the relationship between fatality rates and parameters which describe, in part, the social, physical and economic characteristics of the developing countries. These include vehicle ownership, gross national product per capita, road density, vehicle density (per kilometre of road), population per physician and population per hospital bed. Again, comparisons are made with results obtained on earlier studies.

5E15 JONAH, B.A. and LAWSON, J.J. (1984) The effectiveness of the Canadian mandatory selt belt use laws. *Accident Analysis and Prevention*, **16** (5/6), pp. 433–450.

The impact of four provincial mandatory seat belt use laws passed in 1976 and 1977 on seat belt use and on motor vehicle occupant casualties is examined. Subsequent to the passage of the laws, belt use typically increased from 20 to the 70 per cent level dropping to around 50 per cent over the next several years. Ontario exhibited a clear drop in the fatality and injury rates in the years following the introduction of the law. Quebec experienced little reduction in casualties. The changes in casualties for British Columbia and Saskatchewan were mixed with the former showing a drop only in the fatality rate subsequent to the seat belt law, while the latter experienced a reduction only in the injury rate. The provinces without seat belt use laws also enjoyed some reductions in occupant casualty rates. The changes in occupant casualties in the legislated provinces were also examined relative to the changes in non-occupant casualties and relative to the unlegislated provinces. It was concluded that three provinces experienced some reductions as a result of legislation but not as much as anticipated. It is speculated that the impact of the seat belt use laws fell short of expectations because it was mainly the safe drivers who buckled up in response to the laws.

5E16 KAMERUD, D.B. and VON BUSECK, C.R. (1985) The effects of traffic sound and its reduction on house prices. *Transportation Research Record*, 1033, pp. 16–22.

Sales histories of two residential neighbourhoods bordering on an Interstate highway were examined to determine the effect of traffic sound reduction on house prices. Sound levels were reduced in one of the neighbourhoods by building a barrier along the highway. The second neighbourhood, which remained unshielded, served as a comparison area. Before the barrier was built in the first neighbourhood, sound levels in both neighbourhoods were determined primarily by proximity to the highway. Analysis of house prices showed that, in the absence of shielding, houses nearest the highway sold for less than equivalent houses farther away. The magnitude of this highway-proximity effect, measured in percent of house value per decibel of sound gradient, was consistent with similar estimates previously reported in the literature. The proximity effect on prices appears to have persisted long after the barrier was built. Hence, although the barrier reduced the level of traffic sound and annoyance in the shielded neighbourhood, there was no evidence that these benefits were capitalized into higher house prices. The results of this study therefore suggest that hedonic price regressions (which are not based on true treatment-control data) may overestimate the potential economic benefits of traffic sound reduction.

5E17 KIMBER, R.M. (1984) The effects of wheel clamping in Central London. Transport and Road Research Laboratory, Laboratory Report 1136. Crowthorne: TRRL.

An evaluation of the effect on parking and traffic behaviour of the use of wheel clamps of enforce parking regulations is presented. It was found that the duration, though not the number of parking offences declined and that the reduction in roadside parking densities resulted in a reduction in journey times.

5E18 KORTE, C. and GRANT, R. (1980) Traffic noise, environmental awareness and pedestrian behaviour. *Environment and Behaviour*, **12** (3), pp. 408–420.

Recent research has confirmed that social behaviour, especially helpfulness, is affected by the environmental input level: as the level of environmental bombardment increases, the level of helpfulness decreases. This study was designed to evaluate one explanation for this effect, the restricted awareness explanation. The authors hypothesized that as environmental bombardment increases, people become less aware of peripheral objects and happenings in their immediate surroundings. This characteristic may be part of a general adjustment to high-input levels, which may also include an increase in walking speed and a decrease in visual scanning of the environment. The results confirmed each of these expectations.

During periods of high traffic noise and density, in contrast to low periods, pedestrians were found to be less aware of novel objects placed along their route, to walk faster, and to engage more in a straight-ahead gaze fixation.

5E19 LAMM, R., CHOUEIRI, E.M. and KLOECKNER, J.H. (1985) Accidents in the US and Europe: 1970-1980. *Accident Analysis and Prevention*, **17** (6), pp. 429-438.

This study compares certain demographic and accident characteristics among Western European countries and between Western Europe and the United States. The specific objectives of the study were to: identify various changes in fatalities and fatality rates experienced by each of eleven Western European Countries, by these countries as a whole, and by the United States from 1970 through 1980, with special attention given to the energy crisis and its aftermath from 1974 through 1980; and to determine whether there were statistically significant changes during the 1970-1980 time period in the traffic accident characteristics studied. The findings are as follows: during the decade studied, Western Europe as a whole experienced a fatality rate reduction per 10^9 vehicle-kilometres travelled of 45.8 per cent while the US experienced a 29.1 per cent reduction during this same period. In Western Europe the age groups 0-14, 25-64 and over 64 and its road user groups pedestrians, bicyclists and motorcyclists and moped riders showed statistically significant improvements in the characterists studied. The only US group to experience a significant reduction in fatalities during this period was the age group 0-14; however the 1980 fatality rate per 10^9 vehicle-kilometres of travel of 21.0 for the US, versus 34.8 for Western Europe, indicates that driving in the US is still much safer.

5E20 LUND, A.K. (1986) Voluntary seat belt use among US drivers: geographic, socio-economic and demographic variation. *Accident Analysis and Prevention*, **18** (1), pp. 43-50.

Although voluntary seat belt use rates are low, they are not uniform among different populations of US drivers. In detailed analyses of 1982 data from 12 of the 19 cities in the National Highway Traffic Safety Administration's national seat belt survey and from three of the National Accident Sampling System regions, belt use rates varied greatly by geographic region, socio-economic status and demographic group. These factors also moderated the effects of other factors such as car size and origin of manufacture. Nevertheless, all together, the factors included in the study explained less than 5 per cent of the variation in voluntary seat belt use, and no subpopulation was identified in which seat belts were used by a majority of the members.

5E21 MCKNIGHT, A.J. and MCPHERSON, K. (1986) Evaluation of peer intervention training for high school alcohol safety education. *Accident Analysis and Prevention*, **18** (4), pp. 339–347.

A programme of peer intervention in the drinking and driving of others is compared with a conventional alcohol safety programme in the high school setting. The peer intervention programme led to significant increases in self-reported intervention behaviour, following completion of the course. The conventional alcohol safety programme failed to produce changes in intervention behaviour during this period. Both the peer intervention programme and the conventional alcohol safety programme led to significant knowledge gains. Neither programme led to significant measured shifts in attitudes.

5E22 MACKIE, A.M. and DAVIES, C.H. (1981) Environmental effects of traffic changes. Transport and Road Research Laboratory, Laboratory Report 1015. Crowthorne: TRRL.

The report describes a study of the environmental effects of traffic and traffic changes in nine towns where changes in traffic flow had occurred due to by-pass construction or traffic management schemes. As assessment of the nuisance caused by particular traffic flows has been made. The study also examined the effects of noise and air pollution on people's sensitivity to traffic. Nuisance was measured by means of personal interview surveys of people at home, pedestrians and people working in shops and offices. Nuisance levels changed considerably when the traffic levels changed. The single traffic variable most strongly correlated with nuisance was the number of lorries over 16 tons gvw, but there was also a high correlation between nuisance and total traffic flow, a multiple regression analysis showed that these two variables could explain 85 per cent of the variance in the nuisance data.

5E23 MOHAN, D. and BAWA, P.S. (1985) An analysis of road traffic fatalities in Delhi, India. *Accident Analysis and Prevention*, **17** (1), pp. 33–45.

Road use patterns in Delhi, are very different from those in cities in highly industrialized countries. In Delhi roads are also shared by unmotorized vehicles in large numbers. This study is an attempt to understand fatal crash patterns in the city in 1980 using police data. The results indicate that fatality patterns are very different from those in highly industrialized countries. Pedestrians, two-wheeler riders and bus commuters comprise 80 per cent of fatalities and motor-vehicle occupants a small minority. It appears that priorities for safety countermeasures in Delhi would have to be significantly different from those in more industrialized high-income countries. Some short-term and long-term measures are suggested.

5E24 NELSON, J.P. (1982) Highway noise and property value. A survey of recent evidence. *Journal of Transport Economics and Policy*, **16** (2), pp. 117–138.

This paper critically reviews nine empirical studies of highway noise and property values, conducted since 1974, that use cross-sectional housing data for cities in Canada and the United States. The author first discusses some of the assumptions that underlie the hedonic price model and review highway noise measurement fundamentals. On Walters's noise depreciation sensitivity index, the empirical evidence suggests a depreciation rate of 0.40 ± 0.23 per cent per decibel. The empirical evidence tentatively suggests that highway noise does not lead to increased time on the market for real estate, and should not therefore reduce residential mobility.

5E25 NEMMERS, C.J. and WILLIAMS, W.L. (1983) Guidelines for designating routes for transporting hazardous materials. *Public Roads*, **47** (2), pp. 61–65.

This article summarizes the results of a study by the Federal Highway Administration to develop methods of evaluating roadway and community characteristics which make one route safer than another for transporting hazardous materials. The method accommodates subjective as well as physical and legal restraints on routeing and can be applied to urban, rural and inter-state road.

5E26 ORGANISATION FOR ECONOMIC COOPERATION AND DEVELOPMENT (1986a) *OECD Road Safety Research: A Synthesis*. Paris: OECD, Road Transport Research Group.

This report contains sections on particular age groups (elderly and children) on high-risk road user groups (pedestrians, two-wheelers, the learner driver and trucks), on regulatory action programmes (alcohol legislation, safety belts, speed limits), safety publicity programmes road infrastructure and area-wide measures, and safety improvements during conditions of reduced visibility and night driving.

See also: OECD (1984) *Integrated Road Safety Programmes*. Paris: OECD, Road Transport Research Group.
OECD (1985) *Traffic Safety of Elderly Road Users*. Paris: OECD, Road Transport Research Group.

5E27 ORGANISATION FOR ECONOMIC COOPERATION AND DEVELOPMENT (1986b) *Environmental Effects of Automotive Transport*. Paris: OECD.

This report forms part of the work of the OECD programme on the Comparative Assessment of the Environmental Implications of Various Energy Systems. It establishes a framework for assessment by building a matrix of potential environmental effects at different stages in the production of transport services. The main body of the report examines alternative vehicle technologies. In its concluding chapter it discusses the economic trade-offs which are involved in seeking an environmentally acceptable transport package, and reviews some of the most promising opportunities for obtaining environmental improvements in an economically efficient manner.

5E28 PLOWDEN, S. (1983) Transport efficiency and the urban environment: Is there a conflict? *Transport Reviews*, **3** (4), pp. 363–398.

The main theme of the article is that the traditional idea of an inherent conflict between transport efficiency and the environment is mistaken. Both efficiency and the environment are threatened by the same thing: the excessive and indiscriminate use of vehicles. This comes about because of defects in the fiscal and regulatory framework within which people take transport decisions. Suitable reforms in this framework would simultaneously enhance the environment and improve access for all classes of road user. In the development of this theme, particular attention is paid to transport activities which tend to be neglected by policy-makers, such as walking, cycling and urban goods distribution, and to measures which are not always thought of as instruments of policy at all, such as locational policy and development control, vehicle design, and vehicle taxation, especially of goods vehicles.

See also: Plowden, S. and Hillman, M. (1984) *Danger on the Road: The Needless Scourge*, Policy Studies Institute Report No 627. London: PSI.

5E29 SHANNON, H.S. (1986) Road-accident data: interpreting the British experience with particular reference to the risk homoeostasis theory. *Ergonomics*, **29** (8), pp. 1005–1015.

The risk homoeostasis theory postulates that in any risky situation people will adjust their behaviour to their 'target level' of risk. When applied to road traffic, the theory predicts that conventional safety measures will fail to reduce the accident rate per unit time of road-user exposure. This article examines problems with the analysis of US road accident data which are claimed to support the theory, and analyses comparable British data. This shows a substantial post-war reduction in mortality rate per vehicle distance, and provides little support for risk homoeostasis theory.

5E30 SMITH, A. and STANSFELD, S. (1986) Aircraft noise exposure, noise sensitivity, and everyday errors. *Environment and Behaviour*, **18** (2), pp. 214–226.

The present study compared self-reports of everyday errors given by subjects who lived in an area with a high level of aircraft noise with those of a similar group who lived in an area with a low level of aircraft noise. The subjects were further subdivided into those who considered themselves to be highly sensitive to noise and those who had a lower level of noise sensitivity. The high aircraft noise group reported a higher frequency of occurrence of everyday errors and so did the noise sensitive subjects. However, there was no interaction between noise sensitivity and the level of aircraft noise.

5E31 SURREY, J. (ed.) (1984) *Urban Transportation of Irradiated Fuel*. London: Macmillan.

The transport of irradiated fuel through highly populated areas concerns many people including the authorities who are responsible for it, the people who work with it, and the public, past whose doors it travels. This book reports on an international conference at which all views on the topic are covered within a national and international context. Transport related chapters include the Central Electricity Generating Board's approach, the procedures adopted in France, and different national and local policies on the transport of irradiated fuel. Other contributions cover public concerns on accidents, terrorism and risk perception as well as the industry's procedures on design and safety.

5E32 SVENSON, O. and FISCHHOFF, B. (1985) Perceived driving safety and seat belt usage. *Accident Analysis and Prevention*, **17** (2), pp. 119–134.

Swedish and US subjects judged their own driving skills and safety in relation to other drivers. As in earlier studies, most subjects showed an optimism bias: a tendency to judge oneself as safer and more skillful than the average driver, with a smaller risk of getting involved and injured in an accident. Different measures of the optimism effect were strongly correlated with one another, with driving experience and with the judged importance of human factors (as opposed to technical and chance factors) in causing accidents. Degree of optimism was positively, but weakly, correlated with reported seatbelt usage and worry about traffic accidents. Seatbelt usage was positively related to the extent to which belts are judged to be convenient and popular, and more modestly related to the belt's perceived contributions to safety. These results suggest that providing more information about the effectiveness of seatbelts may not be as efficient a way of increasing seatbelt usage as emphasizing other factors, such as comfort and social norms, which cannot be outweighed by optimism.

5E33 TWEDDLE, G. and COOPER, J.C. (1985) Recent trends in lorry traffic by night. *Traffic Engineering and Control*, **26** (1), pp. 9–12.

Commercial vehicle movements are a major source of environmental deterioration. The dimensions of this deterioration are manifold: visual intrusion, noise pollution, exhaust emissions, accidents and vibration. However there are differences in public perceptions by day and night. Trends in lorry traffic at night have been investigated from census data to establish the current situation in London where a ban on certain night-time movement of lorries has been introduced.

5E34 WHITELEGG, J. (1983) Road safety: defeat, complicity and the bankruptcy of science. *Accident Analysis and Prevention*, **15** (2), pp. 153–160.

Road traffic accidents (RTAs) continue to be a serious problem. The paper argues that much research and effort to minimize this problem is locked into a fundamental misconception in so far as it assumes that blame, responsibility or engineering inadequacies can explain RTAs. The whole system of motorized transport, mobility patterns, land uses, governmental intervention and large company support has deprived society of realistic alternatives to the motor car and bequeathed a deficient technology with several societal disbenefits. Long-term solutions to the problem of RTAs involve basic change to this systems design. Anything less will continue to reinforce the present trajectory.

5F Engineering

5F1 CHATTERJEE, A. and HENDRICKSON, C. (1985) *Innovative Strategies to Improve Urban Transportation Performance*. New York: American Society of Civil Engineers.

Two conflicting objectives often present themselves to engineers, namely how to improve the effectiveness of urban transport modes and how to reduce their costs. There is no panacea for this task and a variety of strategies can be used. These strategies are presented in this book in the form of engineering options, management strategies and transit performance evaluation. Illustrative case study material is also used.

5F2 CLELLAND, A. (1984) A systems approach to Area Traffic Control. *Traffic Engineering and Control*, **25** (4), pp. 171–175.

Area Traffic Control (ATC) systems are now a major part of many a city's infrastructure. Experience gained with these systems has identified limitations in previous ATC system designs. This paper describes a new approach in designing such systems to free the user of limitations imposed by strict traffic control strategies and system architecture. The system concept makes use of the well-known predictable nature of traffic and takes advantage of the application of microprocessor technology in its practical implementation. Examples are given to show the flexibility of such an approach in meeting varying user requirements, yet leaving open the possibility of future enhancements to take advantage of advances in traffic control theory.

5F3 DAWSON, J.A.L. (1986) Electronic road pricing in Hong Kong. *Traffic Engineering and Control*, **27** (2), pp. 79–83.

The demonstration project in Hong Kong has shown that electronic road pricing schemes are now technically feasible. The politics of any scheme are more problematic and it seems unlikely that other cities will build upon this experience. Nevertheless it has been shown that considerable technical advances allow selective charging by vehicle type, by location and by time of day, and that the economic rate of return in a dense and congested city is high.

5F4 HIGGINS, T.J. (1985) Flexible parking requirements for office developments: new support for public parking and ridesharing. *Transportation*, **12** (4), pp. 343–359.

The author examines new, flexible parking requirements in several US cities and Canada. Flexible requirements provide relaxations in zoning code specifications for off-street parking in return for developer commitments to ridesharing measures, support of transit or in-lieu fees for public parking. Issues examined include whether developers take advantage of flexible requirements, whether agreements with developers lead to agreed-upon action, and whether actions lead to desired results. Based on experiences of several cities, implications and cautions are drawn for local planners. The first caution relates to cities using flexible requirements to collect in-lieu fees in support of public parking. Where cities delay providing parking, inflation may make it difficult to provide the desired parking supply. Or, developers may not choose to pay the fee, such as in the case where cities grant relaxations for other measures more attractive than paying the fees.

5F5 MAY, A.D. (1985) Parking restrictions: the case for better enforcement, in Harrison, A.J. and Gretton, J. (eds.) *Transport UK 1985: An Economic Social and Policy Audit*. Newbury: Policy Journals, pp. 81–84.

The benefits of more stringent enforcement of parking control in central London are considerable. This paper outlines the options available within the current legislative framework and discusses whether compliance can be increased by providing more parking spaces and simpler controls, or whether the only way forward is through stiffer penalties and more rigorous enforcement.

5F6 MEYER, M.D. and MCSHANE, M. (1983) Parking policy and downtown economic development. *Journal of Urban Planning and Development*, **109** (1), pp. 27–43.

Policy has switched from accommodating for the car to management strategies as a means to achieving a wide range of community objectives. This paper examines the use of such methods in fostering downtown economic development. Four methods are covered – limiting parking supply; controlling access to parking; the distribution of available parking; and the price of parking. Case studies in Baltimore and Seattle are used.

See also McShane, M. and Meyer, M.D. (1982) Parking policy and urban goals: Linking strategy to needs. *Transportation*, **11** (2), pp. 131–152.

5F7 ORGANISATION FOR ECONOMIC COOPERATION AND DEVELOPMENT (1980) *Evaluation of Urban Parking Systems*. Paris: OECD, Road Research Group.

This review covers parking and the wide range of strategies available for its implementation. The factors needed to determine the appropriate level of parking provision are discussed, and this presentation is complemented by a review of the evaluation methods to assess effectiveness. Research needs are discussed and appendices cover current policies in a cross section of OECD cities.

5F8 ORGANISATION FOR ECONOMIC COOPERATION AND DEVELOPMENT (1983) *Better Use of Vehicles*. Paris: OECD, Group on Traffic Policies.

This paper covers the means by which the use of the car can be better managed in urban areas. It covers safety, energy, car sharing and use of public transport as well as the use of the company car and goods vehicles. Similarly it examines a fuller role for public transport authorities to provide a more comprehensive service for all potential transport users, particularly those who are disadvantaged.

5F9 ORGANISATION FOR ECONOMIC COOPERATION AND DEVELOPMENT (1987) *Dynamic Traffic Management in Urban and Suburban Road Systems*. Paris: OECD, Road Transport Research, Research Group.

The aim is to review and assess dynamic traffic management systems and strategies likely to improve traffic flow and driving conditions on major arterials of urban and suburban road networks. A special focus is placed on the potential of advanced technologies including in-vehicle communication devices and/or road infrastructure equipment.

See also OECD (1979) *Managing Traffic* Paris: OECD.

5F10 STROBEL, H. (1982) *Computer Controlled Urban Transportation: A Survey of Concepts, Methods and International Experiences*. Chichester: Wiley.

This book is concerned with the present and future traffic problems in cities in the developing and developed world. It examines possible solutions to those problems based on technological innovations and implementing large-scale computerized traffic and transport control systems. It discusses the basic concepts and methods for control and automation that have been proposed, developed, and implemented, and experiences from real applications of these in different cities and nations.

5F11 TRANSPORTATION RESEARCH BOARD (1985) *Highway Capacity Manual*. TRB SR 209. Washington, DC: TRB.

This is the third edition of the *Highway Capacity Manual* and forms the basis for the design and operational analysis of highway facilities. The manual reviews traffic characteristics prior to detailed analysis of traffic under uncongested conditions (freeways, multilane and rural highways), and under congested conditions (signalized and non-signalized intersections, arterials, public transport and pedestrian and cyclist facilities). Each chapter introduces appropriate methodologies, procedures for application and examples.

5F12   WATERS, W.G. (1984) Applications of microcomputers in transportation and logistics. *Logistics and Transportation Review*, **20** (4).

A special issue of the journal is devoted to the applications of microcomputers in transport and logistics. Each mode of transport is covered with specific case studies, and the use of general software (e.g. databases and spreadsheets) is considered as well as purpose developed software. Authors include Manheim, M.L. (on management productivity and organization), Belshaw, P.N. (on growth in use of microcomputers), Martland, C.D. (on rail applications), Kimbriel, D.S. (on air) Anderson, D.R. (on freight), and Wyatt, E.M. (on urban transit).

5F13   YEH, C.-I., RITCHIE, S.G. and SCHNEIDER, J.B. (1986) Potential applications of knowledge-based expert systems in transport planning and engineering. *Transportation Research Record*, 1076, pp. 59–65.

The objectives of this paper are to describe the characteristics of knowledge-based expert systems (KBES) and to suggest some applications that appear to have a high potential for development in the field of transport planning and engineering. Such systems represent a rapidly developing branch of artificial intelligence (AI) and computer science that is already having significant impacts in many disciplines. KBES use interactive computer programmes that seek to provide a level of performance and expertise that is matched by only a few human experts in a particular problem domain. An overview is provided of AI and KBES concepts and of existing KBES and their architecture. The current scope of expert systems is described in an attempt to identify high-potential applications in the fields of transport planning and engineering. A number of these applications are identified and discussed. It is concluded that the potential appears high for KBES to become useful tools for practicing transport planners and engineers.

6 Area studies

In addition to the thematic papers outlined in the previous five sections, there are an enormous number of papers published with an area-based focus. In this section, the selection has been limited as only two types of study have been included. Firstly, the references present overviews of the total urban transport situation in particular countries (for example, Khan [6A15], Kolsen [6A16], Said [6A20]). Secondly, some of the references present useful cross-national comparisons (for example, Pandakur [6A19], the Inter-American Development Bank [6A14]. The twenty references selected from the literature cover all five continents and will enable the reader to obtain a grasp of the range of urban transport strategies being pursued worldwide. A majority of the citations concentrate on the role of the transport system in the process of urban development and growth (e.g. Gakenheimer [6A12], Lyons [6A17]), subsequent policy initiatives (e.g. Coombe [6A10]), and implications for issues such as national energy consumption (e.g. Bernard [6A4]). The range of countries covered include the following: developing world – China [6A17], India [6A4], Nigeria [6A5], Brazil [6A6], Bahrain [6A10], Jordan [6A10], Egypt [6A12], Kuwait [6A20] and general comparisons within Latin America [6A14] and South East Asia [6A19]; developed world – Australia [6A16], Canada [6A15], USA [6A9], UK [6A18], USSR [6A11], Japan [6A7], [6A21], South Africa [6A8] and Hong Kong [6A2]. These particular area studies complement other broader based international studies (e.g. Thomson [1B49], [1B50]; World Bank [1B62]).

6A1 ARMSTRONG-WRIGHT, A. (1986) Urban Transit Systems. World Bank, Technical Paper 52. Washington, DC.

This paper compares the characteristics and costs of the main kinds of urban transit systems, including buses, trains, light rail, rapid rail and suburban rail systems. The procedures, analyses and implementation problems associated with setting up new systems are examined together with checklists to ensure that important considerations are not overlooked. Annexes provide a summary of city transport facilities in both developing and developed countries.

6A2 BARDEN, S.A. and RUNNACLES, T.V. (1986) Transport in a high-density urban environment: the experience of Hong Kong. *Transport Reviews* 6 (3), pp. 219–258.

In Hong Kong the high cost of land reclamation servicing has made it necessary to plan land use through zoning commercial and industrial activity and by adopting very high densities for residential accommodation. Traffic has concentrated along particular corridors where its volume now exceeds road capacity. The imperative development of an urban rail system has affected the economic stability of most public transport. Simultaneously, private motoring has increased so rapidly that fiscal restraints have been imposed, generating a serious proposal for electronic road pricing. The future growth of links with China will end Hong Kong's relative isolation and present new transport planning challenges.

6A3 BEED, C. and MORIATY, P. (1986) Transport implications of metropolitan strategy. *Urban Policy and Research*, 4 (2), pp. 30–40.

The transport objectives stated in Melbourne's metropolitan strategy are isolated and an assessment is made of the impacts should the strategy be implemented. Specific transport advantages are likely to flow from the inner and intermediate suburbs component of the strategy, but the advantages to the outer suburbs are less obvious.

6A4 BERNARD, M.J. (1982) India's transportation energy problem. *Transportation Research Record*, 848, pp. 15-20.

The transport sector is the largest and fastest growing imported oil consuming sector in India. This paper reviews the growth of the sector in recent decades and characterizes the current pattern of demand, supply and consumption. Analyses, firstly of the social, political and infrastructure constraints on the sector and secondly of the government's plans and policies are summarized. Without good planning the transport sector may hinder rather than support the country's development because (1) the cost of imported fuels reduced the ability to import other goods needed for development; and (2), the sector could become insufficient for the required internal distribution. Several suggestions for planning and research are presented.

6A5 BOLADE, A.T. (1986) Transport in Metropolitan Lagos. *Transport Reviews*, **6** (1), pp. 1-30.

With an estimated population of 4 million people occupying an area of 1640 sq km, Metropolitan Lagos is the fastest growing urban region in Nigeria. Lagos is still the dual capital city of both the Federal and Lagos State governments of Nigeria; it contains over half of the nation's industrial, commercial and other economic activities. These create transport demands which seem to have exceeded what the available transport infrastructures and services can cope with. The rapid deterioration in the government-owned public transport system and the unorganized operation of numerous private minibuses, the dramatic increase in private car ownership associated with this and with the rapid economic growth after 1970, the inadequacy of road and parking spaces relative to this demand, coupled with unplanned growth and haphazard land use as well as ineffective traffic management and general urban planning, have all combined to compound the metropolitan transport problems. Recent policy initiatives have concentrated on expansion of major routes and some indirect traffic restraint measures. Significant achievements have been made since the worst road traffic chaos of the mid-1970s. But the long-term solutions lie in the promotion of mass transit, comprehensive traffic management and coordinated urban and transport planning and administration of the metropolitan region.

6A6 BRANCO, A.M. and KASSAB, P. (1983) Transport in large cities: a Brazilian point of view. *Transport Reviews*, **3** (2) pp. 117–138.

Following the historical evolution of urban transport in South America, the authors show the economic, technological and cultural facts that have governed its development until today. The paper, mainly based on experience in large Brazilian cities, gives facts and figures about some of the most important towns where different approaches to urban transport were tried. Information about other South American countries is also given and discussed. The article details the evolution, current situation and new plans in Sao Paulo city, describing concession criteria, modal split and the economics of the different modes in operation today and planned for future use, ending with the general influence of Sao Paulo experience of urban transport systems in many other Brazilian cities.

6A7 BRUHL, F. and KATAKURA, M. (1985) Transport in Tokyo. *Transport Reviews*, **5** (4), pp. 345–370.

This paper gives a review of the historical and geographical preconditions as well as of the population and economic development which led to the unique and complex transport systems of Tokyo. Tokyo Metropolis, one of the most populous cities in the world, is located in the National Capital Region of Japan where 32 million people are living today. The special transport problems deriving from this high population density are described in context with the development of employment, transport infrastructure and motorization. Due consideration is given to the influence exerted by the structure of the whole region on the overall traffic behaviour. Several transport phenomena and problem solutions which are typical of the traffic systems in Tokyo are described, such as the change of rush hour congestion rates depending on subway extension, modal split for different trip purposes in the inner urban area, or information via local radio broadcasts with very short range of transmission. The main current transport issues are discussed. Though the transport networks in Tokyo are some of the most developed in the world, there is still heavy congestion in rush hours. The basic policy therefore is the further strengthening and improvement of the public transport network.

6A8 CAMERON, J.W.M. (1980) Transport and city design: recent trends in the design of urban transport facilities. National Institute for Transport and Road Research, Pretoria, South Africa.

This paper reviews the state of the art of long-term structure planning, and advocates the adoption of a total design philosophy for the development of residential areas in the Republic of South Africa. The need for clearer perceptions of current relationships between land use and transport are exemplified and a reappraisal of the urban road classification is suggested, based on the need to differentiate traffic by type, destination and function. A system of design briefs is proposed for township development which will result in more involvement for public sector planners and better guidance to developers.

6A9 CERVERO, R. (1986) Intrametropolitan trends in Sunbelt and western cities: transportation implications. *Transportation Research Record*, 1067, pp. 20–27.

As the nation's economic growth continues to focus on sunbelt and western metropolises, rapid changes are taking place, particularly on the peripheries of these areas, that have major mobility implications. Most notably, jobs are increasingly leaving traditional downtowns for new suburban employment complexes and sprawling office complexes. As a result of this decentralization, predominant trip patterns are becoming more and more diffuse and lateral in direction, not only in burgeoning sunbelt cities but all over the country. Congestion has seemingly lost its directional bias and can now be found in all corners of rapidly expanding metropolises like Houston, Denver, and Orange County, California. All signs suggest, moreover, that the private automobile will continue to gain dominance in commuting markets in the nation's fastest growing areas, largely because of the emerging low-density settlement patterns. From a policy standpoint, emphasis needs to be placed on substantially reorganizing traditional public transit as well as modifying radial-circumferential systems so as to better mimic scattered trip patterns. Busways and timed-transfer arrangements, such as those pioneered in several Canadian cities, are promising. Strong political resistance to radical changes in transport service delivery practices, however, could prove difficult to overcome.

6A10 COOMBE, R.D. (1985) Urban transport policy development: two case studies in the Middle East. *Transport Reviews*, **5** (2), pp. 165–188.

The recent completion of two major transport studies of predominantly urban areas in the Middle East (Amman, Jordan, and Bahrain) has provided the opportunity to compare and contrast the transport characteristics of, and medium-term transport policies for, the two areas. While in structure the two transport systems have many similarities, their base year usage differs significantly. In view of the much lower income levels in Amman, and the resulting lower levels of car ownership, greater reliance is placed on public transport in Amman than in the more car-oriented society in Bahrain. Against this background, and in the context of broadly similar overall levels of growth in travel demand, their development in the medium term future should follow different paths. Amman will need to depend on public transport very heavily, with only limited road building. Bahrain should be able to develop a satisfactory road system, with public transport playing its current role except for the provision of services for some relatively modest number of restrained private vehicle users. In both cases, however, substantial investment in off-street parking spaces is needed. The paper briefly describes the social and economic backgrounds of the two areas, and reviews the transport systems and the organizations responsible for them. Travel demand forecasts are summarized, leading to the transport plan and policy development. The prospects for implementation are discussed, and the paper lastly focuses on some aspects which are key to the development of the transport systems in the two countries.

6A11 CROUCH, M. (1981) Transport policy in Britain and the Soviet Union: a political paradox. *Policy and Politics*, **9** (4), pp. 439–454.

Although heavily criticized, the 'totalitarian' image of the Soviet policy process is still widely accepted, not least for comparative purposes. While British policy-making might be dominated by pluralism and ad hocery, in the Soviet case it is largely a matter of the centralized direction of state power in the service of a controlling ideology. In at least the area of road passenger transport policy this formulation may well be precisely the wrong way round. The Soviet record is one of marked inability and unwillingness to implement declared policy. Bureaucratic pluralism coupled with a distinct disinclination on the part of local agencies to respond to central direction are major inhibiting factors. In the British case, as the 1980 Transport Act illustrated, central government can implement significant legislation despite the articulate opposition of many powerful and directly affected interests.

6A12 GAKENHEIMER, R. (1984) Strategic planning for transportation in the developing world. *Ekistics*, **51** (305), pp. 160–164.

This paper attempts to suggest what strategic planning should be for the developing world. It covers issues of management definition, agency decision targeting, accounting for the positions of the agency that plans, skills and institutional conditions and uncertainty. The question of programming in the strategic planning context is also considered crucial to the successful implementation of proposals in developing countries.

6A13 HART, D.A. (1984) A policy biography of the Greater London Council: planning and transport. *Built Environment*, **10** (2), pp. 100–112.

This paper traces the life of the Greater London Council over its 21-years (1965–1986) and provides a digest of historically significant decisions as they relate to planning and transport. Three broad phases are identified and the key consequences of decisions taken are summarized; its existence has been surrounded by controversey and the text alludes to these.

6A14 INTER-AMERICAN DEVELOPMENT BANK (1982) *The Impact of Energy Costs on Transportation in Latin America*. Washington: IDB.

The purpose of the seminar was to bring together Latin American officials and international experts to discuss the implications of higher energy costs for the transport sector in Latin America. The format of the seminar provided the environment for assessing the impact of scarcity and price escalation of energy, particularly petroleum, on investment policy in the transport sector, modal preference and development, administrative and regulatory policies, technology, and the impact on the transport sector of energy-related decisions in other economic sectors. The proceedings are organized into three parts: Part I contains a summary of the seminar, including background and conclusions; Part II consists of technical papers; and Part III includes a detailed examination of the transport sector and energy issues and policies in four Latin American countries or subregions.

6A15   KHAN, A.M. (1979) Recent transport policy initiatives in Canada: a new role for the Government. *Journal of Advanced Transportation*, **13** (1), pp. 19-37.

Recent transport policy initiatives of the government of Canada suggest a revised mandate that implies an active and interventionist role of the government for guiding future development of the transport system. As major decisions are to be made on strategic options involving capacity expansion, network extensions, service modernization and integration, it is imperative that the government fulfill its leadership role by defining and implementing a process of policy analysis and planning that goes beyond the past practice of 'muddling through'. This paper examines critical issues surrounding the modified role of the government in transport developments in Canada.

6A16   KOLSEN, H.M. (1986) Transport policy in Australia. The role of the interstate commission. *Journal of Transport Economics and Policy*, **20** (2), pp. 275-283.

This article examines the extent to which transport economics is able to influence transport policy, given the existence of historical, institutional, constitutional and political constraints which differ considerably between countries. The Australian Federation has some unique features which include provisions, in the Australian Constitution, for the establishment of an Inter-State Commission. After discussion of the initial reasons for this, the re-establishment of the Commission in 1984, and its activities, are examined in the context of transport policy in the Australian Federation.

6A17   LYONS, T.P. (1985) Transportation in Chinese development, 1952-1982. *Journal of Developing Areas*, **19** (3), pp. 305-327.

China has attempted to develop several modes at the same time and this contrasts with the sequential development typical of many other countries. The current five-year plan calls for increased efforts to develop transport facilities and to operate them effectively. Nevertheless, the Chinese view of transport's role in development remains much narrower than the conventional notion that a well-developed transport system is necessary if modernization is to mean more than a series of scattered modern industrial centres.

6A18 MALTBY, D. and WHITE, H.P. (1982) *Transport in the United Kingdom*. London: Macmillan Press.

This book describes Britain's transport network, industry, and policies and their interaction with other aspects of policy and the economy. The relative roles of the public sector and the private sector are examined, and some trends in passenger transport and freight transport are discussed. The concept of an integrated transport system is considered, and land use, regional development, environmental, investment and other problems examined.

6A19 PENDAKUR, V.S. (1984) Urban Transport in ASEAN. Institute of Southeast Asian Studies, ASEAN Economic Research Unit, Discussion Paper 34. London: ASEAN.

This study focuses on the urban transport sector in the context of urbanization and growth. It describes existing systems and discusses the policy implications of modernization. The emphasis is on the range of vehicles and persons within the secondary transport system. The final section of the paper looks forward and anticipates likely developments and problems in the ASEAN countries.

6A20 SAID, G.M. (1982) An overview of transport in Kuwait. *Transport Reviews*, **2** (4), pp. 321–348.

This paper provides a brief statement of transport in Kuwait. It starts by describing Kuwait's national setting and touches on the economic and social aspects in Kuwait that have an influence on transport patterns and needs. It describes the national transport system and covers road, air, rail and ports. Urban development planning in Kuwait is described and issues related to stages of urban development planning. The Kuwait City Master Plan and new town initiatives are presented. The urban transport system in Kuwait Metropolitan Area is described. In particular the characteristics of the urban road network and public transport facilities are outlined along with recent transport planning studies and new initiatives in the urban transport system. The paper ends with a statement on organizations involved in the transport sector in Kuwait and a note on transport finance.

6A21 WHITE, P.R. (1985) Trends in transport: Japan and Britain compared. *Transportation Planning Technology*, **10** (1), pp. 43-52.

A general comparison which tries to shown how far Japanese approaches could be applied in Britain. The paper covers car ownership, rail transport bus services and the attitudes of both government and the public to private and public transport.

7 Bibliographies and research registers

In English

7A1 ALPERT, M. and LESLEY, L. (1981) *The Role of Public Transport in New Towns, A Bibliography*. Liverpool: Department of Town and Country Planning, Liverpool Polytechnic.

7A2 BAKER, R. and FRASER, C. (1984) *The M25 – Planning and Development Implications: A Bibliography*. London: Environmental Services Unit, Polytechnic of the South Bank.

7A3 BANISTER, D. (1985) *Rural Transport and Planning: An Annotated Bibliography*. London: Mansell.

This companion volume to the current bibliography includes about 600 references on recent research in rural transport and planning. The structure is similar and each section has a brief introductory section highlighting basic themes.

7A4 COUNCIL OF PLANNING LIBRARIANS. Exchange Bibliography Series. Available from the Council at Post Box 229, Monticello, Illinois 61856, USA.

This is a nationally organized group of librarians, planners and organizations interested in the provision of information about city and regional planning. A complete list of over 1000 annotated bibliographies is avaliable on request.

7A5 DOE/DTP (1987) *Annual List of Publications 1986*. Available from DOE/DTP Library Services, 2 Marsham Street, London SW1P 3EB.

The Annual List includes all publications of more than local interest issued or sponsored by the Department of the Environment and the Department of Transport in 1986. HMSO publications, departmental publications, Acts, statutory instruments and departmental circulars are all included.

The Department also produces a series of bibliographies on particular policy areas (such as deregulation) which are of relevance to central and local government, and lists of information and statistical sources in the UK and EEC.

7A6 ELKINGTON, J., MCGLYNN, R. and ROBERTS, J. (1976) *The Pedestrian: Planning and Research*. London: Transport and Environmental Studies.

7A7 EUROPEAN CONFERENCE OF MINISTERS OF TRANSPORT (1986) *Research on Transport Economics: Annual Information Bulletin*, Volume 19. Paris: ECMT.

This bulletin presents a survey of relevant research in the Member countries of the ECMT and certain other industrialized countries. It is published each year (November) on the basis of a survey carried out in the Spring of the same year. The data collected are processed by the OECD.

7A8 GAKENHEIMER, R. and LEWIS, S. (1986) *Urban Transport in Developing Countries: An Annotated Bibliography*. Cambridge, Mass: Massachusetts Institute of Technology.

7A9 *Geographical (Geo) Abstracts*, University of East Anglia, Norwich NR4 7TJ.

A bi-monthly service with three separate sections on human aspects of geography – Part C Economic Geography, Part D Social and Historical Geography, Part F Regional and Community Planning.

Each issue contains about 500 abstracts from journal articles and other sources, national and international. International Development Abstracts focuses exclusively on developing countries. The whole series is now on line as GEOBASE via DIALOG (see Database Search Systems).

7A10 GRAYSON, L. (1986) *The Social and Economic Impact of New Technology 1984–86: A Selected Bibliography*. Letchworth, Herts: Technical Communications.

This is the second edition of the 1978–1984 Bibliography and has 754 references.

7A11 HUXLEY, M. and McLOUGHLIN, J.B. (1985) The new urban studies literature: a review with special reference to Australia. *Progress in Planning*, **24** (3), pp. 163–245.

This paper reviews the 'new urban studies' and planning literature with particular reference to Australia. It surveys traditional work in the field, identifies the paradigm shifts of the 1970s and documents the establishment of the new urban studies point of view. A section on global economic restructuring is followed by a discussion of the effects of these changes on Australia, and comment on the urbanization and planning literature. There is coverage of over 500 references.

7A12 INSTITUTE OF BRITISH GEOGRAPHERS, Transport Geography Study Group (1986) *Research Register 1984*. London: IBG.

This publication is updated regularly and covers the research interests of members of the study group.

7A13 INTERNATIONAL ROAD FEDERATION (1986) *Research and Development on Roads and Road Transport* (prepared in Cooperation with OECD and TRB) Washington, DC: IRF.

This annual report provides a summary of current road research and development throughout the world. Information from each country is generally obtained and presented in a three-year cycle. Year one involves a complete resurvey and the subsequent two years have a supplementary survey.

7A14 MILDREN, K. (1976) *The Use of Engineering Literature*. London: Butterworths.

Contains a 20-page section on highways, traffic and transport engineering.

7A15 PENDAKUR, V.S. (1984) Urban transport in South and Southeast Asia: an annotated bibliography, Library Bulletin - Institute of Southeast Asian Studies (Singapore).

433 references 1970-1984.

7A16 PICKUP, L. and SMITH, D. (1987) *Commuting - The European Dimension - A Bibliography*. Shankill, County Dublin: European Foundation for the Improvement of Living and Working Conditions.

This report presents a selected bibliography of research on commuting in the European community and its consequences for living and working conditions. It contains 500 references of which about 60 per cent have an abstract. It covers research in the last 10 years.

7A17 *Sources and Nature of the Statistics of the United Kingdom*. A series of reviews of statistical sources in particular subject areas. Ones relevant to transport include:

Vol VII	Road Passenger Transport - D.L. Munby
	Road Goods Transport - A.H. Watson
Vol VIII	Land Use - J.T. Coppock
	Town and Country Planning - L.F. Gebbett
Vol X	Ports and Inland Waterways - R.E. Baxter
	Civil Aviation - C. Phillips
Vol XIV	Rail Transport - D.H. Aldcroft
	Sea Transport - D. Mort
Vol XVIII	Posts and Telecommunications - S. Wall and P. Nicholson

All are produced by the Royal Statistical Society and the Social Science Research Council (now the Economic and Social Research Council) and are published by Pergamon Press.

7A18 TOM SHIN, B. (1979) Selected References for Transportation Planning in Developing Countries. Mimeo, Department of Civil Engineering, University of Toronto.

7A19 TRANSPORT AND ROAD RESEARCH LABORATORY, Old Wokingham Road, Crowthorne, Berkshire, RG11 6AU.

A monthly list of all TRRL research reports is produced and the TRRL annual report is also being resurrected. This annual review will describe all research activities at the TRRL including a listing of all publications. The Library operates a computer based data and information retrieval system. Through this, literature searches can be carried out on request, but enquires must be specific and precisely formulated.

7A20 WATERS, W.G. (1984) *Articles Related to Transportation in Major Economic Journals 1960-1981*. Vancouver: Centre for Transportation Studies, University of British Columbia.

7A21 WHITE, P.M. (1979) *Soviet Urban and Regional Planning: A Bibliography with Abstracts*. London: Mansell.

In German (since 1980)

7A22 BERGMANN, U. and KUHN, H. (1980) Forschung in Strassenwesen. Zusammenstellung laufender und abgeschlossener Forschungsarbeiten 1/6/78-30/9/79, Köln: Selbstverlag.

7A23 BUNDESMINISTER FÜR VERKEHR (1986) *Forschung Stadtverkehr*, Vol 37. Bonn - Bad Godesberg.

Part of this publication is an English translation of research commissioned by the Federal Ministry of Transport in Germany. The first part of the English section contains abstracts of the research which has been completed and the second part covers all research and study assignments on urban transport commissioned by the Ministry.

7A24 DEGENKOLBE, H. (1983) *Lärmschutzbauwerke und - massnahmen an Strassen*. Stuttgart: IRB - Verlag.

7A25 DEUTSCHE VERKEHRSWISSENSCHAFTLICHE GESSELLSCHAFT (1983) *Schrifctum aus dem Verkehrswesen 1982*. Köln: Selbstverlag.

Published annually with a timelag of one to two years.

7A26 FRITSCH, H. (1986) *Kosten-Nutzen-Analyse in Verkehrswesen*. Stuttgart: IRB - Verlag.

7A27 KUETING, H.J. (1976) Stress and Strain on drivers: a literature review, Bundesanstalt fuer Strassenwesen, Köln, Germany, 185 references (in German).

The article presents a methodological-critical review of domestic and foreign research concerning stress measurement in drivers of motor vehicles. Among the physiological indicators, heart frequency and electrical conductivity of the skin are dealt with in detail. The possibility of modern traffic being a long term cause of illness is discussed. The psychological indicators are best understood as measures of the capacity to process information and to make decisions.

7A28 ÖSTERREICH, BUNDESMINISTER FÜR BAUTEN UND TECHNIK, STRASSENFORSCHUNG (1983) *Dokumentation 1979–1981 über Forschungsvorhaben und wissenschaftliche Arbeiten in Österreich*. Wien: Selbstverlag.

7A29 PAMPE, U., BEIERSMANN, H. and SCHWANTES, W. (1984) *Stadterneuerung. Eine Literatur über-Sicht*. Stuttgart.

7A30 PANKE, C. (1981) Fussgängerzone und verkehrsberuhigte Stasse im Strassenbaubeitragsrecht nach KAG NW und im Strassenrecht. Angaben zu Literatur und Rechtsprechung, Köln.

7A31 TIMM, J. (1985) *Raumwirksamkeit neuer Technologien*. Literaturquerschnitt, Dortmund.

7A32 WIRZ, S. (1983) *Bibliographie 'Strasse und Umwelt'*. Oppenheim: Selbstverlag.

In French (since 1980)

7A33 CENTRE D'ETUDES DES TRANSPORT URBAINS (1986) *Transport Urbanisme Planification*, Bagneux.

Regular review document on research.

7A34 CLERC-PECHINE (no date) Transport Bibliography, Laboratoire d'Economie des Transports, Université de Lyon II.

7A35 COMMISSION OF THE EUROPEAN COMMUNITIES (1983) *Bibliographie sur les Transports, Documentation Bulletin*. Brussels: Commission of the European Communities.

This bibliography dates back to 1983 and a new one which covers the next three years should be published in 1987.

7A36 INSTITUT NATIONAL DE RECHERCHE SUR LES TRANSPORTS ET LEUR SÉCURITÉ (1986) RTS: Recherche – Transport – Sécurité, Arcueil Cedex.

This review is published annually.

7A37 MERLIN, P. (1984) *Bibliographie sur la Planification des Transport Urbains – Internationale, Retrospective (1950–1983) et Partillement Commentee*. Paris: Presses Universitaires de Vincennes.

7A38 PIOZIN, F. (1984) Les Transports Informels Urbains de Personnes dans les Pays en Developpement, Cent References Bibliographiques, Institut de Recherche des Transports, Arcueil Cedex.

This report on urban paratransit in developing countries presents 100 relevant references.

7B Database search systems

7B1 ACOMPLINE AND URBALINE: All urban abstract items from the research library at the London Research Centre are available on ACOMPLINE with newspaper coverage available on URBALINE.

DATABASE SEARCH SYSTEMS [7B]

Some 250,000 items are documented and are available through Pergamon Orbit Infoline and ESA/IRS systems. Further details are available from the research library on 01-627-9666.

7B2 ATLS: Australian transport literature system is run by the Bureau of Transport Economics.

7B3 Australian Road Research Board, 500 Burwood Road, Vermont South, Victoria 3133, Australia.

7B4 Bureau of Transport Economics, PO Box 84, Canberra ACT 2600, Australia.

7B5 DAI: Dissertation abstracts international is a monthly journal which contains full bibliographic data and abstracts on doctoral dissertations. Dissertation abstracts online produces this information by keyword search. Its scope is mainly North American Universities and can be obtained through University Microfilms International – A catalogue is produced annually for dissertations on transport.
UMI Ltd, White Swan House, Godstone, Surrey, RG9 8 LW.

7B6 HRIS: Highway research information service has some 120,000 items stored on computer tapes, with a further 7500 items added annually. HRIS abstracts are published quarterly and cover highway and non-rail public transport research.

7B7 INROADS: Information on roads is a database system for Australian and related transport research, compiled by the Australian Road Research Board.

7B8 IRRD: The International Road Research Documentation scheme contains abstracts and other details on information sources worldwide on roads and road transport research. The complete IRRD database was started in 1972 and now has some 160,000 records.
OECD, Road Transport Research Programme, 2 Rue Andre-Pascal, 75775 Paris, Cedex 16.
British Library Lending Division, Boston Spa, Wetherby, West Yorkshire, LS23 7BQ.

7B9 TRANSDOC: Covers the main transport economics and policy documents in ECMT member countries, together with selected material from elsewhere. References are in English (40%), French (35%) and German (25%).
ECMT at 19 Rue de Franqueville, 75775 Paris, Cedex 16.

7B10 UMTRIS: Urban mass transportation research information service has approximately 15000 items with about 2500 items added annually. Urban Transportation Abstracts are produced biannually and cover planning, design, finance, control, operations and marketing of public transport.
Contact address for both HRIS and UMTRIS is the Transportation Research Board, National Research Council, 2101 Constitution Avenue NW, Washington, DC 20418.

On line searches can be carried out through DIALOG Information Services Inc, 3460 Hillview Avenue, Palo Alto, California 94304.

7B11 URBAMET: 158 000 references and 108 000 documents, about 10 per cent of which are related to transport.
M Lubin at Direction Regionale de l'Equipment d'Ile de France, Paris, Cedex 15.

Selected periodicals

1 Transport

Australian Road Research
Australian Road Research Board, 500 Burwood Road, Vermont South, Victoria 3133, Australia.
Quarterly, 1964–

Highways and Transportation (from January 1984, formerly *Journal of the Institution of Highway Engineers*, and *Highway Engineer*)
Institution of Highway Engineers, 3 Lygon Place, Ebury Street, London SW1W 0JS.
Monthly, 1954–

SELECTED PERIODICALS

International Journal of Transport Economics
8 Via GA Guattani, Rome 00161, Italy.
Three issues per year, 1974–

Journal of Advanced Transportation (formerly *High Speed Ground Transportation Journal*)
Institute for Transportation, 1410 Duke University Road, Durham, NC 27701, USA.
Three issues per year, 1979–

Journal of Transport Economics and Policy
London School of Economics and Political Science, Houghton Street, Aldwych, London WC2A 2AE.
Three issues per year, 1967–

Journal of Transport History
Manchester University Press, Oxford Road, Manchester M13 OPL.
New series Vol 1 1971–

Logistics and Transportation Review (formerly *Logistics Review*)
University of British Columbia, Vancouver, V6T 1W5, Canada.
Quarterly, 1965–

Planning Transport Research and Computation
PTRC Education and Research Services Ltd, 110 Strand, London WC2.
Irregular.

Proceedings of the American Society of Civil Engineers, Journal of the Engineering Division
American Society of Civil Engineers, 345 East 47th Street, New York, NY 10017.
Quarterly, 1956–

Specialized Transportation Planning and Practice
Gordon Breach Science Publishers Ltd, 42 William IV Street, London WC2.
Quarterly, 1985–

Traffic Engineering and Control
Printerhall Limited, 29 Newman Street, London W1P 3PE.
Monthly, 1959–

Transport (formerly *Journal of the Chartered Institute of Transport*)
Chartered Institute of Transport, 80 Portland Place, London W1N 4DP.
Bimonthly, New Series 1980–

Transport Reviews
Taylor and Francis, 104 John Street, London WC1N 2ET.
Quarterly, 1981–

Transportation
Martinus Nijhoff Publishers, Dordrecht, The Netherlands.
Quarterly, 1972–

Transportation Engineering (formerly *Traffic Engineering*)
Institute of Traffic Engineering, 1815 North Fort Myer Drive, Arlington, BA 22209, USA.
1930–

Transportation Planning and Technology (formerly *Transportation Technology*)
Gordon Breach Science Publishers Ltd, 42 William IV Street, London WC2.
Quarterly, 1972–

Transportation Quarterly (formerly *Traffic Quarterly*)
Eno Foundation for Transportation, Box 55, Saugatuck Station, Westport, Connecticut 06880.
Quarterly, 1947–

Transportation Research
Pergamon Press, Headington Hill Hall, Oxford OX3 0BW.
Bi-monthly, 1967–

Transportation Research Record (formerly *Highway Research Record*)
Transportation Research Board, 2101, Constitution Avenue NW, Washington, DC 20418.
Irregular.

SELECTED PERIODICALS 309

Transportation Science
Operations Research Society of America, 428 East Preston Street, Baltimore, Maryland 21202.
Quarterly, 1967–

2 Planning

Built Environment
Alexandrine Press, PO Box 15, 51 Cornmarket Street, Oxford OX1 3EB.
Quarterly, 1975–

Energy Policy
IPC Business Press, PO Box 63, Guildford, Surrey, GU2 5BH.
Quarterly, 1973–

Environment and Planning
Pion Limited, 207 Brondesbury Park, London NW2 5JN
A Environment and Planning   Monthly, 1974–
B Planning and Design   Quarterly, 1974–
C Government and Policy   Quarterly, 1983–
D Society and Space   Quarterly, 1983–

Futures
IPC Science and Technology Press, PO Box 63, Guildford, Surrey GU2 5BH.
Bimonthly, 1968–

Journal of the American Planning Association
American Planning Association, 1776 Massachusetts Avenue NW, Washington, DC 20036.
Quarterly, 1917–

The Planner
Journal of the Royal Town Planning Institute
26 Portland Place, London W1N 4BE.
Seven issues per year, 1914–

Policy and Politics
School for Advanced Urban Studies, Rodney Lodge, Grange Road, Bristol BS8 4EA.
Quarterly, 1972-

Practicing Planner
American Institute of Planners, 1776 Massachusetts Avenue NW, Washington, DC 20036.
Quarterly, 1971-

Progress in Planning
Pergamon Press Ltd, Headington Hill Hall, Oxford OX3 OBW.
Quarterly, 1973-

Regional Studies
Journal of the Regional Studies Association, Cambridge University Press, Trumpington Street, Cambridge CB2 1RP.
Quarterly, 1967-

Socio-Economic Planning Sciences
Pergamon Press, Headington Hill Hall, Oxford OX3 OBW.
Bi-monthly, 1967-

Surveyor - Public Works Weekly (formerly *Surveyor and Municipal Engineer and Surveyor - Local Government Technology*)
IPC Buildings and Contract Journals Ltd, Surrey House, 1 Throwley Way, Sutton, Surrey, SM1 4QQ.
Weekly, 1892-

Town and Country Planning
TCPA, 17 Carlton House Terrace, London SW1Y 5AS.
Monthly, 1932-

Town Planning Review
Liverpool University Press, 123 Grove Street, Liverpool L7 7AF.
Quarterly, 1910-

Third World Planning Review
Liverpool University Press, 123 Grove Street, Liverpool L7 7AF.
Semi-Annual, 1979-

SELECTED PERIODICALS

Transactions of the Institute of British Geographers
Institute of British Geographers, 1 Kensington Gore, London SW7 2AR.
Quarterly, New Series 1976–

Urban Studies
Longman Group UK Limited, Fourth Avenue, Harlow, Essex CM19 5AA.
Bi-monthly, 1964–

8 Additional entries

8.1 BORINS, S.F. (1988) Electronic road pricing: an idea whose time may never come. *Transportation Research*, **22A** (1), pp. 37–44.

Hong Kong's experiment with electronic road pricing showed that the technology was completely feasible. However, the government was unable to implement the scheme due to strong opposition from a public that perceived it as an invasion of privacy and a tax increase. This outcome was partly a result of forces unique to Kong Kong's political culture as well as both strategic and tactical errors made by the Hong Kong government in presenting its proposal. However, the Hong Kong experience also raises serious questions about whether a sophisticated road pricing scheme will ever be acceptable in a democratic urban polity.

8.2 COHEN, Y. (1987) Commuter welfare under peak-period congestion tolls: who gains and who loses? *International Journal of Transport Economics*, **14** (3), pp. 239–266.

This paper determines some of the welfare effects on road users of levying peak hour congestion tolls. Different motorists are assumed to have different valuations of time and commute to work along a route that contains a point bottleneck such as a bridge or tunnel crossing. Equilibrium travel patterns are derived with individual commuters unable to improve upon their departure schedules. A queue forms whenever vehicular flow exceeds the fixed capacity of the bottleneck. The solution is to impose a smoothly-varying optimal toll schedule which eliminates the queue. It is then shown that higher value of time, higher income motorists are as a group never made worse off by paying efficient tolls, while lower income commuters are never made better off, prior to any redistribution of toll revenues. Since these effects are often non-negligible, then road pricing schemes should involve combining tolls plus disbursements of toll revenues to compensate those who would be made otherwise worse off, enabling every income class to gain.

8.3 CROC, M. (1988) Marseilles integrated transport system. *Journal of Advanced Transportation*, **21** (3), pp. 255–262.

To be fully effective, metro lines must be connected with other modes of transport. This principle has been applied in the city of Marseilles. First, a very good interchange between the two metro lines and the national and suburban railway has been developed in the Saint-Charles main railway station. This interchange connects with the adjacent intercity bus terminal. Second, at every metro station, access facilities and neighbourhood development were planned. Third, bus stations and car parks were installed at main rail-stations. All this was made possible by early coordinated planning.

8.4 DOGAN, M. and KASARDA, J.D. (eds) (1988) *The Metropolis Era*, 2 volumes. London: Sage Publications.

The two volumes describe the consequences of rapid change for the cities and the people who live in them. The contributors look not only at the pathological consequences, but also at the advantages which giant cities have to offer their residents. They present case studies which focus on new challenges to the world's great cities, and discuss the various forms of urban decline in the giant metropolises of developed nations. The first volume examines theories and the issues in each of the main regions of the world, and the second takes individual cities as case studies.

8.5 EUROPEAN CONFERENCE OF MINISTERS OF TRANSPORT (1987) *Transport For Disabled People*. Paris: ECMT.

This document reflects current approaches by ECMT member countries to providing for the transport needs of disabled people.

The situation seems to be supply-led with little concerted research into the methods by which the needs of disabled people can be measured or evaluated. The report outlines the underlying issues and attempts to quantify the numbers of disabled people. It then examines the question of responsibility and the patterns of costs of transport for disabled people. These reviews are then placed in the context of national policies and the role that the ECMT can take in encouraging the provision of transport services that are accessible to disabled people.

8.6 GÄRLING, T. and GÄRLING, E. (1988) Distance minimisation in downtown pedestrian shopping. *Environment and Planning A*, **20** (4), pp. 547-554.

Downtown pedestrian shopping was observed with the purpose of determining whether shoppers attempted to minimize walking distance, and, if so, whether, as has been suggested in previous research, they did that by successively choosing the closest locations. In downtown of an average-sized Swedish city (about 80,000 residents), 150 shoppers were interviewed in a parking lot when they were coming back from shopping rounds. 69 per cent of the shoppers visited more than one location, and 51 per cent visited more than two locations. Of those who visited more than two different locations, 35 (69 per cent) attempted to minimize walking distance. This was most frequently done by first choosing the location farthest away, then minimizing distance successively back to the parking lot. In this way shoppers probably attempted to minimize both the walking distance and the effort to carry goods. Some shoppers managed to choose routes which were shorter than if they had minimized distance successively. This finding was consistent with the results of laboratory studies demonstrating the role of maplike mental representations for distance-minimizing choices.

8.7 GARRISON, W.L. and DEAKIN, E. (1988) Travel, work and telecommunications: a view of the electronics revolution and its potential impacts. *Transportation Research A*, **22** (4), pp. 239-245.

Considerations of the impacts of electronic technologies on transport usually focus on substitution of communications for travel, especially telecommuting. This topic is reviewed briefly, followed by consideration of electronic technology-induced changes in the structure of firms, work by individuals, and consumption. Today's organization of the work place on the basis of time-at-a-place measurements dates from early in the Industrial Revolution; the communications control of production dates from the introduction of the telegraph. Recent and upcoming communications developments may relax time and place requirements while intensifying communications control. Resulting changes in production and consumption may challenge transportation developments in coming decades.

8.8 HANSON, S. (ed.) (1987) *The Geography of Urban Transportation*. London: The Guilford Press.

Three introductory chapters describe the urban transport context, the role of transport in urban form and the urban transport planning process. These are followed by six analytical chapters where a distinction is made in the scale of analysis, whether aggregate or disaggregate. The problem orientation of the book is covered in the third part where each chapter spotlights a particular transport related policy concern: public transport, land-use impacts, energy issues, social and environmental impacts, substituting telecommunications for travel and an overall policy review.

8.9 HARITOS, Z.J. (1987) Public transport enterprises in transition. *Transportation*, **14** (3), pp. 193–207.

Since the mid-1970s many Western governments have felt that liberalization of market forces through deregulation and better control or privatization of public enterprises would raise productivity and reduce inflation and government deficits. This paper reviews the recent literature on public enterprise and draws on the Canadian experience. It discusses the rationale for and concept of public enterprise and focuses on two reform proposals, accountability and privatization. To increase the degree of accountability would require, on the one hand, that the government establish a formal mandate and role for the enterprise and periodically provide formal government directives, and on the other hand, provide an appropriate evaluation framework. Government compensation for imposed public duties is addressed. Full or partial privatization should be pursued when the rationale for a public enterprise has been significantly altered. This applies particularly to public transport enterprises which are in competition with the private sector.

8.10 HENSHER, D.A. (1987) Productive efficiency and ownership of urban bus services. *Transportation*, **14** (3), pp. 209–225.

The established ownership mix of urban bus operations in Australia provides a unique opportunity to investigate the productivity differences between public and private bus service supply. Using duality theory in economics which links economic indices of factor productivity to the cost structure of a firm, empirical measures of total and partial productivity of inputs are developed and the differences are adjusted for the effects of ownership status and operating environment. The evidence supports the notion that private supply of public passenger transport in general has performed more efficiently in the past than public supply, although the differences in productivity need not continue in the future.

8.11 HODGE, D.C. (1988) Fiscal equity in urban mass transit systems: a geographic analysis. *Annals of the Association of American Geographers*, **78** (2), pp. 288–306.

This study clarifies a number of conceptual and methodological questions related to public service equity by analysing the geographic flow of fiscal subsidies for mass transit operations. The analyses focus on cross subsidies between users and between residential locations, on the distribution of non-farebox (tax) revenues between users and locations, and on the total net subsidy. Flows of subsidy between the central city and the suburbs are also establshed. Results indicate that user subsidies are much higher in the suburban areas but that non rider tax revenues in suburbs produce a net flow of subsidies from suburbs to the city centre. Relative to average income value, the tax burden supporting public transport is higher for residents in the central city.

8.12 KAIN, J.F. (1988) Choosing the wrong technology: or how to spend billions and reduce transit use. *Journal of Advanced Transportation*, **21** (3), pp. 197–214.

In spite of a broad consensus among transport analysts that bus rapid transit, whether operating on exclusive rights-of-way or on uncongested high occupancy vehicle lanes or general purpose limited access facilities, provides higher performance and has significantly lower costs per passenger trip than rail transit in medium and low density cities, nearly all Sunbelt cities are building or planning heavy or light rail systems. This paper reviews previous studies of the cost effectiveness of heavy and light rail transit with bus-rapid transit and the growing experience with busways and transitways and concludes, once again, that some form of bus rapid transit would be a far more effective way of providing improved transit in these cities than heavy or light rail transit. Not only would bus rapid transit be substantially cheaper, but it would provide a higher quality of service than light or heavy rail transit for virtually all users. Finally, the paper speculates on the reasons for the continued, 'blind' commitment to rail transit by policymakers in Sunbelt cities and on the refusal of policy-makers in all but a few of these cities to even consider bus rapid transit.

8.13 KITAMURA, R. and VAN DER HOORN, T. (1987) Regularity and irreversibility of weekly travel behaviour. *Transportation*, **14** (3), pp. 227–251.

Dynamic characteristics of travel behaviour are analysed in this paper using weekly travel diaries from two waves of panel surveys conducted six months apart. An analysis of activity engagement indicates the presence of significant regularity in weekly activity participation between the two waves. The analysis also shows a general lack of association between regularity in activity participation and change in person and household attributes, suggesting the presence of behavioural inertia or responses lags. It is further shown that observed trip rates do not exhibit patterns that would be observed if travel behaviour had no response lag and no history dependence. The results point to the needs for models that are capable of representing these aspects of travel behaviour.

8.14 KLAASEN, L.H. and VAN DER MEER, J. (1987) Urban change and public transport. *International Journal of Transport Economics*, **14**(2), pp. 123–132.

In recent years city centres have seen a decline in population and, to a lesser extent, jobs. The increasing spread of population has led to severe peak hour congestion problems as people travel to and from work, with accompanying social, economic and environmental costs. However, recently there has been an increase in the deconcentration of employment, and rising demand for part-time jobs, which may lead to more efficient use of the transport system. The paper argues that this tendency could be reinforced by policy moves to emphasize the role of the city centre as a location for high grade services, which could lead to more balanced transport demands and a gradual change in peak hour demand.

8.15 KROES, E.P. and SHELDON, R.J. (1988) Stated preference methods. An introduction. *Journal of Transport Economics and Policy*, **22** (1), pp. 11–26.

The article is concerned with stated preference methods and their use in the transport sector, particularly within the areas of preference evaluation, demand analysis and forecasting. Drawing upon their collective experience from the past eight years the authors set out to introduce stated preference methods and to discuss how they differ from more conventional revealed preference approaches. Some important transport research areas where stated preference methods have been successfully applied are discussed, illustrated with some appropriate project applications. The paper concludes by referring to some market trends in the use of stated preference methods providing an insight into what can be expected for the future.

This special issue of the journal is concerned with stated preference methods and their use in transport analysis (see also [8.16]).

8.16 LOUVIERE, J. (1988) Conjoint analysis modelling of stated preferences. A review of theory, methods, recent developments and external validity. *Journal of Transport Economics and Policy*, **22** (1), pp. 93–120.

This paper reviews the state-of-the-art in the conjoint analysis paradigm for stated preference research. Communalities and differences among different conjoint analysis techniques are discussed, including the assumptions required to use the techniques and to simulate individuals' choices. The discussion is organized around rating, ranking and discrete response methods of collecting conjoint data. Recent advances in conjoint analysis are discussed, and particular attention is given to the design and analysis of discrete choice experiments. Limitations and problems in the use of conjoint techniques are outlined, and suggestions are made about directions for future research.

8.17 MCCLINTOCK, H. (1987) On the right track? An assessment of recent English experience of innovations in urban bicycle planning. *Town Planning Review*, **58** (3), pp. 267-291.

After reviewing trends in bicycle usage in England, with reference to variations in cycle usage, and the general growth in cycling since the 1970s, the author-discusses the main reasons for planning for cycling. Bicycle planning experience is then discussed with particular reference to new towns and then to older towns and cities. This is followed by discussion of the experience of the Department of Transport-promoted innovatory cycling schemes, both small-scale since 1977 and large-scale since 1984, as well as other recent developments. In conclusion, the experience of cycle planning is assessed in the wider context of town planning, transport planning and traffic management.

8.18 MITCHELSON, R.L. and FISHER, J.S. (1987) Long distance commuting and income change in the towns of upstate New York. *Economic Journal*, **63** (1), pp. 48-65.

Long distance commuting to all levels of the urban hierarchy is a mechanism by which income growth is spread to non-metroplitan peripheries. Attendant income growth multipliers are variable with distance from metropolitan employment centres, with the maximum multipliers being found at the intermediate distances from the metropolitan centre. The increasing potency of multipliers in the 1960s and 1970s and extension of income growth to greater distances are influenced by in-migration, job substitution and increased female participation rates.

8.19 MOGRIDGE, M.J.H. (1987) The use of rail transport to improve accessibility in large conurbations, using London as an example. *Town Planning Review*, **58** (2), pp. 165-182.

London travel data are used to support the idea that only by improving rail services to and through the centre of the conurbation can the accessibility of all the jobs and other facilities in the centre be improved. The idea follows from the fact that an equilibrium in journey speeds is established between road and rail for trips to the centre in congested conditions. Problems of the accessibility of rail travellers using main-line services into central termini to jobs in the centre are revealed with census data. The improvement of accessibility in the suburbs is also discussed.

8.20 MORI, M. and TSUKAGUCHI, H. (1987) A new method for evaluation of level of service in pedestrian facilities. *Transportation Research A*, **21** (3), pp. 223-234.

Safe and comfortable walking is essential for pedestrian movement in modern urban transport systems. Since pedestrian traffic cannot be restricted in some specified streets, some measures for pedestrians have to be taken everywhere in urban areas. This research describes a way to evaluate ordinary pavements, and two different methods are proposed. One is an evaluation based on pedestrian behaviour and the other is an evaluation based on pedestrian opinion. Using the indices of pedestrian density and pavement width one can estimate the level of service of pavement usage. But generally speaking, since it is not often that a pavement is insufficient to deal with pedestrian flow, another approach is necessary for its evaluation, that is, pedestrian awareness of pavement must be taken into account. The former method is recommended for all pavements, especially with comparatively heavy pedestrian traffic, and the latter method is recommended for ones with light pedestrian traffic.

8.21 NEWMAN, P.W.G. and KENWORTHY, J.R. (1988) The transport energy trade-off: fuel efficient traffic versus fuel efficient cities. *Transportation Research A*, **22** (3), pp. 163-174.

Improving fuel efficiency in vehicular traffic by increasing average speeds is shown to have a major trade-off through land-use changes and modal shifts that result in an overall loss in fuel efficiency for the total urban area. In Perth, even though vehicles in central areas have a 19 per cent lower fuel efficiency than average due to congestion, the central area residents still use 22 per cent less actual fuel on average due to their locational advantages. On the other hand, outer suburban traffic is 12 per cent more efficient than average but residents use 29 per cent more actual fuel. A comparison of 32 world cities confirms that there is a trade-off between fuel efficient traffic and fuel-efficient cities. The implications for traffic engineering programmes and road funding are discussed.

8.22 NIJKAMP, P. and REICHMAN, S. (1986) *Transportation Planning in a Changing World*. Aldershot: Gower.

This book on current and future issues in transport planning provides a social science oriented view on mobility and transport. Four major issues are dealt with: an identification of main concerns and dilemmas facing present day transport in industrial economies (with particular emphasis on societal values, individual roles and behaviour, incompatibilities in urban environments, and readjustments in the production system): a description of transport planning as institutionalized procedure in various industrialized countries: a review of new methodological developments in transport analysis (mobility, land use and freight modelling): a discussion of conceptual, institutional and evaluation aspects of policy-making in transport.

8.23 NILLES, J.M. (1988) Traffic reduction by telecommuting: a status review and selected bibliography. *Transportation Research A*, **22** (4), pp. 301-317.

Telecommuting is defined as a subset of teleworking. Two main forms of telecommuting (home and regional centre) are described. The means by which these forms of telecommuting may alter urban transport patterns are outlined, followed by a review of the empirical evidence to date on the impacts and usefulness of telecommuting. Factors affecting the diffusion rate of telecommuting are discussed, including the commuting environment, technological sufficiency, technological familiarity, the social aspects of work, other telecommuter motivations, management issues, legal and regulatory barriers and incentives, and labour entitlement issues. A brief reference to other work in progress is followed by a set of forecasts of possible telecommuting futures.

8.24 NOEL, E.C. (1988) Park and ride: alive, well and expanding in the United States. *Journal of Urban Planning and Development*, **114** (1), pp. 2-13.

Park and ride lots originated in the 1930s as a means for increasing transit ridership. In spite of the increasing availability of cars, interest has grown. This paper reviews the development of park and ride, presents selective statistics on trends in the sizes of lots, discusses more recent issues regarding unsatisfied demand in suburban areas, and makes positive recommendations for increasing their availability. Included here are advanced acquisition of land for park and ride lots, a greater planning role for the regional planning agencies, and more research on demand and location factors.

8.25 OBENG, K. (1987) Economics in US demand responsive transit. *Journal of Advanced Transportation*, **21** (2), pp. 131–146.

This paper develops a neoclassical cost function for demand responsive transit (DRT) system and uses it to test the economies of scale hypothesis. The results show economies of scale and further show that the economies can be explained by speed, local and state subsidies, utilization of seating capacity, fleet utilization and an increase in the number of professionals. Comparison of DRT and bus transit results identifies patterns in policy variables whose effects on cost are the same across modes.

8.26 PERRY, J.L., BABITSKY, T. and GREGERSEN, H. (1988) Organisational form and performance in urban mass transit. *Transport Reviews*, **8** (2), pp. 125–143.

Ownership and management for urban mass transit organizations have taken many forms over the years, with publicly-owned and managed systems now dominant. In recent years, however, strong economic and political forces have increased pressures for privatizing urban mass transit services. This review analyses 20 studies from three countries (predominantly the USA) on the relationship between organizational form and fixed-route bus transit performance. It concludes that previous research has not made a persuasive case for the whole-scale privatization of either ownership or management of urban mass transit organization. Conclusions here are intended to apply to the USA as well as other countries with mixed enterprise systems in which choices about organizational form may have some consequence for performance.

8.27 REID, J. (1987) Negotiating private sector transportation improvements. *Urban Law Policy*, **8** (4), pp. 381–394.

Dallas is among those American cities which has responded to the escalating costs of infrastructure investment by developing negotiated cost sharing agreements in partnership with the private sector.

ADDITIONAL ENTRIES   323

The paper describes the framework for negotiations and illustrates the process with two examples: the Cityplace inner-city redevelopment being carried out by the Southland Corporation, and the suburban development of the Dallas Parkway Center Area.

8.28 SALOMON, I. and KOPPELMAN, F. (1988) A framework for studying teleshopping versus store shopping. *Transportation Research A*, **22** (4), pp. 247–255.

Transport and geography studies of shopping behaviour focus on destination choice assuming a trip had to be made. New telecommunications technologies enable home-based 'teleshopping' to substitute for store shopping. This paper develops a framework for studying the choice between modes of shopping. Shopping activity is defined as information acquisition that precedes purchasing. But, shopping seems to fulfill some psychological and recreational functions in addition to obtaining information. An integration of perspectives from different disciplines results in a conceptual structure which forms a basis for empirical studies of the impact of telecommunications technologies on human travel and activity patterns.

See also: Salomon, I. and Schofer, J.L. (1987) Forecasting telecommunications – travel interactions: the transportation manager's perspective. *Transportation Research A*, **22** (3), pp. 219–229.

8.29 STERN, E. and LEISER, D. (1988) Levels of spatial knowledge and urban travel modelling. *Geographical Analysis*, **20** (2), pp. 140–155.

Models of spatial behaviour implicitly assume a direct connection between the individual's utility function and his actual behaviour. In reality, the link is mediated by the extent and quality of spatial information. Without sufficient knowledge, the chosen behaviour will be selected from a small number of known alternatives. This study demonstrates the different levels of knowledge about particular non-routine travel and suggests that knowledge stabilises at an intermediate level. People acquire a certain amount of information but it is only the professional drivers who have a near complete picture. Consequently, route selection by the general public was found to be largely unpredictable.

8.30 THILL, J.-C. and THOMAS, I. (1987) Towards conceptualising trip-chaining behaviour: a review. *Geographical Analysis*, **19** (1), pp. 1–17.

This paper critically reviews the literature and suggests different ways that trip chaining can be treated and theoretically constructed. The early exploratory studies developed the existence and complexity of travel patterns, but they lacked a comprehensive theoretical framework. Researchers since that time have used stochastic methods and more recently utility maximisation as a basis for analysis. This work has been carried out theoretically and empirically, and this review paper covers all these issues as well as referring to some 120 references.

8.31 VAN REST, D. (1987) Policies for major roads in urban areas in the UK. *Cities*, **4** (3), pp. 236–252.

This paper traces the history of policies for linking urban motorways and dual carriageways with urban areas, using Birmingham and London as examples. The detailed analysis covering the whole post-war period illustrates the concentration of resources on the motorway network and the failure to deal adequately with large volumes of traffic. The motorway programme has contributed significantly to the dispersal of growth from city centres to outlying green belt areas. It emphasizes the difficulties of balancing access and environmental needs in the assessment of new urban roads.

8.32 WEINER, E. (1987*a*) *Urban Transportation Planning in the United States: An Historical Overview*. New York: Praeger.

The development of US urban transport policy over the past 50 years illustrates the changing relationships between Federal, state, and local governments. This comprehensive text examines the evolution of urban transport planning from early developments in highway planning in the 1930s to the shift to decentralisation of authority in the 1980s. Focusing on major national events, the book discusses the influence of legislation, regulations, conferences, Federal programmes, and advances in planning procedures and technology. It offers an in-depth look at the most significant event in transport planning – the Federal-Aid Highway Act of 1962 which was crucial to the spread of urban transport planning across the United States.

Claiming that urban transportation planning is more sophisticated, costly, and complex than its highway and transit planning predecessors, the book demonstrates how urban transport planning evolved in response to changes in such factors as environment, inter governmental coordination, and Federal transit programs.

See also: Weiner, E. (1987*b*) Urban transportation planning since the Federal-Aid Highway Act of 1962. *Journal of Transportation Engineering*, **113** (6), pp. 658–671.

Subject index

Accessibility   1A25, 1B13, 1B42, 2A8, 3A6, 3A8, 3B6, 3C9, 3C11, 3C13, 3C14, 3C16, 3C24, 3C33, 3C35, 3C36, 3C37, 3D9, 3D25, 3D30, 3D33, 5B13, 5B19, 5B46, 5C18, 8.19
Accidents   4D31, 5C7, 5E2, 5E9, 5E12, 5E14, 5E15, 5E19, 5E20, 5E21, 5E23, 5E26, 5E29, 5E3, 5E32
Activity patterns   3C9, 3C16, 5A11, 5A24, 5B24, 5B58, 5E9, 8.13
Age   3C5
Air pollution   5E5, 5E13
Aircraft   5E30
Alcohol   5E21
Analysis *see* methods
Appraisal *see* evaluation
Approaches *see* methods
Artificial intelligence   5F13
Asia   4B16, 6A19
Assignment *see* models
Attitudes   2E3
Australia   1B38, 2D14, 3A6, 3A8, 3D12, 3D32, 4B11, 4C16, 4D12, 4D24, 4D25, 4E4, 4E5, 4F11, 5B1, 5B50, 5B79, 5D15, 5D18, 5D21, 5D22, 6A3, 6A17, 8.10
Automation   5F10
Automobiles *see* cars

Behaviour *see* travel behaviour
Behavioural models   3D19, 5A7, *see also* models
Beltways see motorways
Berlin   1A9
Bias   5B34
Bicycle ownership   4F11
Bicycle use   4F2, 4F3, 4F4, 4F11, 4F12, 5E28, 8.17
Birmingham   3C35
Bogota   5A18
Brazil   5B68, 6A6
Bus planning   4A36
Bus policy   4A36
Bus Stations   3E8
Buses   2A12, 2A13, 2A9, 2D1, 2D5, 2E11, 2E20, 3E8, 4A4, 4A5, 4A8, 4A9, 4A11, 4A17, 4A22, 4A23, 4A25, 4A26, 4A27, 4A29, 4A36, 4A37, 4A41, 4A44, 4A48, 4A49, 4A51, 4A52, 4A55, 4A58, 4C9, 4C14, 5B12, 5B30, 6A21 *see also* public transport
Busway   4C15, 5C6
By-pass   5E22 *see also* roads

Cairo   6A12
California   2B16
Canada   1B7, 3C5, 3D20, 4B3, 4F10, 5B52, 5B64, 5B78, 5C19, 5C24, 5D4, 5D11, 5E15, 5E24, 5F4, 6A15
Capitalism   2E12
Car availability   2A25, 3C18, 5A3, *see also* cars
Car costs   4D1
Car ownership   4A25, 4D9, 4D13, 4D19, 5B8, 5B40, 6A21
Car passenger   3C5, 4D16
Car pooling   4D2, 4D10, 4D14, 4D22, 4D24, 4D28
Car sharing   3D16
Car use   3C18, 3D18, 4D1, 4D9, 4D13, 4D19, 4D30,
Cardiff   3C12
Cars   1B3, 1B9, 1B47, 3D34, 4D5, 4D11, 4D12, 4D16, 4D17, 4D26, 4D27, 5B37, 5E27, 6A2
Case studies   1A15, 1B17, 1B45, 4C13
Central Business District   5B10
Centralization *see* urban change
China   4F12, 6A17

SUBJECT INDEX 329

Cities 1A5, 1A7, 1A9, 1A12, 1A16, 1A20, 1A26, 1B43, 1B60
Cluster analysis 5B52
Cognition 5B22, 5B70, 5B71
Comfort 3E9
Communication 1B34, 3B5, 3B7
Community impacts 5E4, 5F6
Community transport 4C10 *see also* paratransit
Commuters 3C20, 3D1, 4B5, 4B10
Commuting 1B23, 1B52, 1B53, 2A16, 3C1, 3C39, 3D12, 3D13, 3D14, 3D15, 3D16, 3D19, 3D20, 3D21, 3D23, 3D24, 3D29, 3D30, 3D31, 3D4, 3D5, 3D7, 3D8, 3E3, 4B1, 4B7, 4D1, 4D10, 4D20, 4F10, 5B24, 5B63, 8.1, 8.18, 8.23
Commuting costs 3A14, 3D22, 4D2
Company cars 4D25, 4D30, *see also* employer provided transport
Competition 2A10, 2A13, 4A4, 4A8, 4A22, 4A23, 4A26, 4A27, 4A50, 5B30, 5C9, *see also* deregulation
Computer simulation models 5D16, 5B77
Computers 5F2, 5F10, 5F12, 5F13
Concessionary public transport fares 3C19, 3C40, *see also* subsidies
Congestion 1B13, 1B49, 1B57, 3A2, 4D15, 5B16, 5C15, *see also* peak hour
Conjoint measurement 3D26, 8.16
Conservation 2A19, 3D2, 4D11
Consumer behaviour 3C12, 4A38, 5B43, 5B70, 5B72, 5C9, *see also* travel behaviour
Consumer demand *see* demand and supply
Consumer surplus *see* consumer behaviour
Consumption 5D12, 5D20, 5D21, 5D24
Contingency planning 5D14, 5D19
Cost benefit analysis 2A24, 4A20, 4A22, 4A24, 4C6, 5C2, 5C4, 5C5, 5C21, 5C22
Cost estimation techniques 4A17, 5B63
Costs 1B15, 2D14, 3C23, 3D9, 4A9, 4A11, 4A27, 4A29, 4A52, 4C5, 4E5, 5B63, 5C11, 8.4, 8.10, 8.12
Crime 3E1, 3E2, 3E4, 3E6, 3E8
Cross-sectional studies 4A6
Cross-subsidy 4A22, 4A57, *see also* subsidies
Cycling *see* bicycle use
Czechoslovakia 1B7

Decentralization   1A31, 1B52, 2A25, 3D5, *see also* urban change
Decision making   1A11, 1A15, 1B34, 2B16, 2D3, 2E7, 3C36, 4D12
Decision theory   5C19
Delphi techniques   5B20
Demand and supply   1B59, 1B51, 3C5, 3C43, 4A3, 4A5, 4A33, 4A35, 4A37, 4A51, 4A53, 4B15, 5A8, 5A16, 5B36, 5B39, 5B62, 5B75, 5D22
Demand models *see* trip generation models
Demographic Act   5B59
Demographic factors change   2B18, 3C43, 5B59
Density   1B31, 4B16, 5B12
Deregulation   2A1, 2A2, 2A6, 2A10, 2A12, 2A13, 2A20, 2C5, 2E4, 2E9, 4A7, 4A8, 4A22, 4A23, 4A26, 4A50, 4C12 4E2, 8.9 *see also* competition
Design   1A25, 1B18, 1B22, 1B41, 2A7, 3C3, 3C26, 5D4, 5F11, 6A8
Developing countries   1A20, 1B6, 1B8, 1B25, 1B35, 1B50, 1B57, 1B62, 3C8, 4A32, 4A49, 4C8, 4C13, 4D14, 5A12, 5A18, 5C4, 5C7, 5D7, 5E14, 5E23, 6A1, 6A4
Development   1A20, 1A25, 1B4, 1B27, 1B40, 1B48, 2D7, 4B12, 5C23, 5D10, 5E12, 5F6, 6A8, 6A17, 6A18
Dial-a-ride   4C7 *see also* paratransit
Diary data   3D15
Differential fares   4A16 *see also* public transport
Disabled   3B1, 3C3, 3C4, 3C13, 2C22, 3C26, 3C30, 3C44, 3D10, 8.4
Disadvantaged groups   3C12
Disaggregate models   5A7, 5B23, 5B62
Distribution   1B5, 3C2, 3C6, 5B18, 5E7, 8.2
Dualist approach   2A3
Dynamic methods   5A16, 5B11, 5B35, 5B47, 5C18

East Europe   1B4
Econometrics   3A3, 4D12, 5B47, 5B48
Economic activity   5B59
Economic change   1B38
Economic planning   1A8
Economic policy   1A9
Economic theory   2D6
Economic evaluation   5C6 *see also* evaluation

SUBJECT INDEX   331

Economic models   5B30, 5E8
Economics   1B14, 1B15, 1B17, 1B30, 1B37, 1B55, 2D2, 3D9,
    4A38, 4A58, 5C9, 5C13, 5C17
Education   5E21
Efficiency   1A20, 1B39, 1B62, 4A4, 4A15, 4A29, 5D5, 5D11,
    5D22, 5E28, 8.10, 8.12, 8.20
Egypt   6A12
Elasticities   4A4, 4A28, 4A35, 4A36, 4A39, 4A55, 5B46, 5B54,
    5D23, 5E12
Elderly   3B1, 3C18, 3C19, 3C22, 3C23, 3C30, 3C31, 3C43,
    3C44, 3C45, 3E4, 5E26
Electric vehicles   5D13, 5D24
Electronic road pricing *see* road pricing, pricing
El Salvador   5A18
Employer transport   2D12, 3C20
Employment   1A21, 1A28, 2E1, 2E12, 3A10, 3B6, 3C1, 3C15,
    3C17, 3C28, 3C35, 3D1, 3D10, 3D14, 3D24, 5B3, 5B10,
    5B18, 5B21, 5B25, 5B41, 5B56, 5B64, 5B66, 8.7
Employment locations   3A11
Energy   1A25, 1B35, 1B36, 2A19, 2B18, 2C8, 3D23, 3D2, 3D3,
    3D34, 4D11, 4D14, 4D25, 4D29, 5D1, 5D2, 5D3, 5D4, 5D5,
    5D6, 5D7, 5D9, 5D10, 5D11, 5D12, 5D13, 5D14, 5D15,
    5D16, 5D17, 5D18, 5D19, 5D20, 5D21, 5D22, 5D23, 5D24,
    5E27, 6A4, 6A14, 8.20
Engine size   5D12, 5F2
Engineering methods   5F1
Entropy models   5B77
Environment   1B22, 1B28, 1B42, 2A11, 2A26, 5E6, 5E10, 5E13,
    5E16, 5E18, 5E22, 5E25, 5E27, 5E28
Equilibrium   5B3, 5B4, 5B14, 5B15, 5B16, 5B49
Equity   1A20, 1A30, 2E11, 3C2, 3C8, 3C13, 3C21, 3C34, 3C42,
    4A13, 4A20, 4A24, 4A38, 4A42, 8.11
Ethics   2B14
Europe   1B21, 1B23, 2C2, 2C8, 2C13, 3D24, 3E3, 4A21, 4B4,
    4C3, 4C11, 4E2, 5E19
European Community   1A32, 1B15, 1B45, 2C1, 2C3, 2C4, 2C5,
    2C6, 2C12, 2C14, 3C20
Evaluation   1B2, 1B17, 2A24, 2D2, 3A13, 3C2, 3C3, 5C1, 5C2,
    5C3, 5C4, 5C7, 5C8, 5C10, 5C14, 5C16, 5C19, 5C22, 5C25,
    5E10, 5E26, 5F7, 8.20
Expert systems   5F13

Fare Collection 4A1 *see also* public transport
Fares *see* public transport fares
Federal Republic of Germany *see* Germany
Financing 2B13, 2B20, 4A13, 4A20, 4A45, 4B14, 4B19, 4C5, 4D8, 5C4, 5C12, 5C13
Finland 4A47
Fiscal policy 2B13
Flat fares 4B20 *see also* public transport
Flexitime 3D17, 3D32
Footways 4F2
Forecasting 2E11, 4A27, 5A21, 5B17, 5B20, 5B75
France 1A8, 1B7, 3C24, 8.3
Freight 1B15, 1B30, 1B38, 2A11, 2C5, 4E1, 4E2, 4E3, 4E4, 4E5, 5B55, 5B65, 5E6, 5E7, 5E8, 5E11, 5E28, 5E33 *see also* lorries
Fuel 3D34, 5D3, 5D13
Fuel economy 5D8
Fuel prices 4D11
Fuel taxation 4D7
Future 1A16, 1B3, 2B22, 2D8, 4D5, 5A22

Gender *see* women, travel behaviour
General 1A6, 1B7, 1B16, 1B19, 1B20, 1B24, 1B32, 1B33, 1B37, 1B47, 1B48, 1B55, 1B59, 1B60, 3A4, 4A10, 5B39, 5B60, 5E14, 5E34, 6A18
Germany 1A16, 1B7, 1B28, 2B25, 2C7, 2C9, 2C10, 2C13, 3C4, 4C15, 5B74, 5E7
Glasgow 4B19
Goods *see* freight
Government 2A18, 2B23
Government control 2A18
Gravity model 3D26, 5B64
Great Britain 1A4, 1A6, 1A13, 1A14, 1A21, 1A28, 1B16, 1B28, 2A12, 2A14, 2D4, 3B3, 5B18, 6A18

Handicapped *see* disabled
Health and safety 3D24, 3E3, 3E7, 5E13
Heavy goods vehicles *see* lorries
Helicopters 4C6
Heliports 4C6

SUBJECT INDEX 333

Highways *see* roads
Hire cars *see* taxis
History   1A7, 1A9, 1B7, 1B26, 2A15, 2A23, 2B8, 2B24, 2B25, 2C13, 6A7
Home location *see* residential location
Hong Kong   4D6, 4D17, 6A2, 8.1
House prices *see* property values
Household expenditure   5B53
Household travel patterns   3C15, 5A7, 5A11, 5F3, *see also* travel behaviour
Housewives   5B31 *see also* women
Housing   5B3, 5B4, 5B74

Ideology   1B18, 1B54
Impact analysis   4B13, 4F12, 5C23, 5C25, 5E5, 6A3
Implementation   1A1, 1A23, 1A29, 2B5, 2B14, 5D14, 6A10, 6A11
Income   5B53, 8.18
India   6A4
Individual travel patterns   3C16, *see also* travel behaviour
Industry   1B3, 1B17
Inflation   3C43, 5C3
Information   1B34, 4D27, 5B52, 5B70, 5E26, 5F9
Inner cities   3A10, 3C17, 3D6
Institutional frameworks   2B4, 2B24, 2D3
Integration   1B6, 1B9, 8.3 *see also* public transport
International comparison   1A27, 4B9, 4C1, 4D5
Investment *see* financing
Israel   4A46, 5B35

Japan   1B7, 4D18, 6A7, 6A21
Job *see* employment
Job location *see* location, work
Job search *see* unemployment

Kenya   5B40
Kuwait   6A20

Labour   2B18, 2E4, 2E5, 2E7, 2E12, 3C28, 3D10, 4E1
Labour costs   2E9

Labour force   3D7
Labour management   2E2, 3C27
Labour markets   3C29
Labour relations   3C7, 3C25
Land-use impacts   4B3, 4B17
Land-use/transport   1A2, 1A10, 1A18, 1A22, 1B10, 1B11, 1B31, 1B41, 1B56, 2A4, 3A4, 3A5, 3A10, 3B8, 3D34, 4B16, 5B10, 5B12, 5B13, 5B17, 5B20, 5B45, 5B46, 5B59, 5B60, 5B61, 5B74, 5D10, 5D17, 5D20, 6A2
Land values *see* property values
Latin America   3C38, 6A14
Law   1A13, 1B24
Leisure *see* recreation
Licensing   2D1, 4D26   *see also* regulation
Life cycle   5A24, 5B52
Life style   3C45, 3D24, 3D27, 3E3
Lift giving *see* car passenger, car sharing, car pooling
Light rail   4B3, 4B9
Light rapid transit   4B2, 4B18
Local government   1A14
Local decisions   2B23
Local economy   1B55
Local plans   1A18
Location   1B41, 2E12, 3B31, 5B15, 5B36, 5B46, 5B55, 5B61, 5B67
Logistics   5E8
Logit model   5B32, 5B44, 5B51, 5B56, 5B67, 5B68, 5B72
London   1A9, 1B36, 2A3, 2A5, 2A23, 2D4, 5A17, 5B46, 5C2, 5E2, 5E17, 5E33, 5F5, 6A13, 8.19
Long term   5E34
Longitudinal data   5A6, 5B34 *see also* dynamic methods
Lorries   2A11, 5E6, 5E10, 5E22
Los Angeles   3C13, 5C6
Low-income households   3C38, 3E4
Lowry model   5B3, 5B13, 5B77

Management   1B28, 1B57, 1B58, 2B4, 2B5, 2B6, 2B18, 2E2, 2E6, 3C27, 4A7, 4A31, 4A40, 5C15, 5D6, 5D16, 5E11, 5F1, 5F8, 5F9, 6A5, 8.17
Manchester   3D6, 5B6, 5B25

Market approach   2A18
Market economy   1A8, 1B62
Market segmentation   5B9
Marketing   4A31, 4A44
Mathematical methods   1B11, 1B53, 5B77
Methodology   5B2
Methods   1A3, 1A10, 1A12, 1B5, 1B49, 1B50, 2B14, 4A46, 4D23, 4E2, 5A2, 5A6, 5A10, 5B2, 5B13, 5B38, 5B60, 5B72, 5F7, 5F11
Metros   3A3, 3A12, 3C10, 4B15, 8.3   see also light rail transit, rapid transit
Mexico   5B40
Microeconomics   1B55, 5B39
Middle East   6A10
Migration   1A28, 3D31 see also residential mobility
Minibuses   4A8, 4A51
Mobility   1B18, 3C4, 4D17, 8.22 see also travel behaviour
Modal split   5B44, 5B68
Mode choice   3D8, 3D24, 4E2, 5A17, 5B32, 5B43, 5B51, 5B72, 5B78
Models   1A10, 1B10, 1B53, 1B54, 2E5, 3D25, 3D31, 4A23, 4A39, 4A57, 4B5, 4D14, 5A2, 5A15, 5A22, 5B15, 5B24, 5B38, 5B39, 5B40, 5B43, 5B45, 5B59, 5B61, 5B65, 5B67, 5B68, 5B69, 5B72, 5B74, 5B75, 5B77, 5B78, 5B79, 5C23, 5D1, 5D9, 5D21, 5E4, 8.29
Mortgage subsidy   3D2
Motor industry   2E12
Motorists   2E3
Motorways   1B46, 3A11
Multi dimensional scaling   5B9
Multi-purpose trips   3D15, 5A13
Multicriteria analysis   5C8

Netherlands   1B28, 3D30
New Towns   1B22
New transport investments   3A12
New York   1A9, 4B20
New Zealand   5B31, 5B53
New technology   3B5, 3B8, 5D13, 5D24, 5F3
Nigeria   3C11, 6A5

Noise   5E5, 5E16, 5E18, 5E24
Nuclear Fuel   5E31
Nuisance   5E22

O-Bahn *see* busway
Offices   3A2, 3D5, 5F4
One person operations   4A29
Operating costs   3C7, 4A41
Organization   1A27, 2B5, 2B11, 2B12, 2B16, 2D4, 2D9, 2D11, 3C31, 4C4, 8.26 *see also* institutional framework

Panel analysis   4A25, 5B20, 5B29, 5B34, 5B47 *see also* dynamic methods
Paratransit   3C22, 4C3, 4C8, 4C9, 4C11
Pareto optimality   4A39
Paris   1A9, 1B36
Park and ride   4B15, 5B56, 8.24
Parking   5C12, 5E17, 5F4, 5F5, 5F6, 5F7
Part-time labour   2E2, 3C7, 4A54
Peak hour   3D1, 3D16, 3D23, 3D28, 3D34, 4B5, 4D20, 4F10 *see also* congestion
Pedestrianization   1B28, 2C7, 4B2, 4F5, 4F7, 4F8, 4F9
Pedestrians   5B73, 5E18, 8.6, 8.20
Perceptions   3D25, 3E1, 4A30, 5B21, 5B22
Personality scales   3D21
Planning   1A1, 1A3, 1A6, 1A8, 1A10, 1A11, 1A12, 1A13, 1A15, 1A22, 1A24, 1A26, 1A27, 1A28, 1A30, 1A31, 1A32, 1B1, 1B2, 1B34, 1B50, 1B58, 2A5, 2A16, 2B11, 5A12, 5C14, 5D2, 5D17, 5E8, 8.4, 8.17, 8.22
Planning policy   1B5
Police   2E3
Policy   1B4, 1B15, 1B16, 1B20, 1B21, 1B24, 1B27, 1B32, 1B35, 1B42, 1B45, 1B46, 1B47, 1B48, 2A2, 2A4, 2A5, 2A8, 2A12, 2A19, 2A22, 2A26, 2B11, 2B18, 2B22, 2B23, 2B24, 2C1, 2C3, 2C4, 2C6, 2C8, 2C12, 2C13, 2C14, 2E1, 2E7, 3C3, 3C26, 3C42, 3D10, 4A14, 4B4, 4C11, 4D18, 4D26, 4D29, 4E2, 4E3, 4E4, 5A7, 5A8, 5A16, 5A19, 5B17, 5C13, 5D2, 5D18, 5E13, 6A5, 6A7, 6A10, 6A11, 6A15, 6A20, 8.22, 8.30, 8.31, 8.32
Politics   1A12, 1A14, 1A18, 1A21, 1A23, 1A27, 1B2, 1B61, 2A3, 2A16, 2A18, 2A21, 2B2, 2D2, 2E11, 5C1

SUBJECT INDEX

Pollution 3D3
Population movement *see* migration, residential mobility
Population trends 3C18
Ports 4E5
Post 3B5
Practice 1A29, 5A21
Prediction *see* forecasting
Preferences 3D26, 5B19, 5B55, 5B79
Pricing 4A4, 4A18, 4A34, 4C16, 4D23, 4D29, 5C11, 5C12, 5D5, 5D9, 5D23
Private bus operators 2D8, 2D14, 4A47, 4A50
Private capital 2A1, 2B22, 5C13, 8.9, 8.27
Privatization 2A20, 2D5, 2D13, 4A40
Probit models 5B72
Production 1B3
Productivity 3C27, 4A29, 4A47
Profession 2B6
Professionals 2E7
Property values 3A1, 3A3, 3A5, 3A6, 3A12, 3A13, 5C17, 5E24
Protest 2A21
Psychology 5B21, 5B43
Public policy 3C33
Public transport 1B20, 1B25, 1B32, 1B37, 1B39, 1B45, 1B47, 1B51, 1B58, 1B60, 1B61, 2A3, 2A7, 2A14, 2B1, 2B2, 2B5, 2B7, 2B12, 2B20, 2B25, 2C9, 2C11, 2D4, 2E2, 2E11, 3C7, 3C10, 3C19, 3C22, 3C25, 3C34, 3C38, 3D13, 3D18, 3D34, 3E1, 3E2, 3E4, 3E5, 3E6, 3E8, 4A1, 4A2, 4A3, 4A4, 4A6, 4A7, 4A10, 4A13, 4A14, 4A15, 4A16, 4A18, 4A19, 4A20, 4A21, 4A24, 4A30, 4A31, 4A32, 4A33, 4A34, 4A35, 4A40, 4A42, 4A43, 4A45, 4A46, 4A51, 4A53, 4A54, 4A55, 4B9, 4B15, 5B9, 5B44, 5B54, 5B56, 5B63, 5C5, 5C6, 5C12, 5D11, 5D23, 5D24, 6A2, 6A7, 6A21, 8.9, 8.11, 8.12, 8.14, 8.24, 8.26

Qualitative methods 2A14
Quality of service 4A44

Rail 2A15, 2B20, 2C7, 2D13, 4B1, 4B4, 4B5, 4B7, 4B8, 4B10, 4B13, 4B14, 5A17, 5B10, 5C6, 6A2, 6A21, 8.19
Rapid transit 1B61, 4B12, 4B17, 4B19
Recreation 3D21, 3D27, 5B67

Regional policy   2C10
Regulation   1B16, 2C1, 4C13, 4D18 *see also* deregulation
Repertory grid   5B71
Research   2B3, 2E6
Residential choice   3A11, 3A14, 3D14, 3D24
Residential location   3C39, 3D9, 3D19, 3D33, 5B79
Residential mobility   3D20, 3D22, 3D29, 3D30, 5E24
Residential satisfaction   3D12
Residential search   3D33
Residents   5E30
Resources   1B5, 2B15
Responses   5D9
Responsibility   2A22
Restraint   1B28, 4D26
Retail planning   4F1, 5B66
Retailing   3B3, 3B4, 3B6, 5B26
Revealed perference   8.15
Review   1A1, 1A6, 1A32, 1B8, 1B25, 1B29, 1B39, 1B44, 1B51, 1B52, 2B4, 2B24, 3A4, 4A51, 4B16, 4C3, 4C8, 4F9, 5A3, 5A10, 5A11, 5A20, 5A22, 5B38, 5B57, 5B59, 5B73, 5F12, 5F13, 6A6, 6A20, 8.4, 8.8, 8.23, 8.26, 8.29, 8.30, 8.32
Ridesharing   4D3, 4D22, 5F4, *see also* car passenger, car pooling, car sharing, van pooling, shared taxis
Risk   5E1, 5E3, 5E26, 5E29, 5E32
Road construction   3A11, 5B66, 5C3, 5C18
Road haulage   2C1
Road improvements   4D8
Road pricing   2A1, 4D4, 4D6, 4D15, 4D21, 5F3, 8.1 *see also* pricing
Road taxation   4D8
Roads   1B46, 2A21, 2A24, 2B20, 2E1, 5A17, 5C10, 5C16, 5C22, 5C25, 5E11, 5E22, 8.31
Role of transport   6A17
Route choice   4A17, 4F8, 5B69

South Africa   6A8
South East Asia   2D9
Safety   1B9, 2A11, 4D31, 4F2, 5C21, 5E1, 5E26, 5E29, 5E31, 5E34
Safety belts   5E9

SUBJECT INDEX

San Francisco   4B13
Santiago   5A18
Savings   5D6, 5D24
Scaling methods   5B19
Scheduling   4A48, 5A13, 5B24, 5B69
Scotland   4F9
Season tickets   4A19
Seat belts   5E3, 5E15, 5E20
Shared taxis   4C5
Shipping   3D26, 4E5 *see also* ports
Shopping   3B1, 3C10, 3C12, 3D25, 4F1, 4F9, 5B22, 5B70, 5B71, 8.28
Simulation   4A26, 4A50, 5B73, 5D20, 5D22
Singapore   1B17, 4D26, 5A18
Social aspects   1B18, 3A8, 4A37, 5C24, 5E20
Social change   3D27
Social groups   3A8, 3D4, 3D7, 3D14, 3D24, 5B45, 5B50, 5B51
Social welfare   1A22
Society   1B19, 4D27
Sociology   1A7, 1A26, 1B29
Special needs transportation   3C40 *see also* paratransit, disabled
Special transport schemes   3C30
Sri Lanka   3C8
Staggered work hours   3D17, 3D32, 5B27
Stated preference   8.15, 8.16
Statistical analysis   5E12
Stochastic models   5B26
Strategic planning   1A11, 5A20, 6A3, 6A12
Street patterns   5D4, *see* roads
Stress   3E5
Structure   2D9, 5B11
Subsidy   1B25, 1B56, 2A14, 2A26, 2B2, 2B8, 2E10, 3C6, 4A2, 4A6, 4A10, 4A14, 4A15, 4A20, 4A21, 4A24, 4A28, 4A33, 4A38, 4A39, 4A42, 4A43, 4A45, 4A46, 4A58, 4D29, 5C5
Suburban areas   3A2, 3C17, 3D6, 3D12
Surveys   5A11, 5B2
Sweden   3C15, 3C16, 4D27, 5E32, 8.6
Systems approach   1B10, 5B77

Taxation   2C2, 3C2, 4A2, 4A13, 4A24, 4D23, 4D30, 8.11

Taxis   4C1, 4C2, 4C4, 4C12, 4C13, 4C16
Technology   1A5, 1A17, 1B17, 2A8, 3B1, 3B2, 3B3, 3B4, 3B6, 4C15, 5E27, 5F9, 5F10, 8.7, 8.23, 8.28
Telecommunications   3B2, 3B9, 8.7, 8.23, 8.28
Telephone   3B7
Theory   1A4, 1A26, 1B30, 1B61, 2A20, 5A6, 5C20
Third World   1B40, 3A5, 4A32
Ticketing   4A55, 4B7, *see also* public transport
Time   3D16, 5B33, 5B37, 5B42, 5B53, 5C11
Time budgets   5A23, 5A24, 5B31
Time expenditure   5A24
Time lapse photography   5B5
Time of day   3D1, 5A15
Time series   5B1
Time-space   5A15, 5A19
Toll roads   2D6, 5C11, 5C13, 5C20, 8.1, 8.2
Toronto   5C17
Traffic   1B13, 1B49, 1B53, 3D23, 5F9
Traffic congestion   3A2
Traffic control   2A11
Traffic counts   5B76
Traffic flow   3A1
Traffic impacts   3D3
Traffic management   5E22
Traffic peaks *see* peak hour, congestion, time
Traffic speeds   5B5
Training   2E6
Transfer   4A30
Transit *see* public transport
Transport   1A30, 1B14, 1B60, 5B53
Transport improvements   3A14
Transport industry   3C27
Transport/land-use *see* land use
Transport modelling *see* models, trip
Transport planning   1B29, 1B52, 4D31, 4E1, 4F4
Transport policy   4D13, 4D30, 4E1, 4F3, 4F4, 6A21
Transport studies   5A1
Transport trends   6A21 *see also* forecasting, future, trends
Travel   1B8, 3C17, 3C29, 3C32, 3D27, 5B52
Travel behaviour   1B56, 3D15, 4A25, 4A33, 4B3, 4B15, 4B17,

SUBJECT INDEX 341

4B19, 4D3, 4D4, 4D5, 4D9, 4D15, 4D16, 4D19, 4D28, 4D31,
4F1, 4F3, 4F5, 4F7, 4F8, 5A4, 5B23, 5B58, 8.13, 8.15, 8.25
Travel budgets   5A5, 5B33 *see also* time budgets
Travel cards   4A55 *see also* public transport
Travel costs   3D29, 4D15, 5B16
Travel patterns   1B56, 3D3, 3D23, 5A4
Travel speeds   5A17
Travel time   4D2, 5A5, 5A9, 5A13, 5A14, 5A18, 5A25, 5B58 *see also* time
Travelcard   4A27
Trends   1B19, 1B56, 4A43, 5D1, 6A9 *see also* forecasting, future, dynamic methods
Trip generation   3C45, 4B8, 5B65
Trip assignment models   4B49, 4D20, 5B15, 5B16
Trip chains   3C37, 5A4, 8.30 *see also* multi-purpose trips
Trip distribution models   3D4, 5B64, 5B65
Trip generation   5A15
Trip lengths   1B59, 3D2
Trip matrices   5B76
Trip rates   3C24, 5A14
Tyne & Wear   3A12, 3B1

United Kingdom   1A17, 1B22, 1B46, 2A6, 2A7, 2A11, 2A15, 2A16, 2A21, 2A24, 2C7, 3C35, 3D5, 4A7, 4A11, 4B7, 4C2, 4C10, 4D3, 4D9, 4D10, 4F5, 5A25, 5B58, 5B75, 5C20, 5C24, 5D6, 6A11, 6A21, 8.17, 8.31 *see also* Great Britain
Uncertainty   5C14, 5C19
Unemployment   2E5, 3C17, 3C35, 3C36
Union of Soviet Socialist Republics   1B4, 1B7, 6A11
United States of America   1A16, 1A22, 1B2, 1B21, 1B25, 1B26, 1B28, 1B33, 1B39, 1B47, 1B52, 1B61, 2B1, 2B2, 2B4, 2B7, 2B8, 2B11, 2B17, 2B23, 2B24, 2B25, 2D2, 2D11, 2D12, 2E1, 2E9, 2E10, 3A1, 3A3, 3A11, 3B4, 3C34, 3C35, 3C39, 3C41, 3C43, 3D13, 3D17, 3D18, 3E1, 3E2, 3E4, 3E6, 3E8, 4A1, 4A3, 4A13, 4A14, 4A15, 4A16, 4A24, 4A34, 4A40, 4A41, 4A42, 4A48, 4A54, 4B1, 4B2, 4B8, 4B10, 4B16, 4C11, 4C12, 4C13, 4C14, 4D7, 4D8, 4D15, 4D19, 4D22, 4D28, 4E1, 5A1, 5A21, 5A25, 5B4, 5B5, 5B8, 5B9, 5B10, 5B20, 5B24, 5B29, 5B66, 5C16, 5C23, 5D8, 5D10, 5D19, 5D23, 5E1. 5E4, 5E5,

5E16, 5E19, 5E20, 5E25, 5E32, 5F4, 5F6, 5F11, 6A9, 8.12, 8.18, 8.24, 8.25, 8.26, 8.27, 8.32
Uppsala   5A9
Urban familiarity   3C36
Urban development   2B1, 3D13, 3D20, 3D21, 4B2, 6A20, 8.14, 8.21
User benefit   5C9
User-side subsidies   3C40 *see also* subsidies
Utility   5B36, 5B77, 8.29
Utility maximization   5B4, 5B35, 5B41
Utility models   5B18

Value of time   5C1, 5C11
Van pooling   4D2, 4D22 *see also* ridesharing, minibuses
Viewdata   3B3
Visual scan   5E18

Wages   3C29
Walking   4F1, 4F2, 4F5, 4F6, 4F7, 4F8, 4F10, 5E28, 8.20 *see also* pedestrians
Warsaw   2C11
Washington, DC   5D9
Weber   1A7
Welfare   1A22, 1B15, 4A4, 5B54
Wheel clamping   5E17
Women   3C1, 3C9, 3C15, 3C29, 3C32, 3C39, 3C41, 3E2, 3E4
Work *see* employment
Work trips *see* commuting
Working conditions   1B23
Working hours   3D3, 3D18, 3D23, 3D28, 3D34
Working practices   3C7, 4A9, 4A29 *see also* part-time, working hours
World   1A2, 1B3, 1B43, 1B49

Zaire   1B7

Author index

Abelson, P. 5B1
Abkowitz, M.D. 3D1, 4A1
Adam Smith Institute 2A1
Adams, J. 1B1, 5E1
ACOMPLINE and
  URBALINE 7B1
Adiv, A. 4B1, 4D1
Allen, J.G. 2B1, 5A1
Allsop, R.E. 5E2
Alpert, M. 7A1
Altshuler, A. 1B2, 1B3
Amber, J. 1B4
Amico, L.T. 4A2
Ampt, E.S. 5B2
Anas, A. 5B3, 5B4
Anderson, M. 1B3
Anderson, S.C. 2B2
Andrews, H.F. 3C1
Andrle, S. 2B18
Angle, H.L. 2E8
Anjomani, A. 4A2
ARRB: Australian Road
  Research Board 7B3
Ardekani, S. 5B5

Armstrong-Wright, A. 6A1
Arrowsmith, G. 3C2
Ash, T. 3D2
Atherton, T.J. 3D3
Atkins, S.R. 5A2, 5C1
ATLS: Australian transport
  literature system 7B2
Austin, T.L. 3E1

Babitsky, T. 8.26
Bagby, D.G. 3A1
Bailey, J.M. 2A14, 4D2, 5A3
Baker, R. 7A2
Baker, S. 5B1
Balcombe, R.J. 2A2
Banister, C.E. 5B6, 5D1
Banister, D. 1B5, 2A3, 2A4,
  5D1, 7A3
Barat, J. 1B6
Barber, G.M. 4D23
Barden, S.A. 6A2
Barker, T. 1B7
Barnard, P.O. 5B7
Barrett, S. 1A1

Bawa, P.S.   5E23
Bayliss, D.   1B8
Beaumont, J.R.   5D2
Bechdolt, B.V.   4A3
Beed, C.   6A3
Been, C.   3A6
Beesley, M.E.   4A4, 4B11, 5C2
Beiersmann, H.   7A29
Belobaba, P.   5D14
Ben Akiva, M.   3D33, 5B8, 5B35, 5B68
Bendixson, T.   1B9
Benjamin, J.   5B9
Bennett, D.W.   5B40
Berechman, J.   5B10
Berglund, M.   4C11
Bergmann, U.   7A22
Bernard, M.J.   6A4
Bexler, A.   3E2
Bhatt, K.V.   2B9
Bjornson, A.   5D4
Black, J.   1B10, 1B11
Bladikas, A.K.   4A5
Bland, B.H.   5B12
Bloch, A.J.   5D3
Blunden, W.R.   1B11
Bly, P.H.   1B12, 1B56, 4A6, 4A7, 4A8, 4A21, 5B13
Bohlander, G.W.   4E1
Bolade, A.T.   6A5
Bonsall, P.W.   4D3
Borins, S.F.   8.1
Borsay, A.   3C3
Botham, R.   2A4
Bourne, L.S.   1A2
Boyce, D.E.   5B14, 5B15, 5B16
Boyd, C.W.   4A9
Bracken, I.   1A3, 5B17

Bragg, B.W.E.   5E3
Branco, A.M.   6A6
Breheny, M.J.   1A4
Brisbourne, R.H.   2A14
Britton, F.E.K.   4C1
Brog, W.   3C4, 5B2
Brotchie, J.   1A5
Broughton, J.   5B18
Bruhl, F.   6A7
Buchanan, C.   1B13
Buchanan, M.   2A5
Buick, T.R.   3C45
Bundesminister für Verkehr   7A23
Burby, R.J.   4C4
Burkhardt, J.E.   3C23, 5E4
Burnett, P.   5A4
Burns, L.D.   5B19
Bureau of Transport Economics   7B4
Bursey, N.   2A5
Bussiere, Y.   3C5
Butler, S.E.   2E1
Button, K.J.   1B14, 1B15, 1B16, 1B17, 2C1, 4A10, 4A11, 4A12, 5C15, 5C20
Buzawa, E.S.   3E1

Cady, P.D.   5C3
Cameron, J.W.M.   6A8
Campbell, J.   3E5
Carpenter, S.M.   3C6
Carr, J.D.   2A6
Cavalli-Sforza, V.   5B20
Centre d'Etudes des Transport Urbains   7A33
Cervero, R.   3A2, 4A13, 4A14, 4A15, 4A16, 4B2, 4B3, 6A9
Chadda, H.S.   3C31

AUTHOR INDEX

Chang, Y.B.   5B21
Charlton, J.W.   4B15
Chatterjee, A.   5F1
Cherwony, W.   4A17
Chia, L.S.   4D26
Chomitz, K.M.   2E2, 3C7
Choueiri, E.M.   5E19
Christopher, E.J.   2B12
Clarke, M.I.   2A14, 5A11
Clelland, A.   5F2
Clerc-Pechine   7A34
Clough, W.S.   2A2
Coe, G.A.   4C2
Coelho, J.D.   5B77
Cohen, Y.   8.2
Cohn, L.F.   5E5
Commission of the European Communities   7A35
Confederation of British Road Passenger Transport   2A7
Coombe, R.D.   6A10
Cooper, J.C.   5E6, 5E33
Cooper, S.   3E2
Copeland, D.   3C10
Coshall, J.T.   5B22
Council of Planning Librarians   7A4
Council for Science and Society   2A8
Cousins, S.   2C2
Cribbins, P.D.   5C16
Croc, M.   8.3
Crouch, M.   6A11
Crowell, W.H.   4A5
Cubukgil, A.   3D4
Cullingworth, J.B.   1A6
Curtis, F.A.   5D4
Cutting, C.A.   5E14

D'Este, G.   5B27

Daganzo, C.F.   5B37
DAI: Dissertation abstracts international   7B5
Daly, A.   5B23
Damm, D.   3A3, 5B24
Daniels, P.W.   3A4, 3D5
Dasgupta, M.   1B56, 3D6, 3D7, 3D8, 5B25
Daskin, M.S.   4A18
Davies, B.C.L.   2C8
Davies, C.H.   5E22
Davies, R.B.   5B26
Davies, R.L.   3B1
Dawson, J.A.   4A19, 5F3
Deakin, E.   8.7
De Boer, E.   1B18
De Vore, P.W.   1B19
Deadman, D.   5C20
Dean, D.L.   3E8
Deen, T.B.   2B3
Degenkolbe, H.   7A24
Demetsky, M.J.   2D7
Department of the Environment   7A5
Department of Transport   7A5
Deutsche Verkehrswissenschaftliche Gessellschaft   7A25
Diandas, J.   3C8
Dickey, J.W.   1B20, 5C4
Diewald, W.J.   1B20
Dillon, W.R.   5B51
Dix, M.C.   2E3, 5A6, 5A11, 5A16
Dodgson, J.S.   4A20, 5C5
Dogan, M.   8.4
Donnison, J.R.   2A14
Dooley, T.   4A54
Downes, J.D.   5B28
Dubin, R.A.   3D9

Duncan, G.J. 5B29
Dunkerley, J. 5D5
Dunlop, J.T. 2E4
Dunn, J.A. 1B21
Dupree, H. 1B22
Dziewonski, K. 1A2

Eagle, D.M. 2E5, 5B66
Echenique, M. 3A5
Eckstein, W.E. 5E7
Elkington, J. 7A6
Elliott, B. 1A7
Else, P.K. 4D4
Emmerson, P. 4A21, 5B28
Erdmenger, J. 2C3
Ergun, G. 3D11, 5B67
Estrin, S. 1A8
European Community 2C4
European Conference of Ministers of Transport 2C5, 3D10, 4A22, 4B4, 4C3, 4D5, 4E2, 5E8, 7A7, 8.5
European Foundation 1B23, 3E3
Evans, A. 2A9, 3A6, 4A23, 5B30
Evans, L. 5E9
Ewers, H.-J. 1A9

Farris, M.T. 4E1
Faulks, R.W. 1B24
Feibel, C.E. 4C4
Ferreira, L.J.A. 5D6
Fiegel, N. 3D12
Finn, P. 5E3
Fischhoff, B. 5E32
Fisher, J.S. 8.18
Fisher, R.J. 1B25
Flink, J.A. 1B26
Fong, P.K.W. 4D6

Foot, D.H.S. 1A10
Forer, P.C. 5B31
Forkenbrock, D.J. 4A24, 4D7
Foster, C. 2A10
Fouracre, P.R. 4A32
Fowkes, A.S. 4A12
Fox, M.B. 3C9
Fraser, C. 7A3
Friend, J.K. 1A11
Fritsch, H. 7A26
Frost, M. 3D8, 5B25
Fudge, C. 1A1
Fullerton, J. 3C10
Fulton, P.N. 3D13

Gaj, S. 4D8
Gakenheimer, R. 2B4, 6A12, 7A8
Gallagher, M.A. 3C21
Garelik, S. 3E2
Gärling, E. 8.6
Gärling, T. 8.6
Garrison, W.L. 8.7
Geltner, D. 1B35, 5D7
Geographical abstracts 7A9
Gensch, D.H. 5B32
Gera, S. 3D14
Ghoneim, N.S.A. 4B5
Giannopoulos, G.A. 3B2, 4B6
Gihring, T. 3C11
Gilbert, G. 4C4
Gillespie, A. 1A28
Gillingwater, D. 1B16
Gist, P. 5C2
Giuliano, G. 2E10
Glaister, S. 2D1, 4A4, 4A25, 4B7, 5C2
Gleichman, G. 4A17
Goddard, J. 1A9, 1A28

AUTHOR INDEX

Golay, J.   2A10
Goldberg, L.   4D8
Goldsmith, M.   1A12
Gomez-Ibanez, J.A.   1B32, 4B8
Goodwin, P.B.   2A14, 4A26, 4D9, 5A5, 5A6, 5A16
Gordon, P.   4B9, 5C6
Gordon, S.   2B5
Gourvish, T.R.   2A15
Grant, J.   2A16
Grant, M.   1A13
Grant, R.   5E18
Grayson, L.   7A10
Great Britain Dept. of Environment   7A5
Great Britain Dept. of Transport   2A11, 2A12, 5E10, 7A5
Great Britain House of Commons   2A13
Greene, D.L.   5D8
Greening, P.A.   4C5, 4D10
Gregerson, H.   8.26
Gunn, H.F.   5B33
Guy, C.M.   3B3, 3C12, 4F1
Gwilliam, K.M.   2A17, 2C6, 4A27
Gyford, J.   1A14

Hahn, H.   3C13
Hall, P.   1A5, 1A15, 1A16, 1A17, 1B5, 1B27, 2C7
Hall, R.W.   3C14
Hanson, P.   3C15
Hanson, S.   3C15, 3C16, 3D15, 5A4, 5A9, 8.8
Haritos, Z.J.   8.9
Harland, D.G.   4F2
Harris, D.J.   2C8

Harris, R.A.   5E5
Harrison, F.D.   3D17
Hart, D.A.   6A13
Hass-Klau, C.   1B28, 2C7, 2C9
Hawkins, D.   3D3
Hay, A.   4A28
Healey, P.   1A18, 1B29
Hedges, B.   3C17
Hedges, C.A.   5E11
Heggie, I.G.   3C6, 5A7, 5A8
Heinila, A.   4A47
Heinze, G.W.   2C10
Hendrickson, C.   3D16, 5F1
Henning-Hager, U.   5E12
Hensher, D.A.   1B30, 4D11, 4D12, 5B34, 5B48, 8.10
Herbert, J.D.   1A19
Herman, R.   5B5
Herz, R.K.   4F3
Hibbs, J.   2A18
Higgins, T.J.   5F4
Higginson, M.P.   4A29
Hillman, M.   2A19
Hills, P.J.   5C7
Hirsh, M.   5A15, 5B35
Hobeika, A.G.   1B20
Hoch, I.   5D5
Hodge, D.C.   8.11
Hoefer, C.A.   4D7
Hoel, L.A.   2B6
Holden, D.J.   5A17
Holmes, P.   1A8
Hopkin, J.M.   2A2, 3C17, 3C18, 3C19, 3C20
Horowitz, A.D.   5B37
Horowitz, A.J.   4A30
Horowitz, J.L.   5B36, 5D9, 5E13
Hovell, P.J.   4A31

Howard, E.B.   3B4
HRIS: Highway Research Information Service   7B6
Hu, P.S.   5D8
Hudson, M.   4F4
Huff, J.O.   5A9
Hurst, C.J.   1B20
Hutchinson, B.G.   5A10, 5B52, 5B64
Huxley, M.   7A11
Hyman, W.A.   2B6

INROADS: Information on roads   7B7
Institut National de Recherche sur les Transports et leur sécurité 7A36
Institute of British Geographers   7A12
Inter-American Development Bank   6A14
International Road Federation 7A13
Ircha, M.C.   3C21
IRRD: International Road Research Documentation 7B8

Jackson, R.   3C22, 4C5, 4D10
Jacobs, G.D.   4A32, 4A49, 5E14
Jacoby, R.G.   4F2
Janarthanan, N.   5C8
Jansen, G.R.M.   5B38
Jara-Diaz, S.R.   5C9
Jarrett, R.G.   5D21
Johnson, C.   3C30
Johnson, C.M.   2D8
Johnson, G.T.   2B7
Johnson, I.   5B46

Johnston, R.H.   1B56
Johnston, R.R.M.   5D21
Jonah, B.A.   5E15
Jones, D.W.   2B8, 3D17
Jones, M.   1B3
Jones, P.M.   3A7, 5A8, 5A11
Jones-Lee, M.W.   5C7
Jovanis, P.   3D17, 3D18
Juster, F.T.   5B29

Kain, J.F.   1B33, 8.12
Kamerud, D.B.   5E16
Kanafani, A.   5B39
Kanarek, J.M.   4B10
Kasarda, J.D.   8.4
Kassab, P.   6A6
Katakura, M.   6A7
Kay, M.A.   3D12
Keasey, K.   2A20
Kemp, M.A.   2B9
Kennett, S.   1A28
Kenworthy, J.   5D15, 8.21
Keppleman, F.S.   4A33
Kettle, P.B.   4B11
Keyes, D.L.   5D10
Keys, E.C.   5B40
Keys, P.   5D2
Khan, A.M.   4D13, 5C19, 5D11, 6A15
Khisty, C.J.   5A12
Kim, T.J.   5B16
Kimber, R.M.   5E17
King, R.J.   3A8
Kirby, R.F.   2B9, 4A34
Kitamura, R.   5A13, 5B41, 5B42, 8.13
Kivell, H.   5B31
Klaassen, L.H.   1B31, 8.14
Kloeckner, J.H.   5E19
Knapp, S.F.   3C23

AUTHOR INDEX

Knight, R.L.   4B12
Keonig, J.G.   3C24
Kolsen, H.M.   6A16
Koppelman, F.S.   5B43, 5B44, 5B58, 8.28
Kornhauser, A.L.   3D2
Korte, C.   5E18
Koshi, M.   4D18
Kostyniuk, L.P.   3D25, 5A13
Koutsopoulos, H.N.   3C25
Kroes, E.P.   8.15
Kueting, H.J.   7A27
Kuhn, H.   7A22
Kuhn, P.   3D14
Kulash, D.J.   2B6

Lago, A.M.   4A35
Lam, T.N.   1B54, 5D12
Lamm, R.   5E19
Landau, U.   5A15
Landrock, J.N.   5A14
Larson, T.D.   2B13
Lave, C.A.   2D2, 2E2, 3C7
Lawrence, D.S.   4C6
Lawson, J.J.   5E15
Layzell, A.D.   2E3, 5A6, 5A16
Le Clercq, F.   3A9
Lee, A.M.   3B5
Lee, L.W.   4D14
Lee, W.   3C26
Leiser, D.   8.29
Lerman, S.R.   3A3, 3D33, 5B24
Lerner-Lam, E.   3A3
Lesley, L.   7A1
Lessieu, E.J.   4D15
Leutzbach, W.   4E3
Levin, P.H.   2D3
Levine, N.   3E4

Levinson, H.S.   2B10, 4D15
Levy, C.   4F4
Lewis, J.C.   3B6
Lewis, K.   2A5
Lewis, S.   7A8
Lieb, R.C.   3C27, 3C28
Lijewski, T.   2C11
Lillydahl, J.H.   3C39
Lim, Y.H.   5B53
Lima, P.M.   5C10
Linn, J.F.   1A20
Louviere, J.   8.16
Lucas, G.G.   5D13
Lund, A.K.   5E20
Lundin, O.   4D18
Lyons, T.P.   6A17

Mace, S.   4D17
Macgill, S.M.   5B77
Mackett, R.L.   5B45, 5B46
Mackie, A.M.   5E22
Mackie, P.J.   2A17, 4A27
Macrory, R.   4F4
Maddala, G.S.   5B47
Madden, J.F.   3C29
Madden, T.J.   5B51
Maltby, D.   6A18
Mannering, F.   4D19, 5B48
Manski, C.F.   5B8
Markham, J.   3D22
Markowitz, J.E.   4B13
Markusen, A.   1A17
Massey, D.   1A21
Matsoukis, E.C.   5B49
Matzerath, H.   1A9
Maunder, D.A.C.   4A32
May, A.   2D4, 3A10, 5F5
Mayworm, P.   4A35, 4A36
McCarthy, P.   3D19
McClintock, H.   8.17

McCollom, B.   4A54
McCoomb, L.A.   4D16
McCrone, D.   1A7
McDonnell, J.J.   2B14
McDowell, B.D.   2B11
McEnroe, J.M.   4A35
McGillivray, R.G.   2B9
McGlynn, R.   7A6
McKnight, A.J.   5E21
McKnight, C.   2B12, 3C30
McLoughlin, J.B.   7A11
McPherson, K.   5E21
McShane, M.   4D18, 5F6
Meegan, R.   1A21
Meltzer, J.   1A22
Merlin, P.   7A37
Meyburg, A.H.   3B5
Meyer, J.R.   1B32, 1B33
Meyer, M.   1B34, 2B4, 2B5, 2D12, 5D14, 2E7, 5F6
Mihalcin, E.   4F10
Mildren, K.   7A14
Miller, C.E.   3B7
Miller, E.J.   1B34, 3D4
Miller, L.H.   5C4
Mills, F.   3A11
Miron, J.R.   3D20
Mitchell, C.G.B.   4A37, 4F5
Mitchelson, R.L.   8.18
Moavenzadeh, F.   1B35
Mogridge, M.J.H.   1B36, 3D21, 4D9, 5A17, 8.19
Mohan, D.   5E23
Moran, A.J.   4A31
Morgan, J.N.   5B29
Mori, M.   8.20
Moriaty, P.   6A3
Morrall, J.F.   4F8
Morris, J.M.   5A24, 5B50
Morris, P.   4A38

Mullen, P.   2A5
Mulley, C.   2A20, 2D1, 2D5
Muretta, P.   5C6

Nakamura, R.T.   1A23
Naroff, J.L.   5B51
Nash, C.A.   1B37, 4A27, 4B14
National Consumer Council   4F6
Naylor, M.L.   3D12
Neale, J.L.   5B52
Neff, C.   5C24
Neilsen, L.   5D4
Nelson, J.P.   5E24
Nemmers, C.J.   5E25
Newell, J.   4D20
Newman, P.   5D15, 8.21
Newton, P.   1A5
Nicholson, A.J.   4F4, 5B53
Nilles, J.M.   8.23
Nijkamp, P.   1A5, 5B38, 8.22
Niskanen, E.   5C11
Noel, E.C.   3C31, 8.24
Novaco, R.W.   3E5

O'Donnell, K.J.   4A11
O'Farrell, P.   3D22
Obeng, K.   4A39, 5B54, 8.25
Ogden, K.W.   1B38, 4E4, 4E5, 5B55
Oldfield, R.H.   4A7, 4A8
Organization for Economic Cooperation and Development   2D6, 4D21, 5C12, 5C13, 5D16, 5E26, 5E27, 5F7, 5F8, 5F9
Orski, C.K.   1B39
Ortolano, L.   5B20
Ortuzar, J. de.D.   5B56

Österreich, Bundesminister für Bauten und Technik Strassenforschung 7A28
Ott, M. 3D23
Owen, W. 1A24, 1B40
Owens, D.D. 4D22
Owens, S. 1A25, 5D17
Oxley, P.R. 4C7

Paaswell, R.E. 5B10
Pagano, A.M. 3C30
Page, J.H. 2D7
Painter, M. 2A21
Pampe, U. 7A29
Pang, L.M.G. 5C25
Panke, C. 7A30
Park, C.Y. 2B13
Pas, E.I. 5B57, 5B58
Patterson, N.S. 3A10
Paulley, N. 1B56
Pearlstein, A. 3E6
Pearman, A.D. 1B15, 1B17, 4A12, 5C14, 5C15
Peiser, R.B. 1B41
Pendakur, V.S. 6A19, 7A15
Perrett, K.E. 2A2, 3A12, 3C10, 4B15
Perry, J.L. 2E8, 4A40, 8.26
Pickering, D. 4F2
Pickett, M.W. 3A12, 4B15
Pickles, A.R. 5B26
Pickrell, D.H. 4A41
Pickup, L. 3C20, 3C32, 3D24, 7A16
Pignataro, L.J. 5D3
Pikarsky, M. 2D8
Pinch, S. 1A28
Piozin, F. 7A38
Pirie, G.H. 3C33
Plank, E. 3D16

Plowden, S. 1B42, 2A22, 5E28
Politano, A. 4D8
Poole, M.R. 5C16
Porter, A.L. 2B13
Porter, B. 4A17
Potter, S. 2C2
Poulton, M.C. 3B8
Prashker, J.N. 5A15, 5B35
Pucher, J. 1B2, 3C34, 4A42, 4A43
Putman, S.H. 5B59, 5B60, 5B61

Quarmby, D.A. 4A44
Quinn, D.J. 3C35, 3C36

Rallis, T. 1B43
Ralston, B.A. 4D23
Rao, S. 2B13
Rasbash, D.L. 3A13
Reason, J. 3E7
Recker, W.W. 3D25
Rees, L.P. 2B13
Regan, E.J. 4D15
Reichman, S. 8.22
Reid, J. 8.27
Render, T.E. 2A14
Ribbeck, K. 3C4
Ribu, E. 2C12
Richards, M. 5B62
Richards, W.L. 5D13
Richardson, A.J. 3C37, 4D24, 5B2, 5B79
Riley, N.E. 3E8
Rimmer, P.J. 1B44, 2D9
Ritchie, S.G. 5F13
Robbins, M. 2A23
Roberts, J. 7A6
Robins, L. 3C30
Robinson, J.B. 5B78

Rock, S.M.   4A45
Rodriguez, C.G.   2B14
Rooney, S.   5B63
Roos, D.   1B3
Rose, G.   4A33
Ross, H.E.   5C21
Roth, G.   2D10, 5A18
Ruijgrok, C.J.   5B38
Runnacles, T.V.   6A2
Rusch, G.   5A19

Saccomanno, F.F.   5C17
Said, G.M.   6A20
Salomon, I.   3B9, 8.28
Sanderson, I.R.   4A57
Saunders, P.   1A26
Schevernstuhl, G.J.   3D3
Schmitt, R.P.   2D11
Schneider, C.G.   2E1
Schneider, J.B.   5C8, 5F13
Schnuerer, H.   5C18
Schofer, J.L.   2B15
Schofer, J.O.   5A20
Schou, K.   4D25
Schreffler, E.   2D12
Schuler, H.J.   3D26
Schuurman, F.J.   3C38
Schwab, M.   3C16
Schwantes, W.   7A29
Schweiterman, J.P.   2E9
Self, P.   1A27
Sen, L.   5B9
Seneviratne, P.N.   4F7, 4F8
Shallal, L.A.Y.   5C19
Shannon, H.S.   5E29
Sharp, C.   5C20
Sharpe, R.   5D18
Shaw, D.J.B.   1B4
Shaw, P.L.   2B16
Sheldon, R.L.   8.15

Sherman, L.   5B8
Sicking, D.L.   5C21
Sikdar, P.K.   5B64
Silcock, D.T.   4C8, 4C9
Simon, R.B.   2B16
Simpson, B.J.   1B45
Sinclair, R.   1A2
Singell, L.D.   3C39
Skinner, D.   5D23
Slavin, H.   3D23
Smallwood, F.   1A23
Smerk, G.M.   2B17
Smith, A.   5E30
Smith, D.   7A16
Smith, J.   4F9
Smith, W.S.   4B16
Snelson, P.   4F4
Sonntag, H.   5B65
Sources and nature of the
  statistics of the U.K.   7A17
Spear, B.D.   3C40
Spence, N.   1A28, 3D8, 5B25
Spencer, A.   4D3, 4D26
Spielberg, F.   2B18
St Clair, D.J.   1B47
Standing Advisory Committee
  on Trunk Road
  Assessment   2A24
Stansfeld, S.   5E30
Starkie, D.   1B46, 2D13
Stephanedes, Y.J.   2E5, 5B66
Stephens, N.T.   1B20
Stern, E.   4A46, 8.29
Steuart, G.N.   4D16
Stevens, A.M.   5B78
Stewart, G.   4F10
Stimpson, C.   3C41
Stokes, R.G.F.   4F5
Stokols, D.   3E5
Stoner, J.W.   4A24

AUTHOR INDEX

Stopher, P.R.   3D11, 5A20, 5A21, 5B21, 5B67
Stringham, M.G.P.   4B17
Strobel, H.   5F10
Stuart, R.C.   1B20
Stucker, J.   3A14
Studnicki-Gizbert, K.W.   1B48, 3C42
Sullivan, E.C.   5D19
Supernak, J.   5A22
Surrey, J.   5E31
Sutton, J.C.   4C10
Svenson, O.   5E32
Sviden, O.   4D27
Swait, J.   5B68
Symons, L.   1B4

Talvitie, A.   4A47
Tang, W.S.   4D3
Tanner, J.C.   5A23, 5B18
Taylor, J.C.   1A29
Taylor, W.C.   3D34
Teal, R.   2E10, 4C12, 4D28, 5B63
Teodorovic, D.   5B69
Theologitis, J.M.   3D27
Thill, J.-C.   8.30
Thomas, I.   8.30
Thomson, J.M.   1B49, 1B50
Till, L.   5D8
Timm, J.   7A31
Timmermans, H.   5B70, 5B71
Tom Shin, B.   7A18
Tomazinis, A.R.   5D20
Topham, N.   4A20, 5C5
Town, S.W.   3A15
Train, K.   5B72
TRANSDOC: ECMT Database   7B9
Transportation Research Board   2B19, 3D28, 4A48, 4B18, 5F11
Trayford, R.S.   5D21
Troy, P.N.   1A30
TRRL   1B51, 7A19
Truncellito, V.J.   4B10
Trygg, L.L.   4B12
Tsukaguchi, H.   8.20
Turner, E.D.   5E2
Turner, G.E.   5B73
Tweddle, G.   5E33
Tyson, W.   5C22
Tzedakis, A.   2A5

Ueberschaer, M.   2C13
UMTRIS: Urban mass transportation research information service   7B10
United States Department of Transportation   1B52, 3C43, 3C44, 4C12, 4C13
URBAMET   7B11

Van den Berg, L.   5B11
Van der Heijden, R.   5B71
Van der Hoorn, T.   8.13
Van der Meer, J.   8.14
Van Rest, D.   8.31
Van der Touw, J.W.   5D21
Vaughan, R.J.   1B53
Vaziri, M.   1B54
Verster, A.C.P.   3D29, 3D30
Vickerman, R.W.   1B55, 3D31
Victoria Ministry of Transport   3D32
Vijayakumar, S.   4A49, 4C14
Viton, P.A.   4A50
Von Buseck, C.R.   5E16
Vuchic, V.R.   2B20, 4C15

Wachs, M. 2B21, 2E11, 3E4, 3E6, 4D29
Wadhwa, L.C. 5D22
Walker, R.D. 1B20
Wallis, J.P. 2D14
Walmsley, D.A. 4B19
Walters, A.A. 4A51
Wang, G.H.K. 5D23
Ward, D. 3D23
Ward, M.F. 2E12
Warnes, A.M. 3A4
Waters, W.G. 5F12, 7A20
Watterson, W.T. 5C23
Weant, R.A. 2B10
Webber, M.M. 1A31
Webster, F.V. 1B56, 2A25, 4A52, 5B13
Wegener, M. 5B74
Weiner, E. 2B22, 2B23, 2B24, 8.32
Weisbrod, G.E. 3D33
Weisman, M. 4A53
Wells, M.J. 4A54
Werlin, H.H. 1B57
Westerveld, H. 5B71
Whalley, A. 2A19
White, H.P. 6A18
White, P.M. 7A21
White, P.R. 1B58, 1B59, 4A29, 4A55, 4A56, 5D24, 6A21
Whitelegg, J. 1B60, 2C14, 4D30, 4D31, 5E34
Whiteley, G.K. 2A14
Whitt, J.A. 1B61
Wigan, M.R. 4F11, 5A24, 5B50
Williams, A. 1A28

Williams, D.G. 1A29
Williams, D.J. 4C16
Williams, H.C.W.L. 4A57, 5B75, 5B77
Williams, M. 4A3, 4A58
Williams, R.H. 1A32
Williams, W.L. 5E25
Willson, R. 4B9
Willumsen, L.G. 4D13, 5B76
Wilson, A.G. 5B77
Wilson, F.R. 5B78
Wilson, N.H.M. 3C25
Wilson, T. 5C24
Wirasinghe, S.C. 4B5
Wirz, S. 7A32
Wiseman, F. 3C28
Wistrich, E. 2A26
Witkowski, J.M. 3C45, 3D34
Wohl, M. 1B33, 2B9
Womack, J. 1B2, 1B3
World Bank 1B62
Wozny, M.C. 3C23, 5E4
Wright, M. 2D5
Wrigley, N. 4F1

Yago, G. 2B25
Yamada, T. 4B20
Yang, J.M. 4F12
Yeh, C.-I. 5F13
Young, J. 3A3
Young, W. 3C37, 4D24, 5B55, 5B79
Yu, J.C. 5C25

Zahavi, Y. 5A18, 5A25
Zavattero, D.A. 2B12
Zehner, R.B. 3D12
Zlosel, D.J. 4A30

NOV 0 9 1990